I FIRST SAW THAT GIRL ON A SNOWY DAY LAST YEAR.

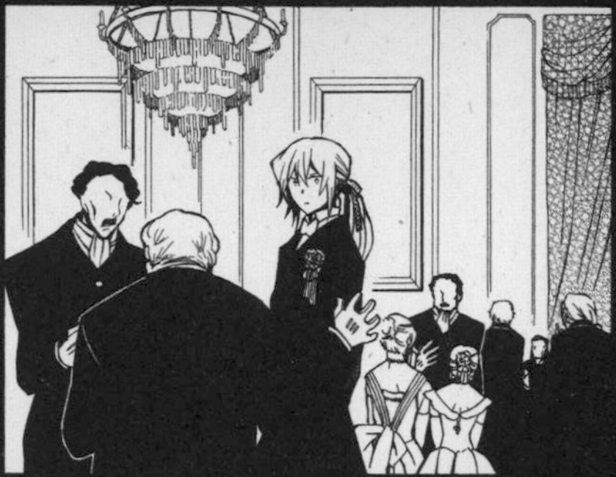

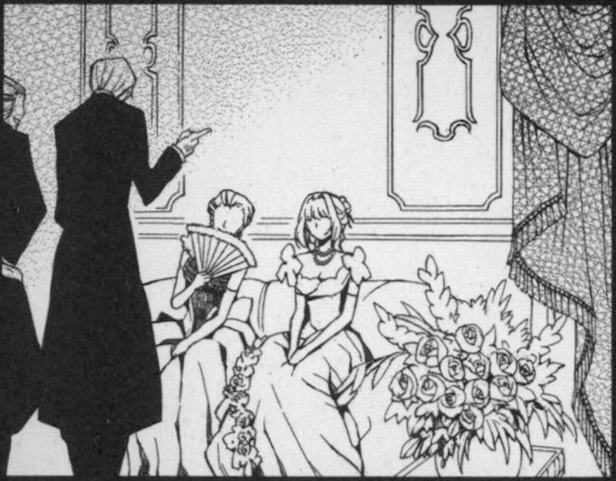

THOSE EMERALD EYES SO LIKE "HIS"
LOOKED AS IF THEY WERE ACCUSING ME.

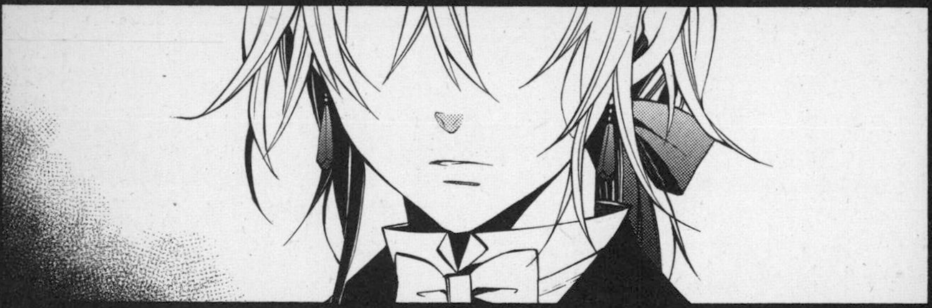

TO AVERT MY OWN EYES FROM MY SINS, I...

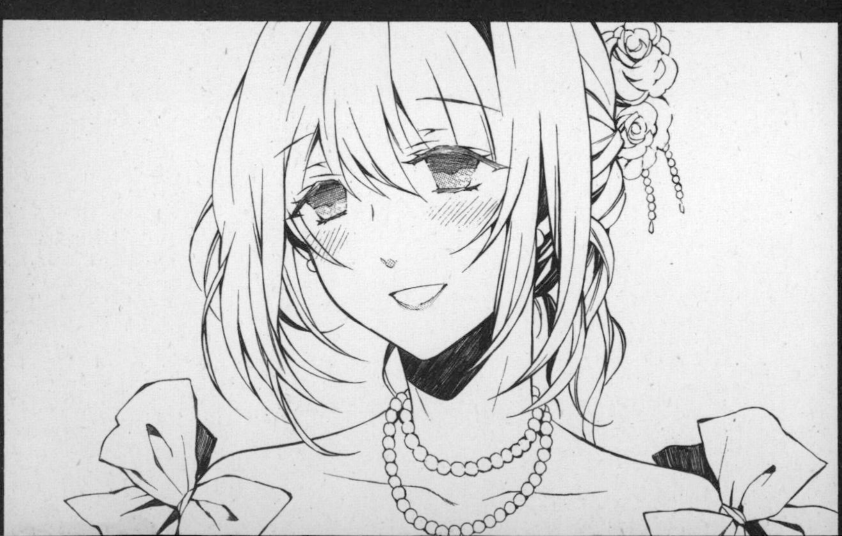

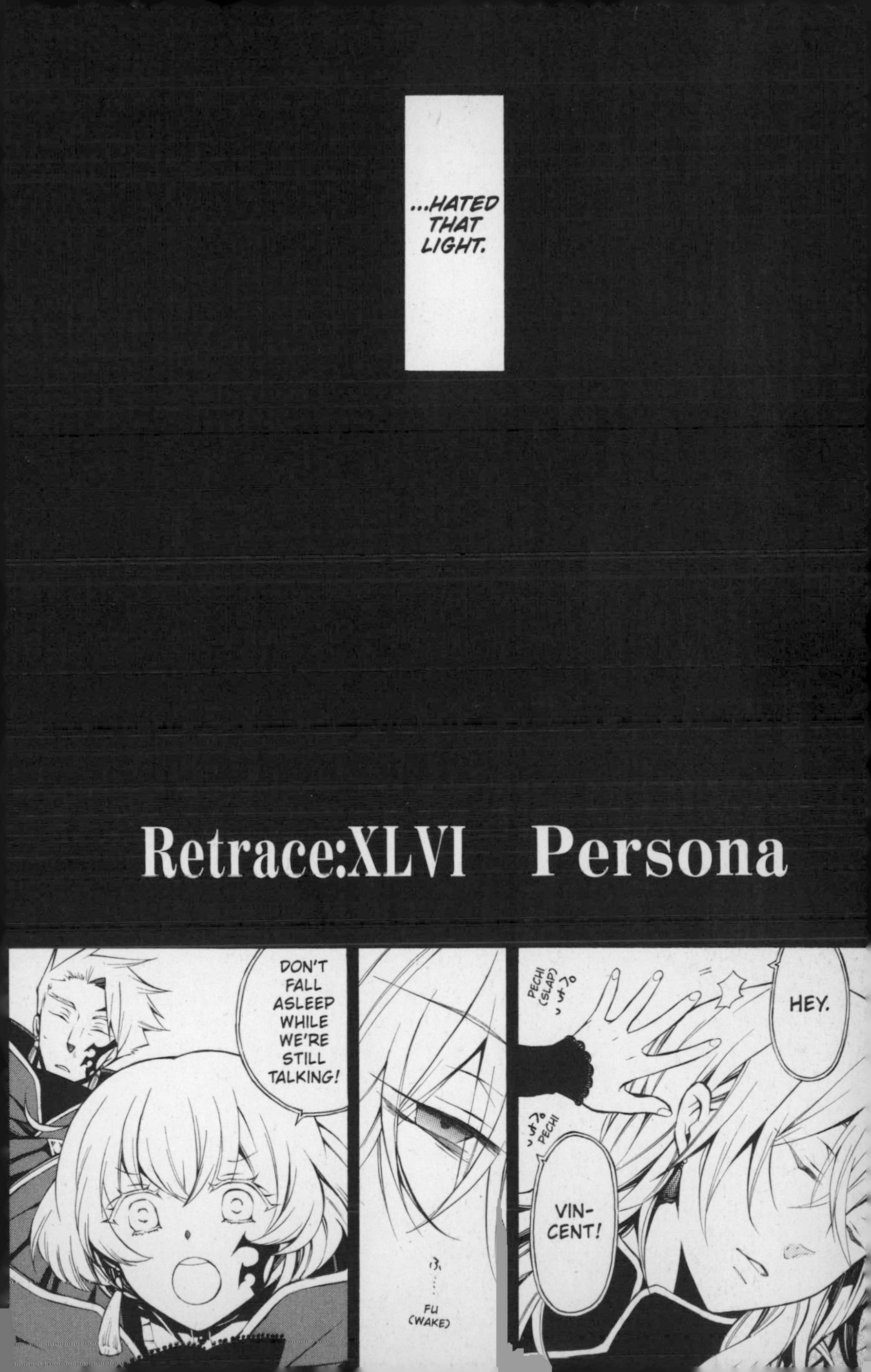
...HATED THAT LIGHT.
Retrace:XLVI Persona
HEY.
PECHI (SLAP)
PECHI
VIN-CENT!
FU (WAKE)
DON'T FALL ASLEEP WHILE WE'RE STILL TALKING!

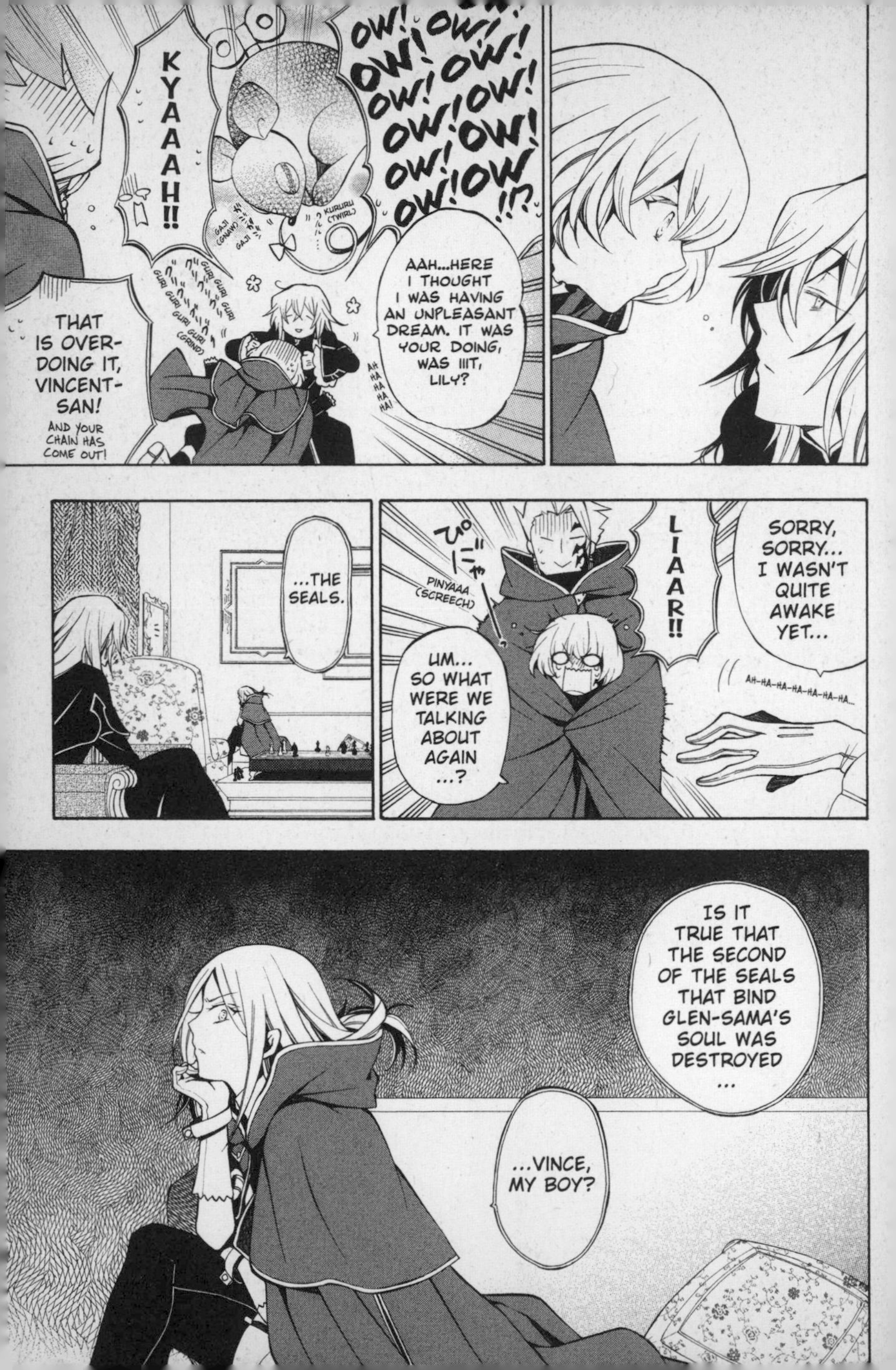

OW! OW! OW! OW! OW! OW! OW! OW! OW! OW! OW! OW! !!?
KYAAAH!!
AAH...HERE I THOUGHT I WAS HAVING AN UNPLEASANT DREAM. IT WAS YOUR DOING, WAS IIIT, LILY?
KURURU (TWIRL)
GAJI (GNAW) GAJI
AH HA HA HA HA!
GURI GURI GURI GURI GURI GURI (GRIND)
THAT IS OVER-DOING IT, VINCENT-SAN!
AND YOUR CHAIN HAS COME OUT!
SORRY, SORRY... I WASN'T QUITE AWAKE YET...
AH-HA-HA-HA-HA-HA-HA...
LIAAR!!
PINYAAA (SCREECH)
UM... SO WHAT WERE WE TALKING ABOUT AGAIN...?
...THE SEALS.
IS IT TRUE THAT THE SECOND OF THE SEALS THAT BIND GLEN-SAMA'S SOUL WAS DESTROYED...
...VINCE, MY BOY?

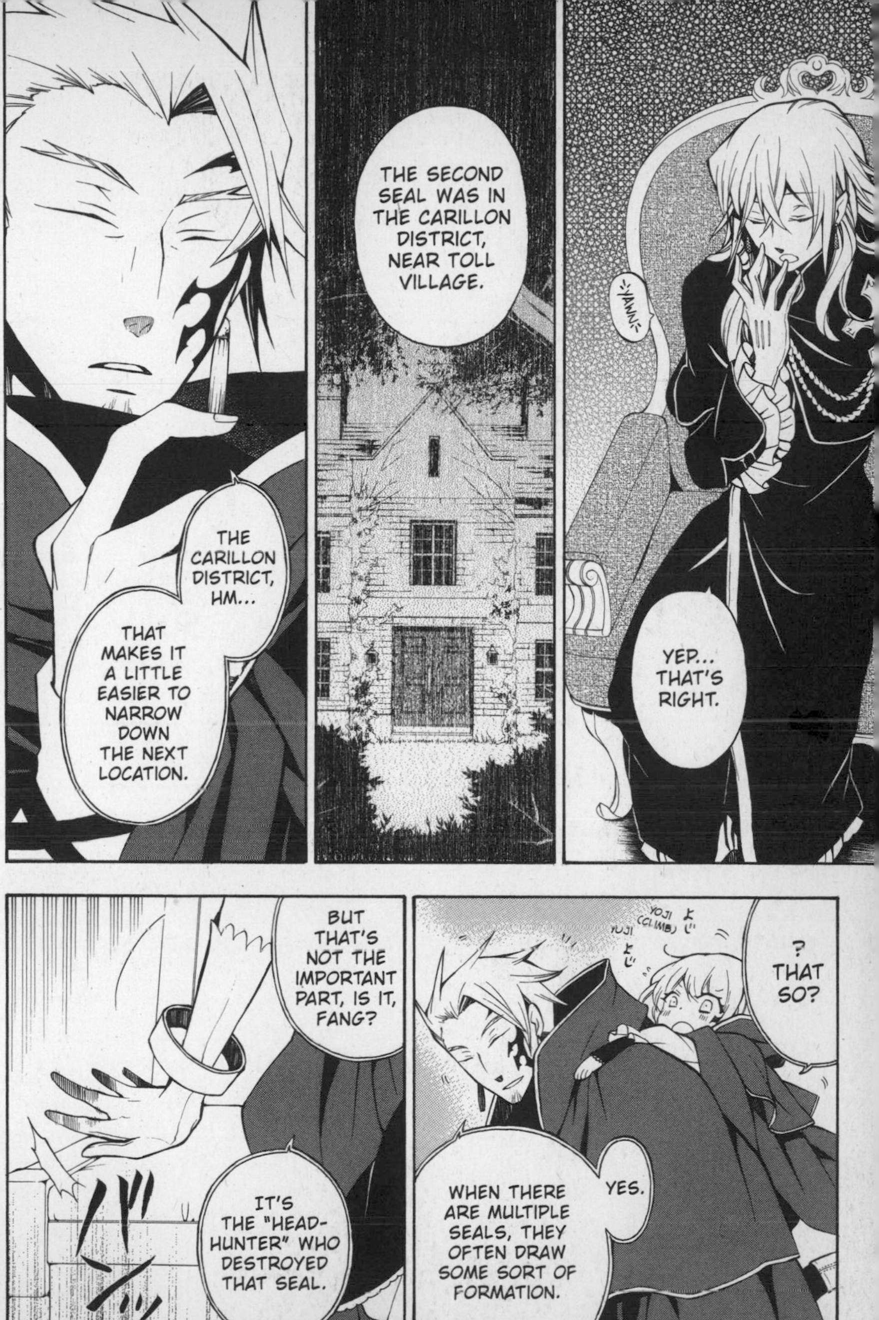
YAWN
YEP... THAT'S RIGHT.
THE SECOND SEAL WAS IN THE CARILLON DISTRICT, NEAR TOLL VILLAGE.
THE CARILLON DISTRICT, HM...
THAT MAKES IT A LITTLE EASIER TO NARROW DOWN THE NEXT LOCATION.
? THAT SO?
YOJI (CLIMB) よじ
YUJI よじ
YES.
WHEN THERE ARE MULTIPLE SEALS, THEY OFTEN DRAW SOME SORT OF FORMATION.
BUT THAT'S NOT THE IMPORTANT PART, IS IT, FANG?
IT'S THE "HEAD-HUNTER" WHO DESTROYED THAT SEAL.
BAN (WHAM)

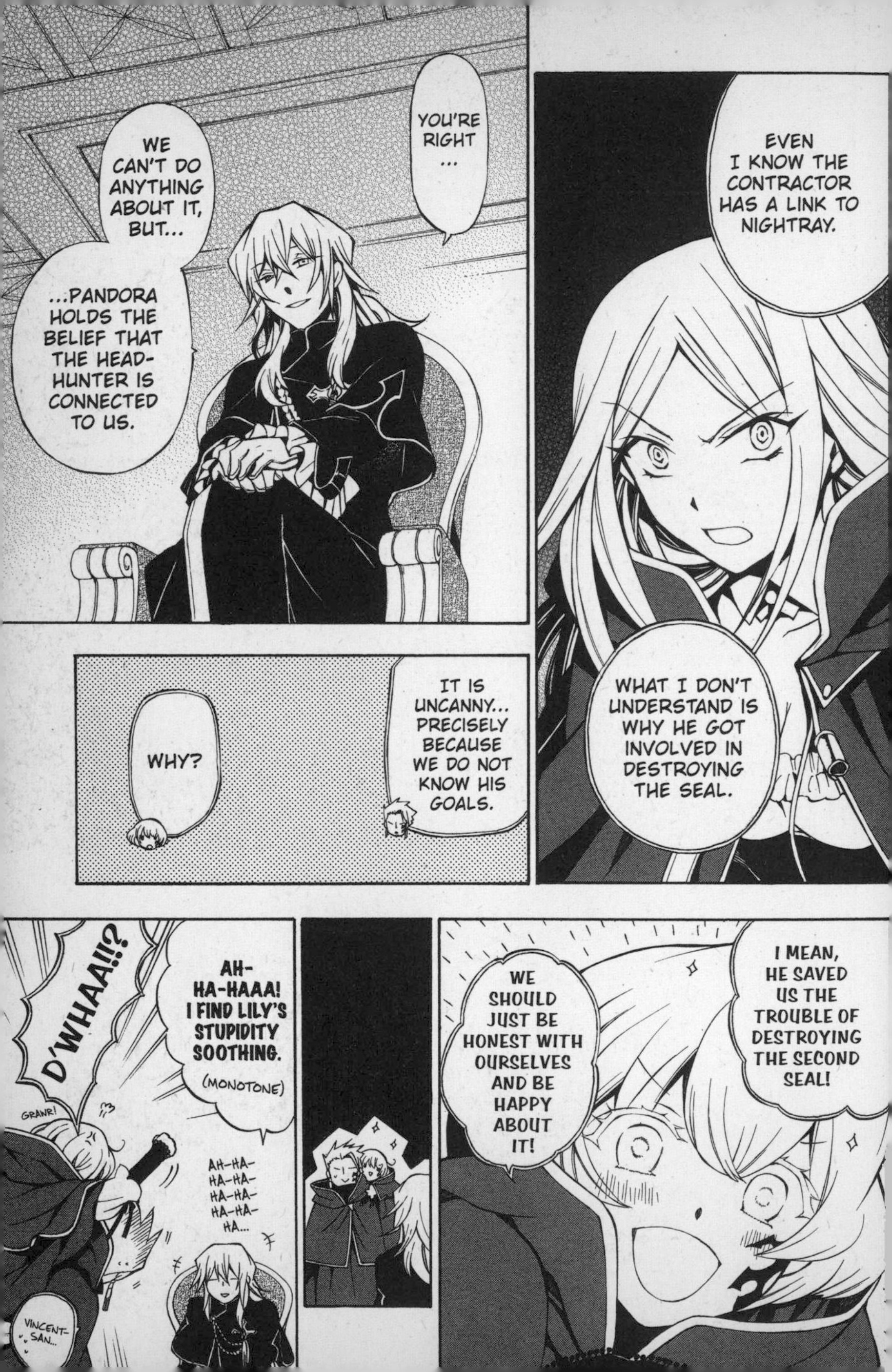

EVEN I KNOW THE CONTRACTOR HAS A LINK TO NIGHTRAY.
WHAT I DON'T UNDERSTAND IS WHY HE GOT INVOLVED IN DESTROYING THE SEAL.
YOU'RE RIGHT ...
WE CAN'T DO ANYTHING ABOUT IT, BUT...
...PANDORA HOLDS THE BELIEF THAT THE HEAD-HUNTER IS CONNECTED TO US.
IT IS UNCANNY... PRECISELY BECAUSE WE DO NOT KNOW HIS GOALS.
WHY?
I MEAN, HE SAVED US THE TROUBLE OF DESTROYING THE SECOND SEAL!
WE SHOULD JUST BE HONEST WITH OURSELVES AND BE HAPPY ABOUT IT!
AH-HA-HAAA! I FIND LILY'S STUPIDITY SOOTHING.
(MONOTONE)
D'WHAA!!?
GRAWR!
AH-HA-HA-HA-HA-HA-HA-HA-HA...
VINCENT-SAN...

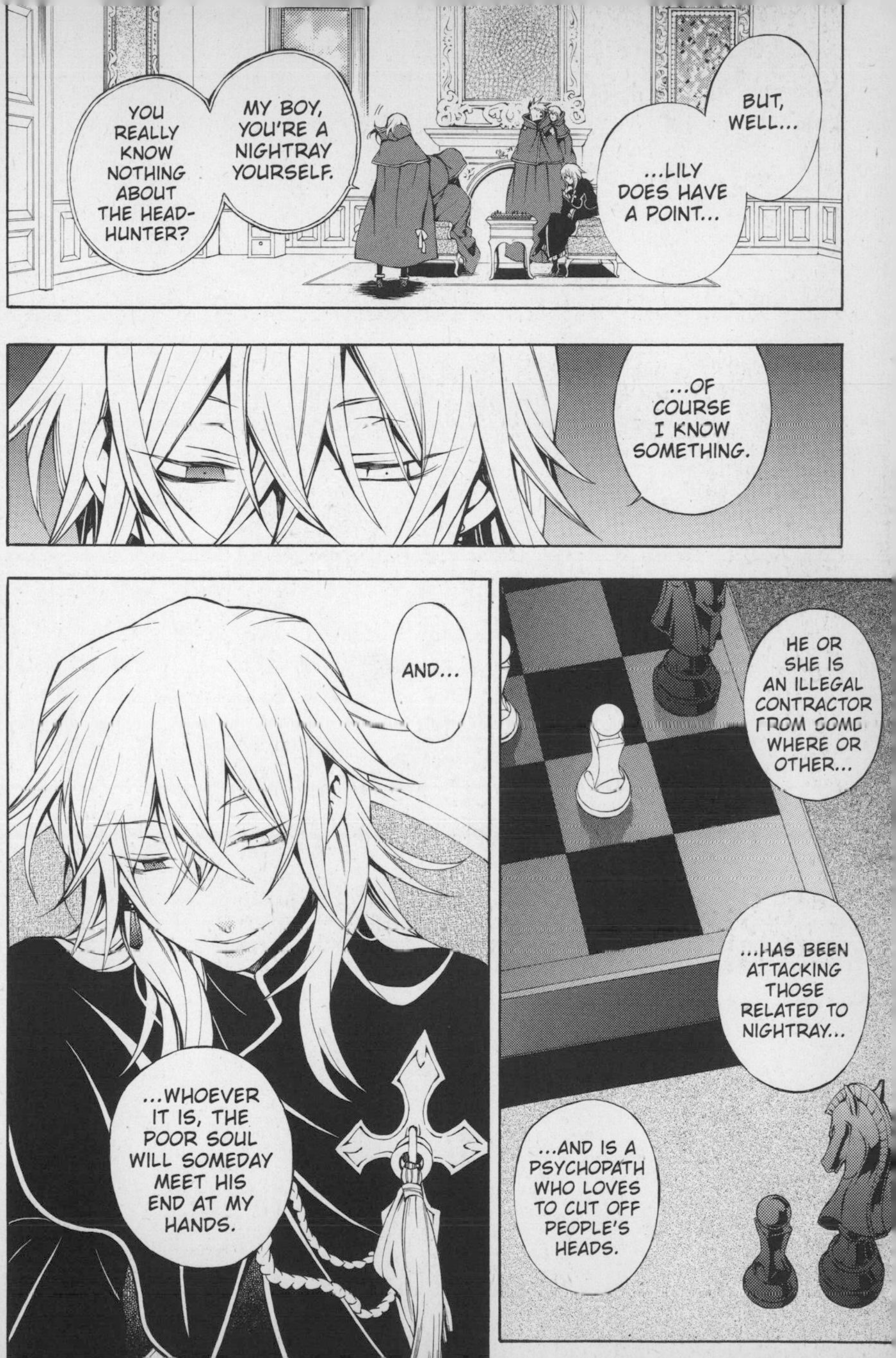
BUT, WELL...
...LILY DOES HAVE A POINT...
MY BOY, YOU'RE A NIGHTRAY YOURSELF.
YOU REALLY KNOW NOTHING ABOUT THE HEAD-HUNTER?
...OF COURSE I KNOW SOMETHING.
HE OR SHE IS AN ILLEGAL CONTRACTOR FROM SOME WHERE OR OTHER...
...HAS BEEN ATTACKING THOSE RELATED TO NIGHTRAY...
...AND IS A PSYCHOPATH WHO LOVES TO CUT OFF PEOPLE'S HEADS.
AND...
...WHOEVER IT IS, THE POOR SOUL WILL SOMEDAY MEET HIS END AT MY HANDS.

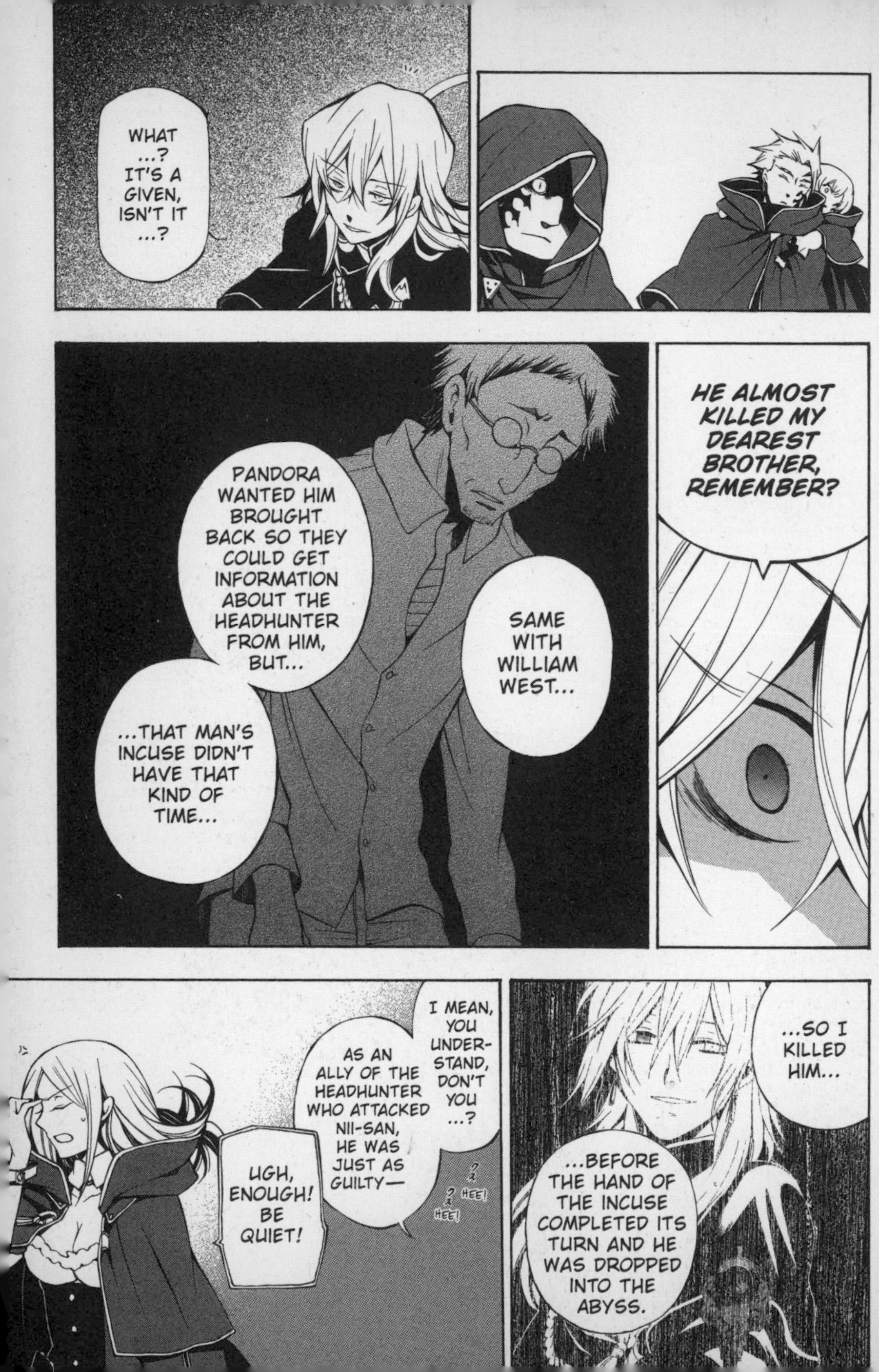
WHAT ...? IT'S A GIVEN, ISN'T IT ...?
HE ALMOST KILLED MY DEAREST BROTHER, REMEMBER?
SAME WITH WILLIAM WEST...
PANDORA WANTED HIM BROUGHT BACK SO THEY COULD GET INFORMATION ABOUT THE HEADHUNTER FROM HIM, BUT...
...THAT MAN'S INCUSE DIDN'T HAVE THAT KIND OF TIME...
...SO I KILLED HIM...
...BEFORE THE HAND OF THE INCUSE COMPLETED ITS TURN AND HE WAS DROPPED INTO THE ABYSS.
I MEAN, YOU UNDER-STAND, DON'T YOU ...?
AS AN ALLY OF THE HEADHUNTER WHO ATTACKED NII-SAN, HE WAS JUST AS GUILTY—
HEE! HEE!
UGH, ENOUGH! BE QUIET!

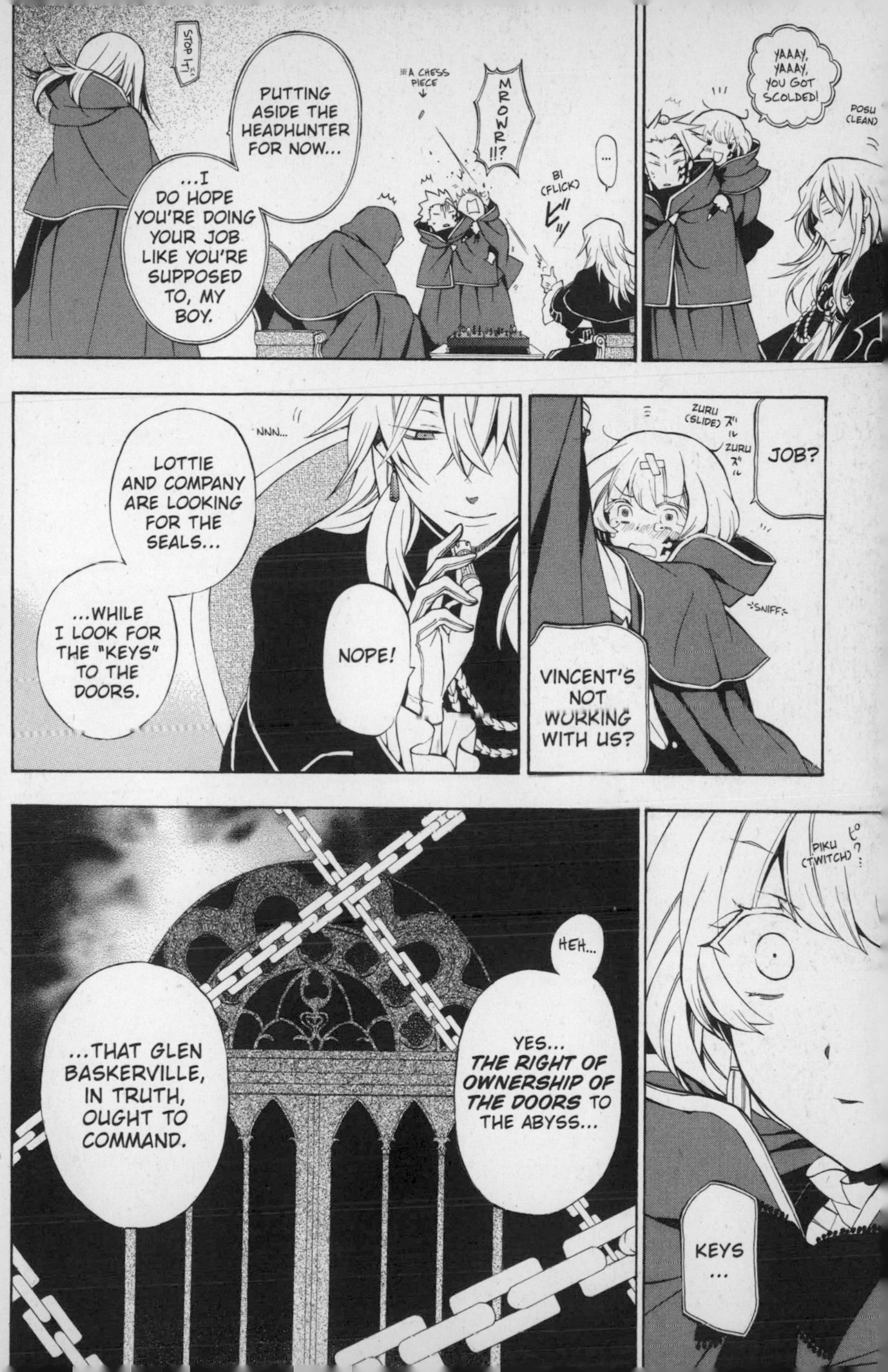

YAAAY, YAAAY, YOU GOT SCOLDED!
POSU (LEAN)
※A CHESS PIECE
MROWR!!?
...
BI (FLICK)
PUTTING ASIDE THE HEADHUNTER FOR NOW...
...I DO HOPE YOU'RE DOING YOUR JOB LIKE YOU'RE SUPPOSED TO, MY BOY.
STOP IT
ZURU (SLIDE) ZURU
JOB?
VINCENT'S NOT WORKING WITH US?
SNIFF
NNN...
LOTTIE AND COMPANY ARE LOOKING FOR THE SEALS...
NOPE!
...WHILE I LOOK FOR THE "KEYS" TO THE DOORS.
PIKU (TWITCH)
KEYS...
HEH...
YES... THE RIGHT OF OWNERSHIP OF THE DOORS TO THE ABYSS...
...THAT GLEN BASKERVILLE, IN TRUTH, OUGHT TO COMMAND.

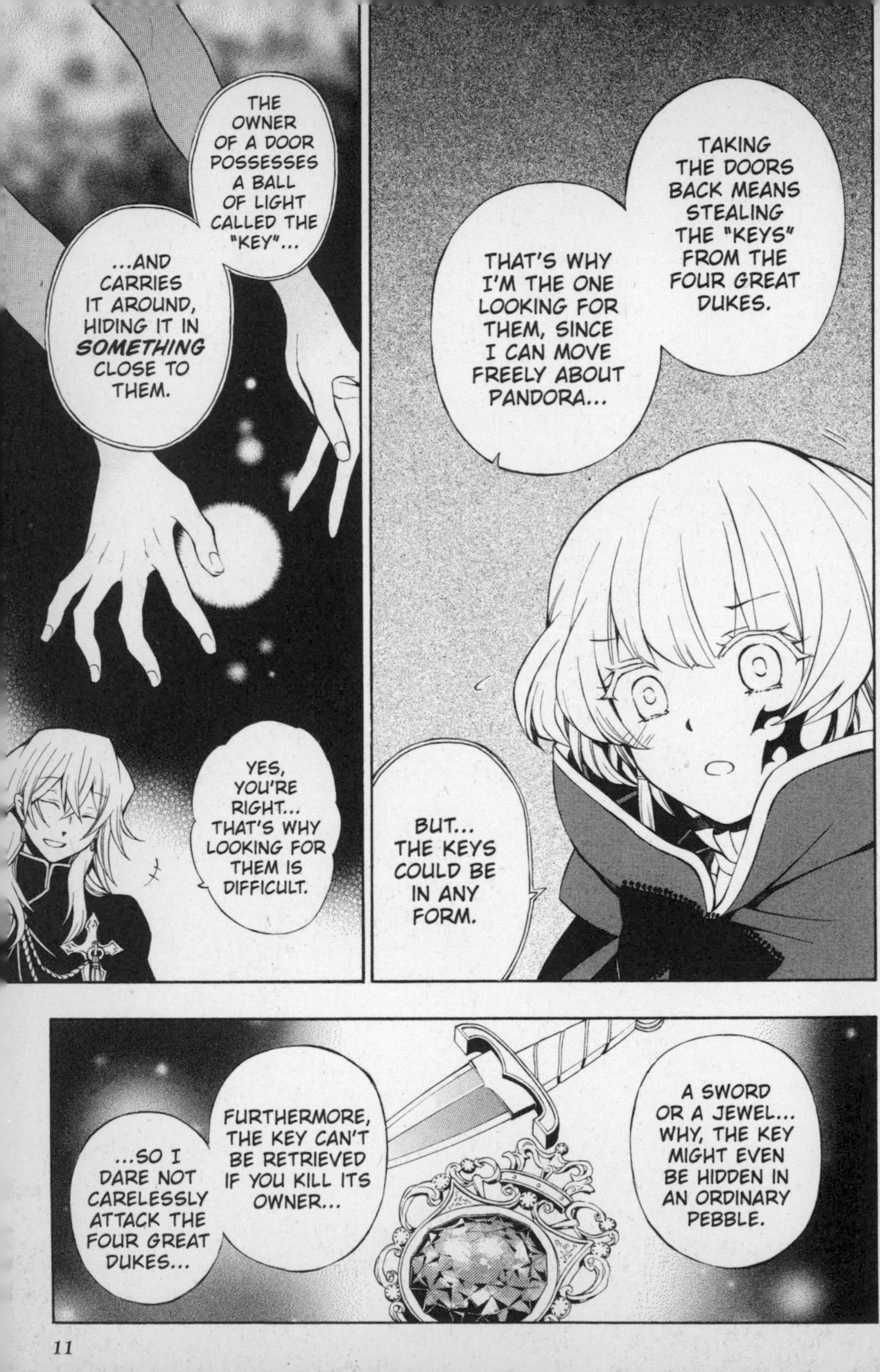
TAKING THE DOORS BACK MEANS STEALING THE "KEYS" FROM THE FOUR GREAT DUKES.
THAT'S WHY I'M THE ONE LOOKING FOR THEM, SINCE I CAN MOVE FREELY ABOUT PANDORA...
BUT... THE KEYS COULD BE IN ANY FORM.
THE OWNER OF A DOOR POSSESSES A BALL OF LIGHT CALLED THE "KEY"...
...AND CARRIES IT AROUND, HIDING IT IN *SOMETHING* CLOSE TO THEM.
YES, YOU'RE RIGHT... THAT'S WHY LOOKING FOR THEM IS DIFFICULT.
A SWORD OR A JEWEL... WHY, THE KEY MIGHT EVEN BE HIDDEN IN AN ORDINARY PEBBLE.
FURTHERMORE, THE KEY CAN'T BE RETRIEVED IF YOU KILL ITS OWNER...
...SO I DARE NOT CARELESSLY ATTACK THE FOUR GREAT DUKES...

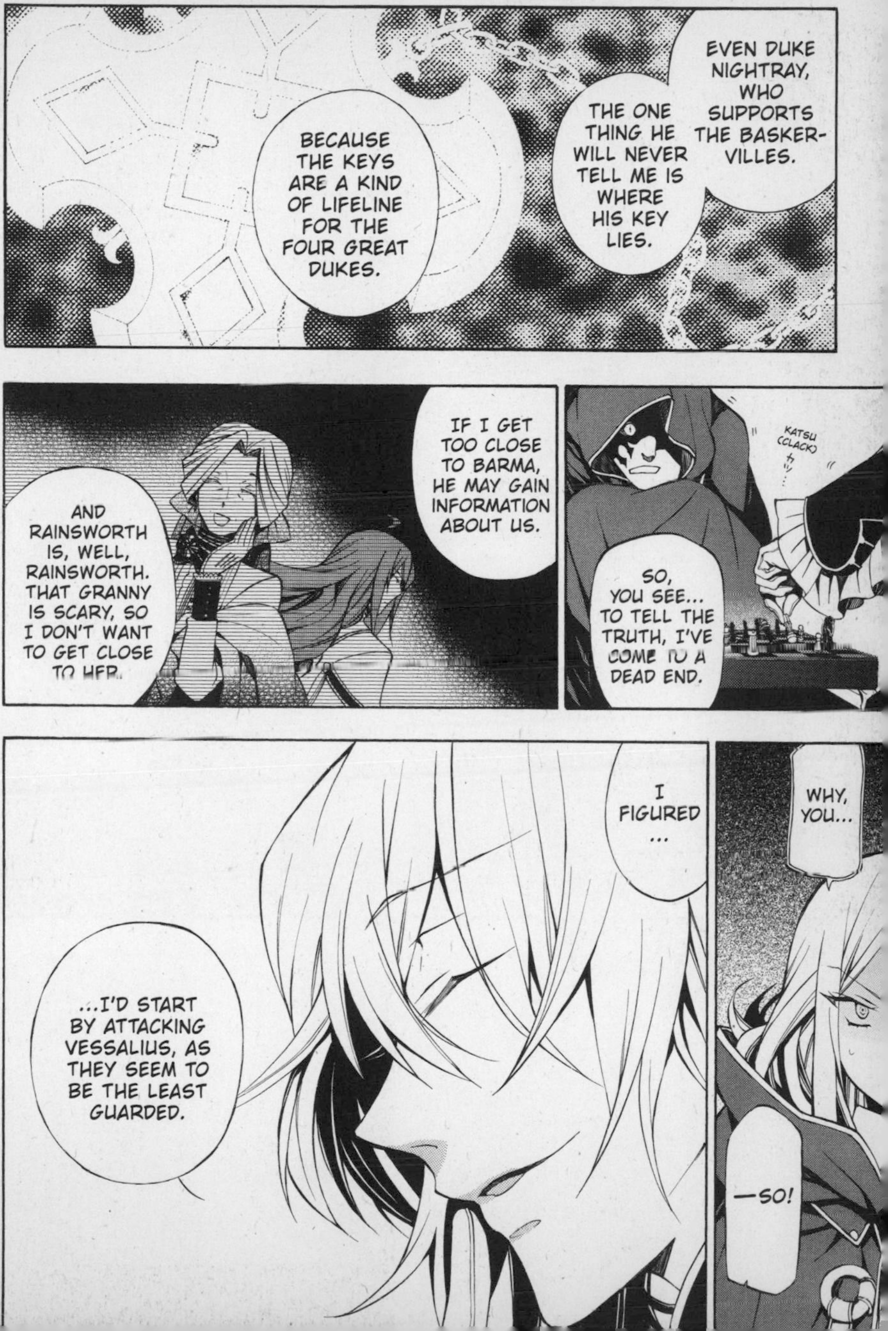
EVEN DUKE NIGHTRAY, WHO SUPPORTS THE BASKER-VILLES.
THE ONE THING HE WILL NEVER TELL ME IS WHERE HIS KEY LIES.
BECAUSE THE KEYS ARE A KIND OF LIFELINE FOR THE FOUR GREAT DUKES.
KATSU (CLACK)
SO, YOU SEE... TO TELL THE TRUTH, I'VE COME TO A DEAD END.
IF I GET TOO CLOSE TO BARMA, HE MAY GAIN INFORMATION ABOUT US.
AND RAINSWORTH IS, WELL, RAINSWORTH. THAT GRANNY IS SCARY, SO I DON'T WANT TO GET CLOSE TO HER.
WHY, YOU...
—SO!
I FIGURED ...
...I'D START BY ATTACKING VESSALIUS, AS THEY SEEM TO BE THE LEAST GUARDED.

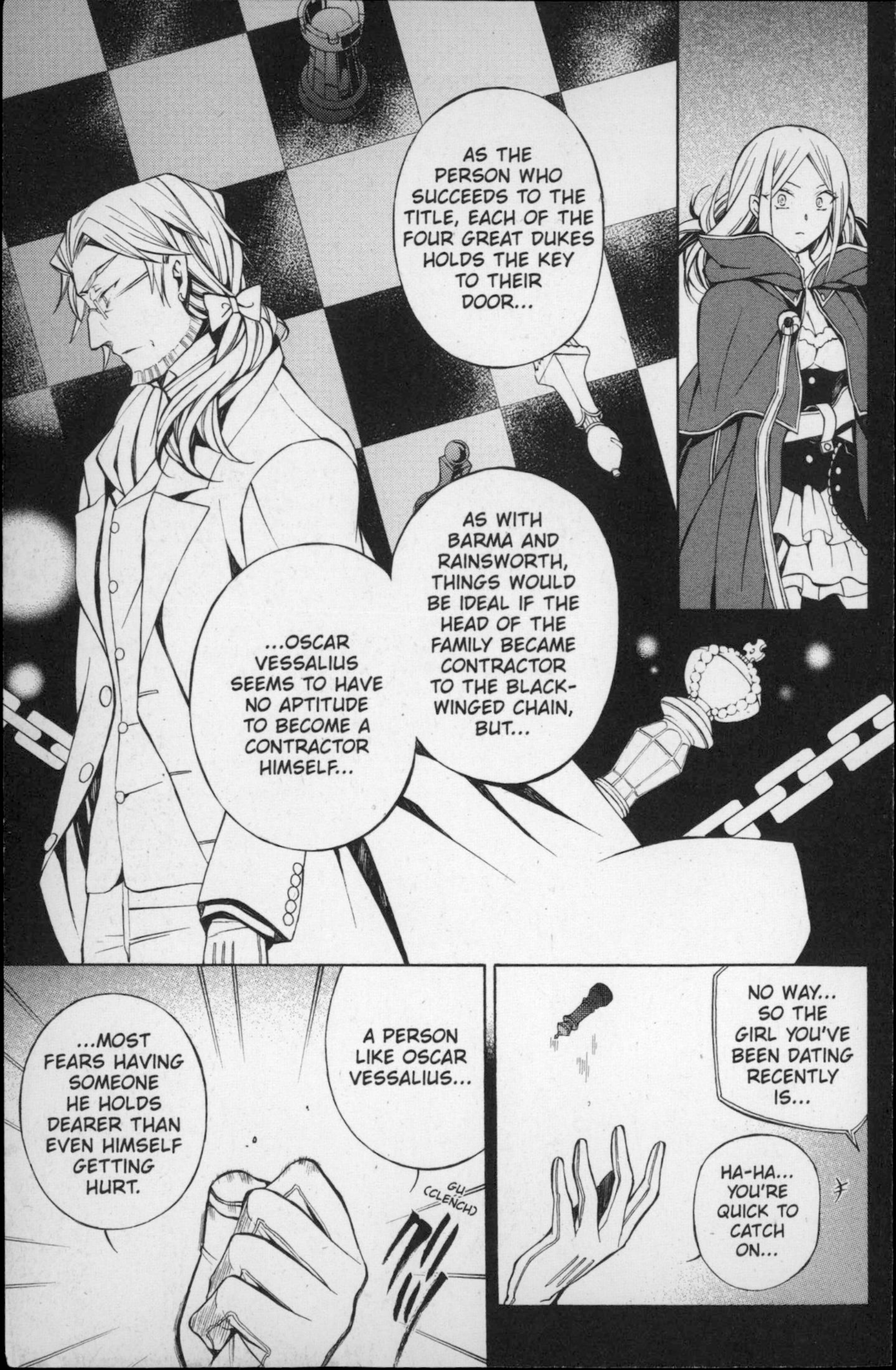
AS THE PERSON WHO SUCCEEDS TO THE TITLE, EACH OF THE FOUR GREAT DUKES HOLDS THE KEY TO THEIR DOOR...
AS WITH BARMA AND RAINSWORTH, THINGS WOULD BE IDEAL IF THE HEAD OF THE FAMILY BECAME CONTRACTOR TO THE BLACK-WINGED CHAIN, BUT...
...OSCAR VESSALIUS SEEMS TO HAVE NO APTITUDE TO BECOME A CONTRACTOR HIMSELF...
NO WAY... SO THE GIRL YOU'VE BEEN DATING RECENTLY IS...
HA-HA... YOU'RE QUICK TO CATCH ON...
A PERSON LIKE OSCAR VESSALIUS...
...MOST FEARS HAVING SOMEONE HE HOLDS DEARER THAN EVEN HIMSELF GETTING HURT.
GU (CLENCH)

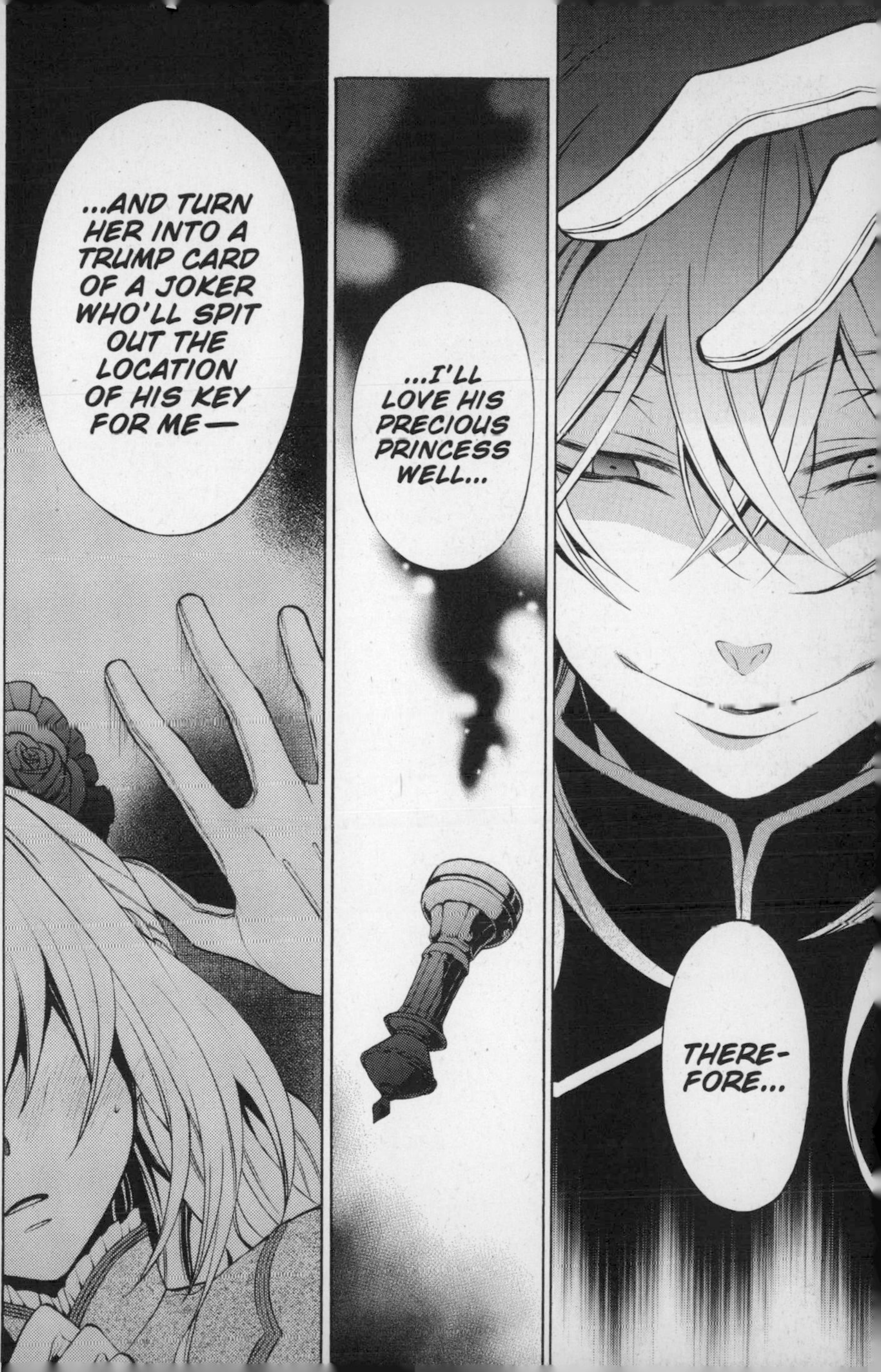
THERE-
FORE...
...I'LL LOVE HIS PRECIOUS PRINCESS WELL...
...AND TURN HER INTO A TRUMP CARD OF A JOKER WHO'LL SPIT OUT THE LOCATION OF HIS KEY FOR ME—

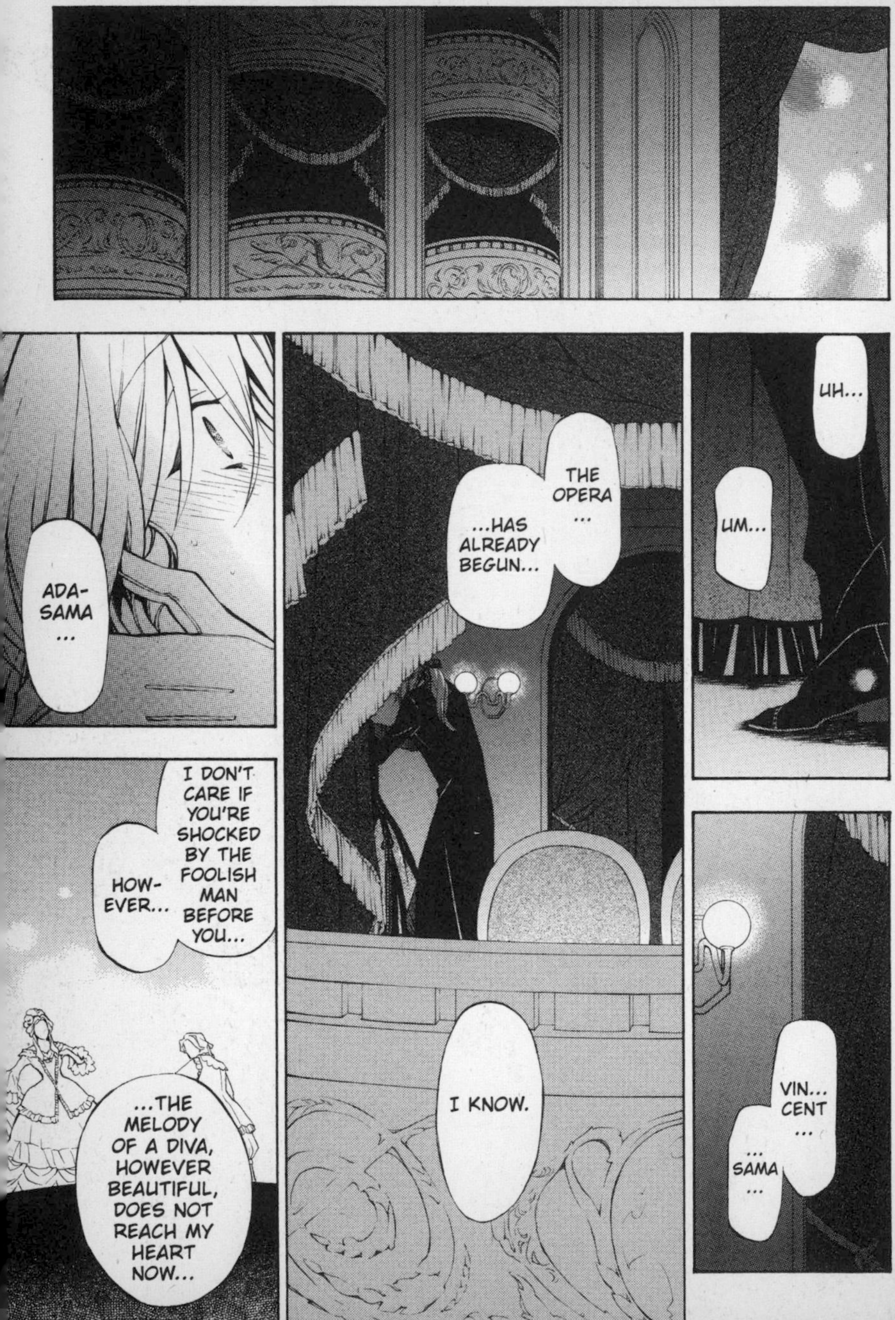
UH...
UM...
VIN... CENT...
... SAMA...
THE OPERA...
...HAS ALREADY BEGUN...
I KNOW.
ADA-SAMA...
I DON'T CARE IF YOU'RE SHOCKED BY THE FOOLISH MAN BEFORE YOU...
HOW-EVER...
...THE MELODY OF A DIVA, HOWEVER BEAUTIFUL, DOES NOT REACH MY HEART NOW...

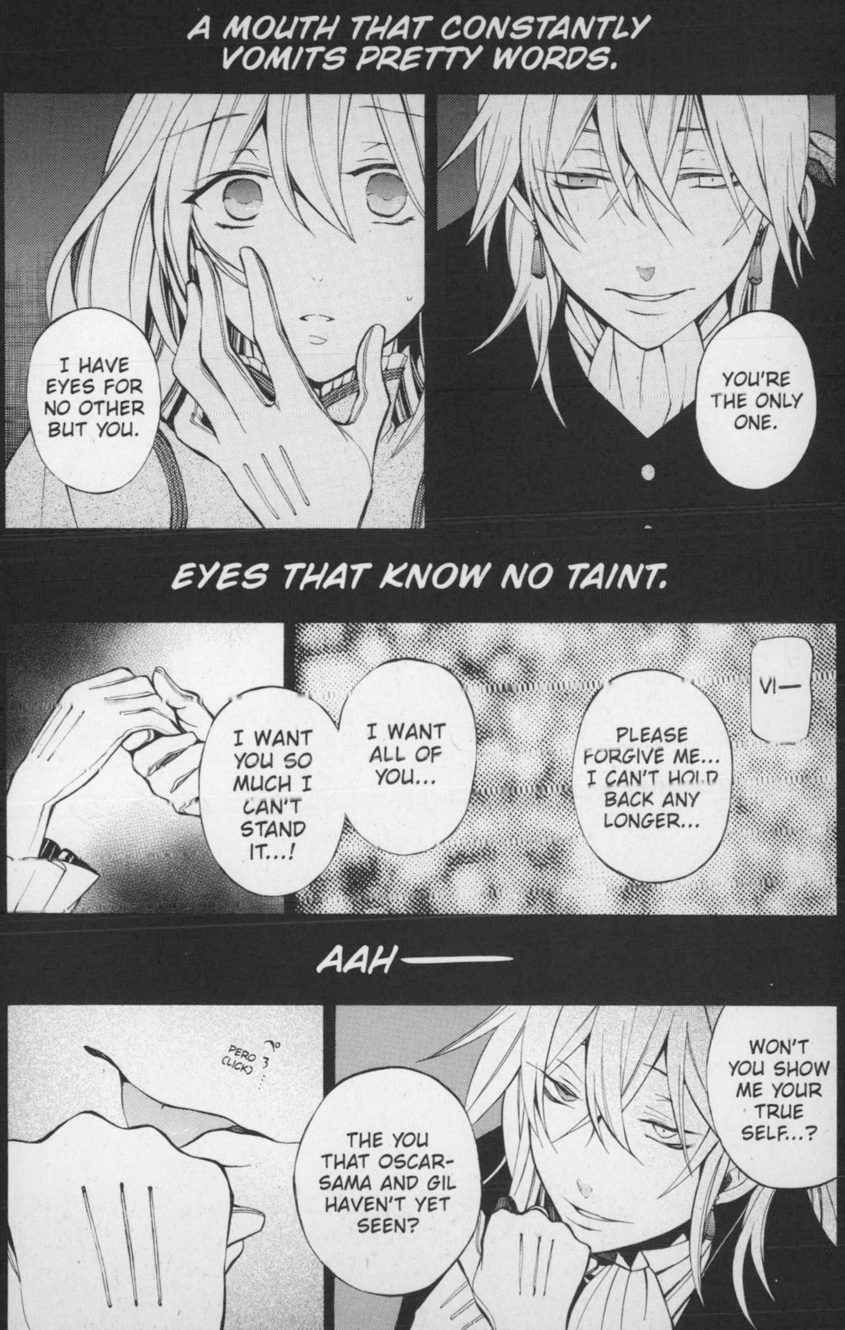
A MOUTH THAT CONSTANTLY VOMITS PRETTY WORDS.
YOU'RE THE ONLY ONE.
I HAVE EYES FOR NO OTHER BUT YOU.
EYES THAT KNOW NO TAINT.
VI—
PLEASE FORGIVE ME... I CAN'T HOLD BACK ANY LONGER...
I WANT ALL OF YOU...
I WANT YOU SO MUCH I CAN'T STAND IT...!
AAH——
WON'T YOU SHOW ME YOUR TRUE SELF...?
THE YOU THAT OSCAR-SAMA AND GIL HAVEN'T YET SEEN?
PERO (LICK)

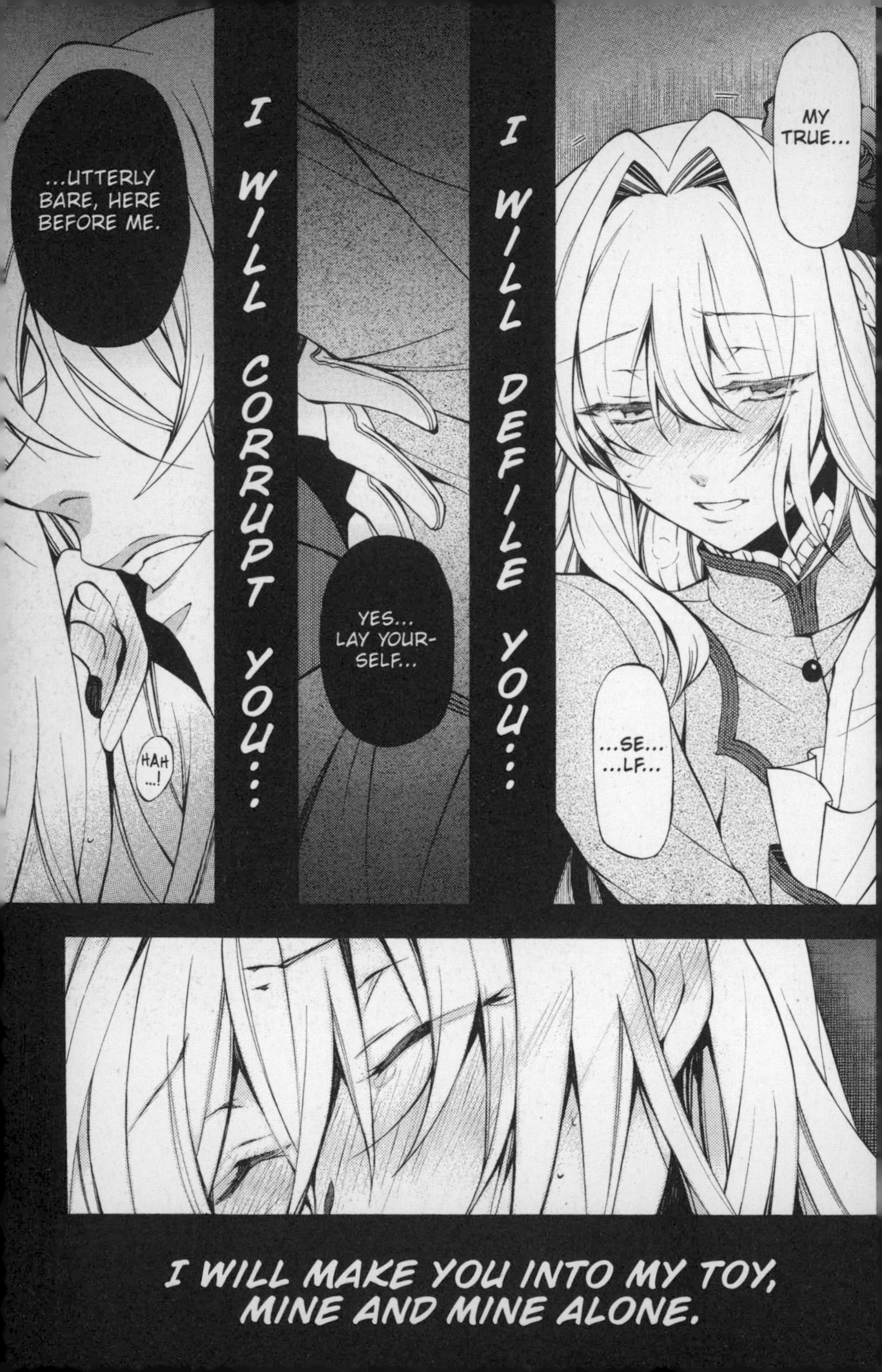
MY TRUE...
...SE... ...LF...
I WILL DEFILE YOU...
YES... LAY YOUR-SELF...
I WILL CORRUPT YOU...
...UTTERLY BARE, HERE BEFORE ME.
HAH ...!
I WILL MAKE YOU INTO MY TOY, MINE AND MINE ALONE.

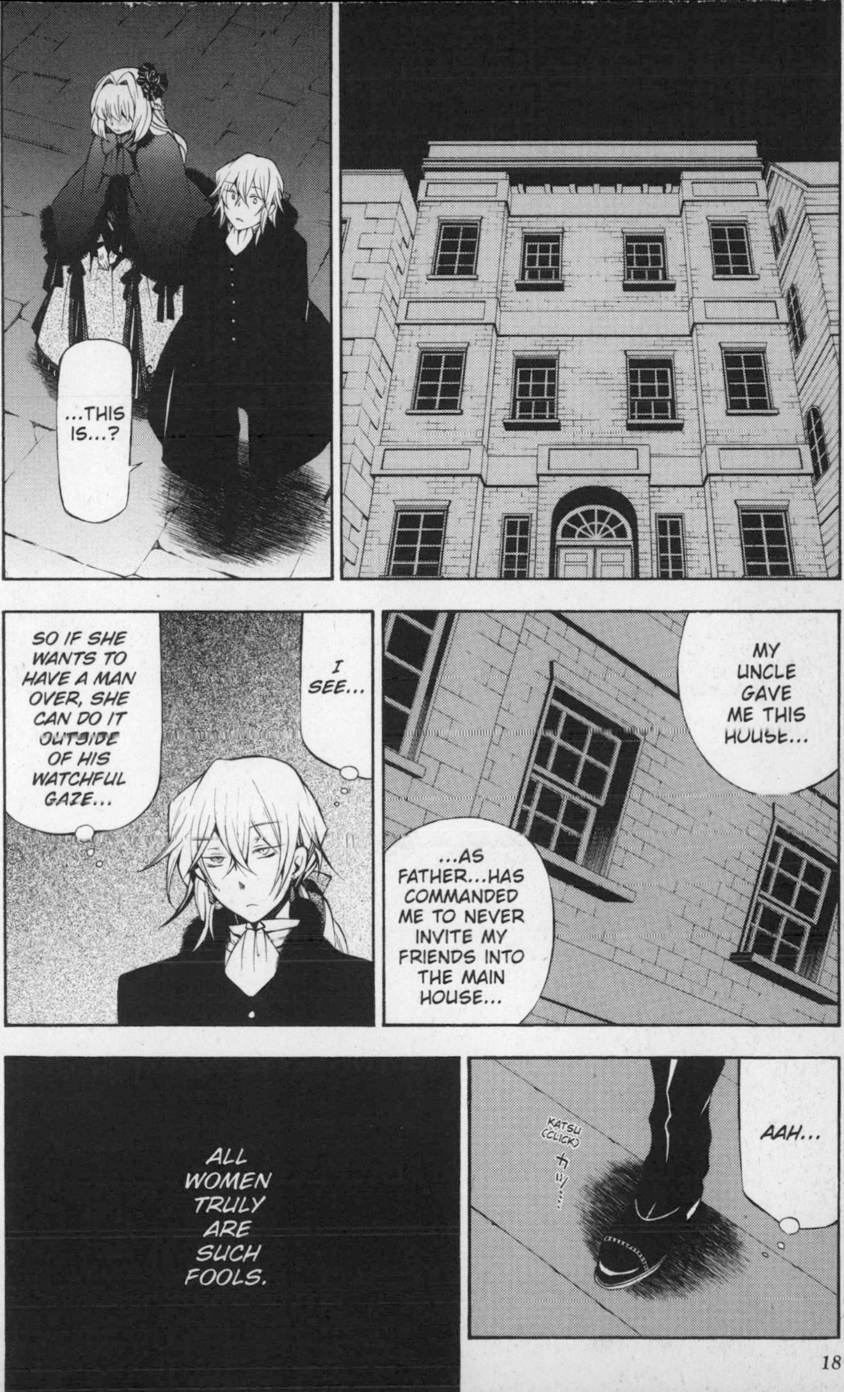
...THIS IS...?
MY UNCLE GAVE ME THIS HOUSE...
...AS FATHER...HAS COMMANDED ME TO NEVER INVITE MY FRIENDS INTO THE MAIN HOUSE...
I SEE...
SO IF SHE WANTS TO HAVE A MAN OVER, SHE CAN DO IT OUTSIDE OF HIS WATCHFUL GAZE...
AAH...
KATSU (CLICK)
カツ…
ALL WOMEN TRULY ARE SUCH FOOLS.

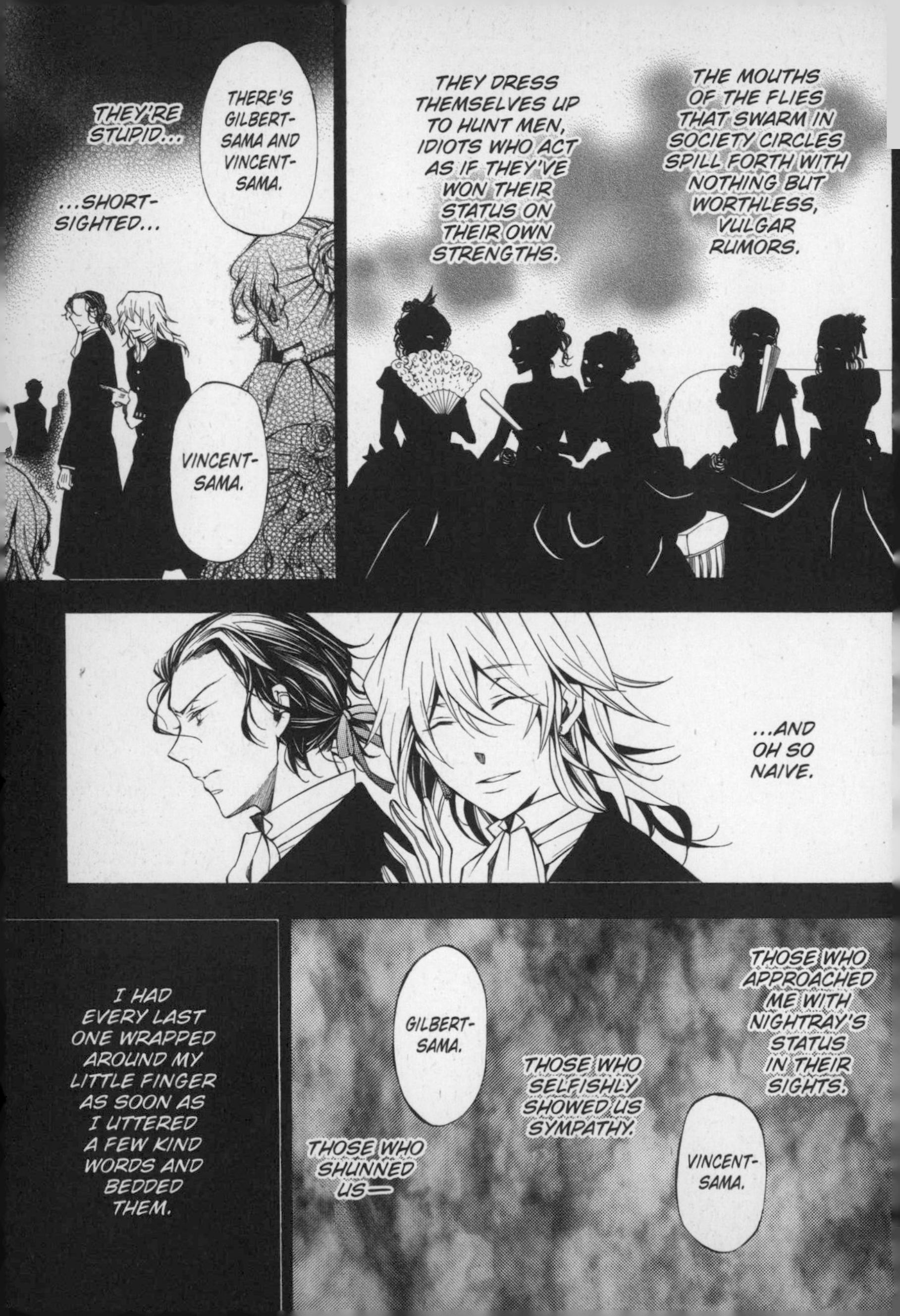
THE MOUTHS OF THE FLIES THAT SWARM IN SOCIETY CIRCLES SPILL FORTH WITH NOTHING BUT WORTHLESS, VULGAR RUMORS.
THEY DRESS THEMSELVES UP TO HUNT MEN, IDIOTS WHO ACT AS IF THEY'VE WON THEIR STATUS ON THEIR OWN STRENGTHS.
THERE'S GILBERT-SAMA AND VINCENT-SAMA.
THEY'RE STUPID...
...SHORT-SIGHTED...
VINCENT-SAMA.
...AND OH SO NAIVE.
THOSE WHO APPROACHED ME WITH NIGHTRAY'S STATUS IN THEIR SIGHTS.
GILBERT-SAMA.
THOSE WHO SELFISHLY SHOWED US SYMPATHY.
VINCENT-SAMA.
THOSE WHO SHUNNED US—
I HAD EVERY LAST ONE WRAPPED AROUND MY LITTLE FINGER AS SOON AS I UTTERED A FEW KIND WORDS AND BEDDED THEM.

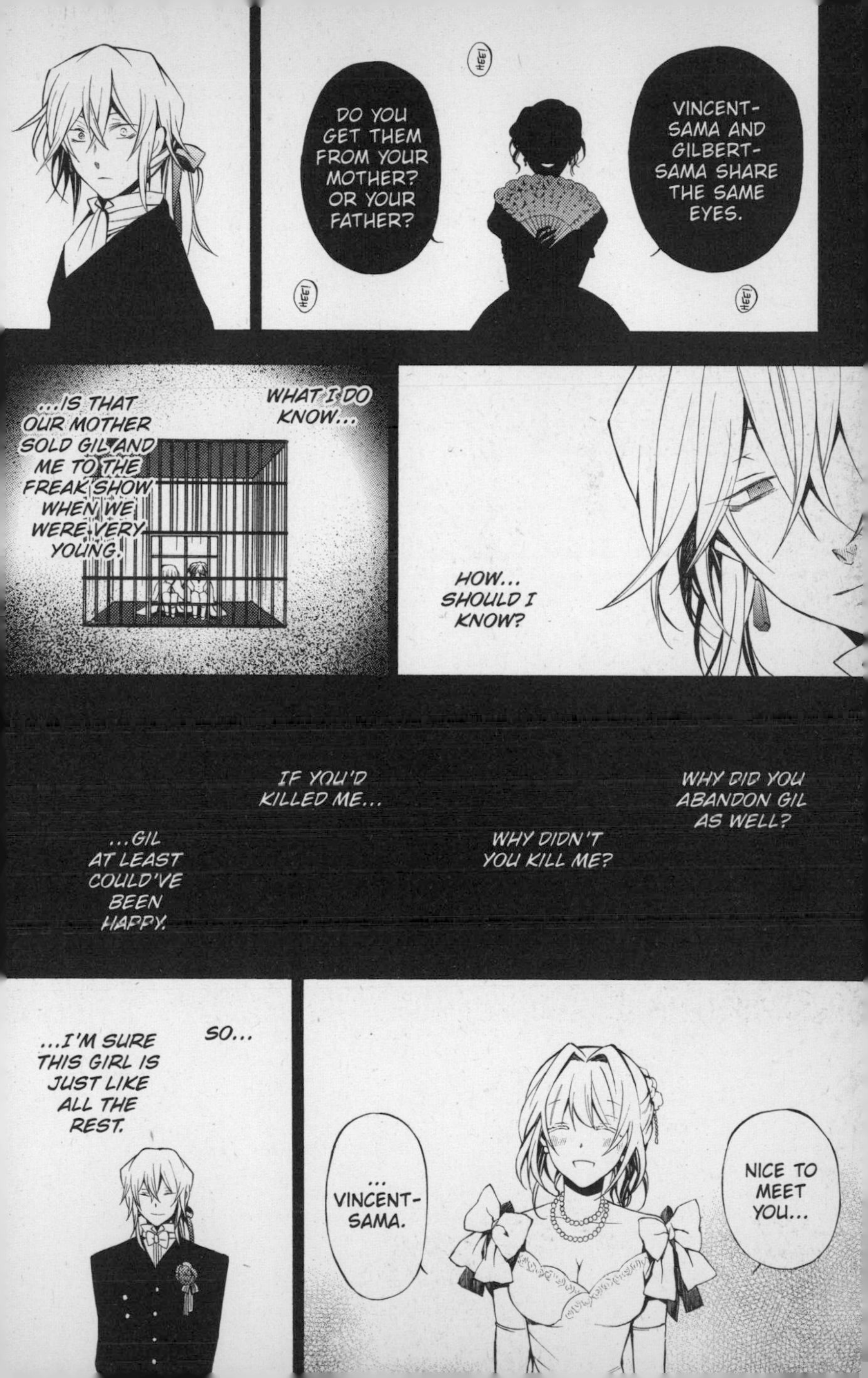
HEE!
VINCENT-SAMA AND GILBERT-SAMA SHARE THE SAME EYES.
HEE!
DO YOU GET THEM FROM YOUR MOTHER? OR YOUR FATHER?
HEE!
HOW... SHOULD I KNOW?
WHAT I DO KNOW...
...IS THAT OUR MOTHER SOLD GIL AND ME TO THE FREAK SHOW WHEN WE WERE VERY YOUNG.
WHY DID YOU ABANDON GIL AS WELL?
WHY DIDN'T YOU KILL ME?
IF YOU'D KILLED ME...
...GIL AT LEAST COULD'VE BEEN HAPPY.
NICE TO MEET YOU...
... VINCENT-SAMA.
SO...
...I'M SURE THIS GIRL IS JUST LIKE ALL THE REST.

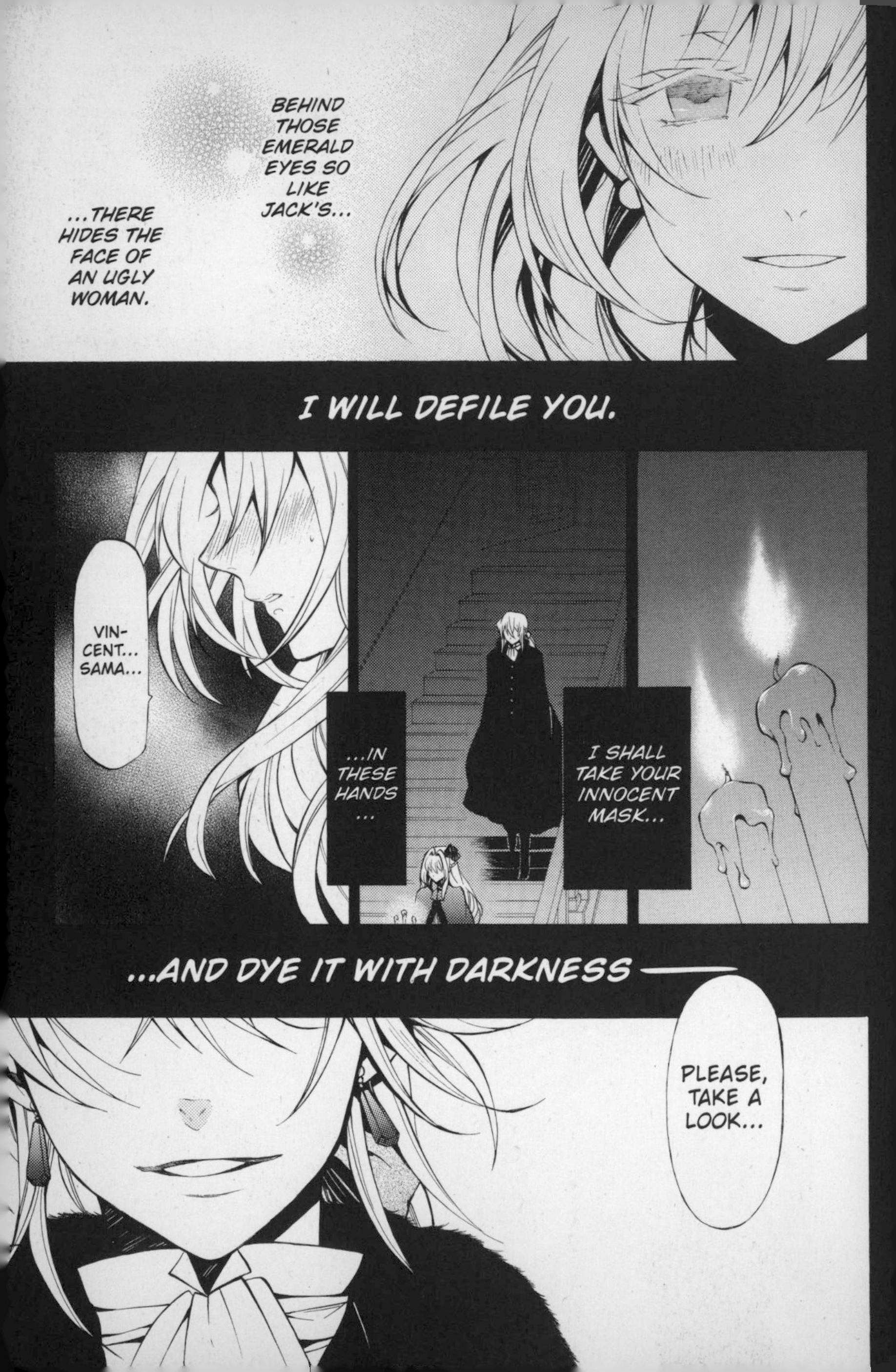
BEHIND THOSE EMERALD EYES SO LIKE JACK'S...
...THERE HIDES THE FACE OF AN UGLY WOMAN.
I WILL DEFILE YOU.
I SHALL TAKE YOUR INNOCENT MASK...
...IN THESE HANDS ...
VIN-CENT... SAMA...
...AND DYE IT WITH DARKNESS—
PLEASE, TAKE A LOOK...

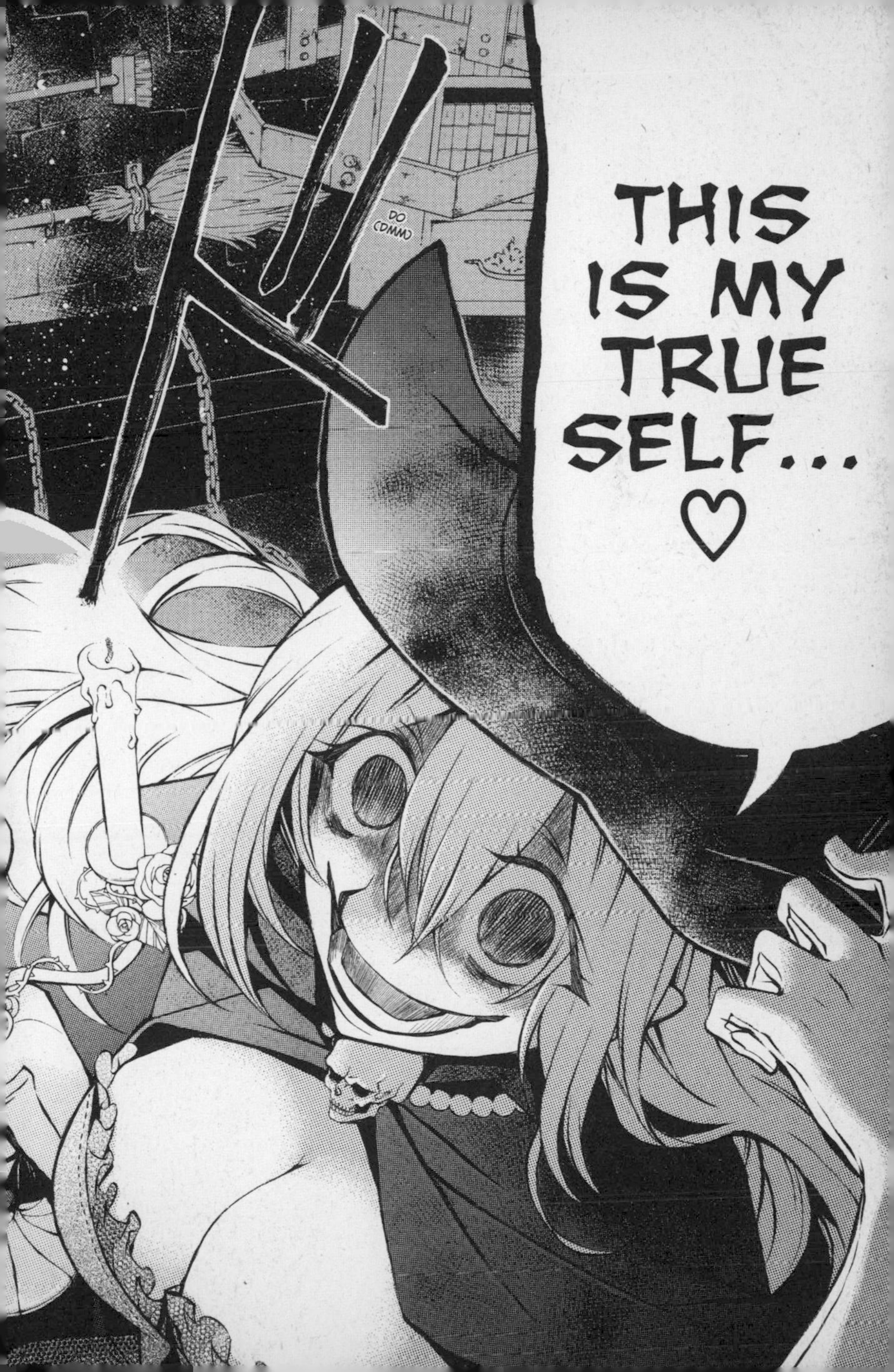
THIS IS MY TRUE SELF... ♡
DO (DMM)

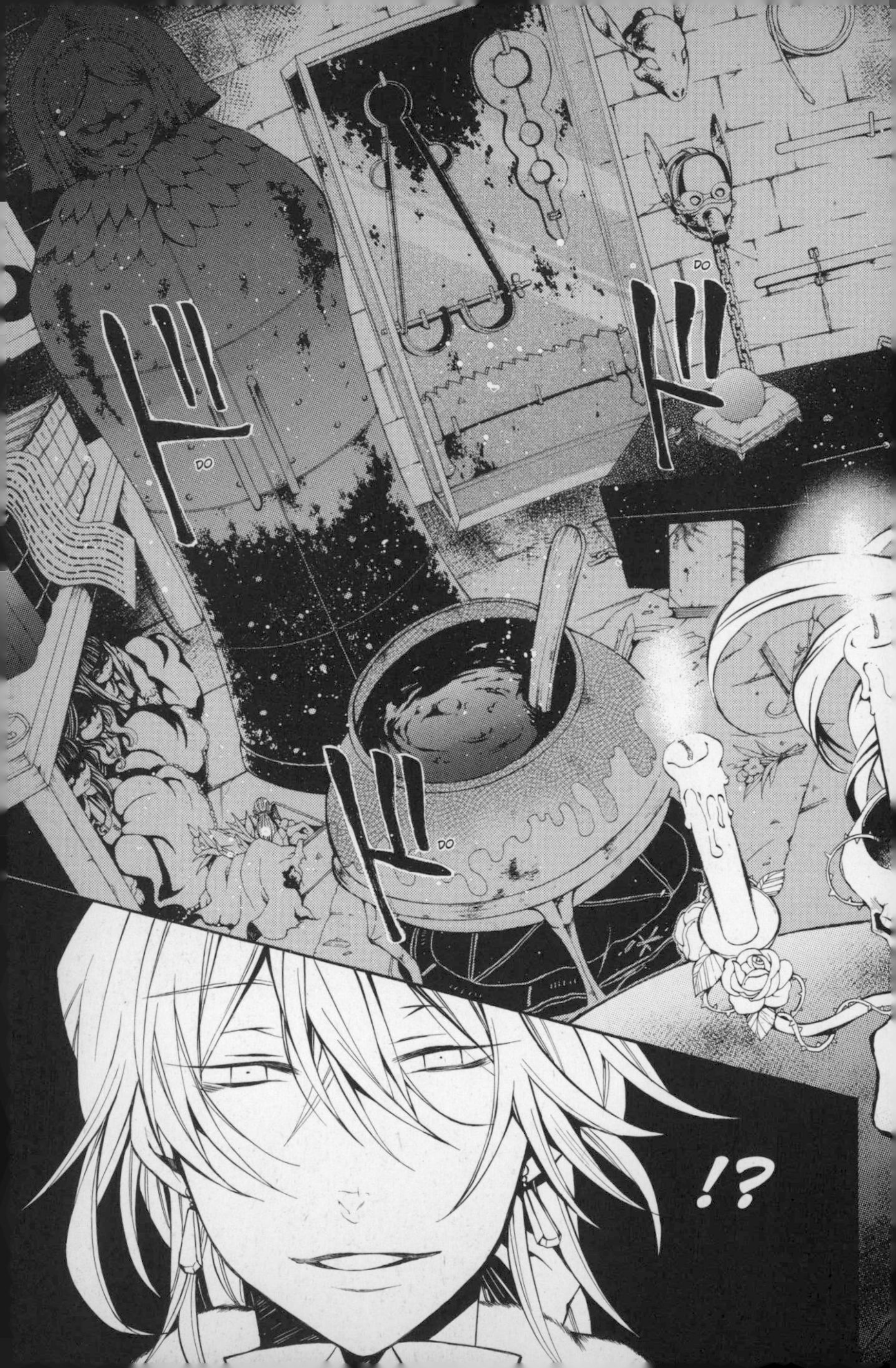
ド
DO
ド
DO
ド
DO
!?

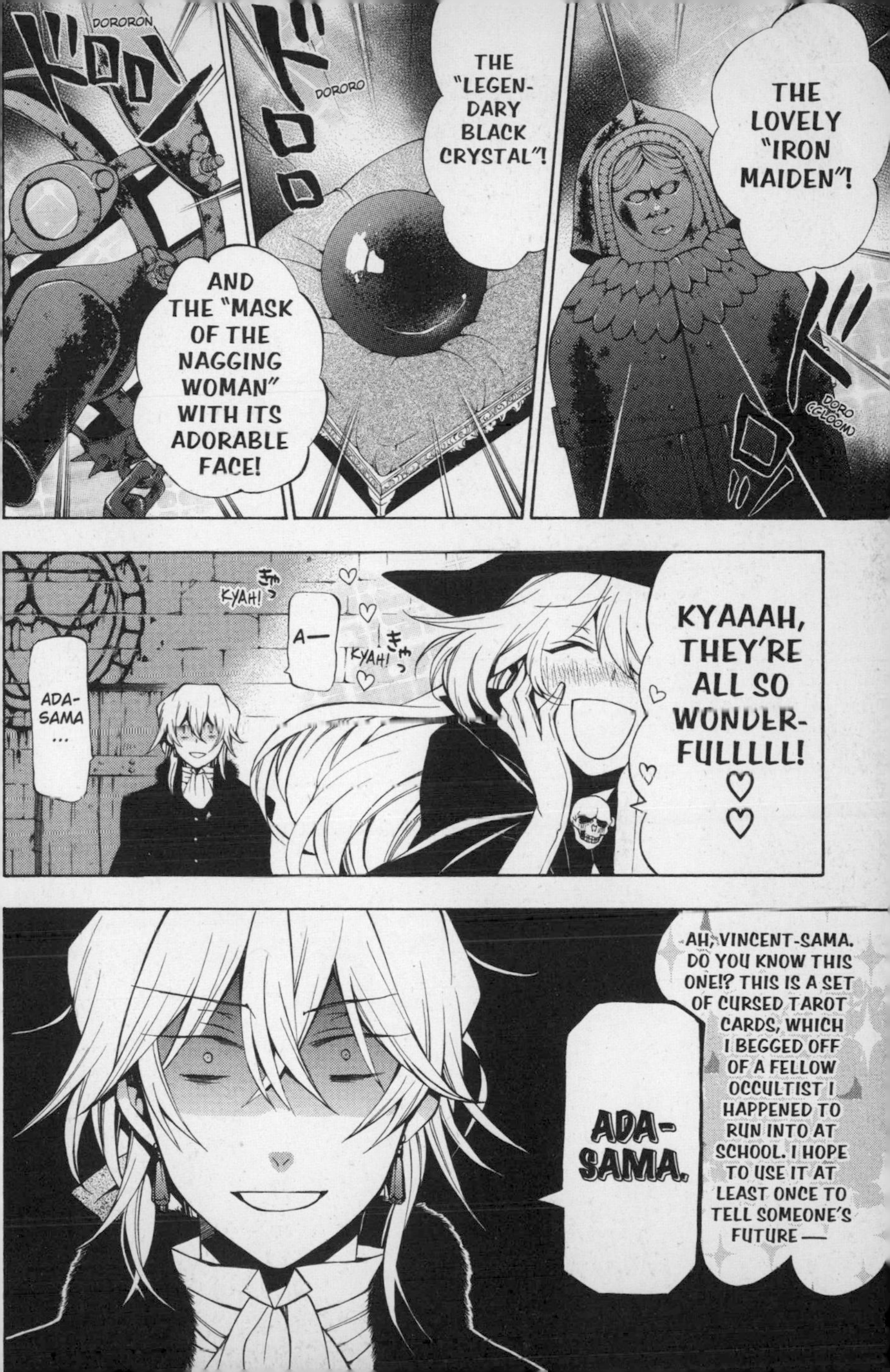
THE LOVELY "IRON MAIDEN"!
DORO (GLOOM)
THE "LEGEN-DARY BLACK CRYSTAL"!
DORORO
DORORON
AND THE "MASK OF THE NAGGING WOMAN" WITH ITS ADORABLE FACE!
KYAAAH, THEY'RE ALL SO WONDER-FULLLLLL! ♡ ♡
きゃっ KYAH!
A—
きゃっ KYAH!
ADA-SAMA ...
AH, VINCENT-SAMA. DO YOU KNOW THIS ONE!? THIS IS A SET OF CURSED TAROT CARDS, WHICH I BEGGED OFF OF A FELLOW OCCULTIST I HAPPENED TO RUN INTO AT SCHOOL. I HOPE TO USE IT AT LEAST ONCE TO TELL SOMEONE'S FUTURE—
ADA-SAMA.

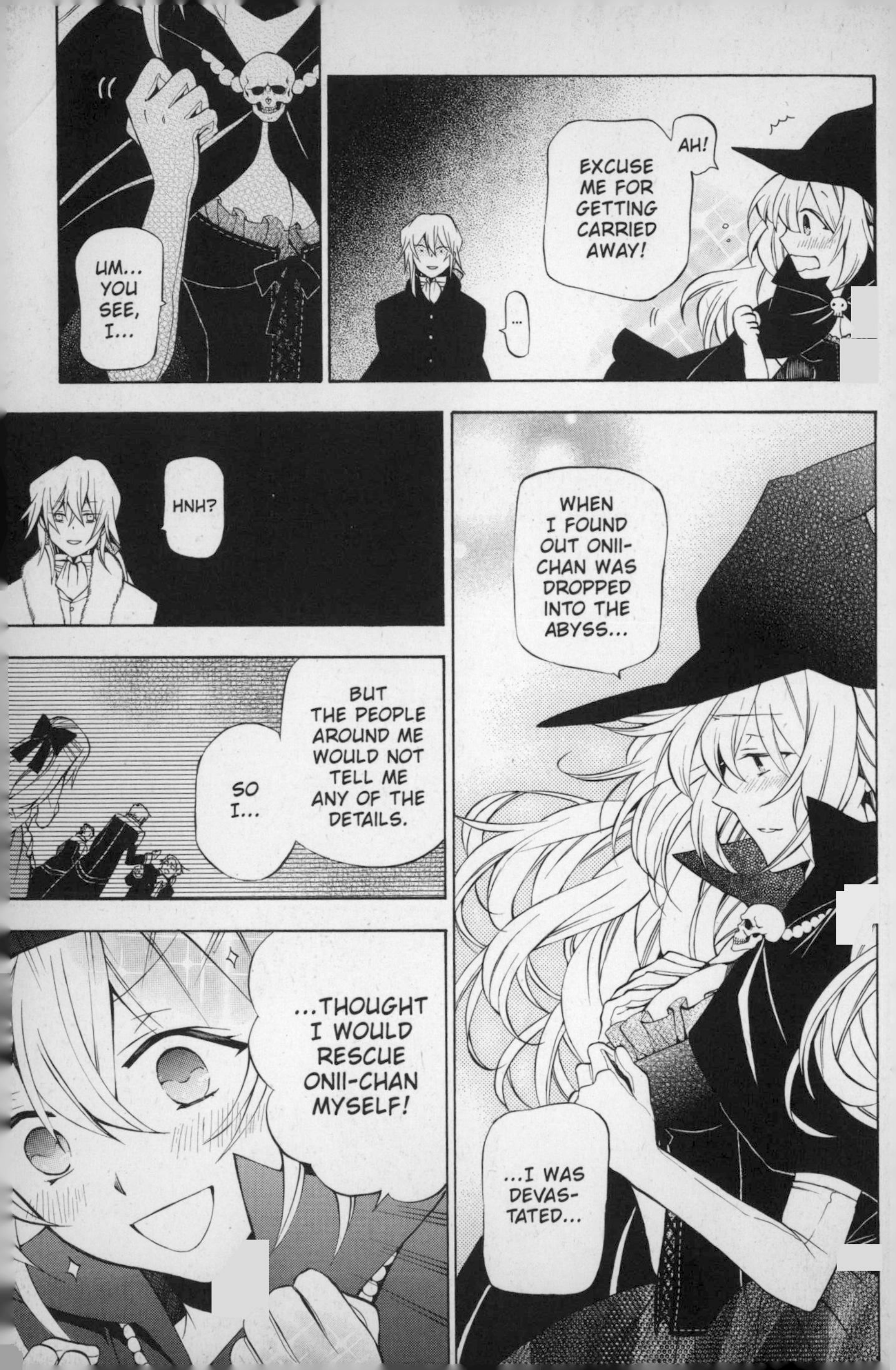
AH!
EXCUSE ME FOR GETTING CARRIED AWAY!
...
UM... YOU SEE, I...
WHEN I FOUND OUT ONII-CHAN WAS DROPPED INTO THE ABYSS...
...I WAS DEVASTATED...
HNH?
BUT THE PEOPLE AROUND ME WOULD NOT TELL ME ANY OF THE DETAILS.
SO I...
...THOUGHT I WOULD RESCUE ONII-CHAN MYSELF!

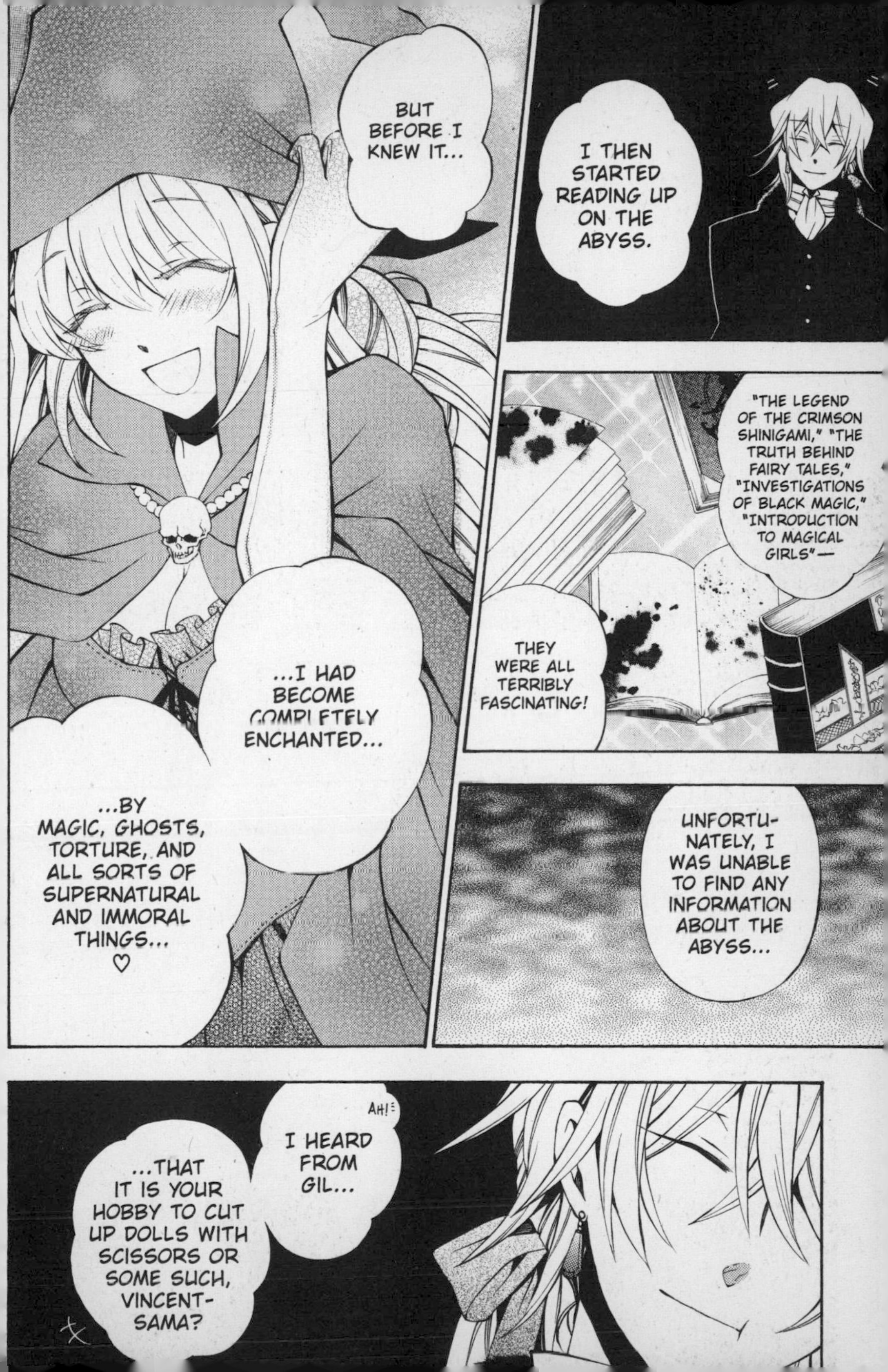
I THEN STARTED READING UP ON THE ABYSS.
"THE LEGEND OF THE CRIMSON SHINIGAMI," "THE TRUTH BEHIND FAIRY TALES," "INVESTIGATIONS OF BLACK MAGIC," "INTRODUCTION TO MAGICAL GIRLS"—
THEY WERE ALL TERRIBLY FASCINATING!
UNFORTUNATELY, I WAS UNABLE TO FIND ANY INFORMATION ABOUT THE ABYSS...
BUT BEFORE I KNEW IT...
...I HAD BECOME COMPLETELY ENCHANTED...
...BY MAGIC, GHOSTS, TORTURE, AND ALL SORTS OF SUPERNATURAL AND IMMORAL THINGS... ♡
AH!
I HEARD FROM GIL...
...THAT IT IS YOUR HOBBY TO CUT UP DOLLS WITH SCISSORS OR SOME SUCH, VINCENT-SAMA?

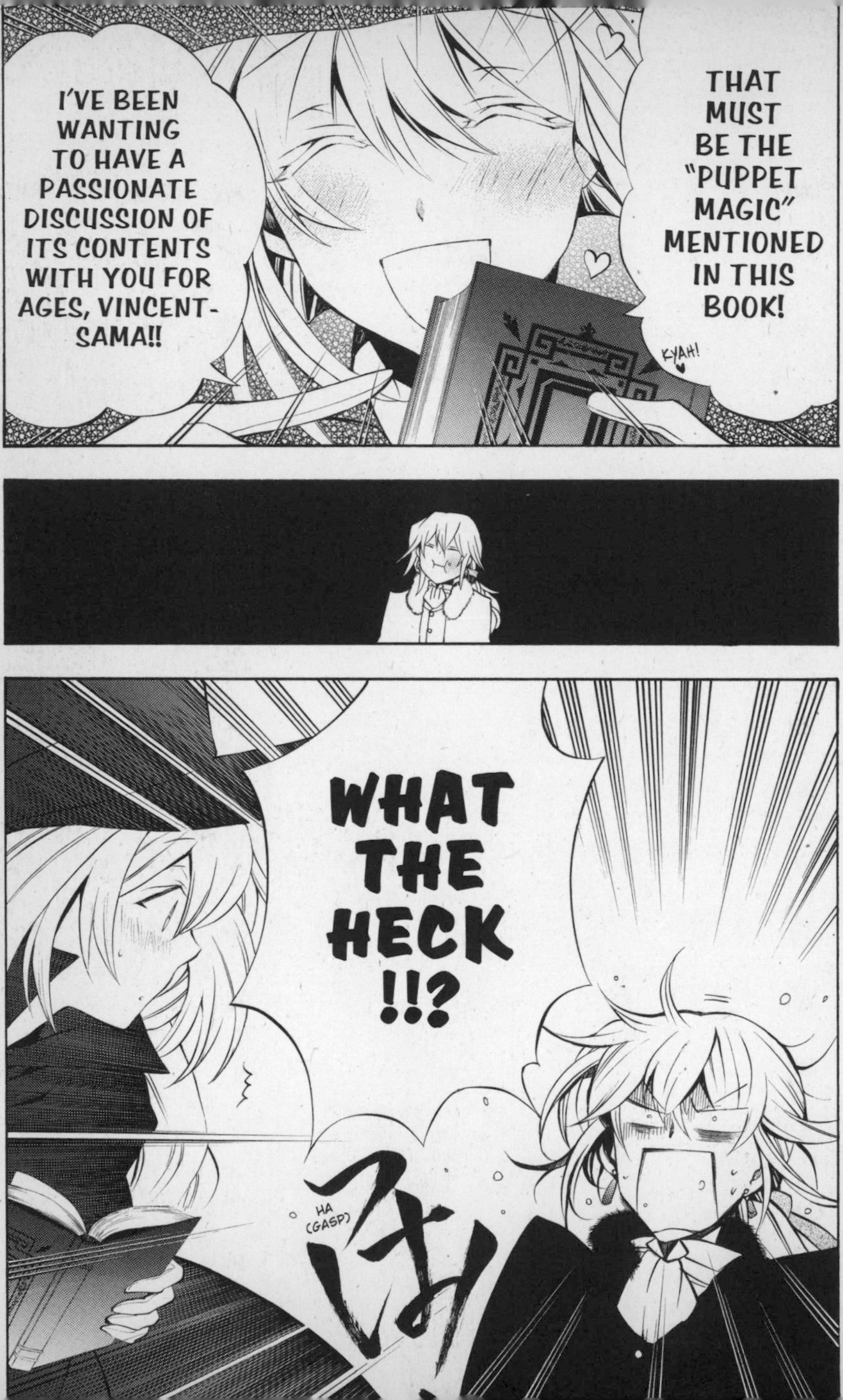
THAT MUST BE THE "PUPPET MAGIC" MENTIONED IN THIS BOOK!
KYAH!
I'VE BEEN WANTING TO HAVE A PASSIONATE DISCUSSION OF ITS CONTENTS WITH YOU FOR AGES, VINCENT-SAMA!!
WHAT THE HECK!!?
HA (GASP)

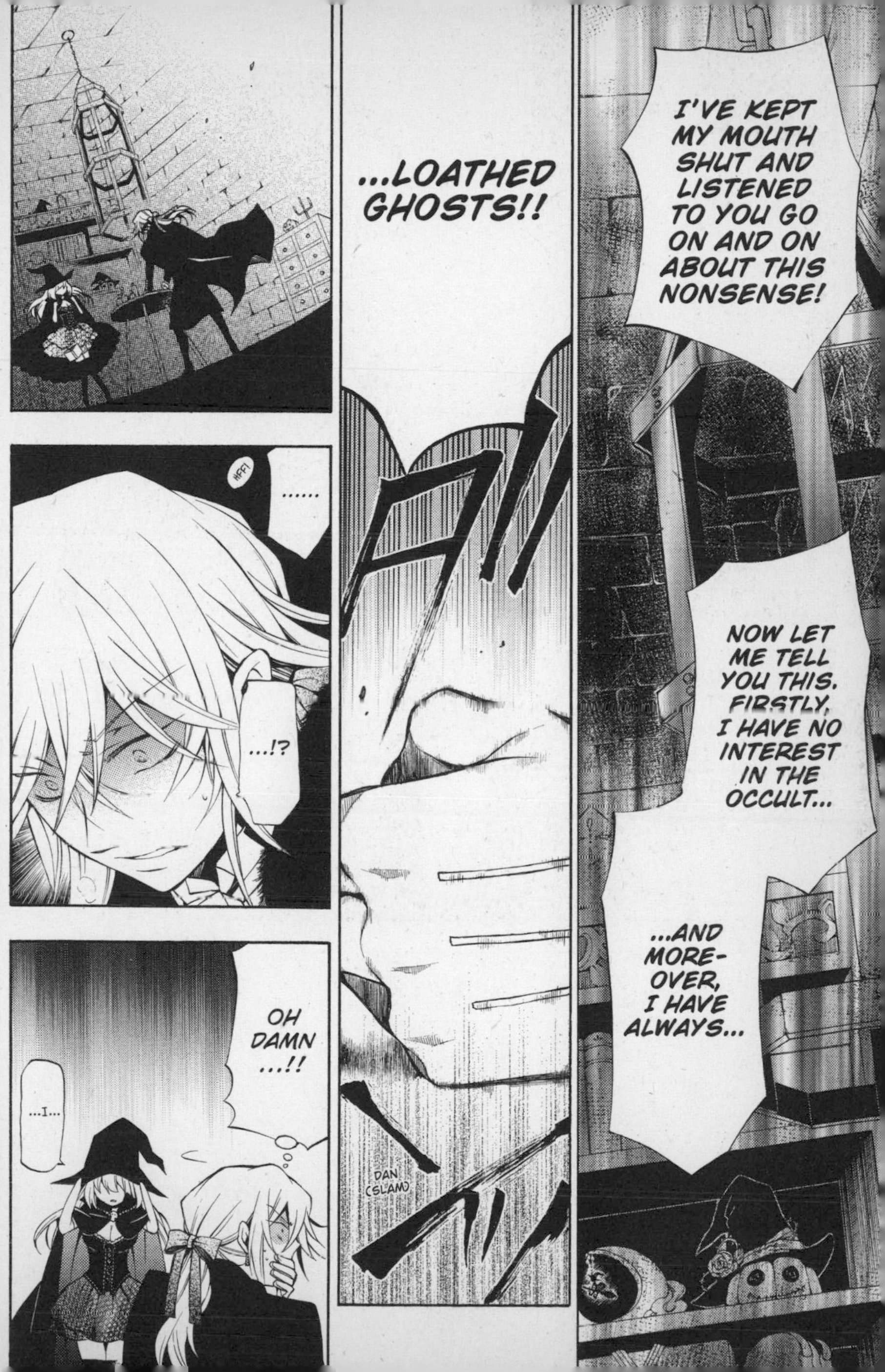
I'VE KEPT MY MOUTH SHUT AND LISTENED TO YOU GO ON AND ON ABOUT THIS NONSENSE!
NOW LET ME TELL YOU THIS. FIRSTLY, I HAVE NO INTEREST IN THE OCCULT...
...AND MORE-OVER, I HAVE ALWAYS...
...LOATHED GHOSTS!!
DAN (SLAM)
HFF!
......
...!?
OH DAMN ...!!
...I...

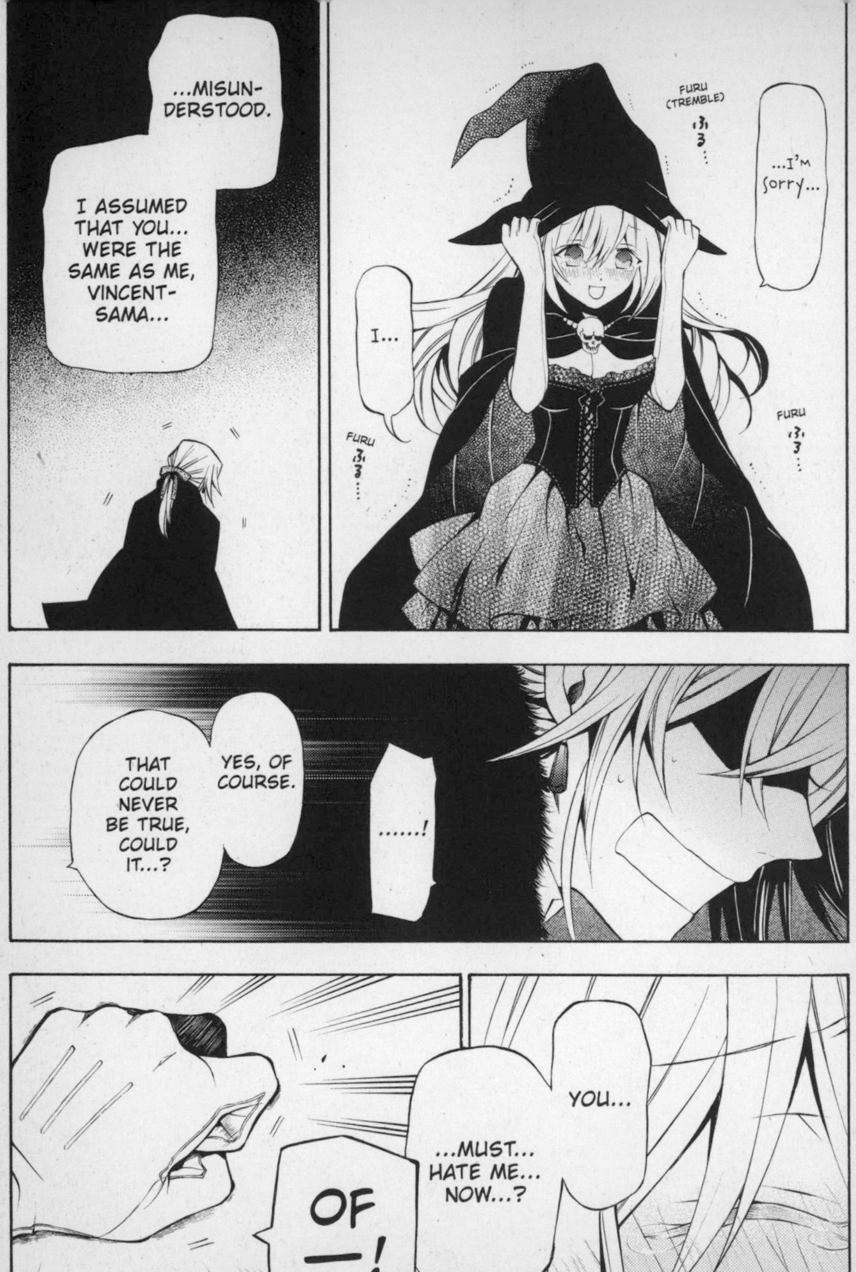
...I'M
sorry...
FURU
(TREMBLE)
ふる...
I...
FURU
ふる...
FURU
ふる...
...MISUNDERSTOOD.
I ASSUMED THAT YOU... WERE THE SAME AS ME, VINCENT-SAMA...
......!
YES, OF COURSE.
THAT COULD NEVER BE TRUE, COULD IT...?
YOU...
...MUST... HATE ME... NOW...?
OF—!

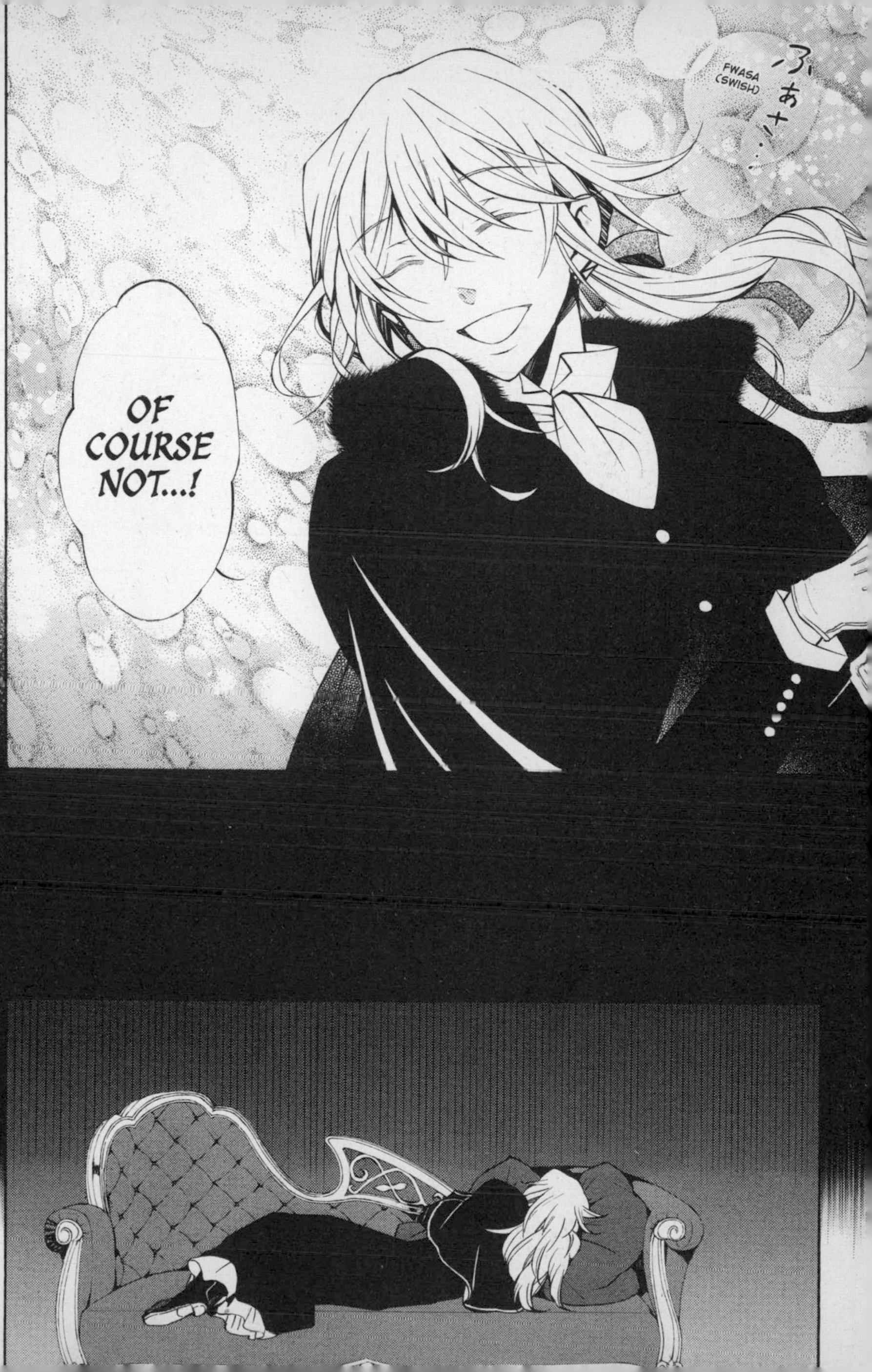
ふぁさ…
FWASA (SWISH)
OF COURSE NOT...!

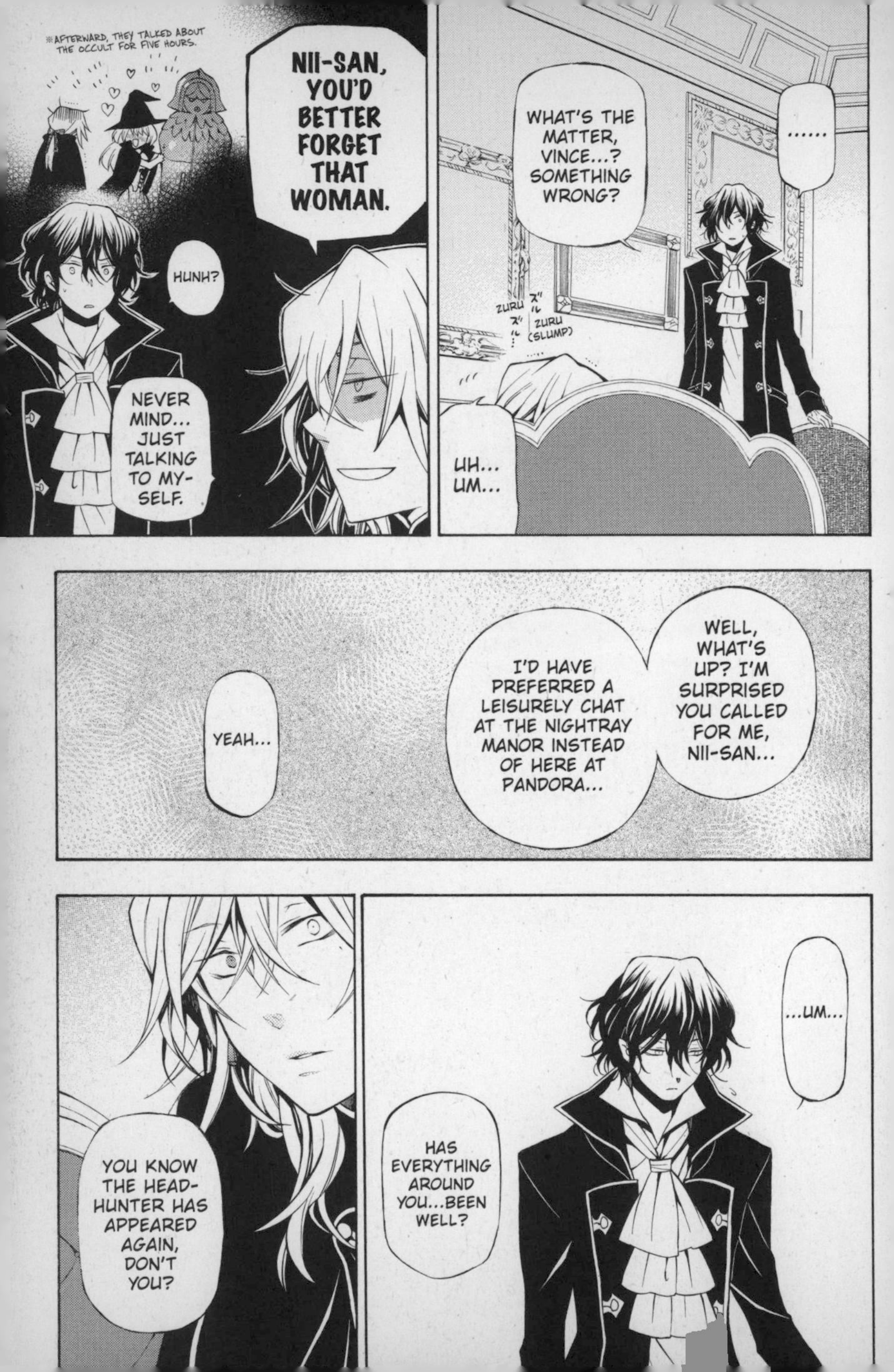
......
WHAT'S THE MATTER, VINCE...? SOMETHING WRONG?
ZURU ZURU (SLUMP)
UH... UM...
NII-SAN, YOU'D BETTER FORGET THAT WOMAN.
※AFTERWARD, THEY TALKED ABOUT THE OCCULT FOR FIVE HOURS.
HUNH?
NEVER MIND... JUST TALKING TO MY-SELF.
WELL, WHAT'S UP? I'M SURPRISED YOU CALLED FOR ME, NII-SAN...
I'D HAVE PREFERRED A LEISURELY CHAT AT THE NIGHTRAY MANOR INSTEAD OF HERE AT PANDORA...
YEAH...
...UM...
HAS EVERYTHING AROUND YOU...BEEN WELL?
YOU KNOW THE HEAD-HUNTER HAS APPEARED AGAIN, DON'T YOU?

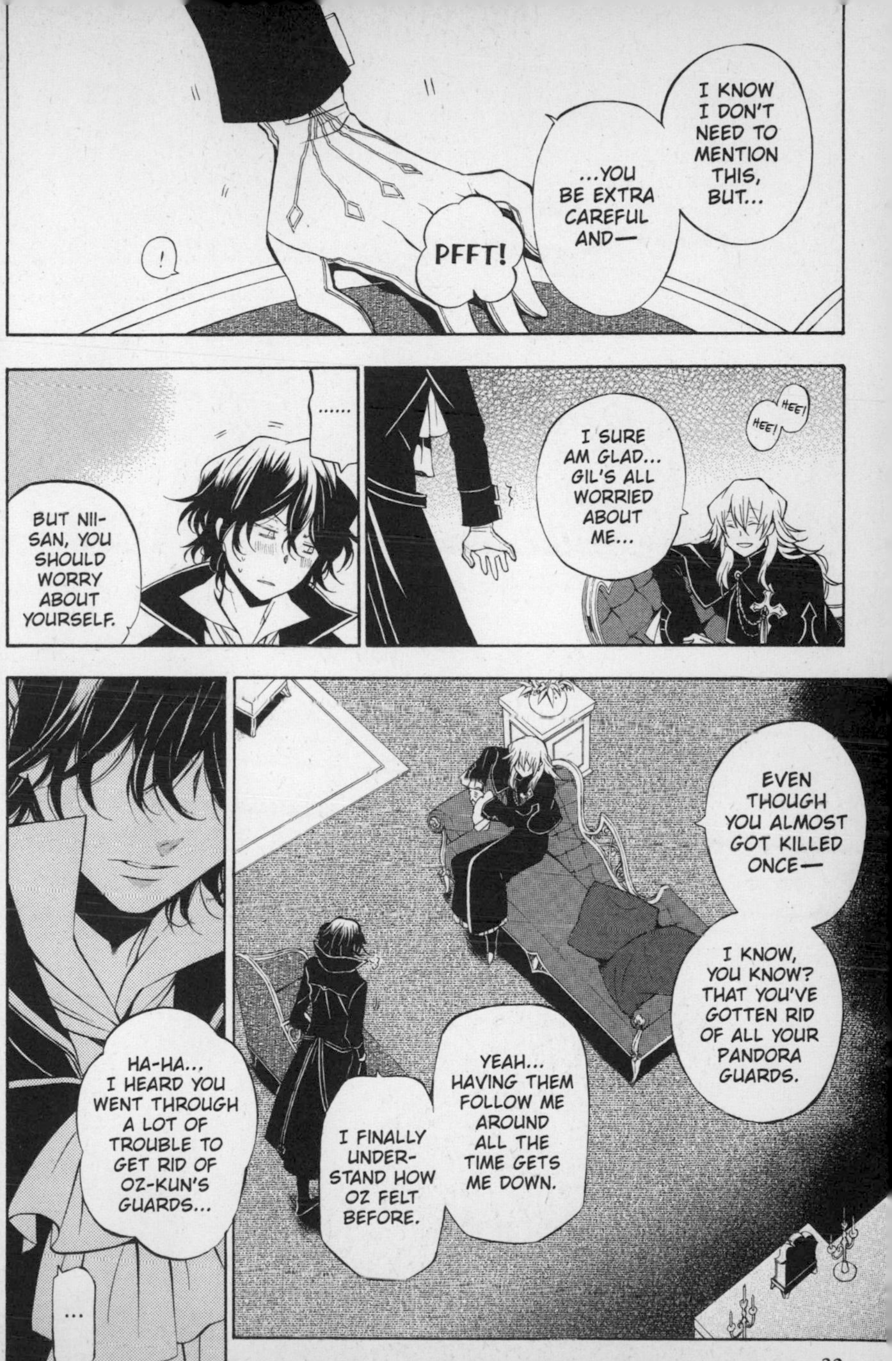
I KNOW I DON'T NEED TO MENTION THIS, BUT...
...YOU BE EXTRA CAREFUL AND—
PFFT!
!
HEE! HEE!
I SURE AM GLAD... GIL'S ALL WORRIED ABOUT ME...
......
BUT NII-SAN, YOU SHOULD WORRY ABOUT YOURSELF.
EVEN THOUGH YOU ALMOST GOT KILLED ONCE—
I KNOW, YOU KNOW? THAT YOU'VE GOTTEN RID OF ALL YOUR PANDORA GUARDS.
YEAH... HAVING THEM FOLLOW ME AROUND ALL THE TIME GETS ME DOWN.
I FINALLY UNDER-STAND HOW OZ FELT BEFORE.
HA-HA... I HEARD YOU WENT THROUGH A LOT OF TROUBLE TO GET RID OF OZ-KUN'S GUARDS...
...

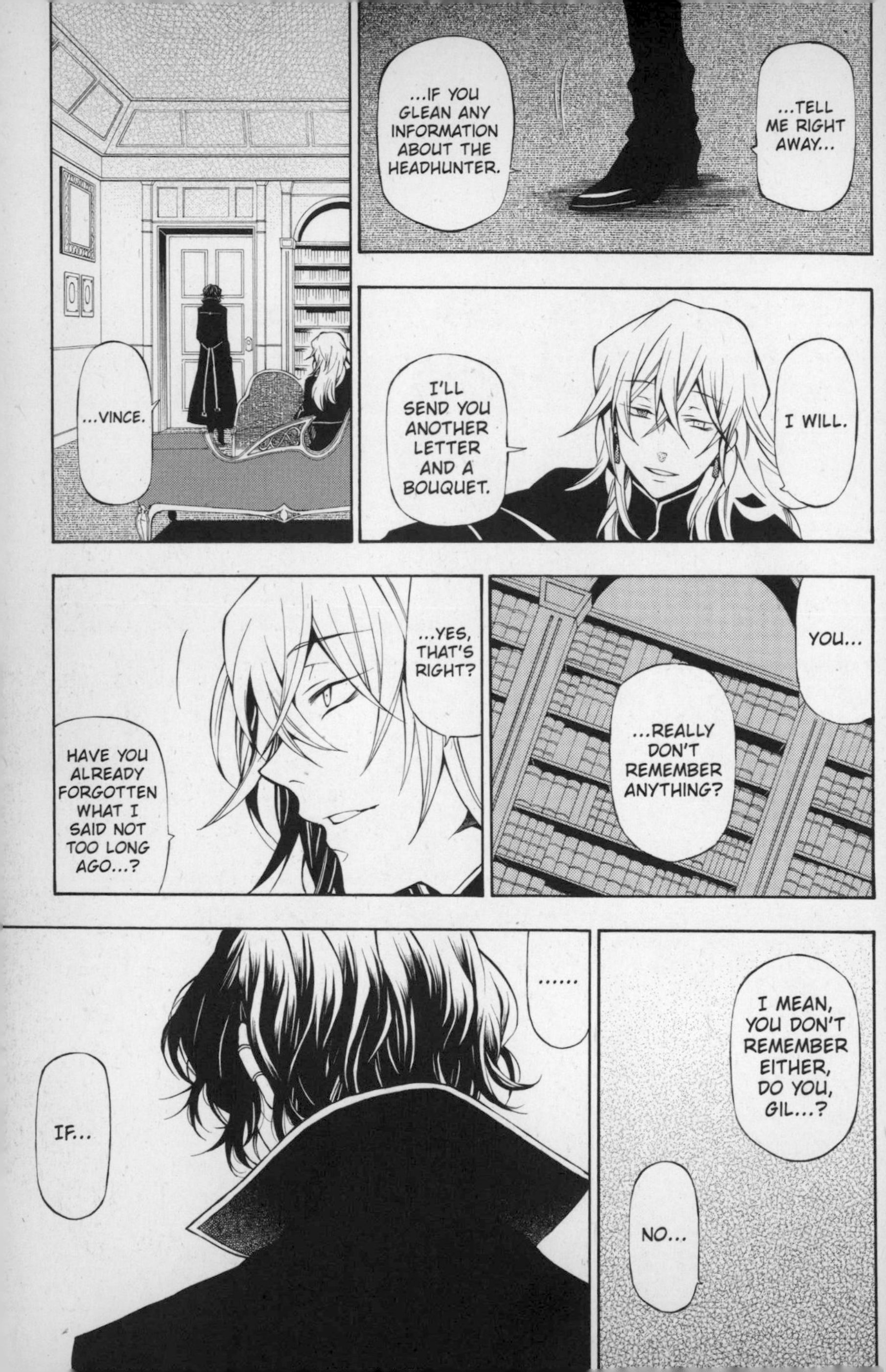
...TELL ME RIGHT AWAY...
...IF YOU GLEAN ANY INFORMATION ABOUT THE HEADHUNTER.
I WILL.
I'LL SEND YOU ANOTHER LETTER AND A BOUQUET.
...VINCE.
YOU...
...REALLY DON'T REMEMBER ANYTHING?
...YES, THAT'S RIGHT?
HAVE YOU ALREADY FORGOTTEN WHAT I SAID NOT TOO LONG AGO...?
I MEAN, YOU DON'T REMEMBER EITHER, DO YOU, GIL...?
NO...
......
IF...

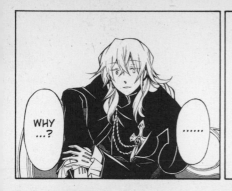

WHY
...?

......

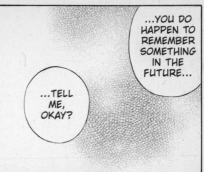

...TELL
ME,
OKAY?

...YOU DO
HAPPEN TO
REMEMBER
SOMETHING
IN THE
FUTURE...

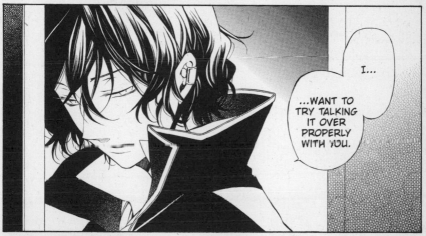

I...

...WANT TO
TRY TALKING
IT OVER
PROPERLY
WITH YOU.

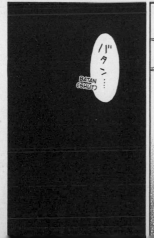

バタン...

BATAN
(SHUT)

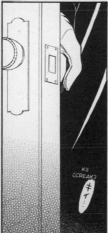

キィ...

KII
(CREAK)

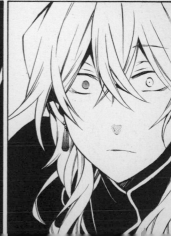

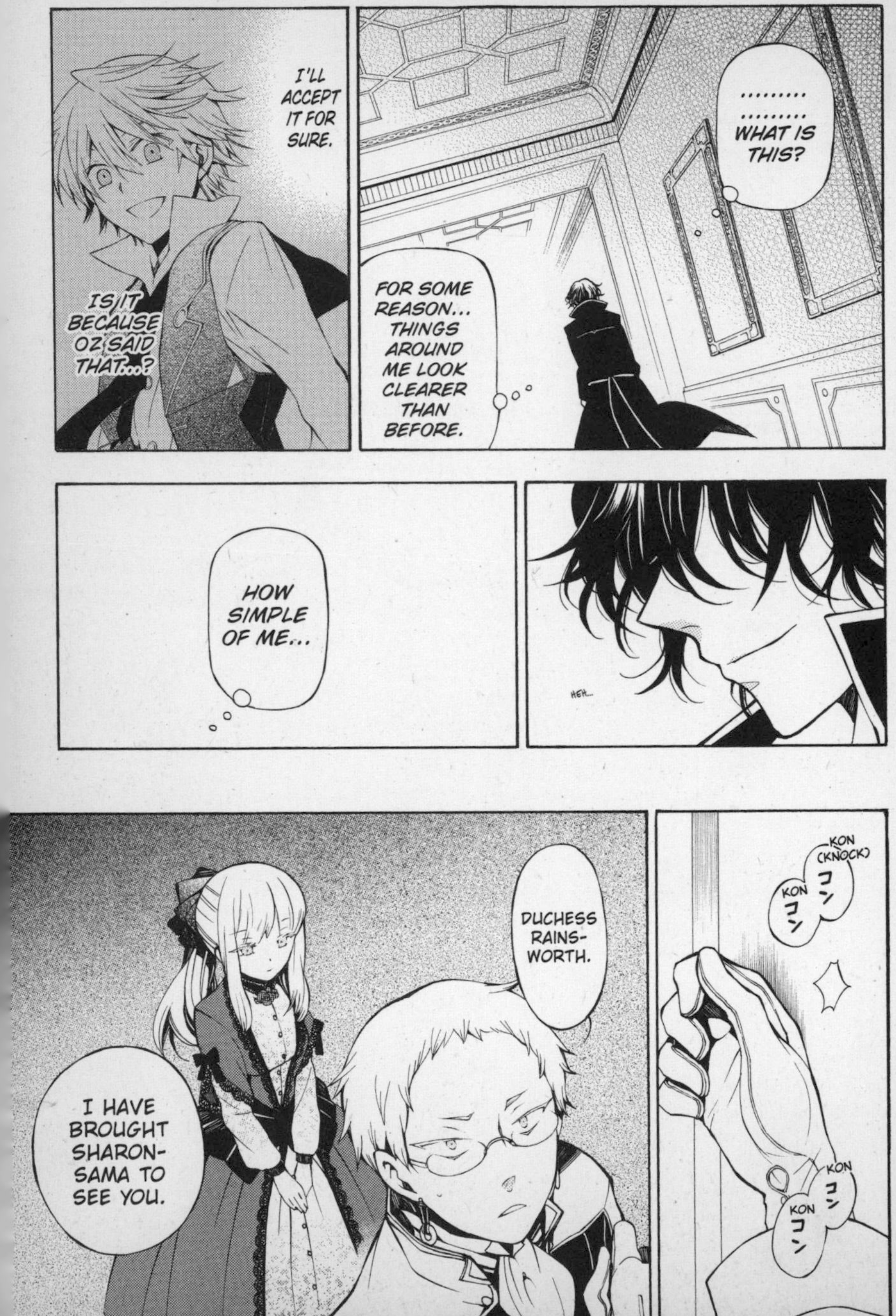

....
....
WHAT IS THIS?
FOR SOME REASON... THINGS AROUND ME LOOK CLEARER THAN BEFORE.
I'LL ACCEPT IT FOR SURE.
IS IT BECAUSE OZ SAID THAT...?
HEH...
HOW SIMPLE OF ME...
KON (KNOCK) コン
KON コン
KON コン
KON コン
DUCHESS RAINSWORTH.
I HAVE BROUGHT SHARON-SAMA TO SEE YOU.

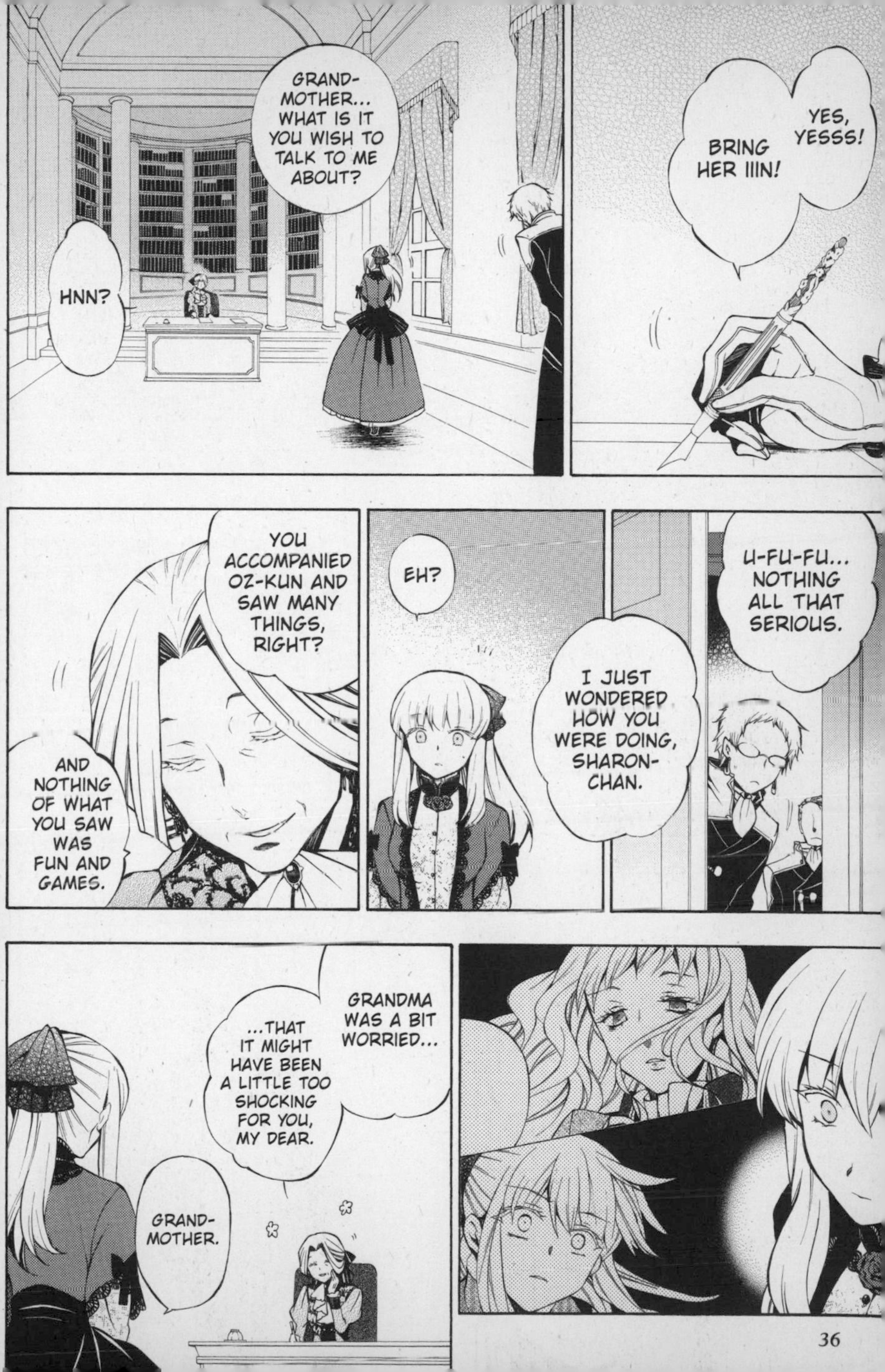
YES, YESSS!
BRING HER IIIN!
GRAND-MOTHER... WHAT IS IT YOU WISH TO TALK TO ME ABOUT?
HNN?
U-FU-FU... NOTHING ALL THAT SERIOUS.
I JUST WONDERED HOW YOU WERE DOING, SHARON-CHAN.
EH?
YOU ACCOMPANIED OZ-KUN AND SAW MANY THINGS, RIGHT?
AND NOTHING OF WHAT YOU SAW WAS FUN AND GAMES.
GRANDMA WAS A BIT WORRIED...
...THAT IT MIGHT HAVE BEEN A LITTLE TOO SHOCKING FOR YOU, MY DEAR.
GRAND-MOTHER.

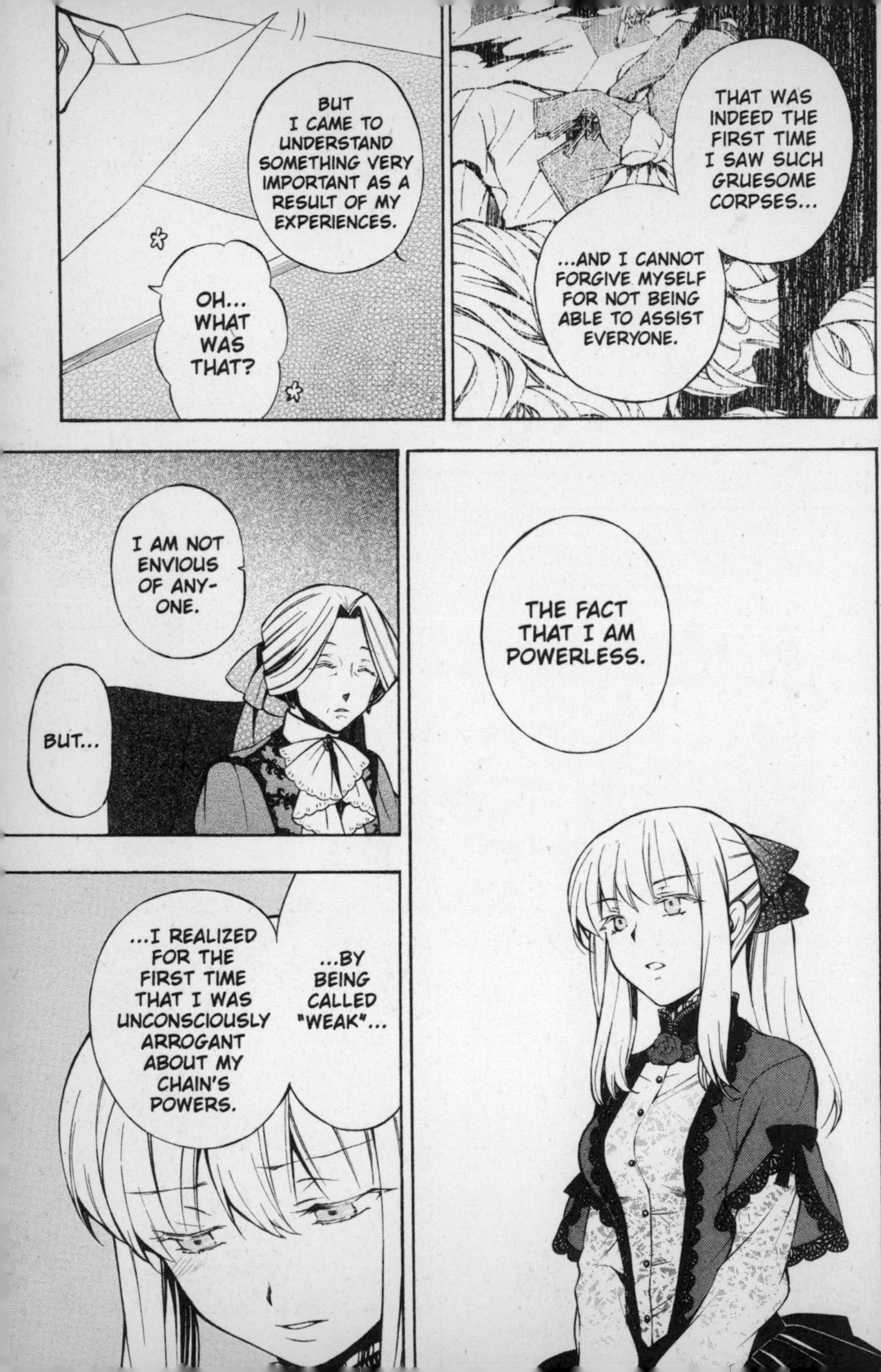
THAT WAS INDEED THE FIRST TIME I SAW SUCH GRUESOME CORPSES...
...AND I CANNOT FORGIVE MYSELF FOR NOT BEING ABLE TO ASSIST EVERYONE.
BUT I CAME TO UNDERSTAND SOMETHING VERY IMPORTANT AS A RESULT OF MY EXPERIENCES.
OH... WHAT WAS THAT?
THE FACT THAT I AM POWERLESS.
I AM NOT ENVIOUS OF ANY-ONE.
BUT...
...BY BEING CALLED "WEAK"...
...I REALIZED FOR THE FIRST TIME THAT I WAS UNCONSCIOUSLY ARROGANT ABOUT MY CHAIN'S POWERS.

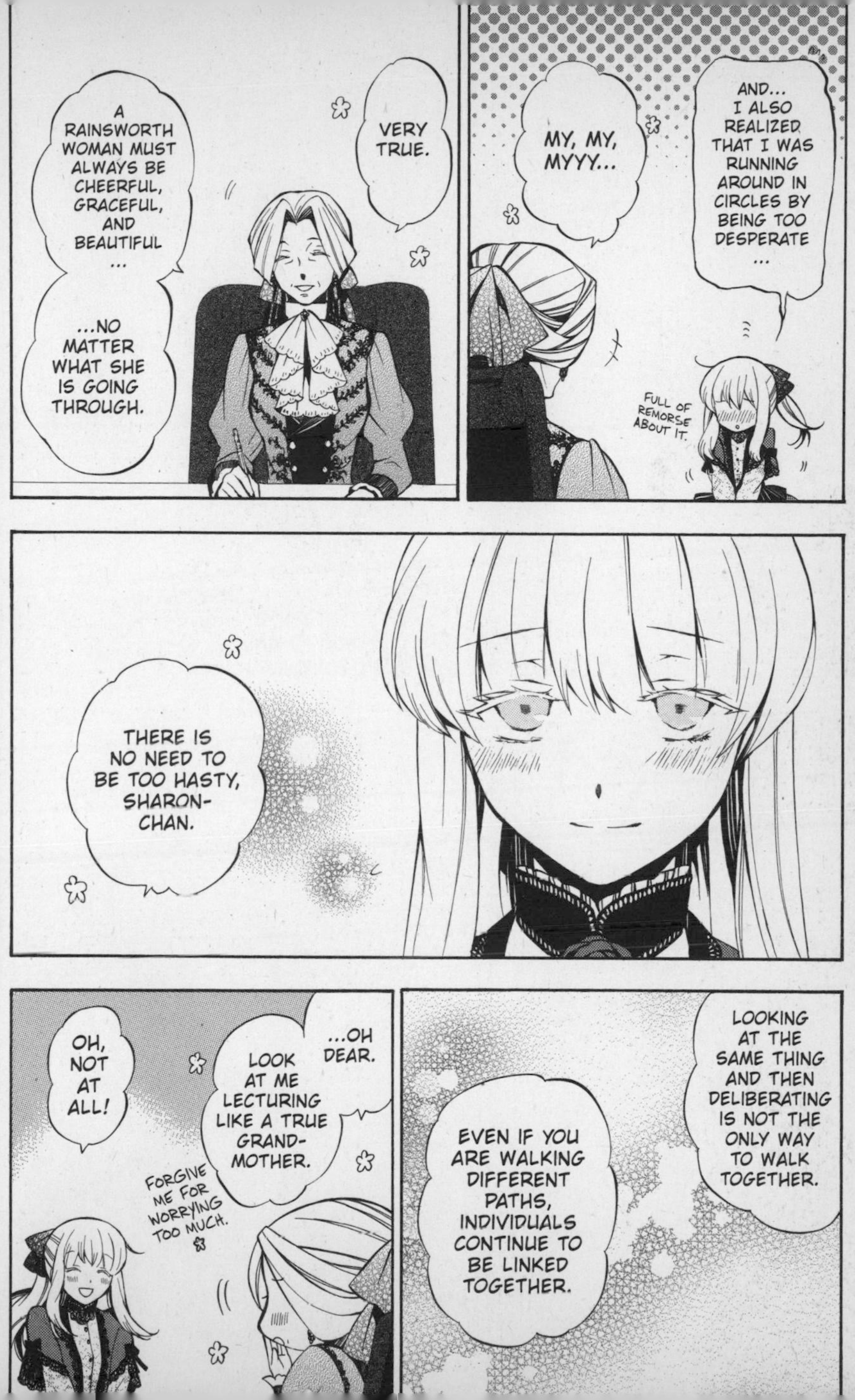
AND... I ALSO REALIZED THAT I WAS RUNNING AROUND IN CIRCLES BY BEING TOO DESPERATE ...
FULL OF REMORSE ABOUT IT.
MY, MY, MYYY...
VERY TRUE.
A RAINSWORTH WOMAN MUST ALWAYS BE CHEERFUL, GRACEFUL, AND BEAUTIFUL ...
...NO MATTER WHAT SHE IS GOING THROUGH.
THERE IS NO NEED TO BE TOO HASTY, SHARON-CHAN.
LOOKING AT THE SAME THING AND THEN DELIBERATING IS NOT THE ONLY WAY TO WALK TOGETHER.
EVEN IF YOU ARE WALKING DIFFERENT PATHS, INDIVIDUALS CONTINUE TO BE LINKED TOGETHER.
...OH DEAR.
LOOK AT ME LECTURING LIKE A TRUE GRAND-MOTHER.
FORGIVE ME FOR WORRYING TOO MUCH.
OH, NOT AT ALL!

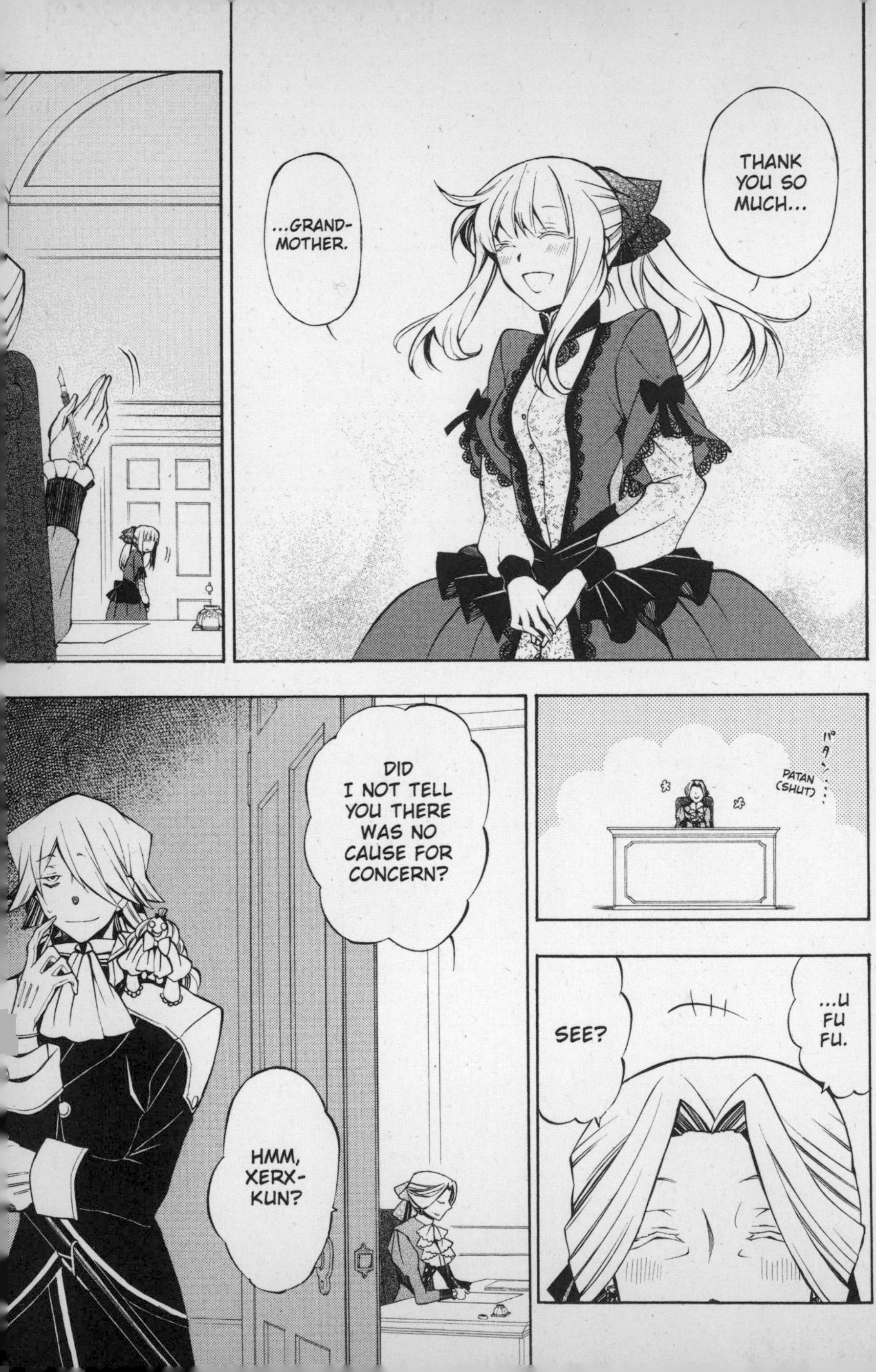
THANK YOU SO MUCH...
...GRAND-MOTHER.
PATAN (SHUT)
...U FU FU.
SEE?
DID I NOT TELL YOU THERE WAS NO CAUSE FOR CONCERN?
HMM, XERX-KUN?

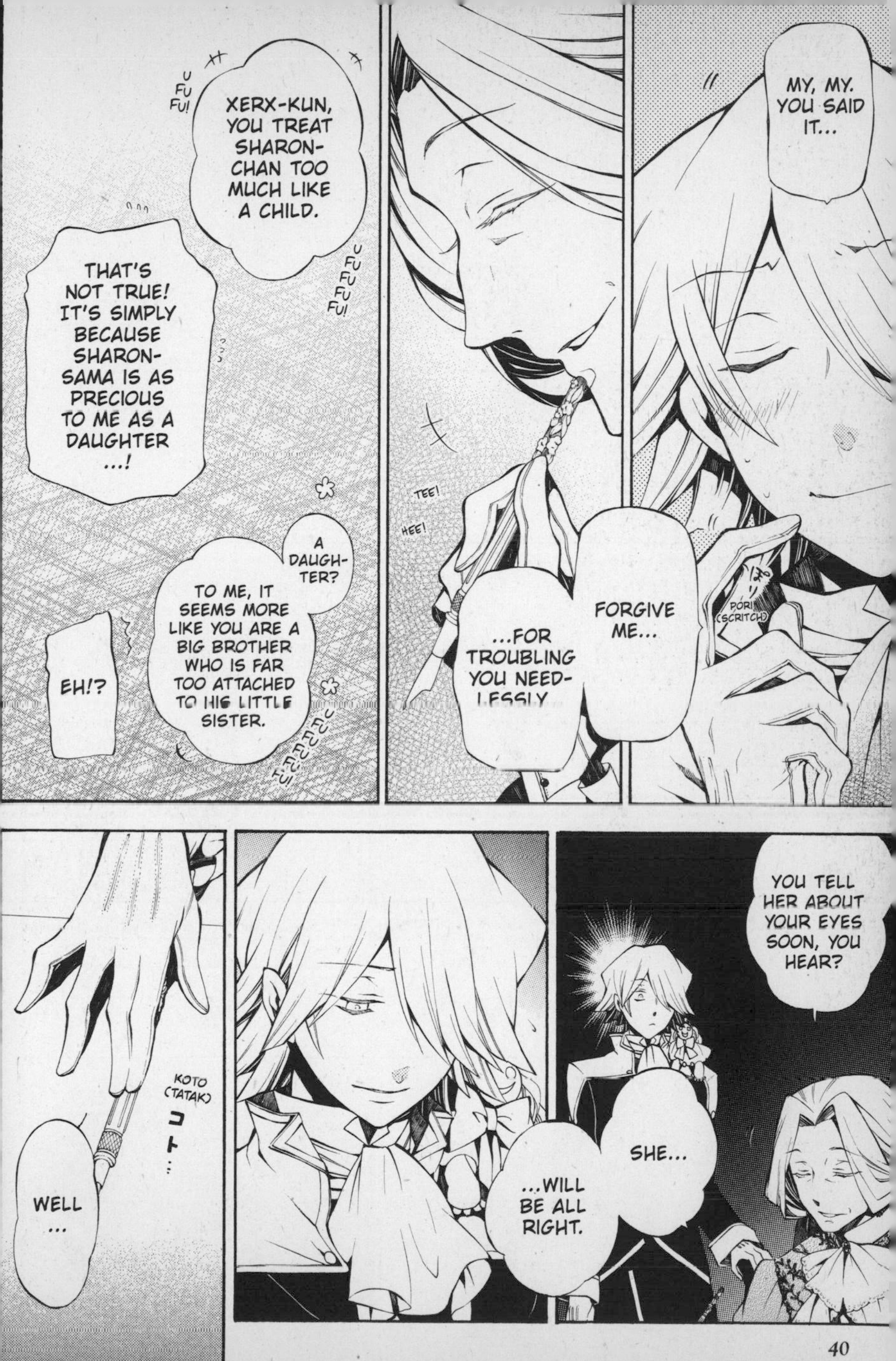
MY, MY. YOU SAID IT...
FORGIVE ME...
PORI (SCRITCH)
...FOR TROUBLING YOU NEED-LESSLY
TEE!
HEE!
XERX-KUN, YOU TREAT SHARON-CHAN TOO MUCH LIKE A CHILD.
U FU FU!
U FU FU FU FU!
THAT'S NOT TRUE! IT'S SIMPLY BECAUSE SHARON-SAMA IS AS PRECIOUS TO ME AS A DAUGHTER ...!
A DAUGH-TER?
TO ME, IT SEEMS MORE LIKE YOU ARE A BIG BROTHER WHO IS FAR TOO ATTACHED TO HIS LITTLE SISTER.
EH!?
U FU FU FU FU FU!
YOU TELL HER ABOUT YOUR EYES SOON, YOU HEAR?
SHE...
...WILL BE ALL RIGHT.
KOTO (TATAK)
WELL ...

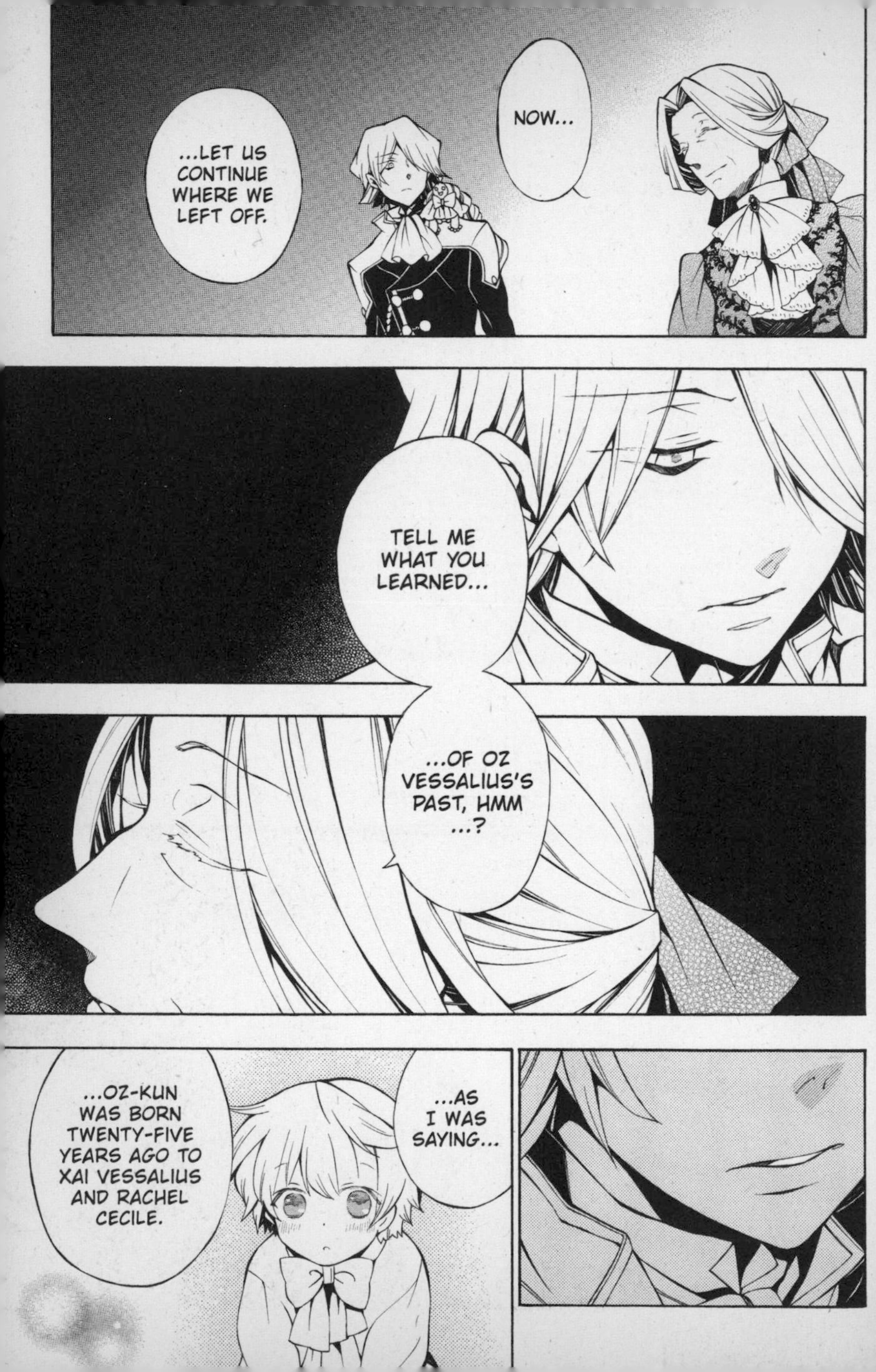
NOW...
...LET US CONTINUE WHERE WE LEFT OFF.
TELL ME WHAT YOU LEARNED...
...OF OZ VESSALIUS'S PAST, HMM ...?
...AS I WAS SAYING...
...OZ-KUN WAS BORN TWENTY-FIVE YEARS AGO TO XAI VESSALIUS AND RACHEL CECILE.

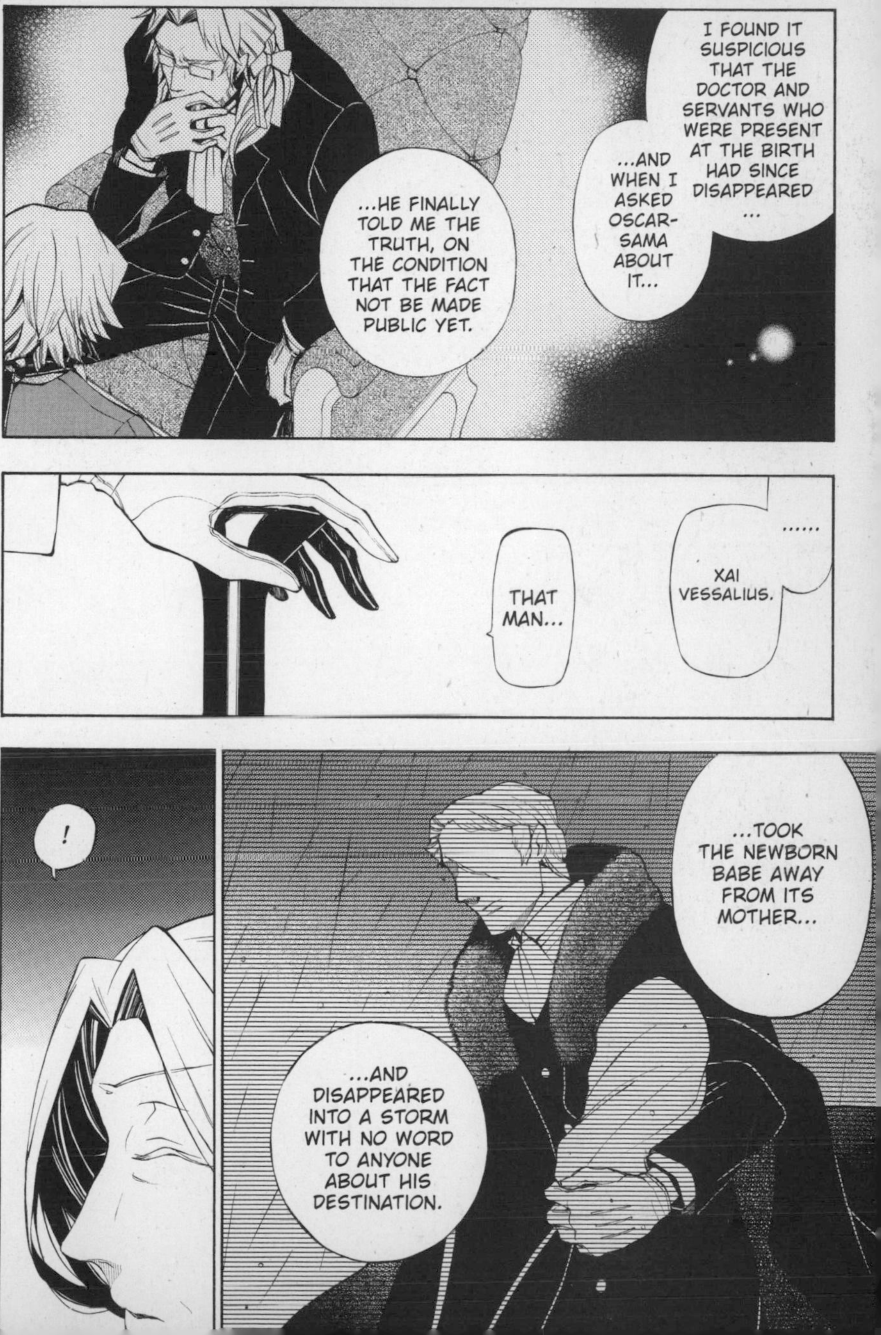
I FOUND IT SUSPICIOUS THAT THE DOCTOR AND SERVANTS WHO WERE PRESENT AT THE BIRTH HAD SINCE DISAPPEARED...
...AND WHEN I ASKED OSCAR-SAMA ABOUT IT...
...HE FINALLY TOLD ME THE TRUTH, ON THE CONDITION THAT THE FACT NOT BE MADE PUBLIC YET.
......
XAI VESSALIUS.
THAT MAN...
...TOOK THE NEWBORN BABE AWAY FROM ITS MOTHER...
...AND DISAPPEARED INTO A STORM WITH NO WORD TO ANYONE ABOUT HIS DESTINATION.
!

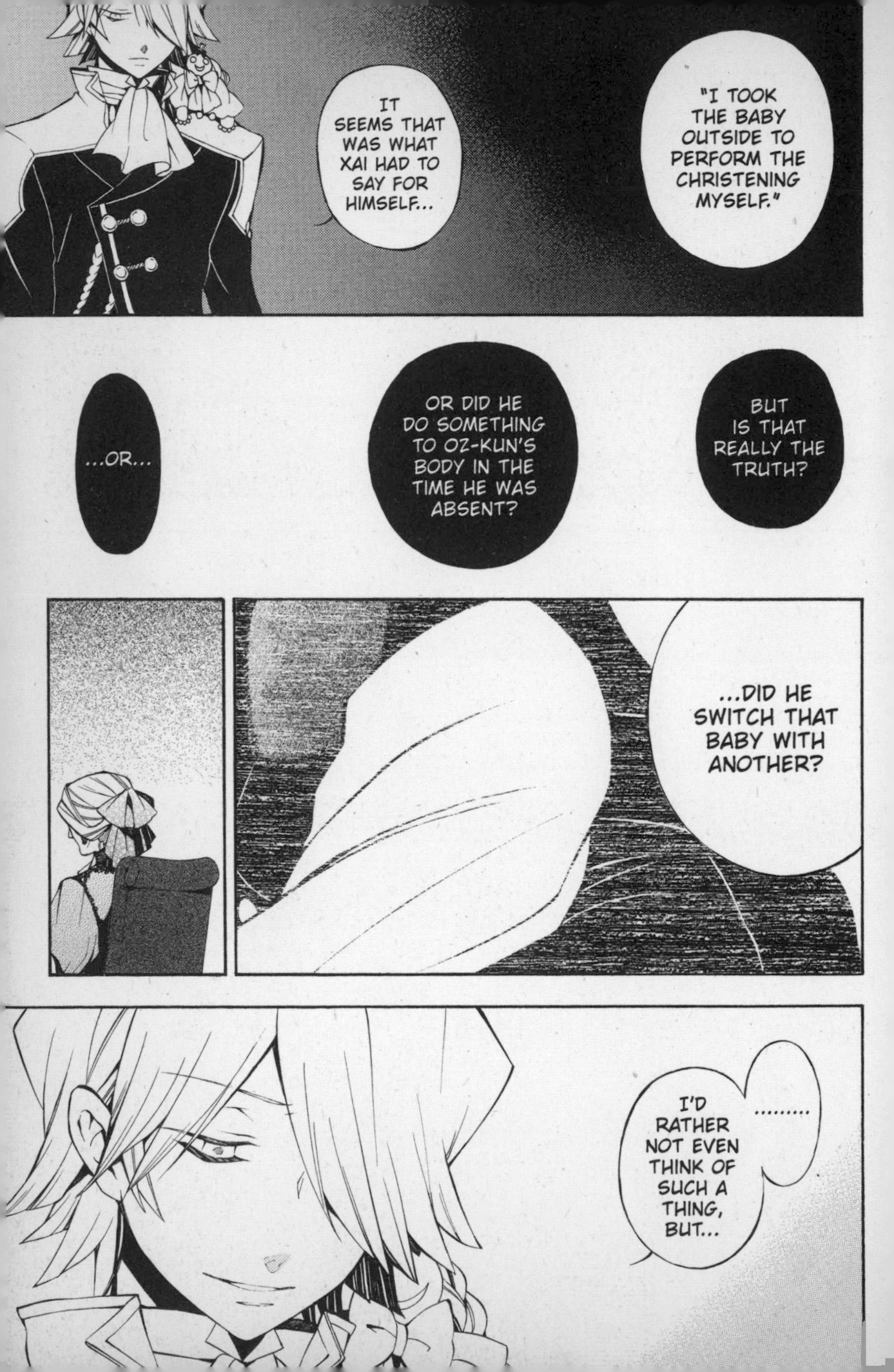
"I TOOK THE BABY OUTSIDE TO PERFORM THE CHRISTENING MYSELF."
IT SEEMS THAT WAS WHAT XAI HAD TO SAY FOR HIMSELF...
BUT IS THAT REALLY THE TRUTH?
OR DID HE DO SOMETHING TO OZ-KUN'S BODY IN THE TIME HE WAS ABSENT?
...OR...
...DID HE SWITCH THAT BABY WITH ANOTHER?
....
I'D RATHER NOT EVEN THINK OF SUCH A THING, BUT...

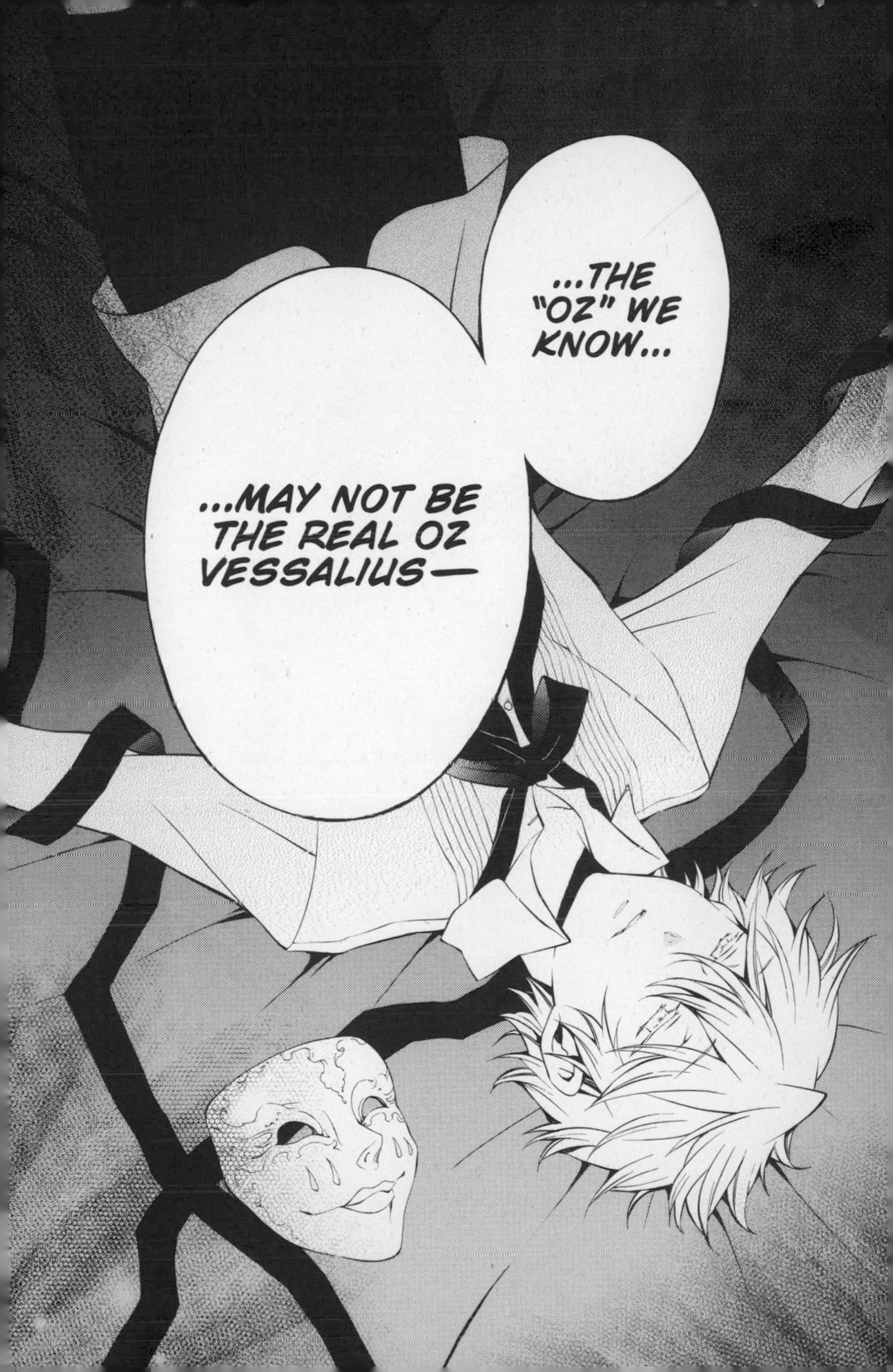
...THE "OZ" WE KNOW...
...MAY NOT BE THE REAL OZ VESSALIUS—

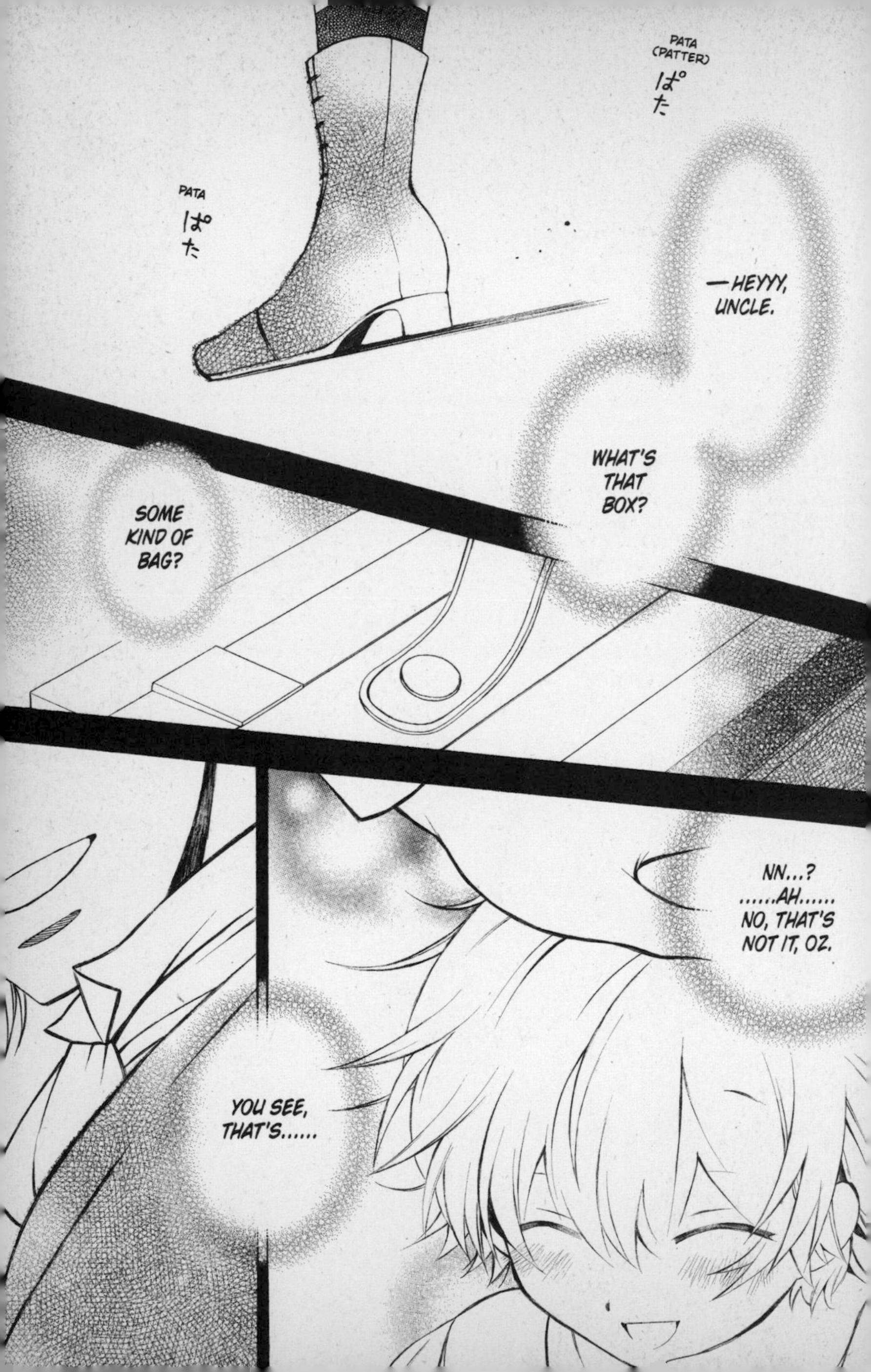
PATA (PATTER)
ぱた
—HEYYY, UNCLE.
PATA
ぱた
WHAT'S THAT BOX?
SOME KIND OF BAG?
NN...? ......AH...... NO, THAT'S NOT IT, OZ.
YOU SEE, THAT'S......

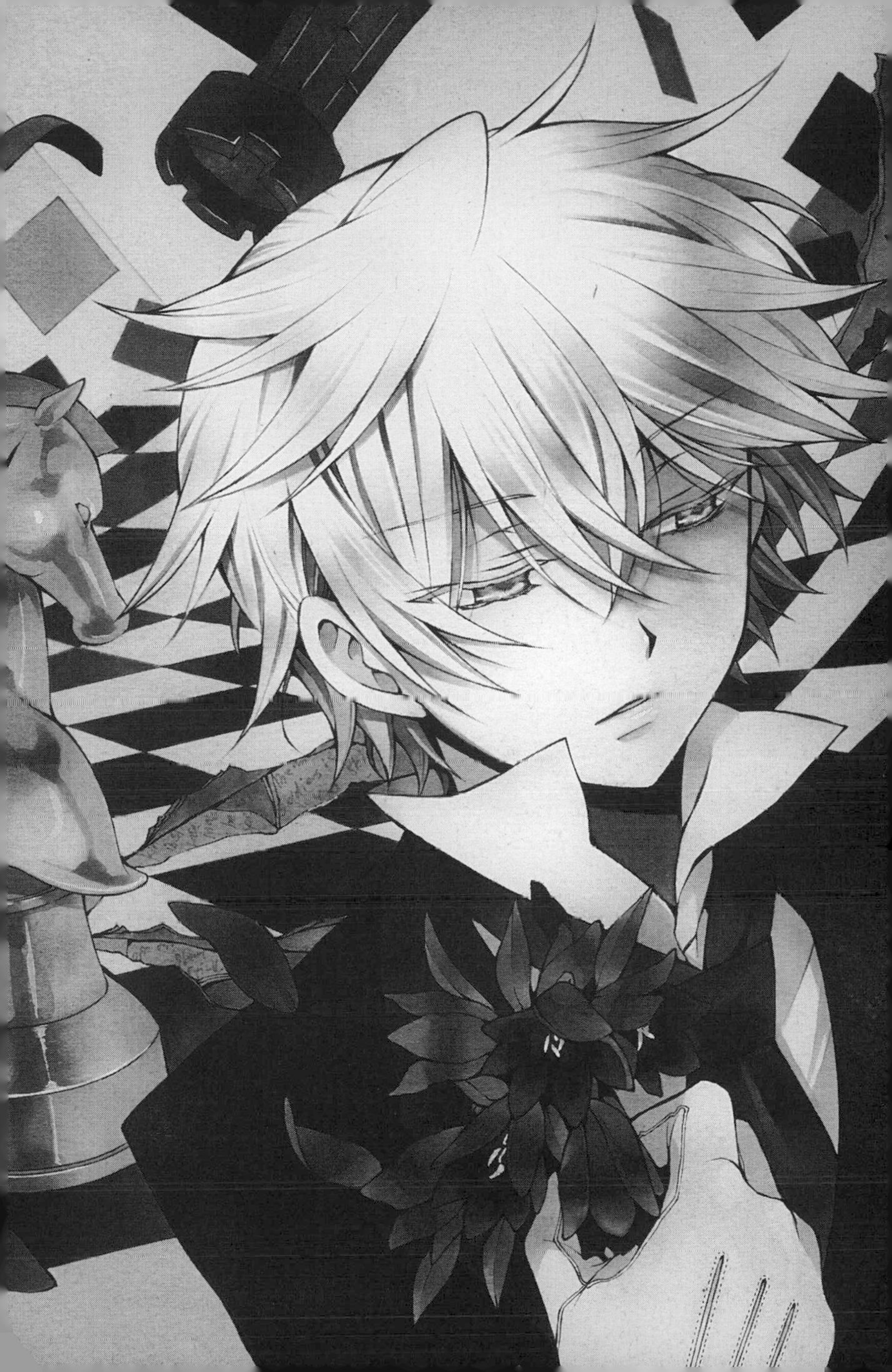

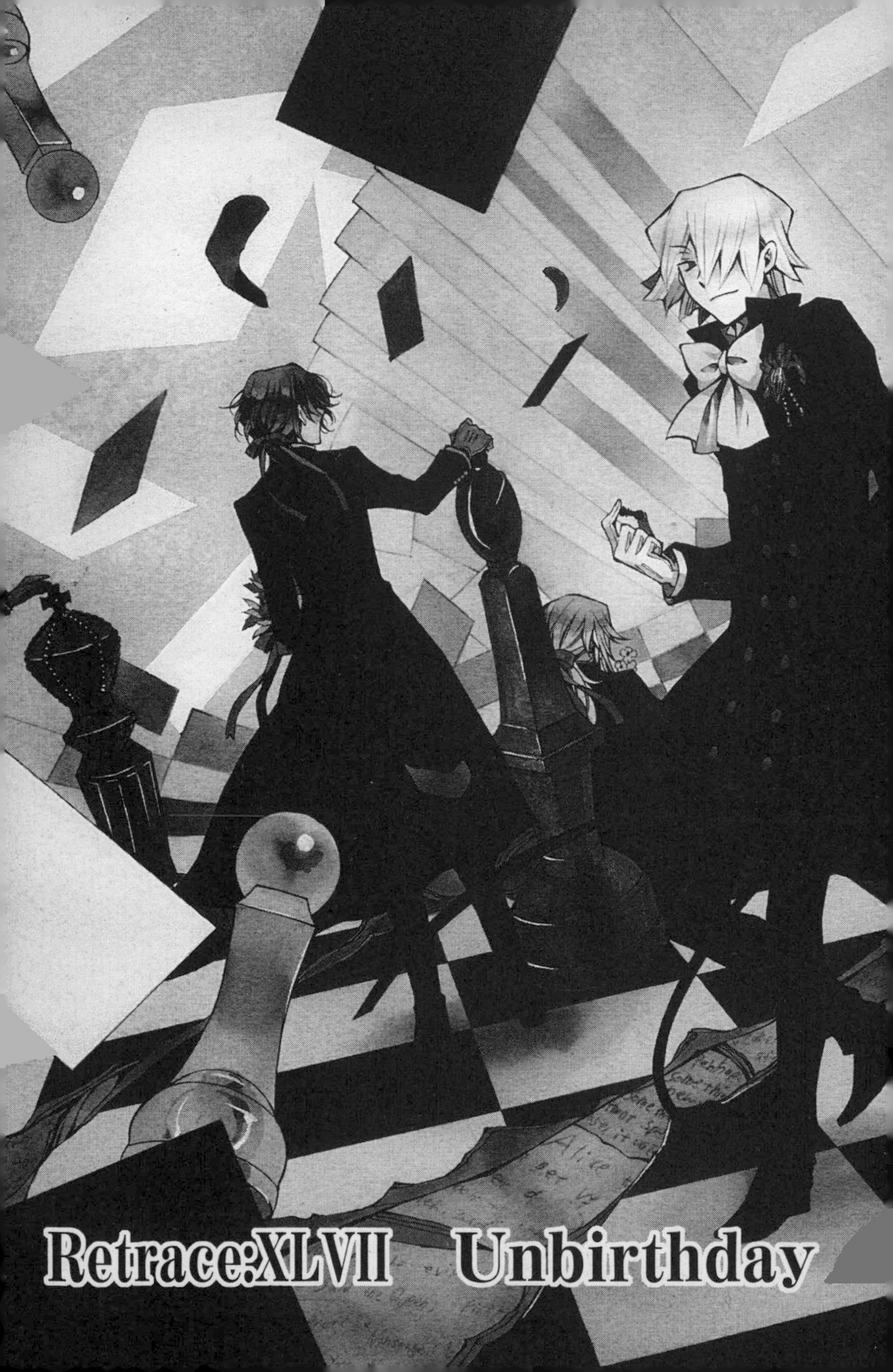

Retrace:XLVII Unbirthday

BONUS MANGA: "I DON'T GET IT...I JUST DON'T GET IT, NII-SAN......"

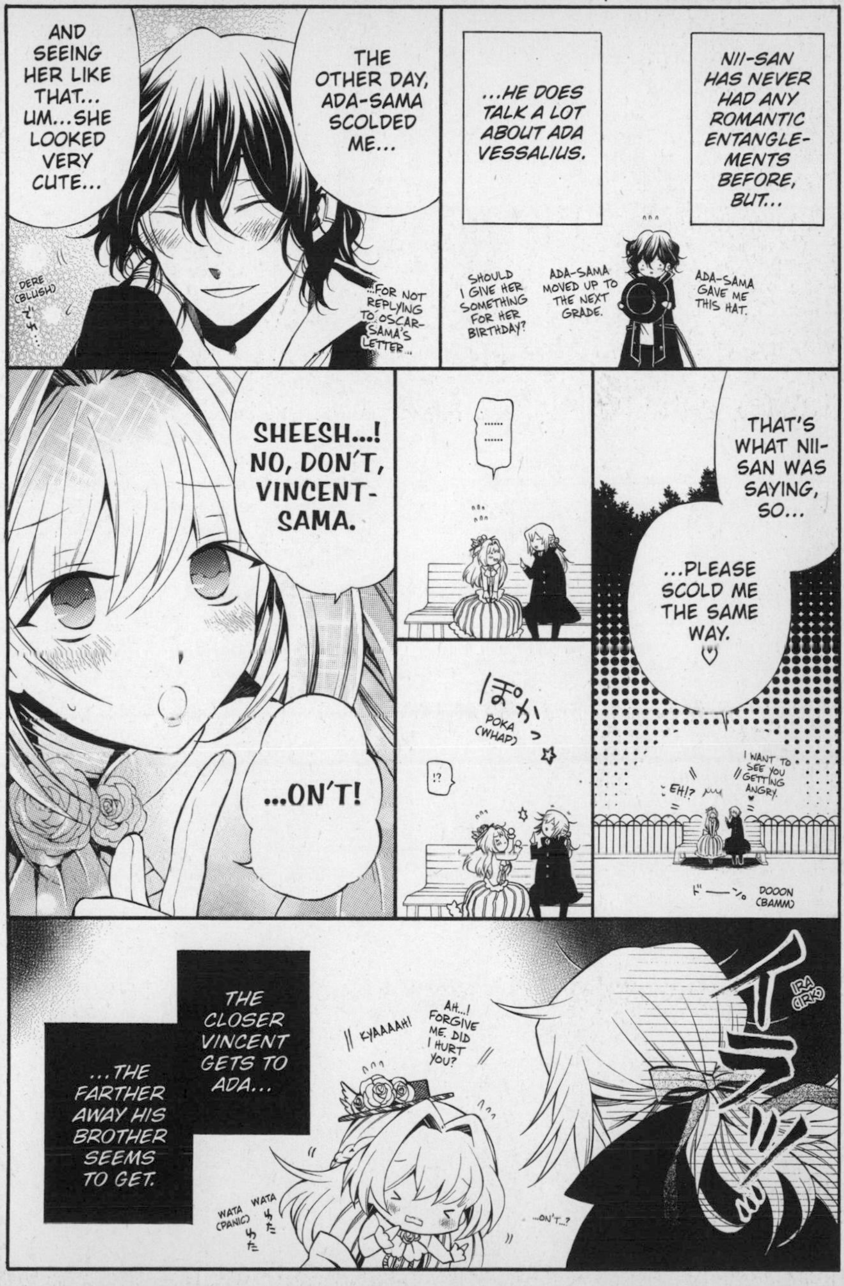
NII-SAN HAS NEVER HAD ANY ROMANTIC ENTANGLE-MENTS BEFORE, BUT...
...HE DOES TALK A LOT ABOUT ADA VESSALIUS.
ADA-SAMA GAVE ME THIS HAT.
ADA-SAMA MOVED UP TO THE NEXT GRADE.
SHOULD I GIVE HER SOMETHING FOR HER BIRTHDAY?
THE OTHER DAY, ADA-SAMA SCOLDED ME...
...FOR NOT REPLYING TO OSCAR-SAMA'S LETTER...
AND SEEING HER LIKE THAT... UM...SHE LOOKED VERY CUTE...
DERE (BLUSH)
THAT'S WHAT NII-SAN WAS SAYING, SO...
...PLEASE SCOLD ME THE SAME WAY.
I WANT TO SEE YOU GETTING ANGRY.
EH!?
ドーン。 DOOON (BAMM)
......
......
ぽかっ
POKA (WHAP)
!?
SHEESH...! NO, DON'T, VINCENT-SAMA.
...ON'T!
IRA (IRK)
...ON'T...?
AH...! FORGIVE ME. DID I HURT YOU?
KYAAAAH!
WATA WATA (PANIC)
THE CLOSER VINCENT GETS TO ADA...
...THE FARTHER AWAY HIS BROTHER SEEMS TO GET.

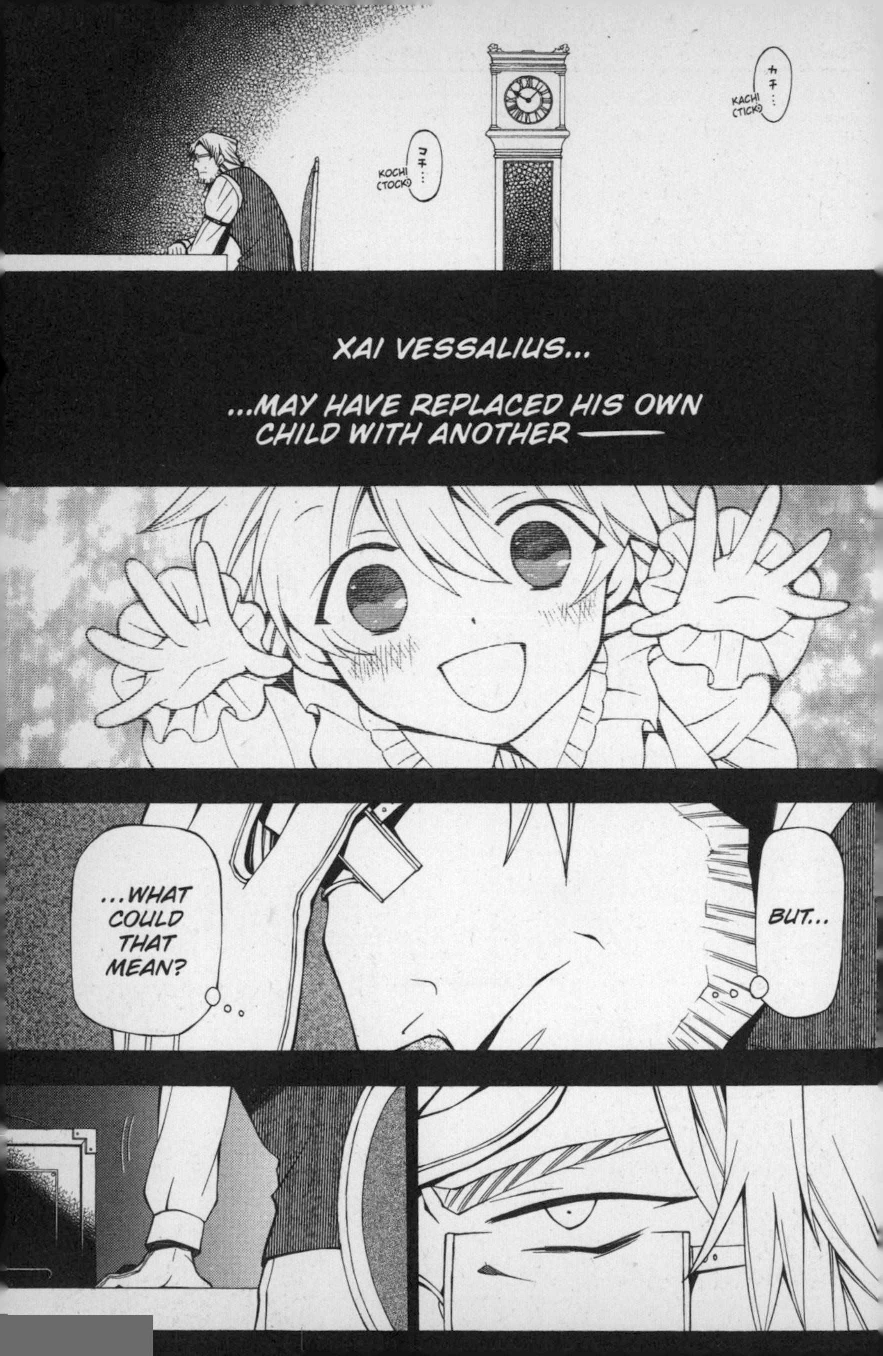
カチ…
KACHI (TICK)
コチ…
KOCHI (TOCK)
XAI VESSALIUS...
...MAY HAVE REPLACED HIS OWN CHILD WITH ANOTHER—
BUT...
...WHAT COULD THAT MEAN?

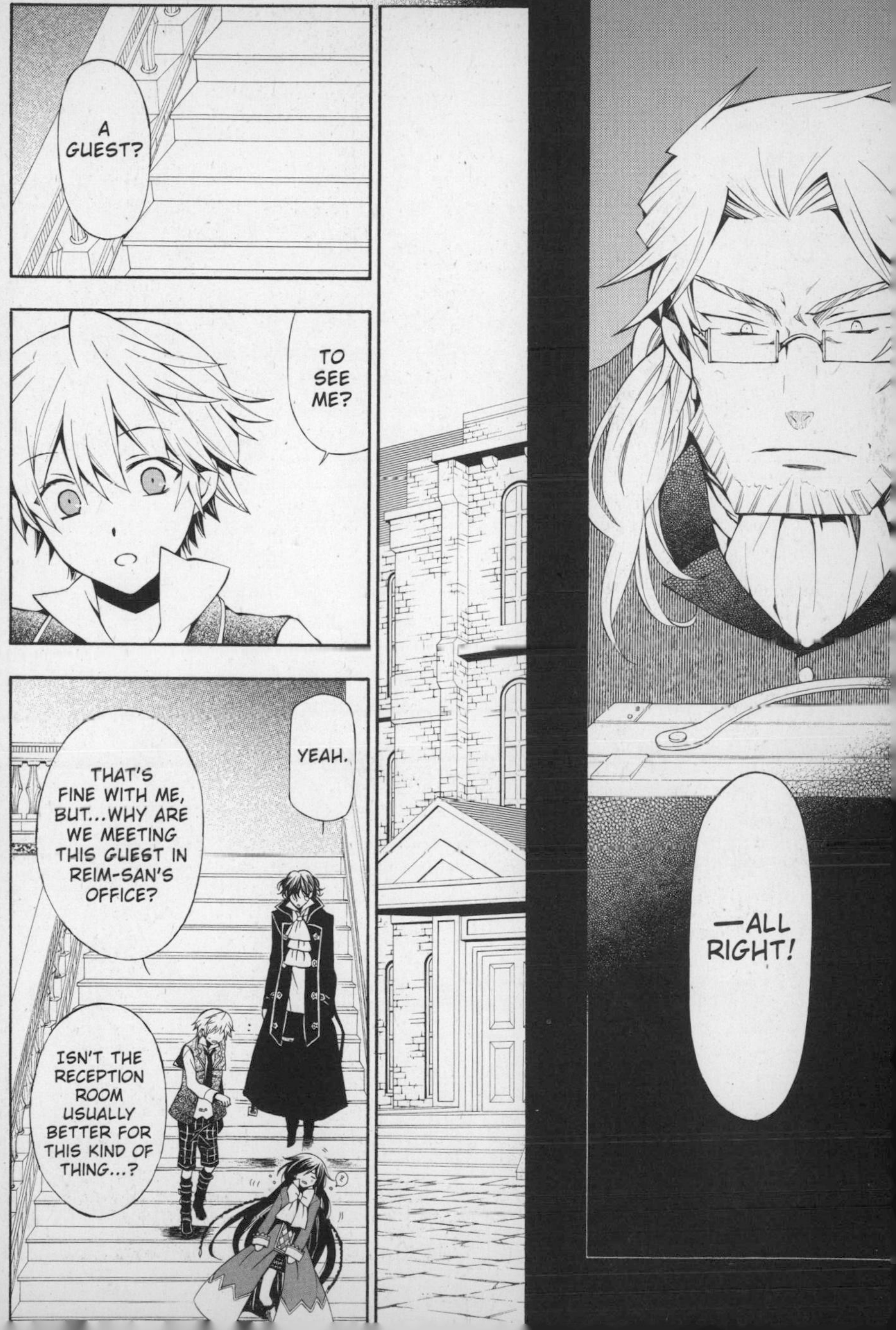
—ALL RIGHT!
A GUEST?
TO SEE ME?
YEAH.
THAT'S FINE WITH ME, BUT...WHY ARE WE MEETING THIS GUEST IN REIM-SAN'S OFFICE?
ISN'T THE RECEPTION ROOM USUALLY BETTER FOR THIS KIND OF THING...?

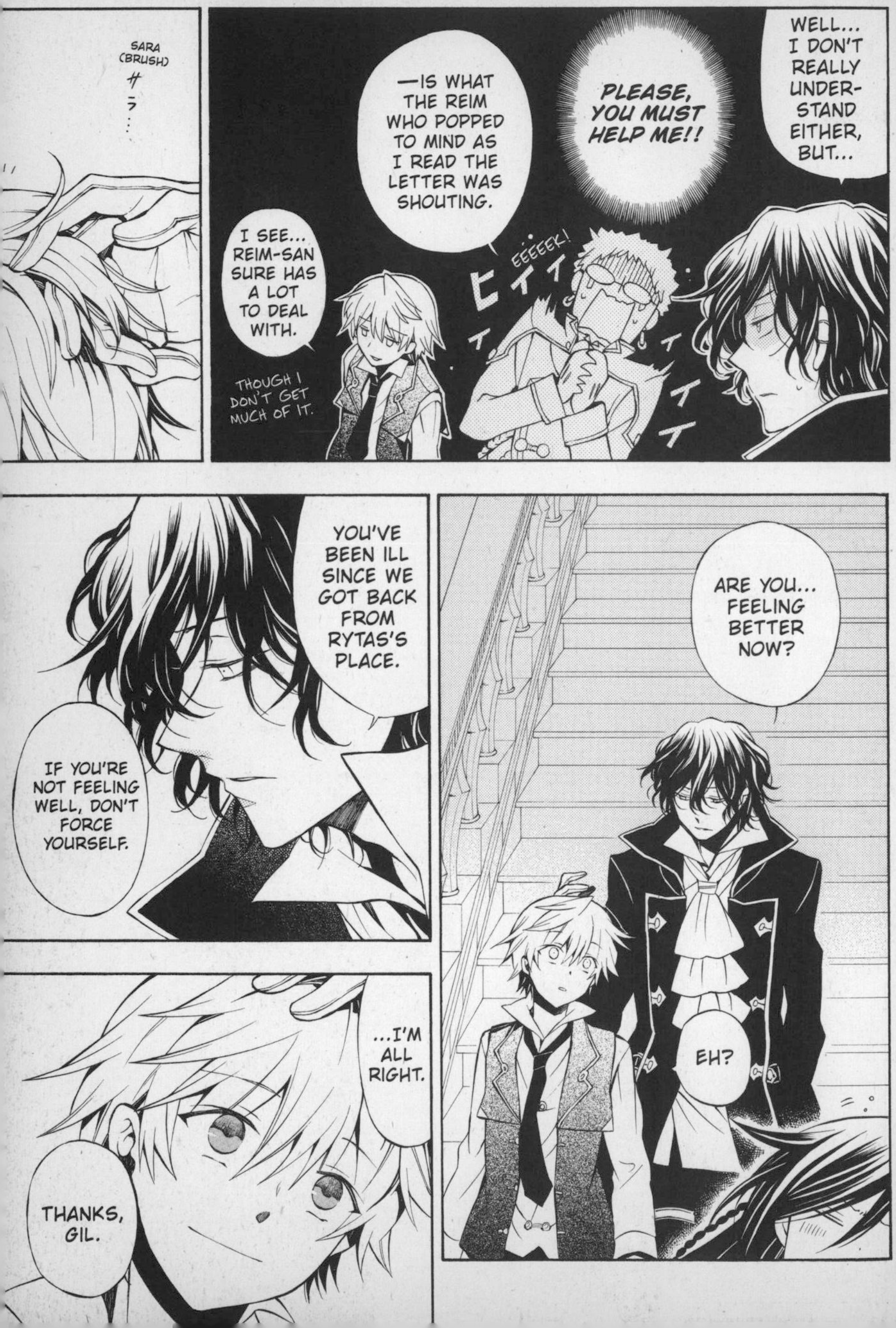
WELL... I DON'T REALLY UNDER-STAND EITHER, BUT...
PLEASE, YOU MUST HELP ME!!
—IS WHAT THE REIM WHO POPPED TO MIND AS I READ THE LETTER WAS SHOUTING.
EEEEEK!
I SEE... REIM-SAN SURE HAS A LOT TO DEAL WITH.
THOUGH I DON'T GET MUCH OF IT.
SARA (BRUSH)
サラ…
ARE YOU... FEELING BETTER NOW?
EH?
YOU'VE BEEN ILL SINCE WE GOT BACK FROM RYTAS'S PLACE.
IF YOU'RE NOT FEELING WELL, DON'T FORCE YOURSELF.
...I'M ALL RIGHT.
THANKS, GIL.

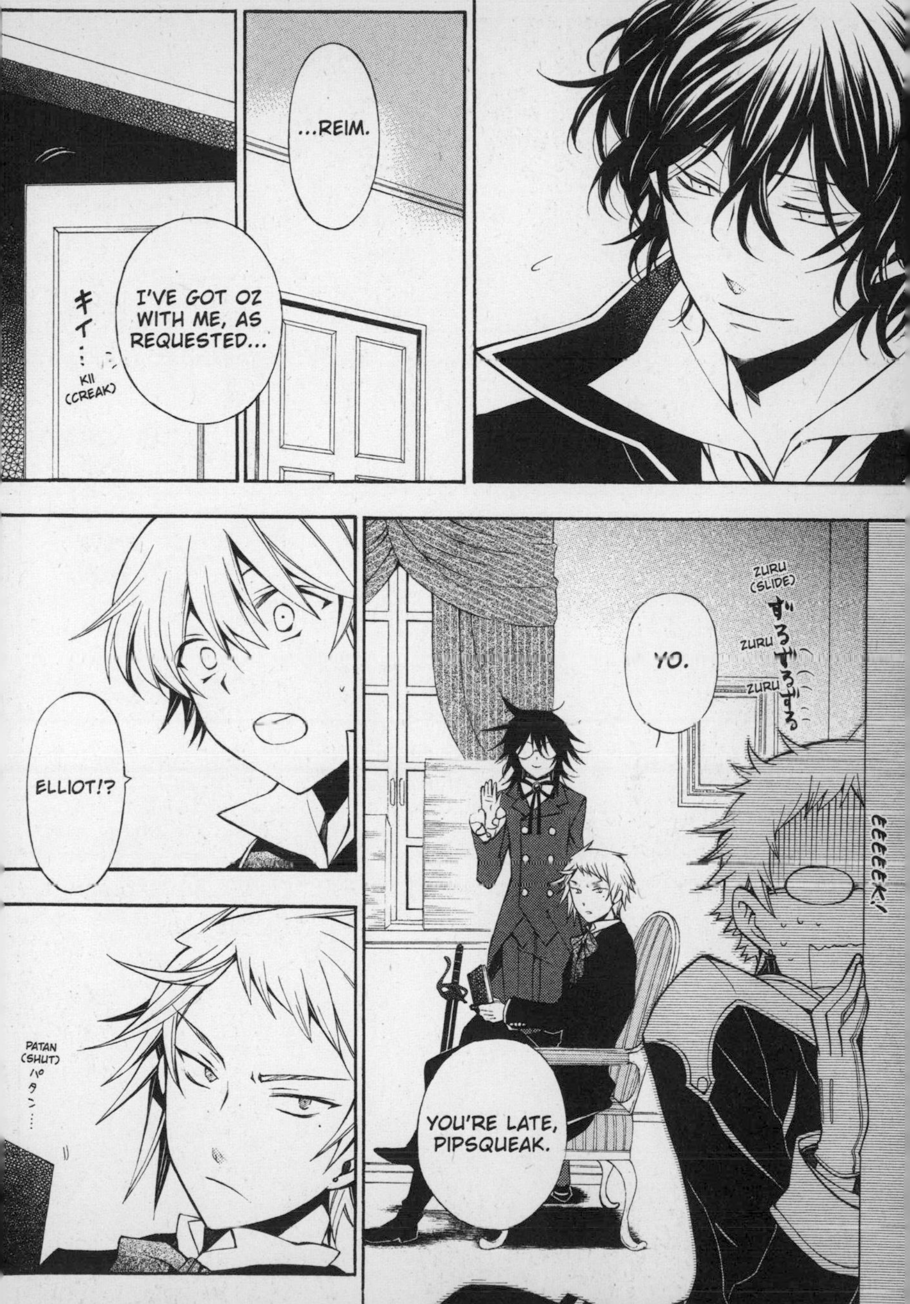
...REIM.
I'VE GOT OZ WITH ME, AS REQUESTED...
キイ…
KII (CREAK)
YO.
ZURU (SLIDE) ずるずるずる ZURU ZURU
EEEEEEK!
YOU'RE LATE, PIPSQUEAK.
ELLIOT!?
PATAN (SHUT) パタン…

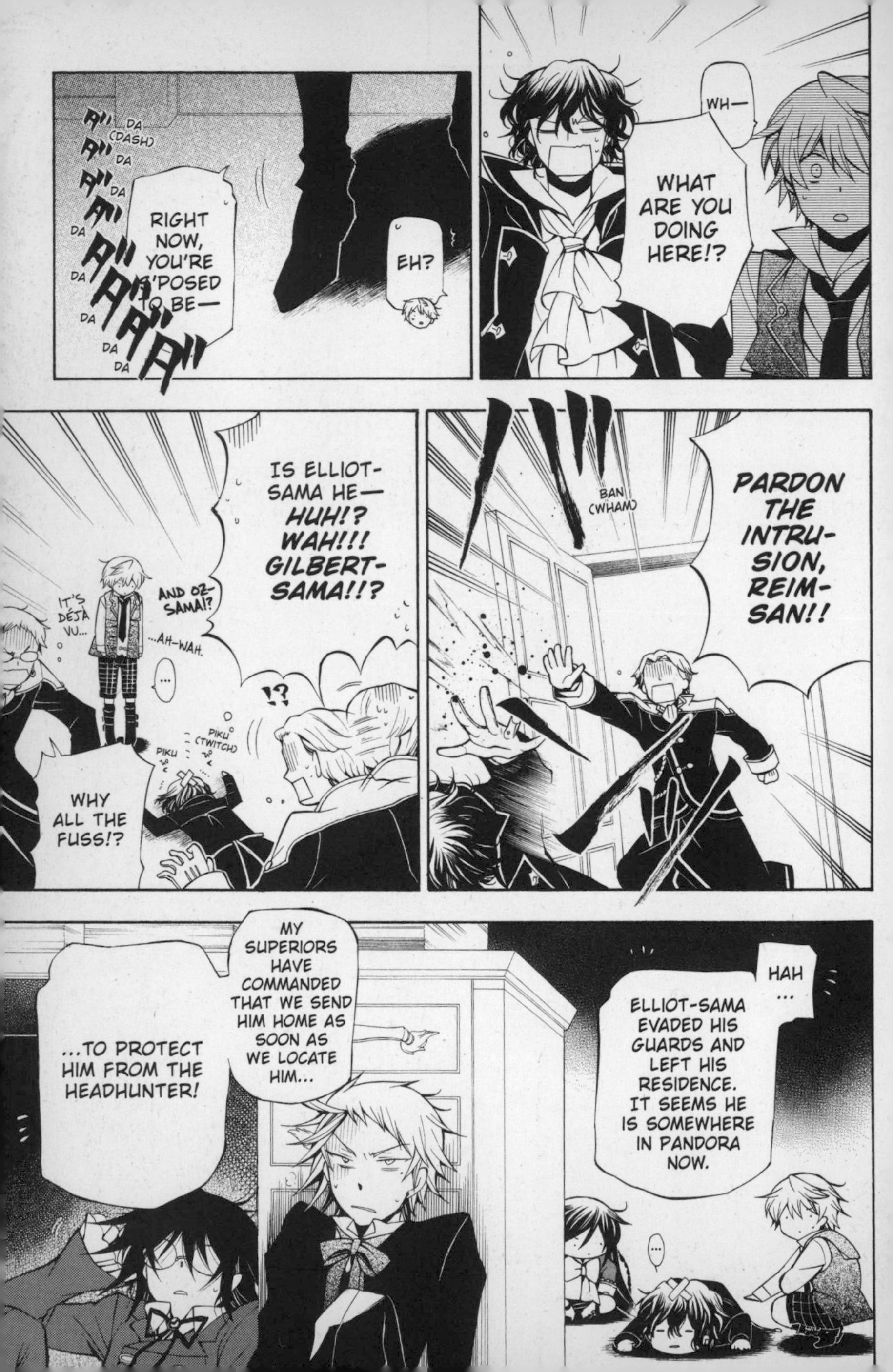
WH—
WHAT ARE YOU DOING HERE!?
EH?
RIGHT NOW, YOU'RE S'POSED TO BE—
DA (DASH) DA DA DA DA DA DA DA
BAN (WHAM)
PARDON THE INTRUSION, REIM-SAN!!
IS ELLIOT-SAMA HE— HUH!? WAH!!! GILBERT-SAMA!!?
!?
AND OZ-SAMA!?
...AH-WAH.
IT'S DÉJÀ VU...
...
PIKU (TWITCH) PIKU
WHY ALL THE FUSS!?
HAH ...
ELLIOT-SAMA EVADED HIS GUARDS AND LEFT HIS RESIDENCE. IT SEEMS HE IS SOMEWHERE IN PANDORA NOW.
...
MY SUPERIORS HAVE COMMANDED THAT WE SEND HIM HOME AS SOON AS WE LOCATE HIM...
...TO PROTECT HIM FROM THE HEADHUNTER!

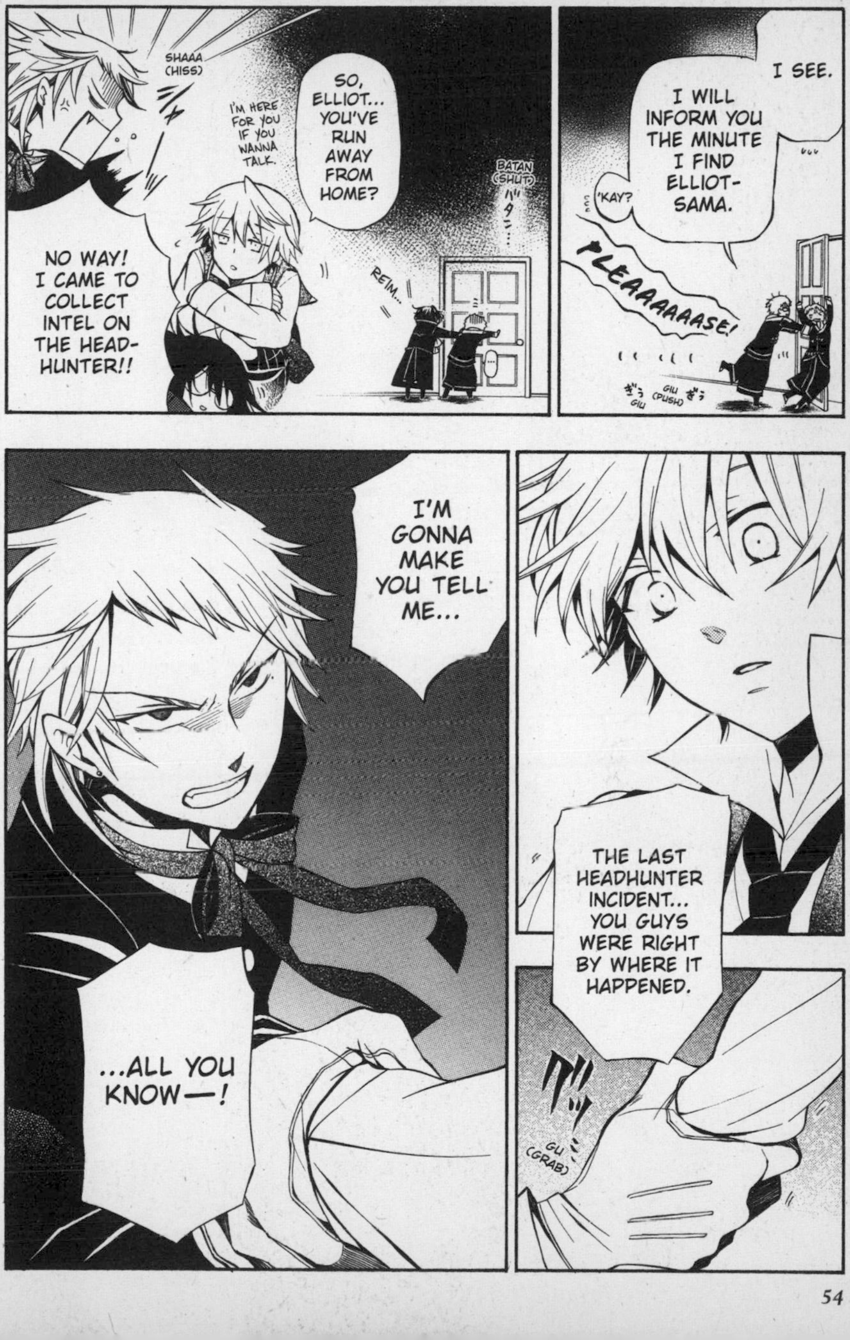
I SEE.
I WILL INFORM YOU THE MINUTE I FIND ELLIOT-SAMA.
'KAY?
PLEAAAAAASE!
GIU GIU (PUSH)
BATAN (SHUT)
SO, ELLIOT... YOU'VE RUN AWAY FROM HOME?
I'M HERE FOR YOU IF YOU WANNA TALK.
SHAAA (HISS)
REIM...
NO WAY! I CAME TO COLLECT INTEL ON THE HEAD-HUNTER!!
THE LAST HEADHUNTER INCIDENT... YOU GUYS WERE RIGHT BY WHERE IT HAPPENED.
GU (GRAB)
I'M GONNA MAKE YOU TELL ME...
...ALL YOU KNOW—!

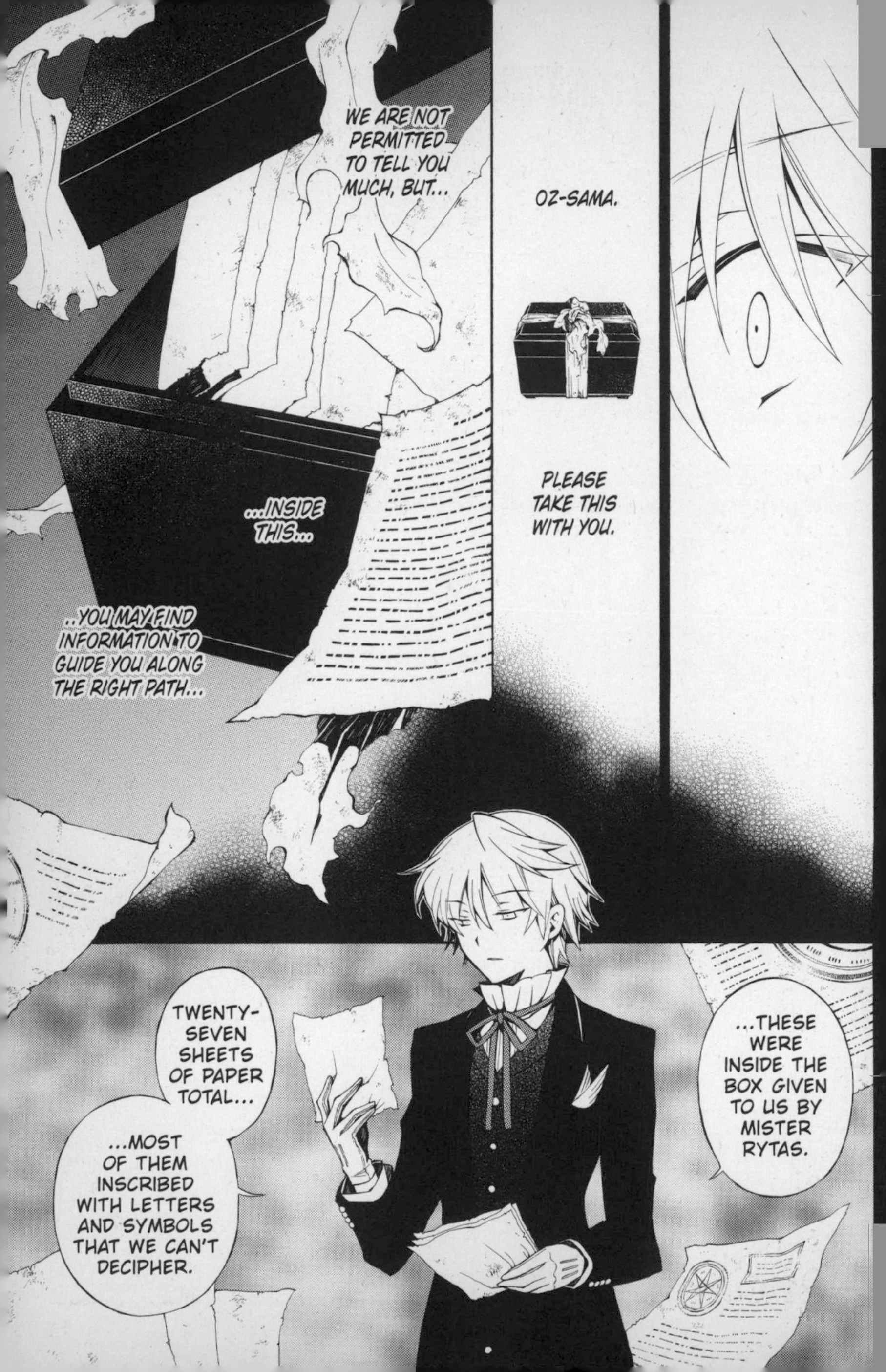
OZ-SAMA.
PLEASE TAKE THIS WITH YOU.
WE ARE NOT PERMITTED TO TELL YOU MUCH, BUT...
...INSIDE THIS...
...YOU MAY FIND INFORMATION TO GUIDE YOU ALONG THE RIGHT PATH...
...THESE WERE INSIDE THE BOX GIVEN TO US BY MISTER RYTAS.
TWENTY-SEVEN SHEETS OF PAPER TOTAL...
...MOST OF THEM INSCRIBED WITH LETTERS AND SYMBOLS THAT WE CAN'T DECIPHER.

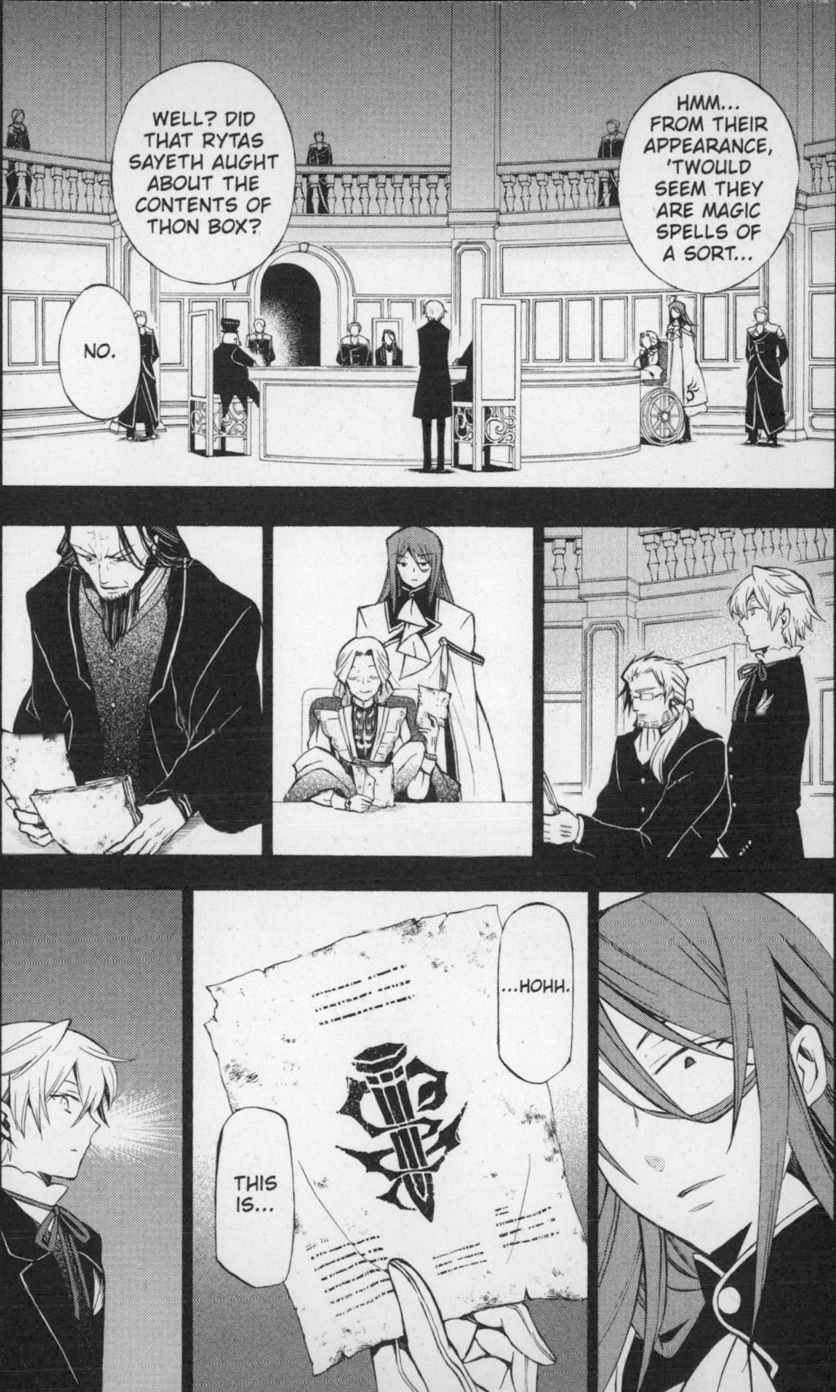
HMM... FROM THEIR APPEARANCE, 'TWOULD SEEM THEY ARE MAGIC SPELLS OF A SORT...
WELL? DID THAT RYTAS SAYETH AUGHT ABOUT THE CONTENTS OF THON BOX?
NO.
...HOHH.
THIS IS...

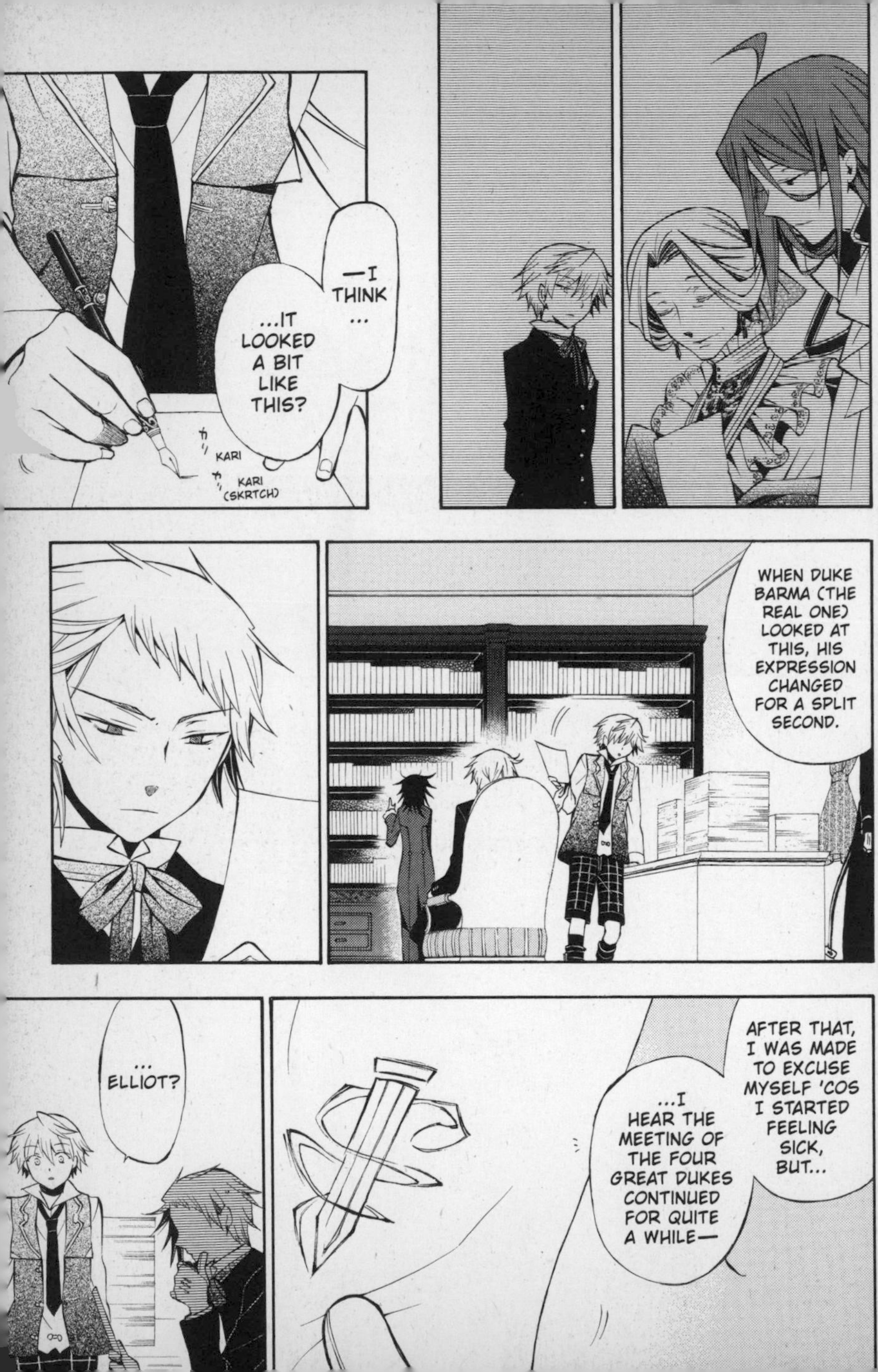
—I THINK...
...IT LOOKED A BIT LIKE THIS?
KARI KARI (SKRTCH)
WHEN DUKE BARMA (THE REAL ONE) LOOKED AT THIS, HIS EXPRESSION CHANGED FOR A SPLIT SECOND.
AFTER THAT, I WAS MADE TO EXCUSE MYSELF 'COS I STARTED FEELING SICK, BUT...
...I HEAR THE MEETING OF THE FOUR GREAT DUKES CONTINUED FOR QUITE A WHILE—
...ELLIOT?

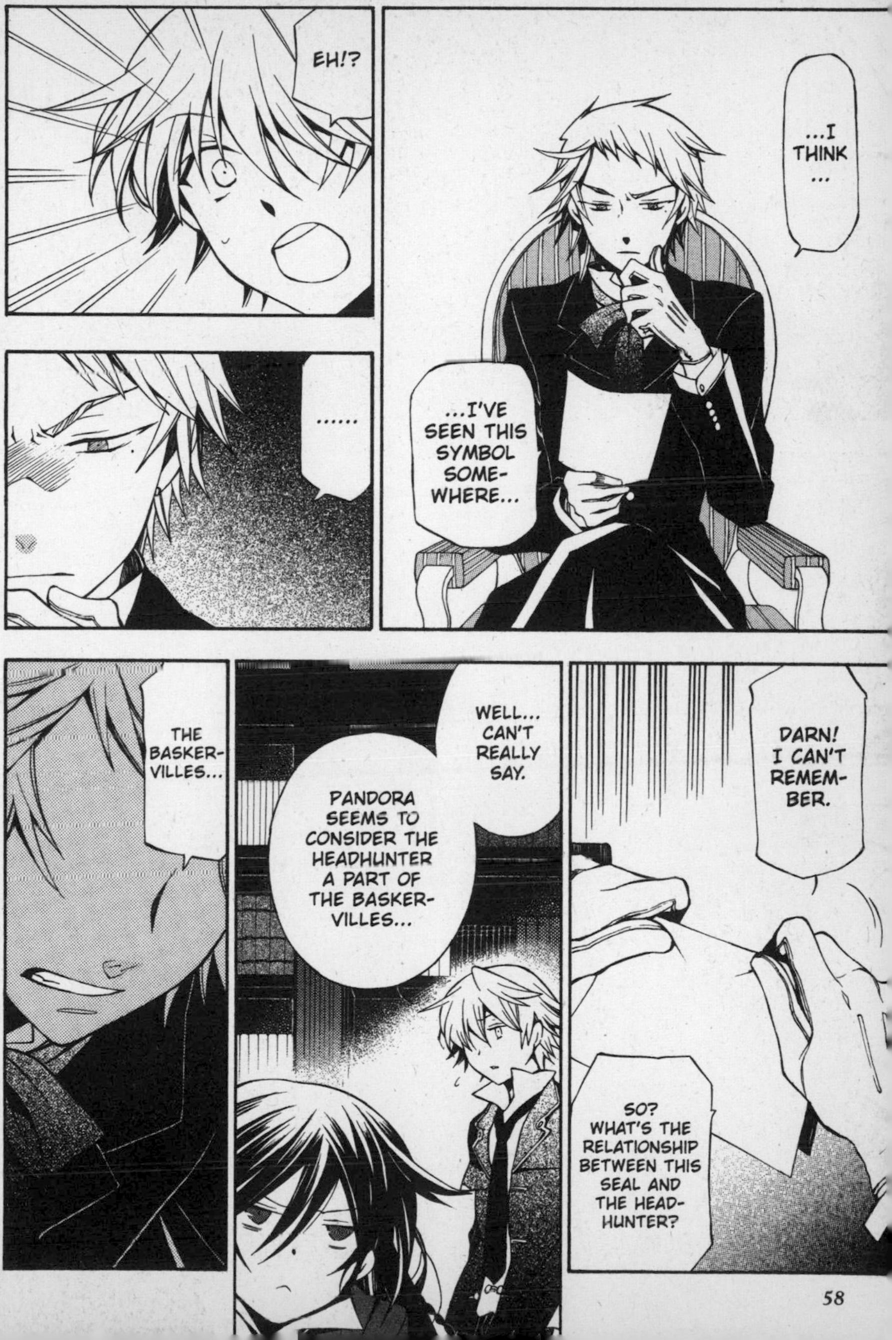
...I THINK ...
...I'VE SEEN THIS SYMBOL SOME-WHERE...
EH!?
......
DARN! I CAN'T REMEM-BER.
SO? WHAT'S THE RELATIONSHIP BETWEEN THIS SEAL AND THE HEAD-HUNTER?
WELL... CAN'T REALLY SAY.
PANDORA SEEMS TO CONSIDER THE HEADHUNTER A PART OF THE BASKER-VILLES...
THE BASKER-VILLES...

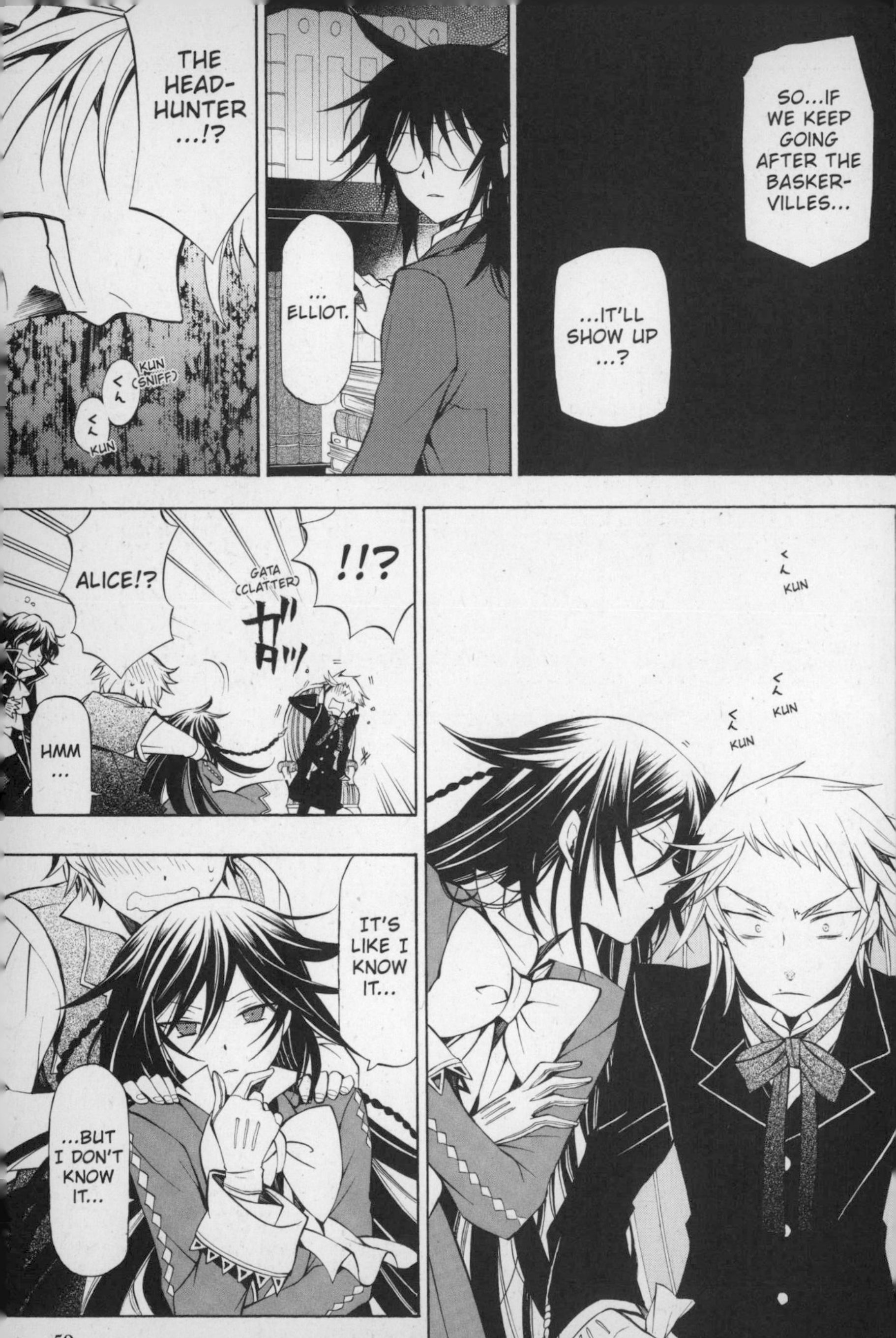
SO...IF WE KEEP GOING AFTER THE BASKER-VILLES...
...IT'LL SHOW UP ...?
... ELLIOT.
THE HEAD-HUNTER ...!?
くん KUN (SNIFF)
くん KUN
くん KUN
くん KUN
くん KUN
!!?
ガタッ GATA (CLATTER)
ALICE!?
HMM ...
IT'S LIKE I KNOW IT...
...BUT I DON'T KNOW IT...

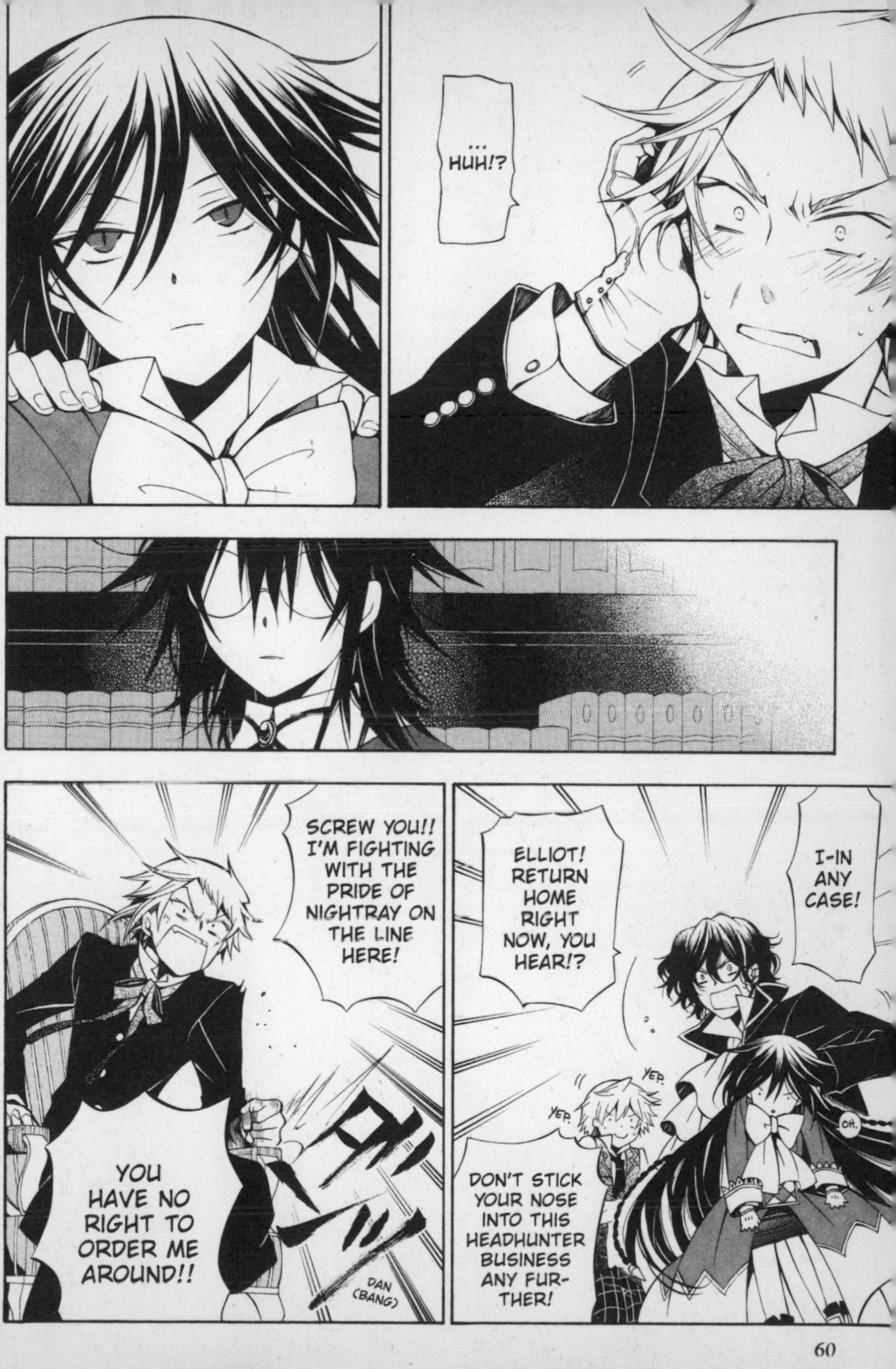
... HUH!?
I-IN ANY CASE!
ELLIOT! RETURN HOME RIGHT NOW, YOU HEAR!?
YEP.
YEP.
OH.
DON'T STICK YOUR NOSE INTO THIS HEADHUNTER BUSINESS ANY FURTHER!
SCREW YOU!! I'M FIGHTING WITH THE PRIDE OF NIGHTRAY ON THE LINE HERE!
DAN (BANG)
YOU HAVE NO RIGHT TO ORDER ME AROUND!!

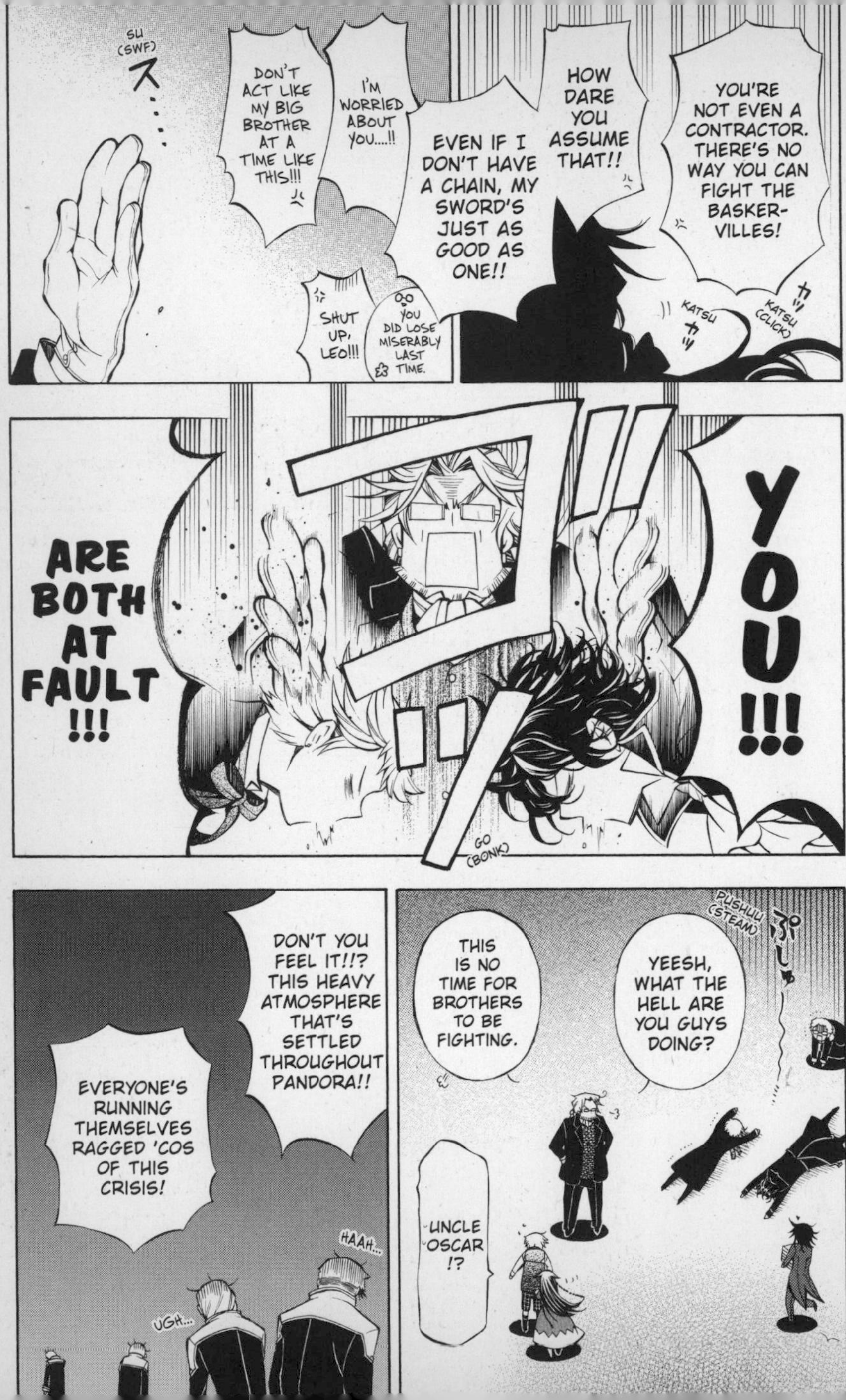

YOU'RE NOT EVEN A CONTRACTOR. THERE'S NO WAY YOU CAN FIGHT THE BASKER-VILLES!
HOW DARE YOU ASSUME THAT!!
EVEN IF I DON'T HAVE A CHAIN, MY SWORD'S JUST AS GOOD AS ONE!!
KATSU (CLICK)
KATSU
I'M WORRIED ABOUT YOU....!!
DON'T ACT LIKE MY BIG BROTHER AT A TIME LIKE THIS!!!
SU (SWF)
SHUT UP, LEO!!!
YOU DID LOSE MISERABLY LAST TIME.
YOU
!!!
ARE BOTH AT FAULT !!!
GO (BONK)
PUSHUU (STEAM)
YEESH, WHAT THE HELL ARE YOU GUYS DOING?
THIS IS NO TIME FOR BROTHERS TO BE FIGHTING.
UNCLE OSCAR !?
DON'T YOU FEEL IT!!? THIS HEAVY ATMOSPHERE THAT'S SETTLED THROUGHOUT PANDORA!!
EVERYONE'S RUNNING THEMSELVES RAGGED 'COS OF THIS CRISIS!
HAAH...
UGH...

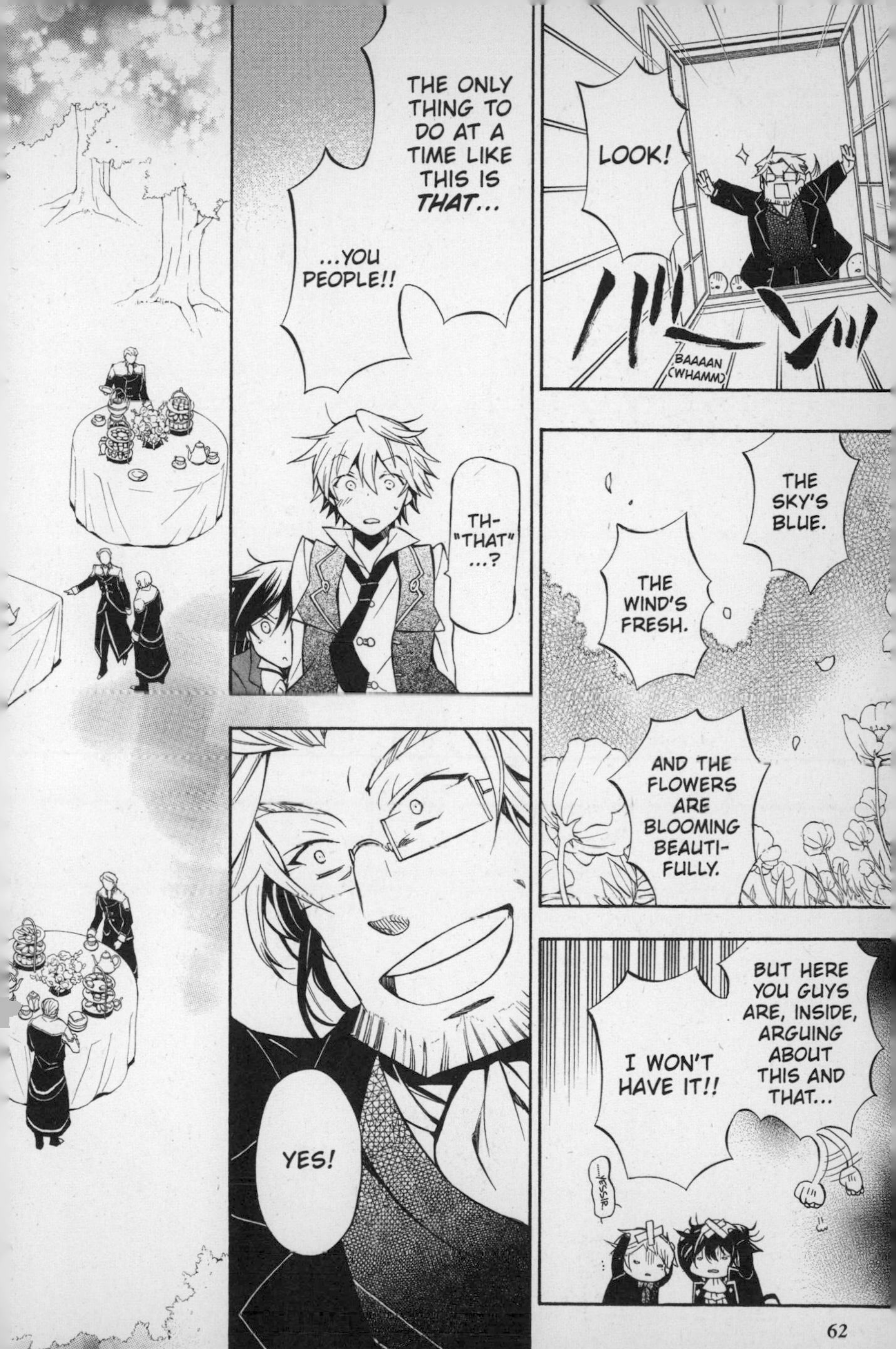
LOOK!
BAAAAN (WHAMM)
THE SKY'S BLUE.
THE WIND'S FRESH.
AND THE FLOWERS ARE BLOOMING BEAUTI-FULLY.
BUT HERE YOU GUYS ARE, INSIDE, ARGUING ABOUT THIS AND THAT...
I WON'T HAVE IT!!
...YESSIR.
THE ONLY THING TO DO AT A TIME LIKE THIS IS *THAT*...
...YOU PEOPLE!!
TH- "THAT" ...?
YES!

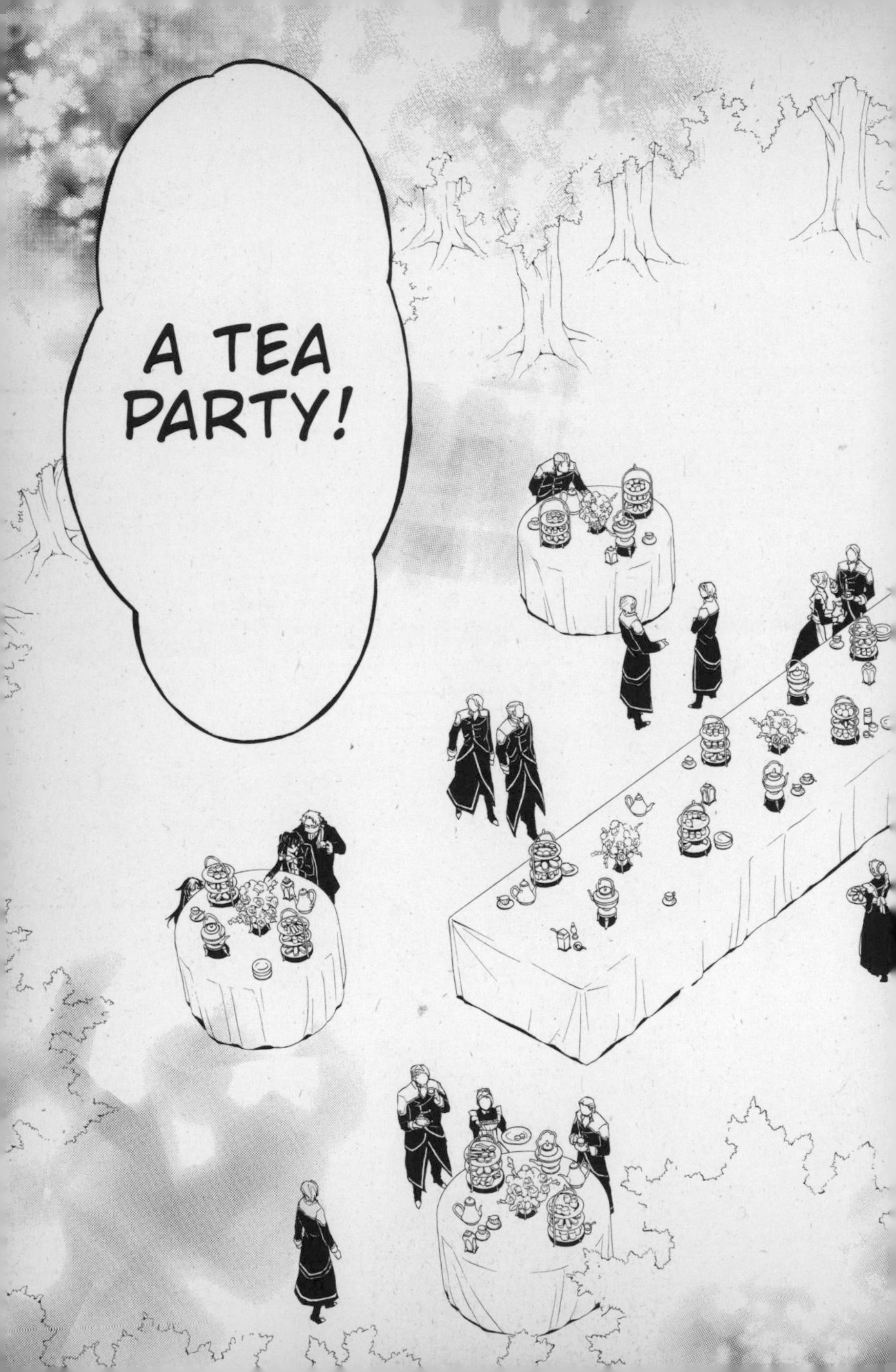
A TEA PARTY!

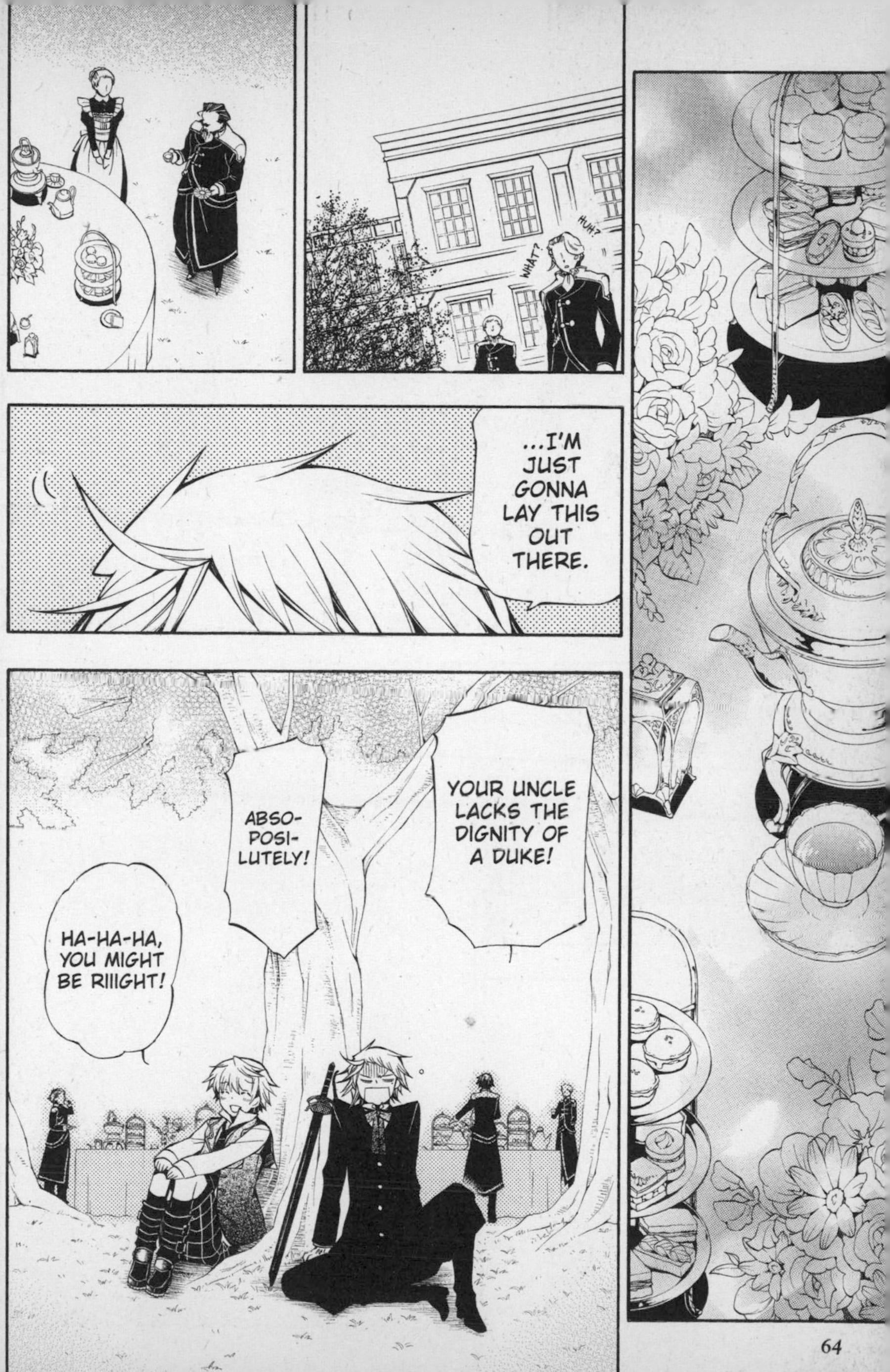
HUH?
WHAT?
...I'M JUST GONNA LAY THIS OUT THERE.
YOUR UNCLE LACKS THE DIGNITY OF A DUKE!
ABSO-POSI-LUTELY!
HA-HA-HA, YOU MIGHT BE RIIIGHT!

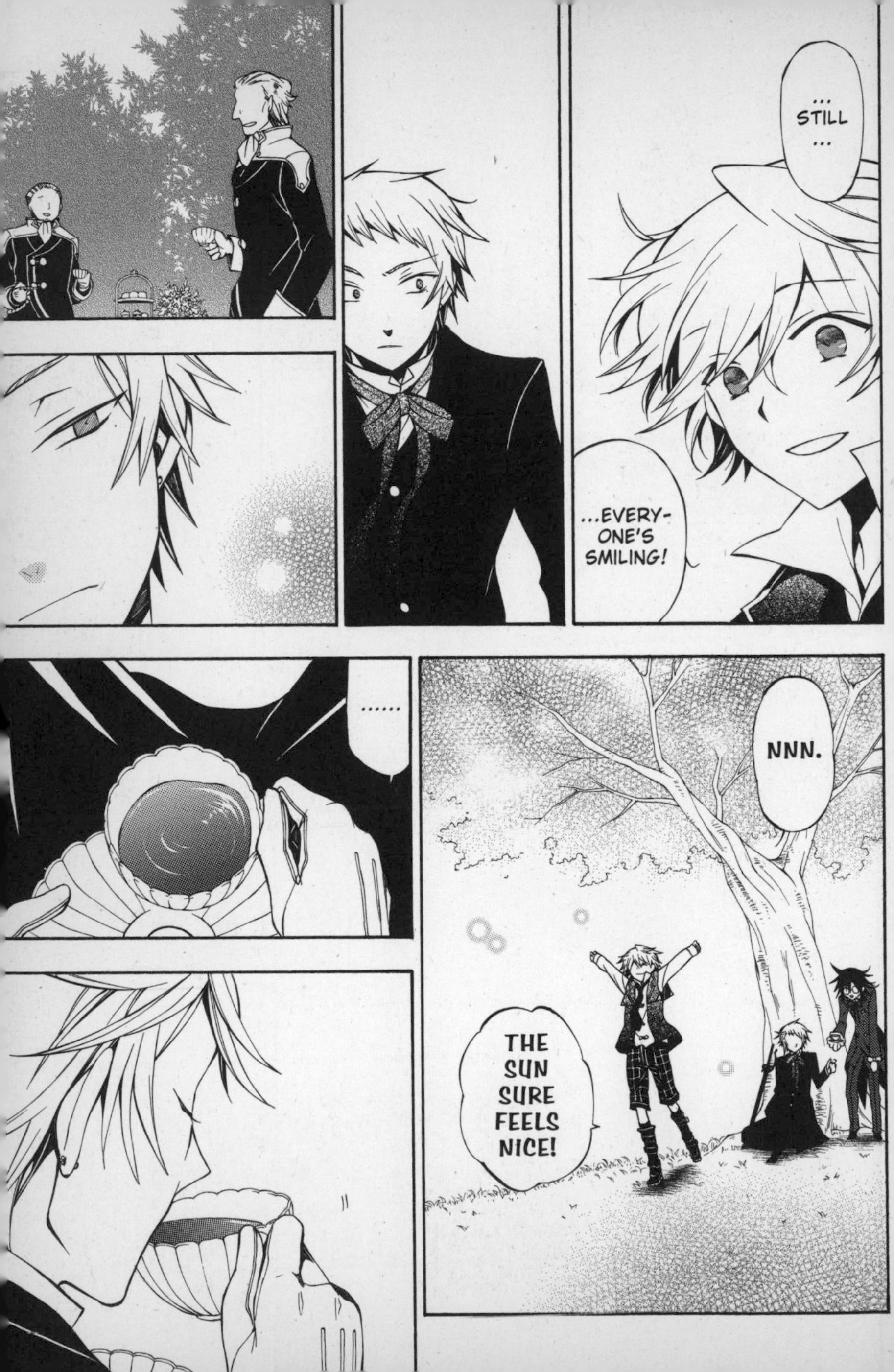
...STILL...
...EVERY-ONE'S SMILING!
NNN.
THE SUN SURE FEELS NICE!
......

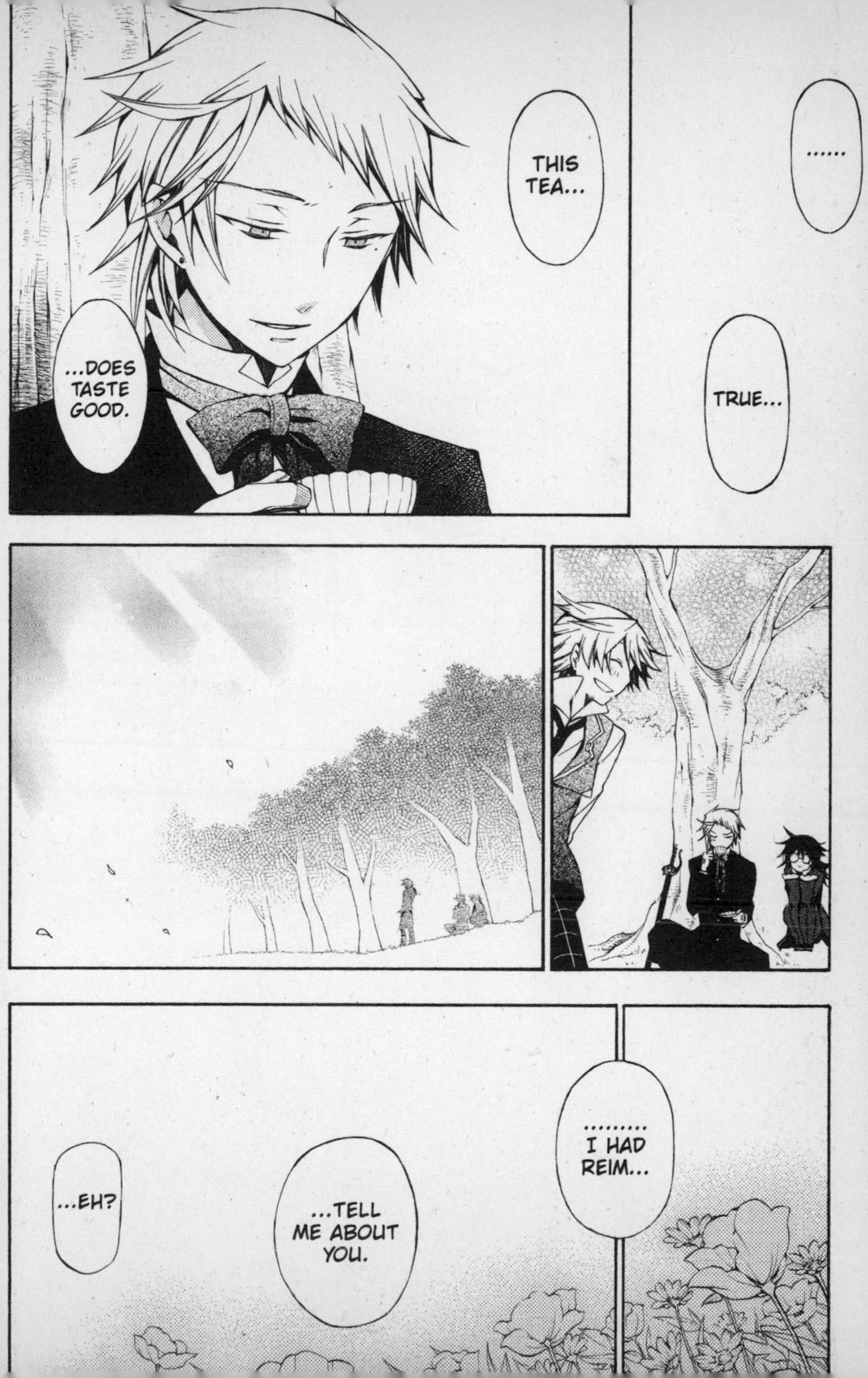
......
TRUE...
THIS TEA...
...DOES TASTE GOOD.
....
I HAD REIM...
...TELL ME ABOUT YOU.
...EH?

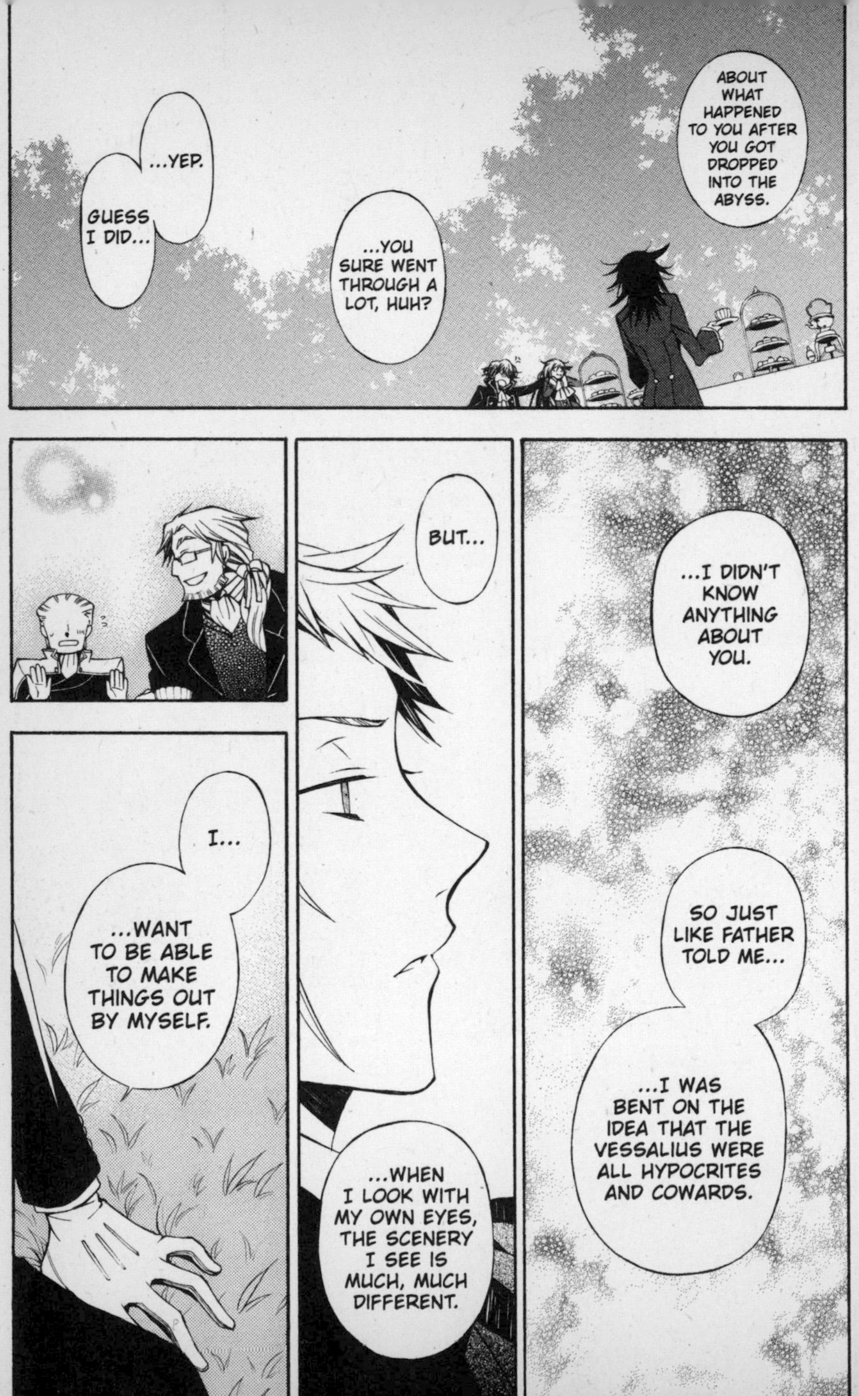
ABOUT WHAT HAPPENED TO YOU AFTER YOU GOT DROPPED INTO THE ABYSS.
...YOU SURE WENT THROUGH A LOT, HUH?
...YEP.
GUESS I DID...
...I DIDN'T KNOW ANYTHING ABOUT YOU.
SO JUST LIKE FATHER TOLD ME...
...I WAS BENT ON THE IDEA THAT THE VESSALIUS WERE ALL HYPOCRITES AND COWARDS.
BUT...
...WHEN I LOOK WITH MY OWN EYES, THE SCENERY I SEE IS MUCH, MUCH DIFFERENT.
I...
...WANT TO BE ABLE TO MAKE THINGS OUT BY MYSELF.

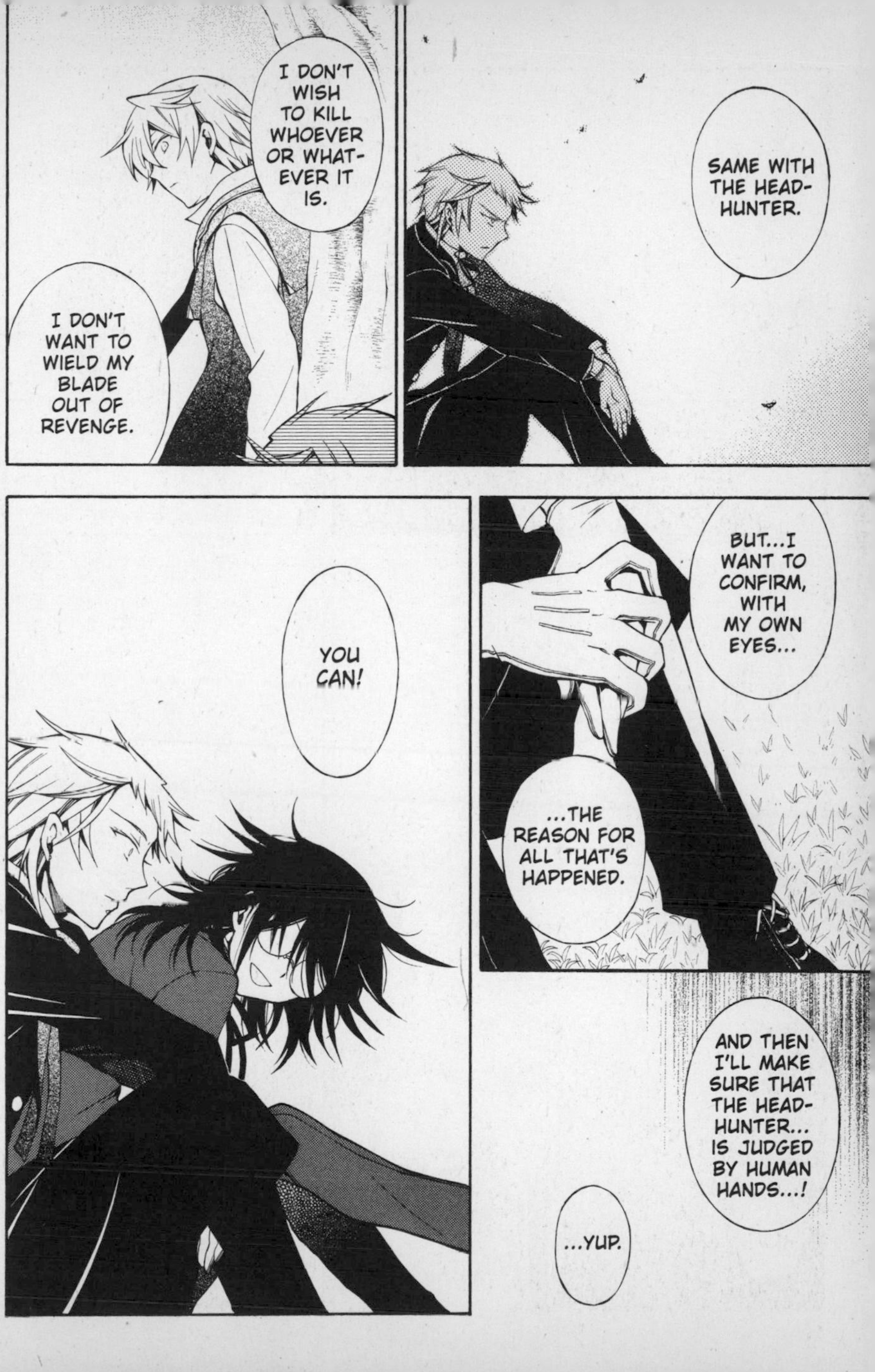
SAME WITH THE HEAD-HUNTER.
I DON'T WISH TO KILL WHOEVER OR WHAT-EVER IT IS.
I DON'T WANT TO WIELD MY BLADE OUT OF REVENGE.
BUT...I WANT TO CONFIRM, WITH MY OWN EYES...
...THE REASON FOR ALL THAT'S HAPPENED.
AND THEN I'LL MAKE SURE THAT THE HEAD-HUNTER... IS JUDGED BY HUMAN HANDS...!
...YUP.
YOU CAN!

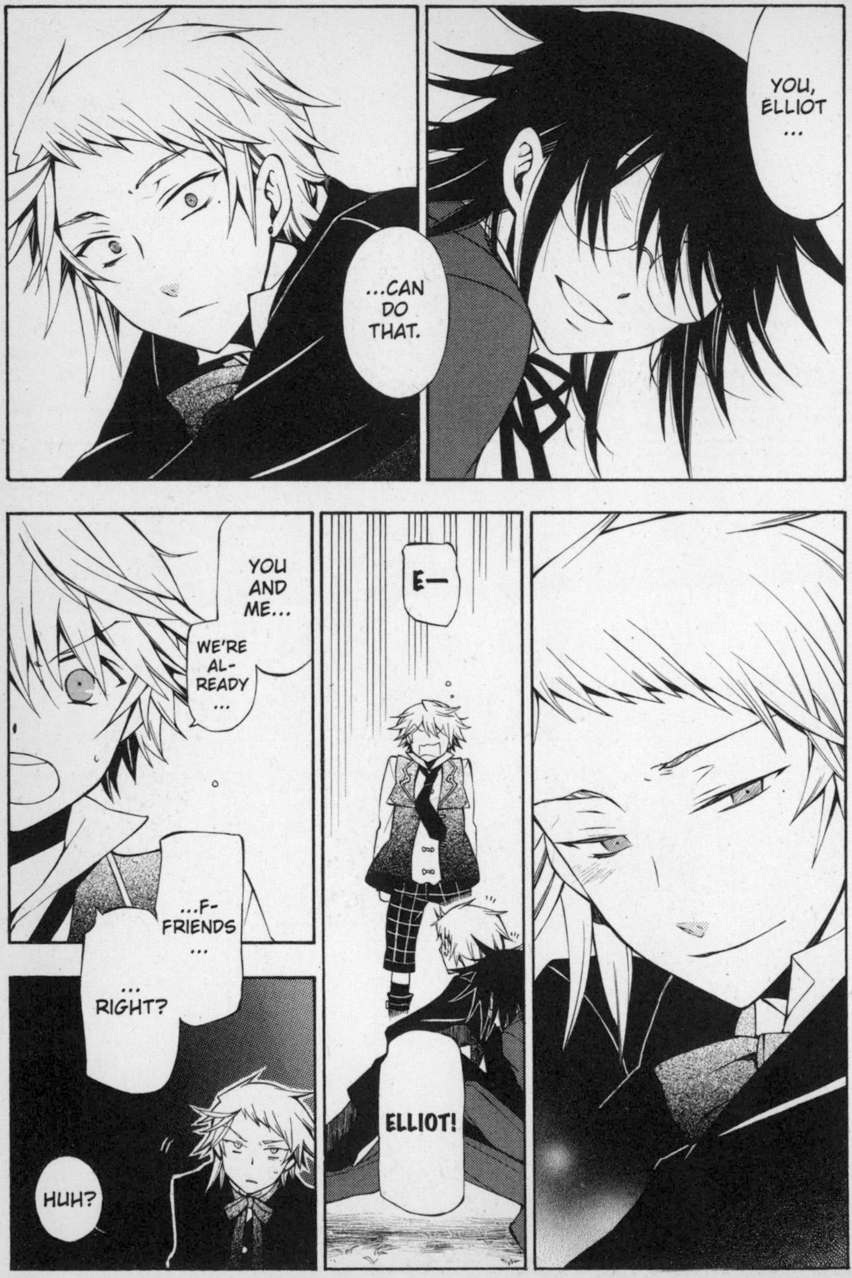
YOU, ELLIOT ...
...CAN DO THAT.
E—
ELLIOT!
YOU AND ME...
WE'RE AL-READY ...
...F- FRIENDS ...
... RIGHT?
HUH?

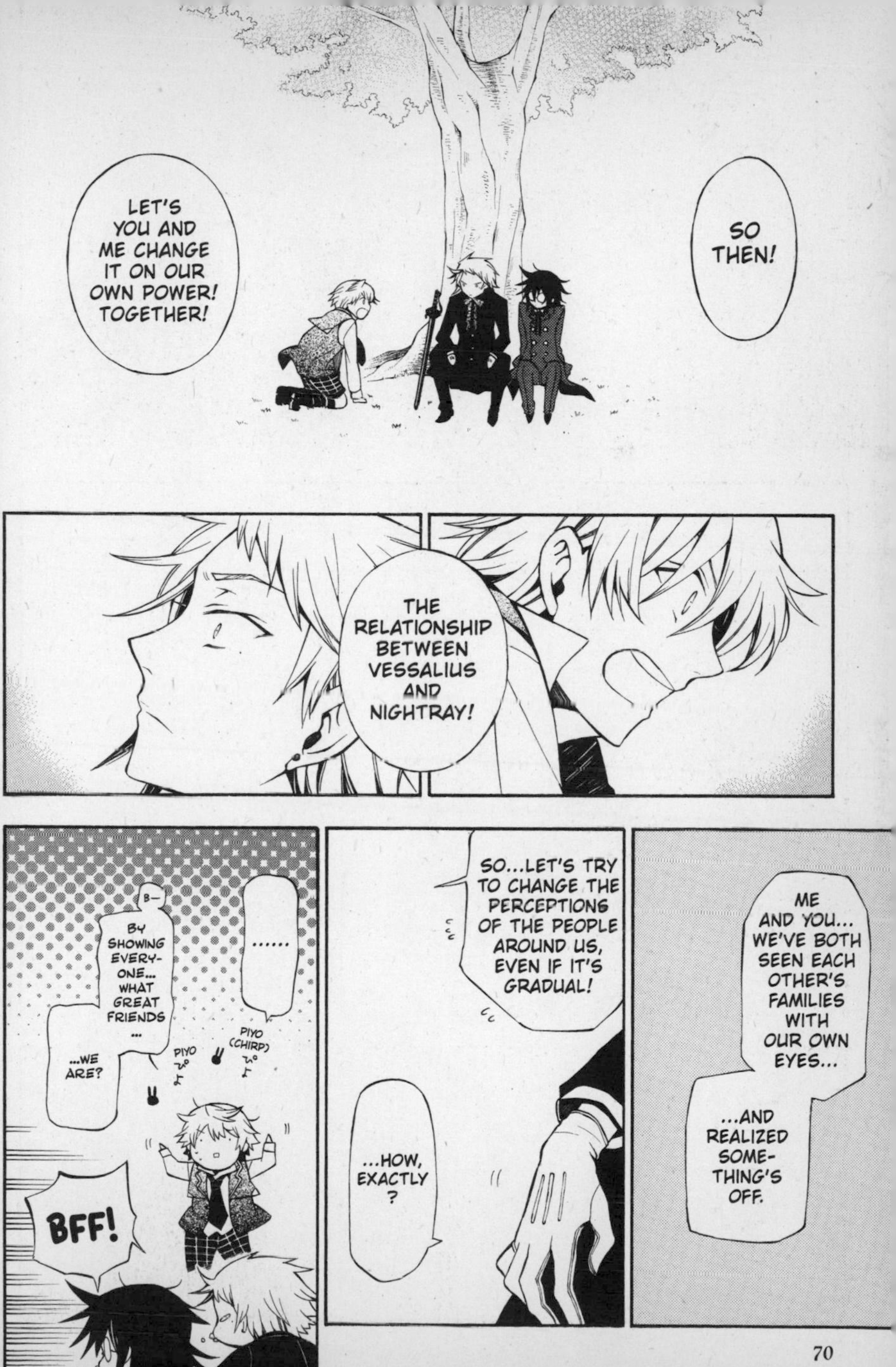
SO THEN!
LET'S YOU AND ME CHANGE IT ON OUR OWN POWER! TOGETHER!
THE RELATIONSHIP BETWEEN VESSALIUS AND NIGHTRAY!
ME AND YOU... WE'VE BOTH SEEN EACH OTHER'S FAMILIES WITH OUR OWN EYES...
...AND REALIZED SOME-THING'S OFF.
SO...LET'S TRY TO CHANGE THE PERCEPTIONS OF THE PEOPLE AROUND US, EVEN IF IT'S GRADUAL!
...HOW, EXACTLY?
......
B—
BY SHOWING EVERY-ONE... WHAT GREAT FRIENDS ...
...WE ARE?
PIYO (CHIRP)
PIYO
BFF!

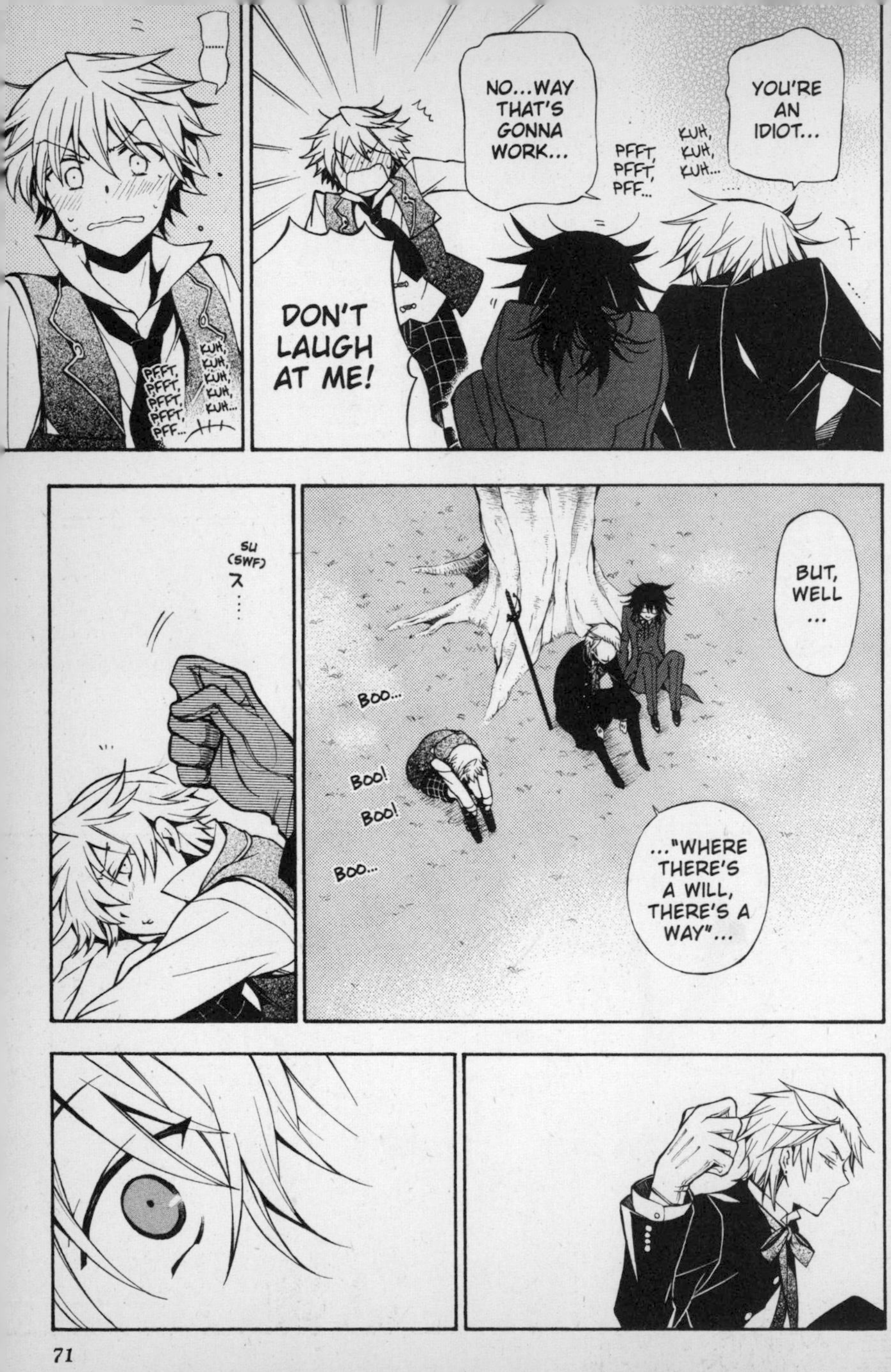
YOU'RE AN IDIOT...
KUH, KUH, KUH...
PFFT, PFFT, PFF...
NO...WAY THAT'S GONNA WORK...
DON'T LAUGH AT ME!
......
KUH, KUH, KUH, KUH, KUH...
PFFT, PFFT, PFFT, PFFT, PFF...
BUT, WELL ...
..."WHERE THERE'S A WILL, THERE'S A WAY"...
BOO...
BOO!
BOO!
BOO...
SU (SWF)
ス…

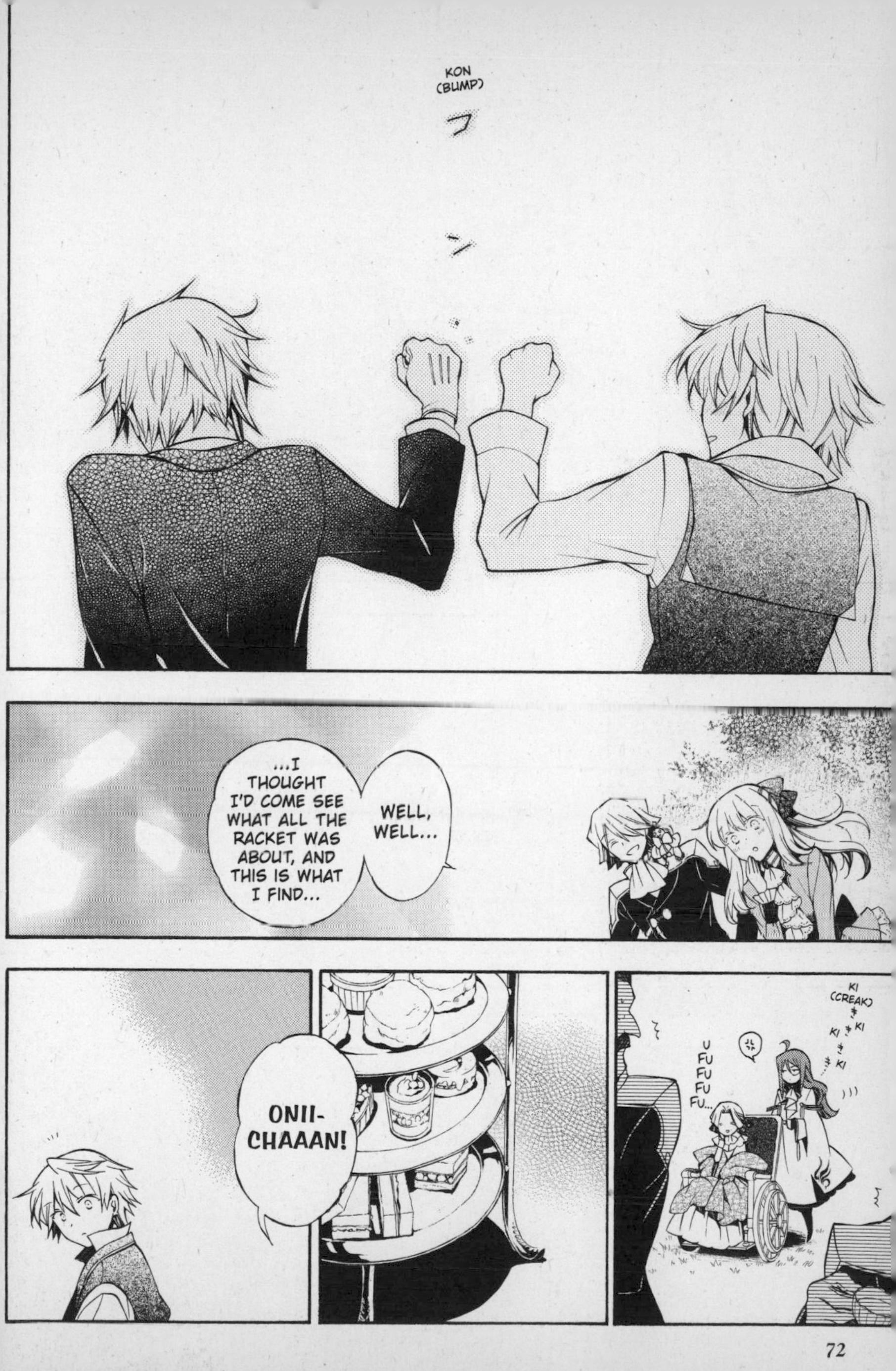
KON (BUMP)
WELL, WELL...
...I THOUGHT I'D COME SEE WHAT ALL THE RACKET WAS ABOUT, AND THIS IS WHAT I FIND...
KI (CREAK) KI KI KI
U FU FU FU FU...
ONII-CHAAAN!

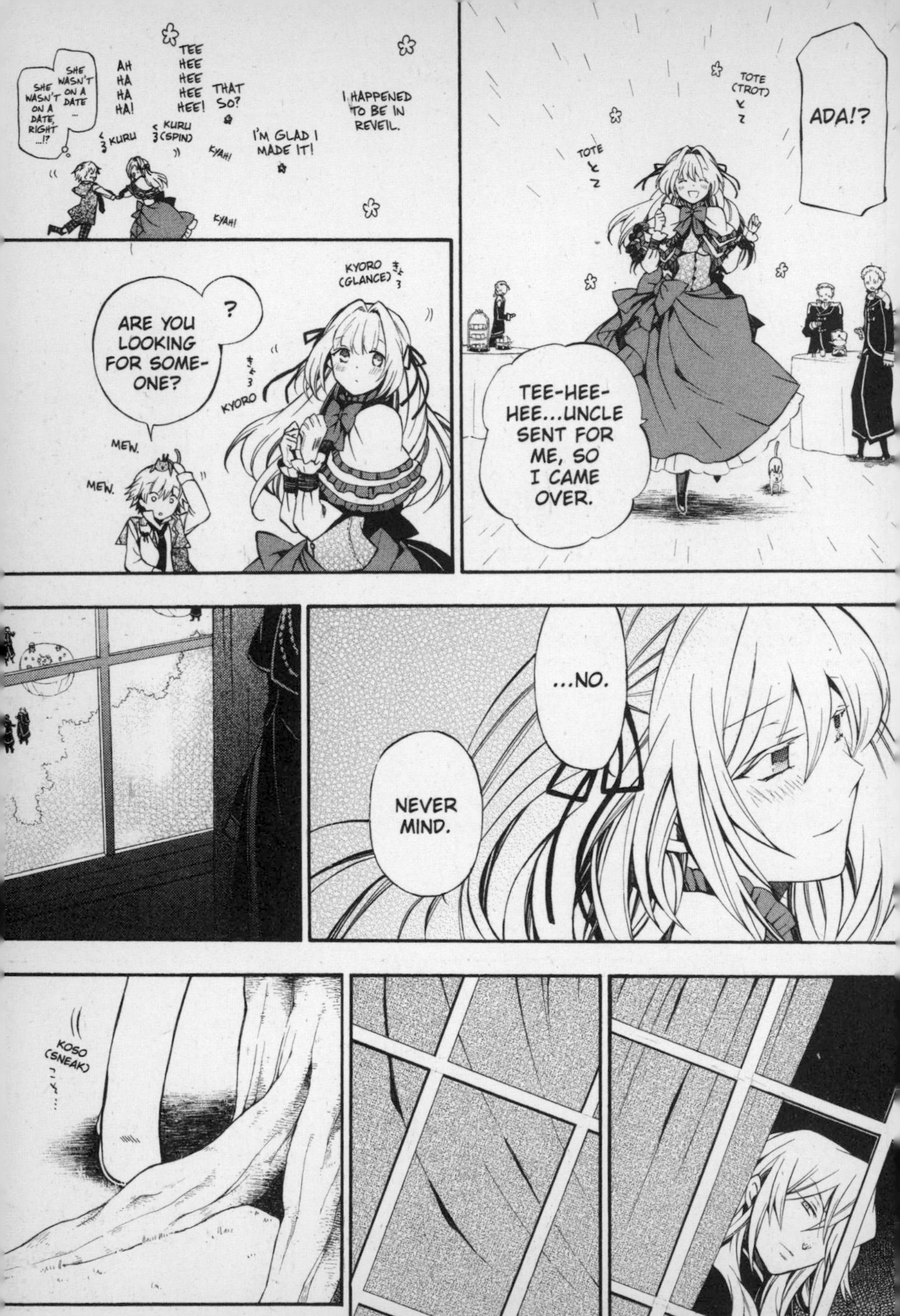

ADA!?
TOTE (TROT)
TOTE
TEE-HEE-HEE...UNCLE SENT FOR ME, SO I CAME OVER.
I HAPPENED TO BE IN REVEIL.
I'M GLAD I MADE IT!
THAT SO?
TEE HEE HEE HEE HEE!
AH HA HA HA!
KURU (SPIN)
KURU
KYAH!
KYAH!
SHE WASN'T ON A DATE ...
SHE WASN'T ON A DATE, RIGHT ...!?
KYORO (GLANCE)
KYORO
?
ARE YOU LOOKING FOR SOME-ONE?
MEW.
MEW.
...NO.
NEVER MIND.
KOSO (SNEAK)

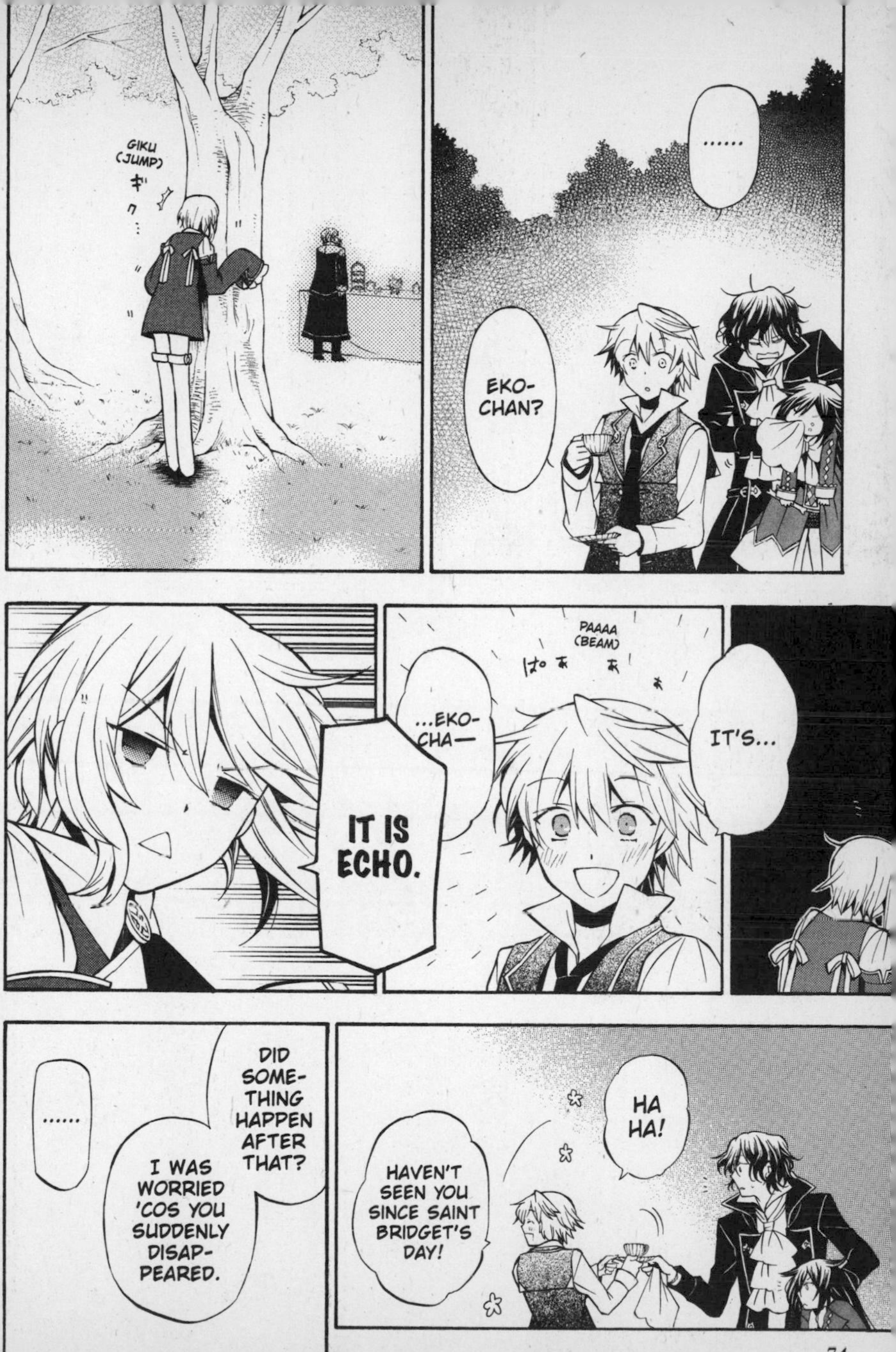
......
EKO-CHAN?
GIKU (JUMP)
ギク
IT'S...
PAAAA (BEAM)
ぱあああ
...EKO-CHA—
IT IS ECHO.
HA HA!
HAVEN'T SEEN YOU SINCE SAINT BRIDGET'S DAY!
DID SOMETHING HAPPEN AFTER THAT?
I WAS WORRIED 'COS YOU SUDDENLY DISAPPEARED.
......

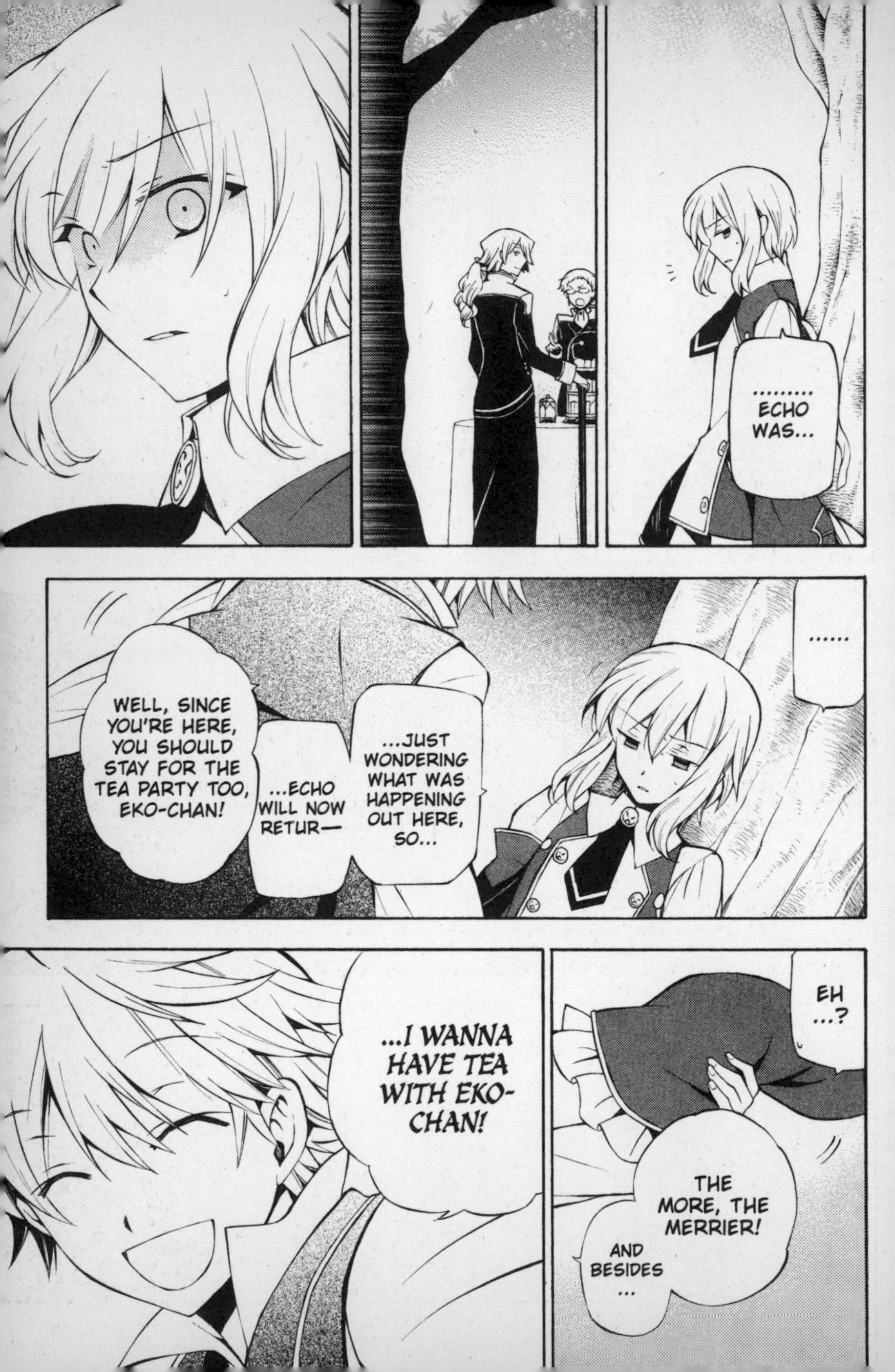
.... ECHO WAS...
......
...JUST WONDERING WHAT WAS HAPPENING OUT HERE, SO...
...ECHO WILL NOW RETUR—
WELL, SINCE YOU'RE HERE, YOU SHOULD STAY FOR THE TEA PARTY TOO, EKO-CHAN!
EH ...?
THE MORE, THE MERRIER!
AND BESIDES ...
...I WANNA HAVE TEA WITH EKO-CHAN!

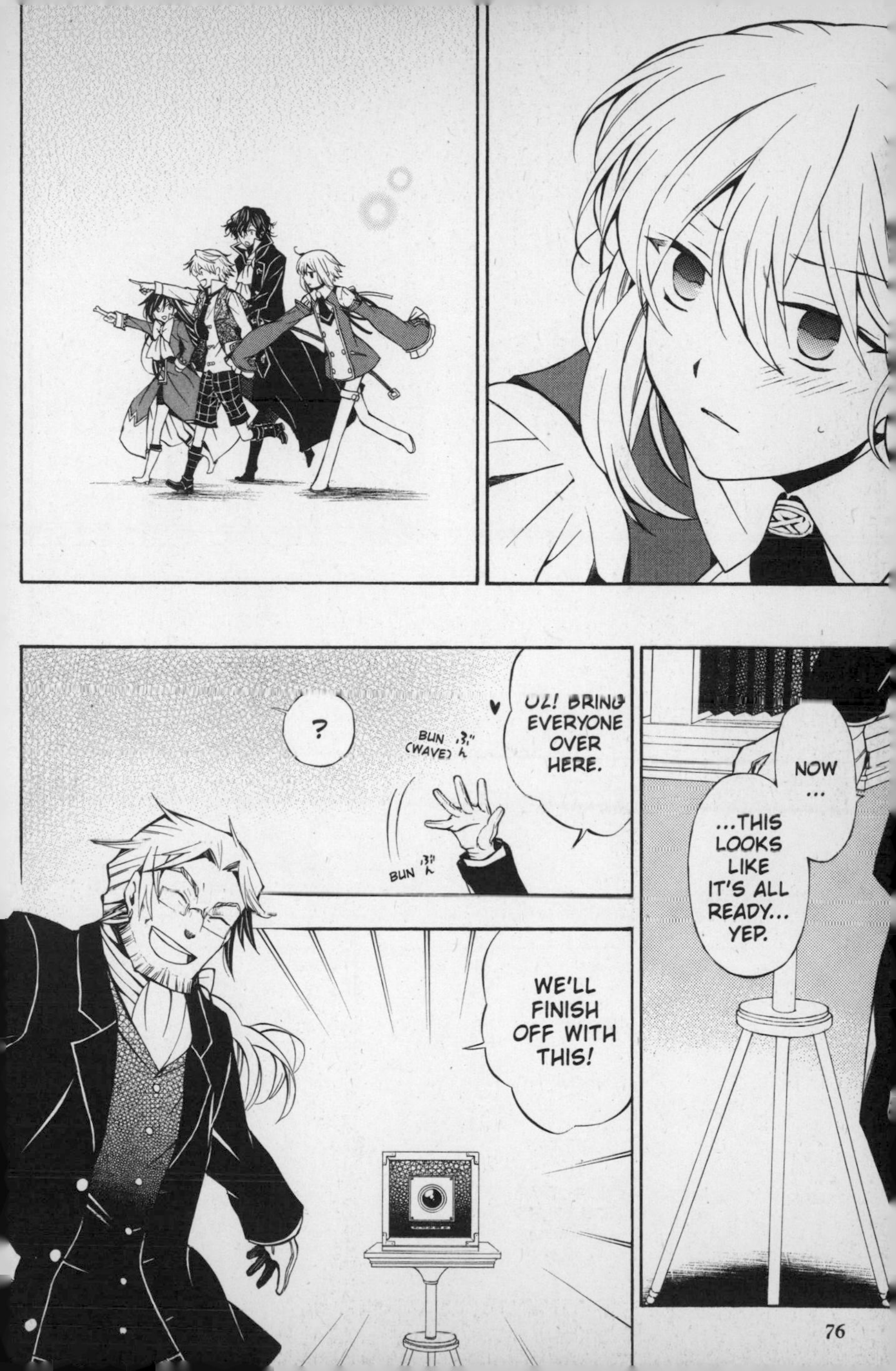
NOW ...
...THIS LOOKS LIKE IT'S ALL READY... YEP.
OZ! BRING EVERYONE OVER HERE.
?
BUN (WAVE)
BUN
WE'LL FINISH OFF WITH THIS!

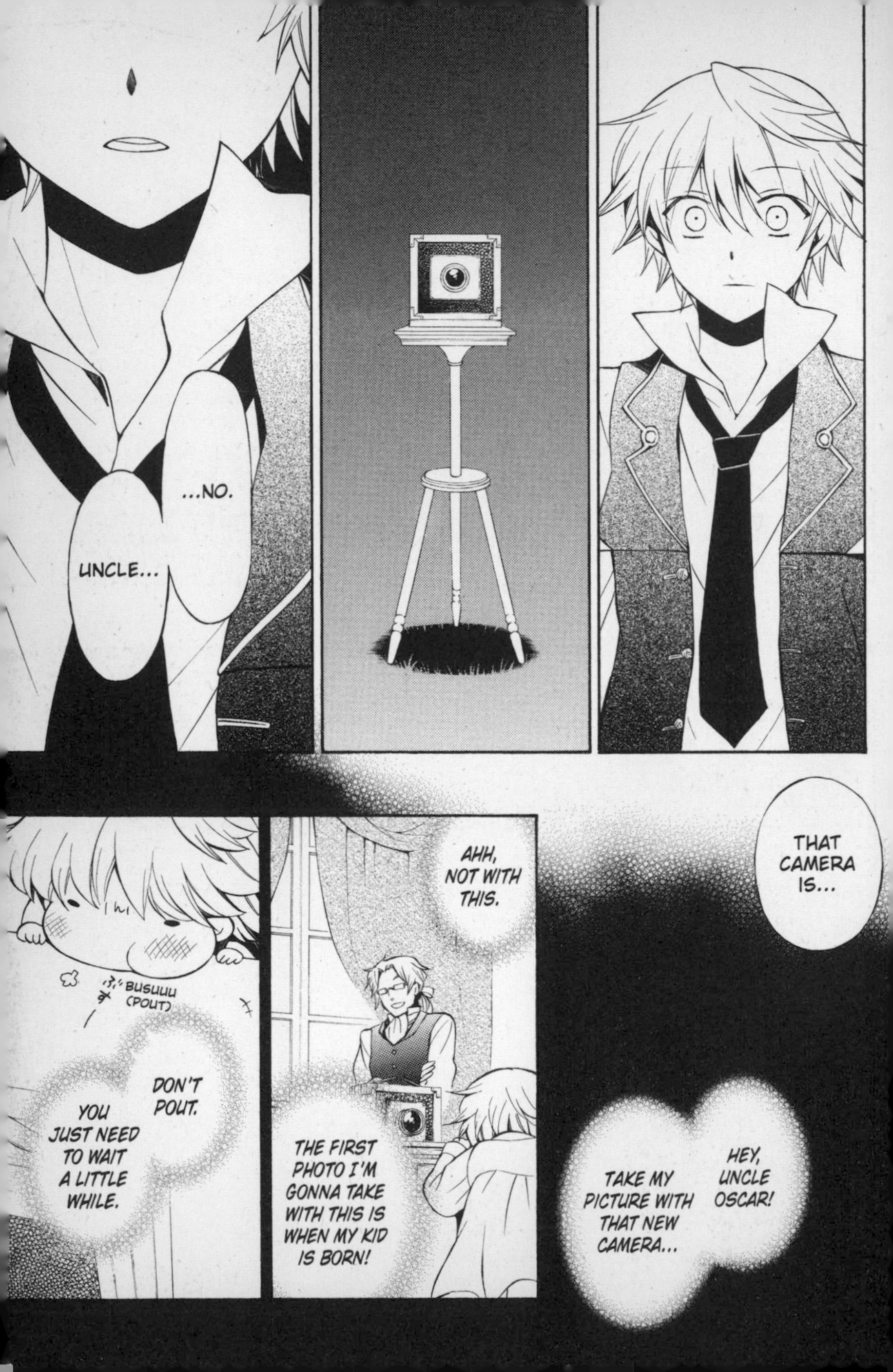
...NO.
UNCLE...
THAT CAMERA IS...
HEY, UNCLE OSCAR!
TAKE MY PICTURE WITH THAT NEW CAMERA...
AHH, NOT WITH THIS.
THE FIRST PHOTO I'M GONNA TAKE WITH THIS IS WHEN MY KID IS BORN!
BUSUUU (POUT)
DON'T POUT.
YOU JUST NEED TO WAIT A LITTLE WHILE.

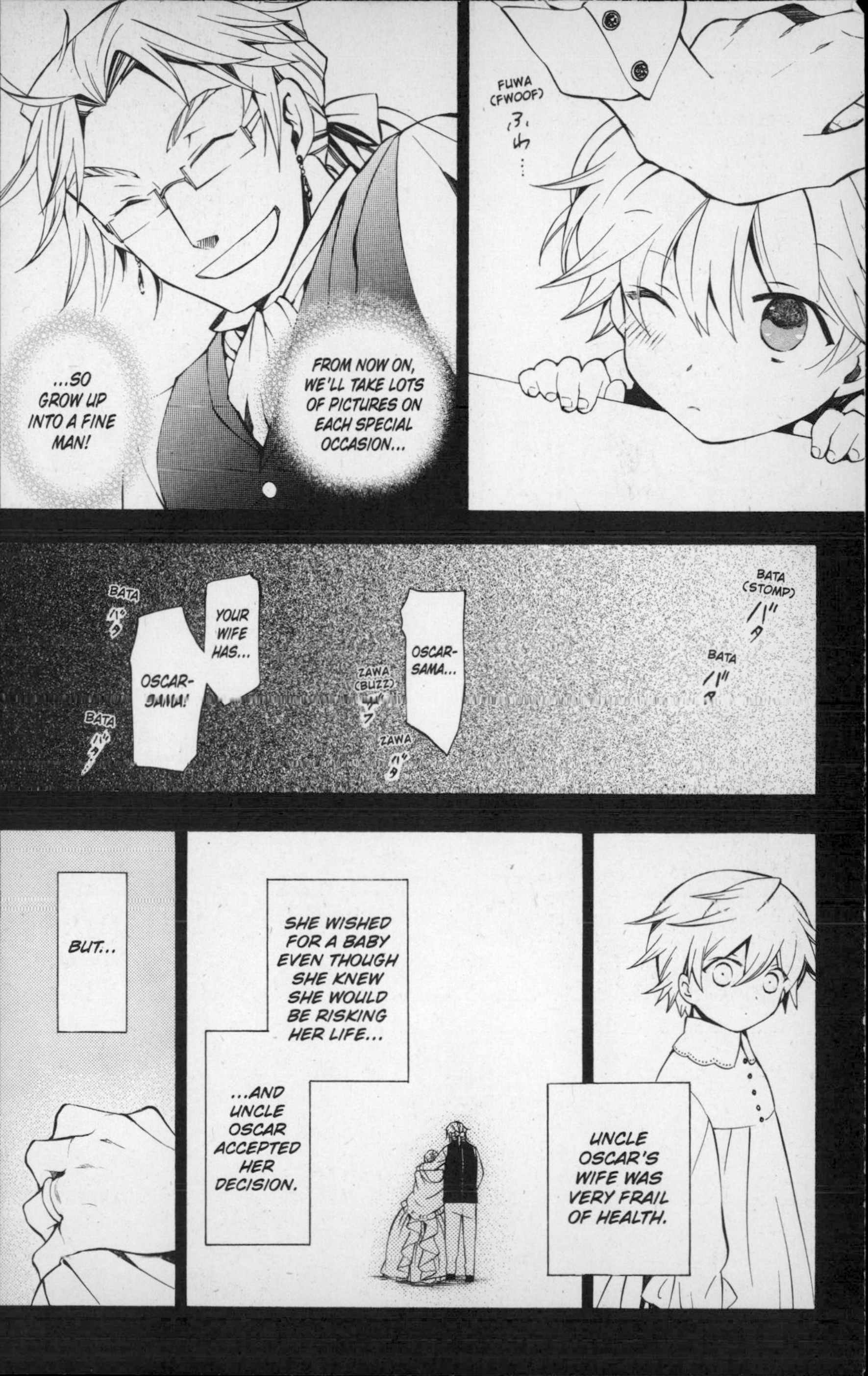
FUWA
(FWOOF)
FROM NOW ON, WE'LL TAKE LOTS OF PICTURES ON EACH SPECIAL OCCASION...
...SO GROW UP INTO A FINE MAN!
BATA
(STOMP)
BATA
OSCAR-SAMA...
ZAWA
(BUZZ)
ZAWA
YOUR WIFE HAS...
OSCAR-SAMA!
BATA
BATA
UNCLE OSCAR'S WIFE WAS VERY FRAIL OF HEALTH.
SHE WISHED FOR A BABY EVEN THOUGH SHE KNEW SHE WOULD BE RISKING HER LIFE...
...AND UNCLE OSCAR ACCEPTED HER DECISION.
BUT...

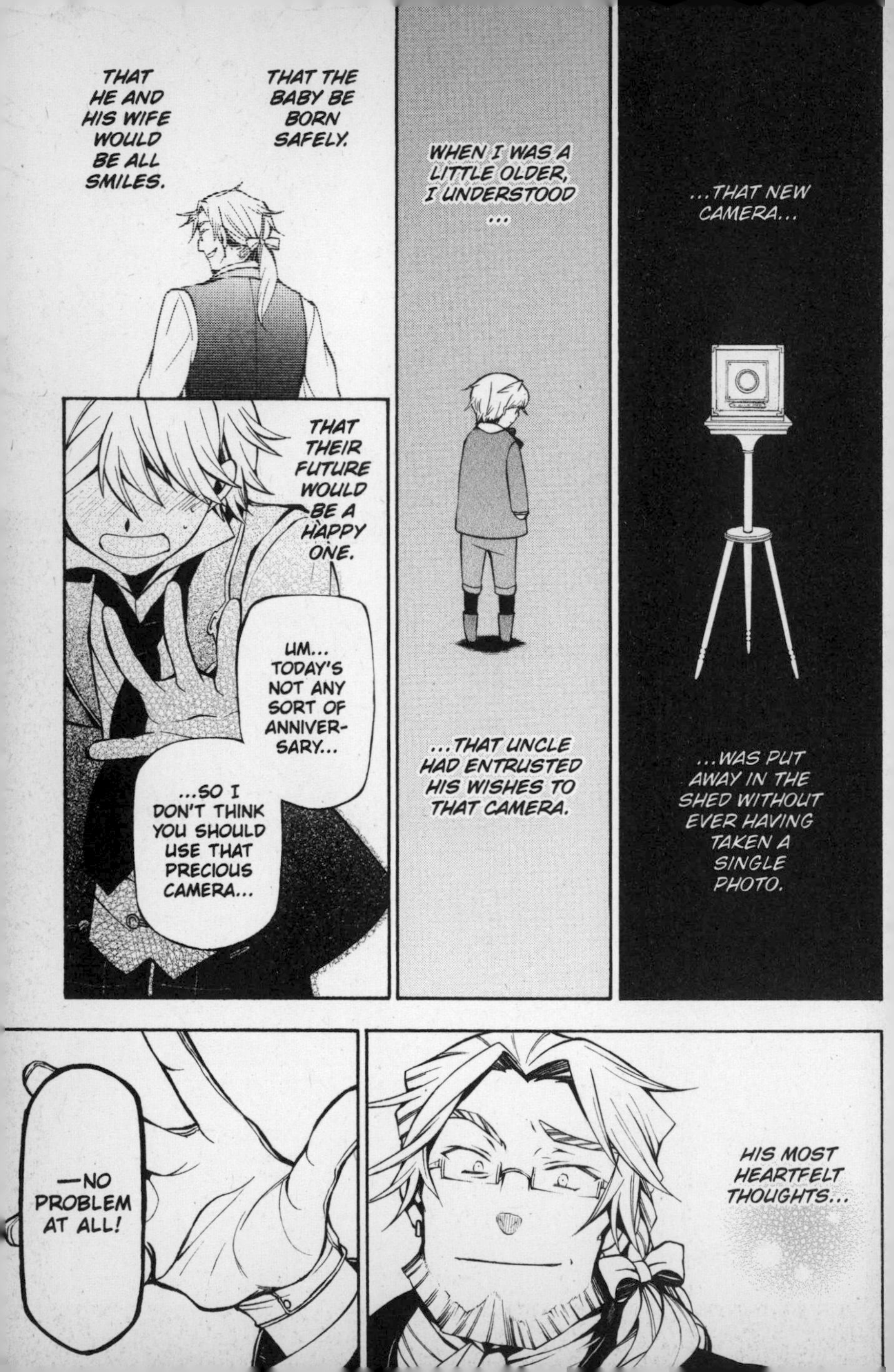
...THAT NEW CAMERA...
...WAS PUT AWAY IN THE SHED WITHOUT EVER HAVING TAKEN A SINGLE PHOTO.
WHEN I WAS A LITTLE OLDER, I UNDERSTOOD...
...THAT UNCLE HAD ENTRUSTED HIS WISHES TO THAT CAMERA.
THAT THE BABY BE BORN SAFELY.
THAT HE AND HIS WIFE WOULD BE ALL SMILES.
THAT THEIR FUTURE WOULD BE A HAPPY ONE.
UM... TODAY'S NOT ANY SORT OF ANNIVERSARY...
...SO I DON'T THINK YOU SHOULD USE THAT PRECIOUS CAMERA...
HIS MOST HEARTFELT THOUGHTS...
—NO PROBLEM AT ALL!

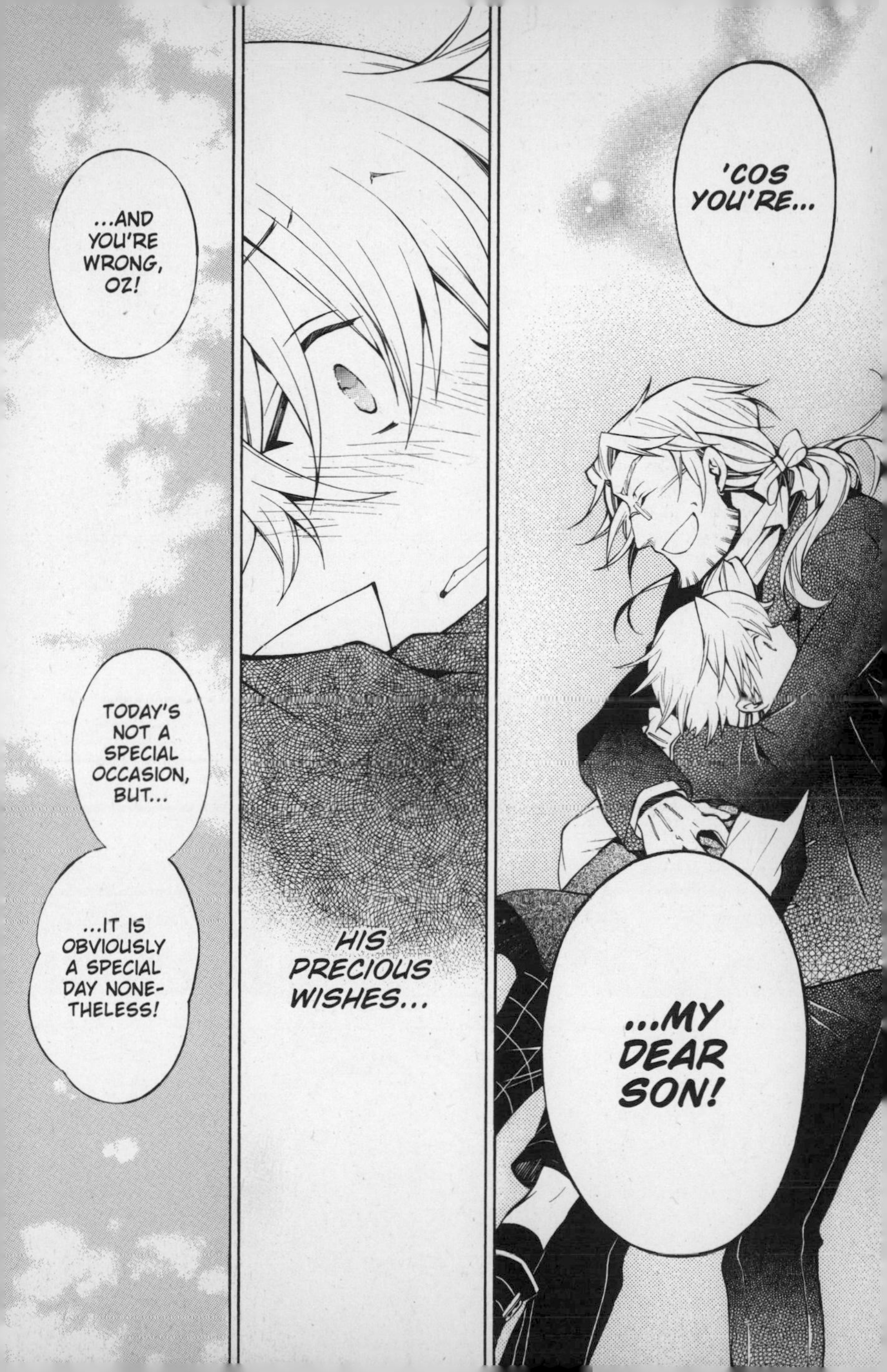
'COS YOU'RE...
...MY DEAR SON!
HIS PRECIOUS WISHES...
...AND YOU'RE WRONG, OZ!
TODAY'S NOT A SPECIAL OCCASION, BUT...
...IT IS OBVIOUSLY A SPECIAL DAY NONE-THELESS!

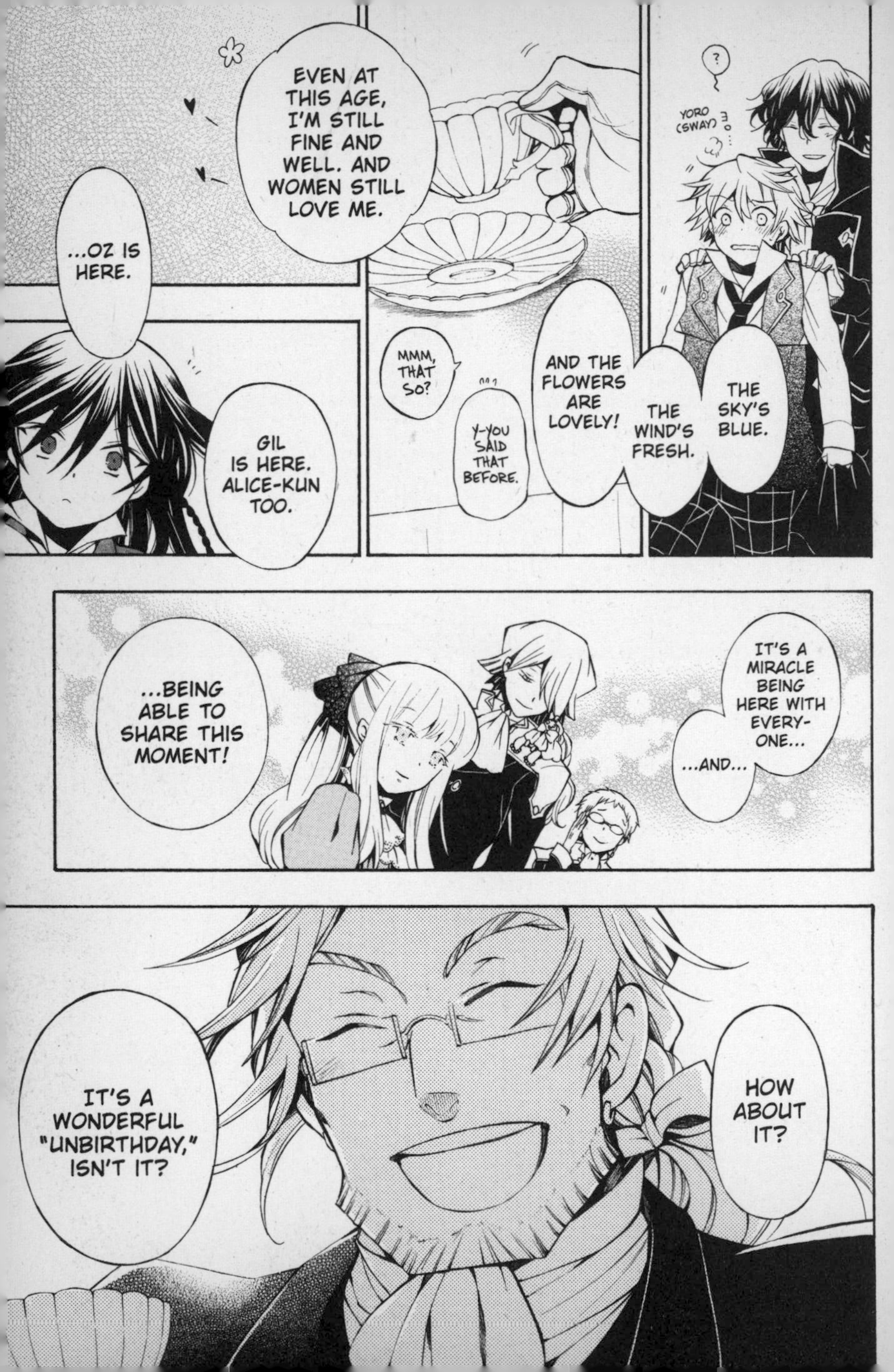

?
YORO (SWAY)
EVEN AT THIS AGE, I'M STILL FINE AND WELL. AND WOMEN STILL LOVE ME.
THE SKY'S BLUE.
THE WIND'S FRESH.
AND THE FLOWERS ARE LOVELY!
Y-YOU SAID THAT BEFORE.
MMM, THAT SO?
...OZ IS HERE.
GIL IS HERE. ALICE-KUN TOO.
IT'S A MIRACLE BEING HERE WITH EVERY-ONE...
...AND...
...BEING ABLE TO SHARE THIS MOMENT!
HOW ABOUT IT?
IT'S A WONDERFUL "UNBIRTHDAY," ISN'T IT?

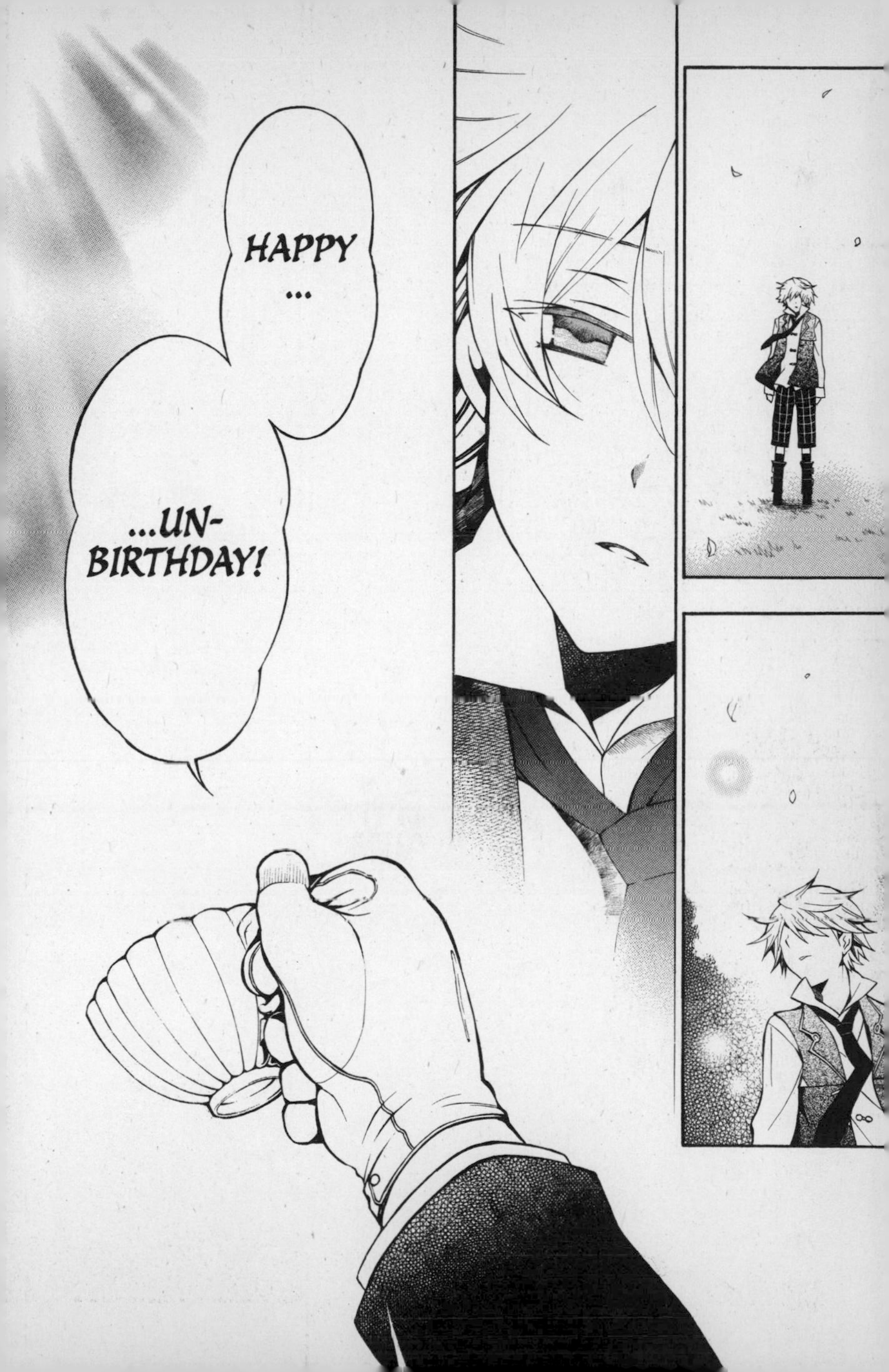
HAPPY ...
...UN-BIRTHDAY!

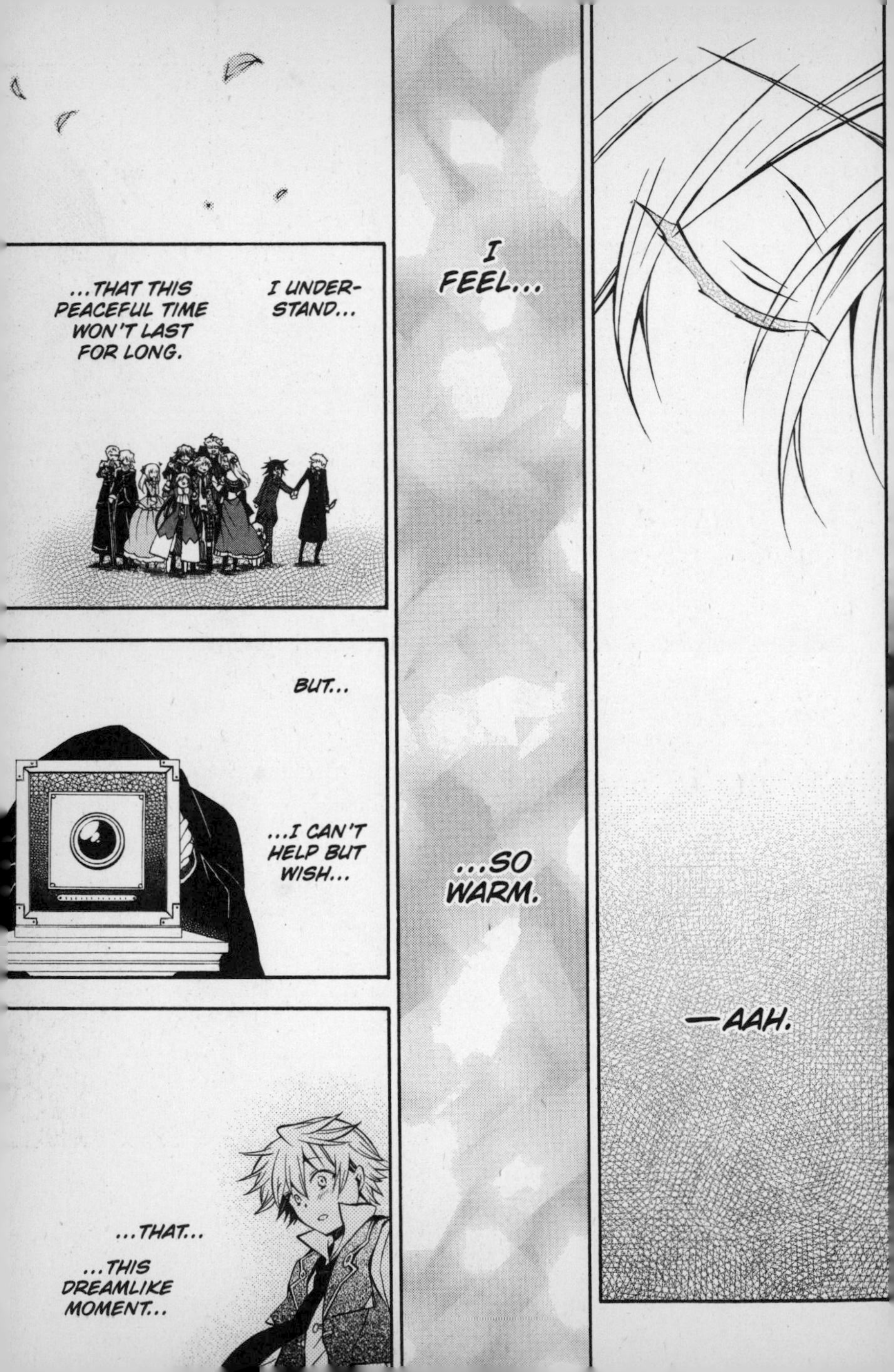
—AAH.
I FEEL...
...SO WARM.
I UNDER-STAND...
...THAT THIS PEACEFUL TIME WON'T LAST FOR LONG.
BUT...
...I CAN'T HELP BUT WISH...
...THAT...
...THIS DREAMLIKE MOMENT...

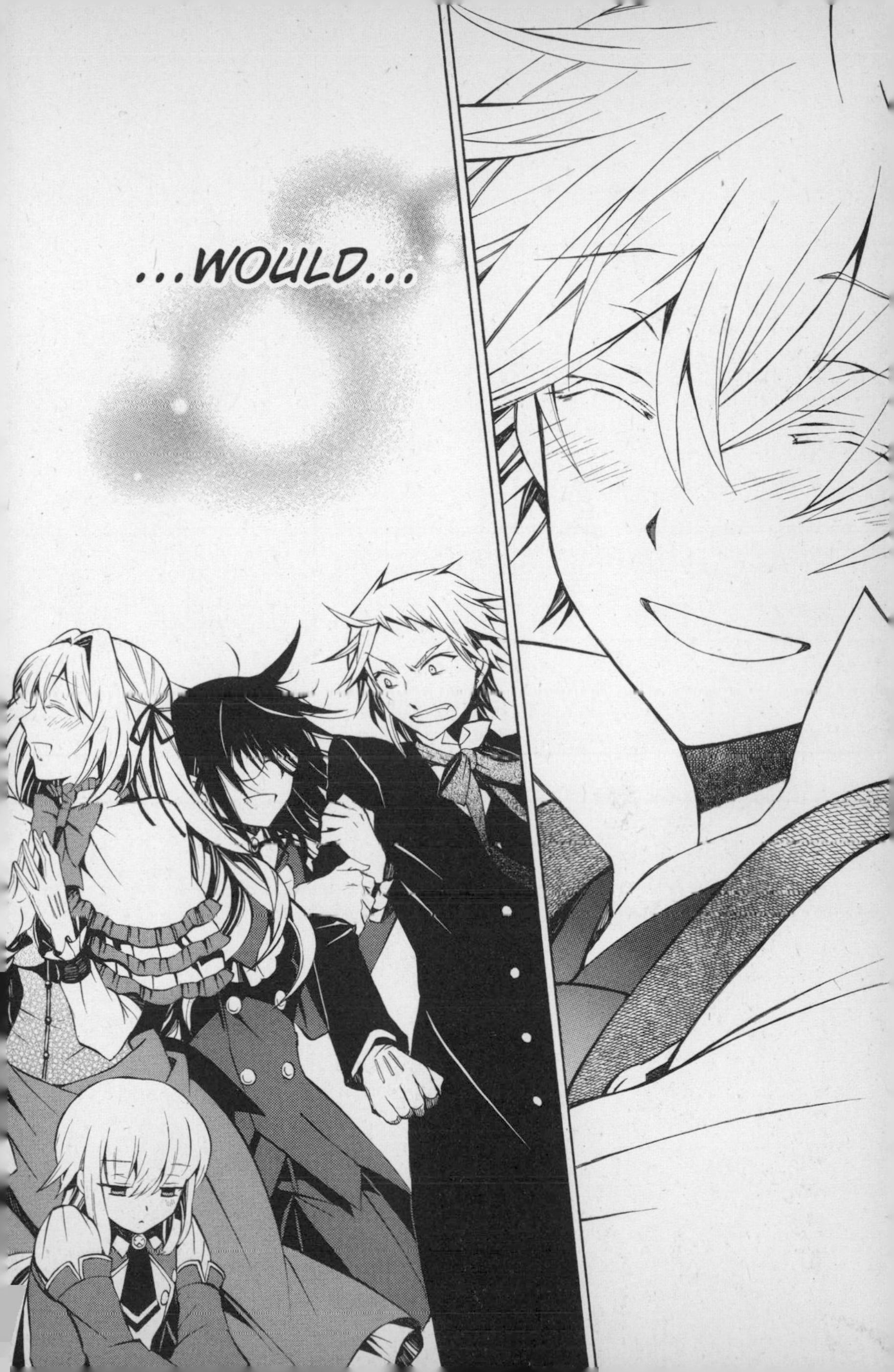
...WOULD...

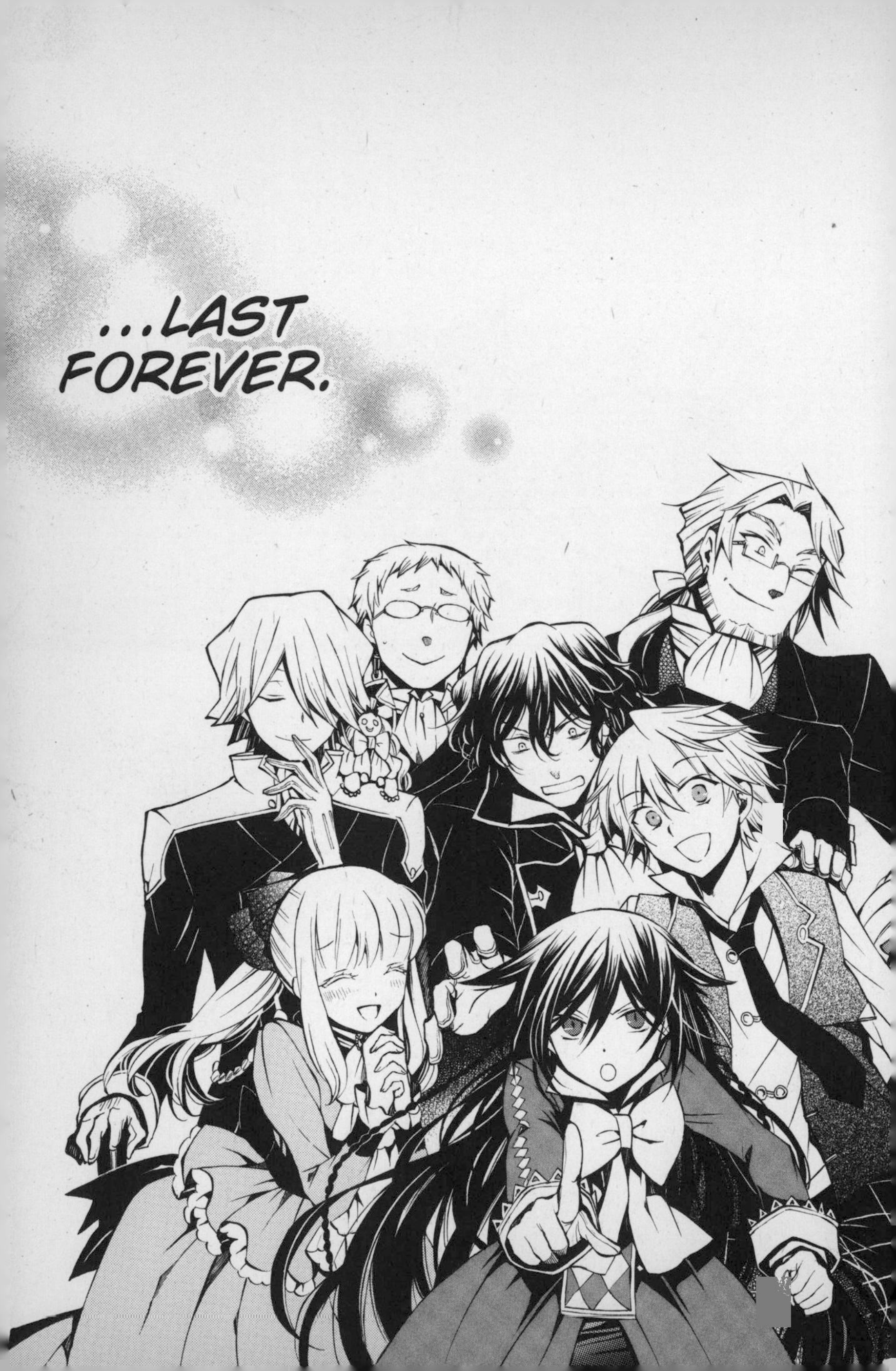
...LAST FOREVER.

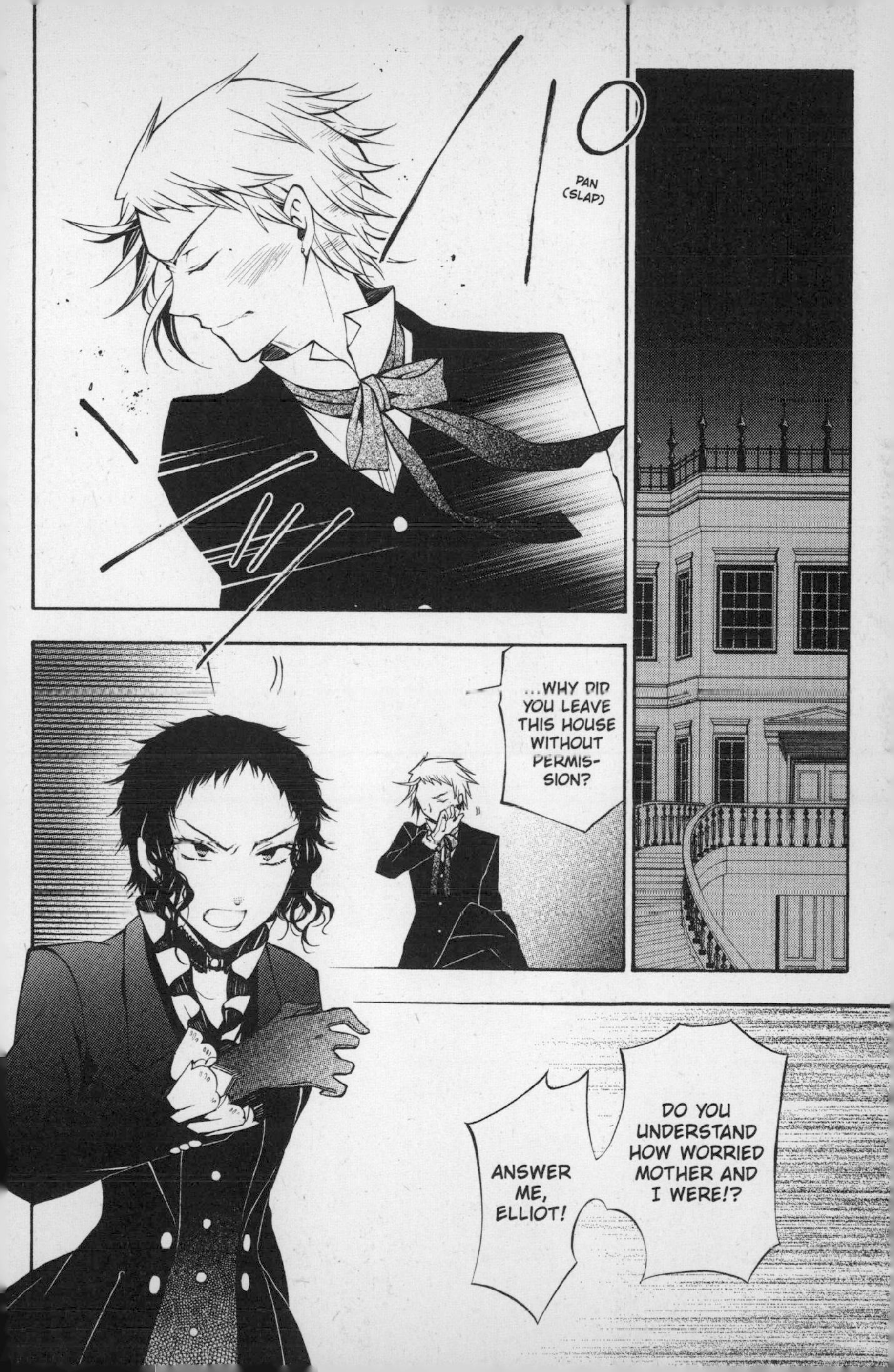
PAN (SLAP)
...WHY DID YOU LEAVE THIS HOUSE WITHOUT PERMIS-SION?
DO YOU UNDERSTAND HOW WORRIED MOTHER AND I WERE!?
ANSWER ME, ELLIOT!

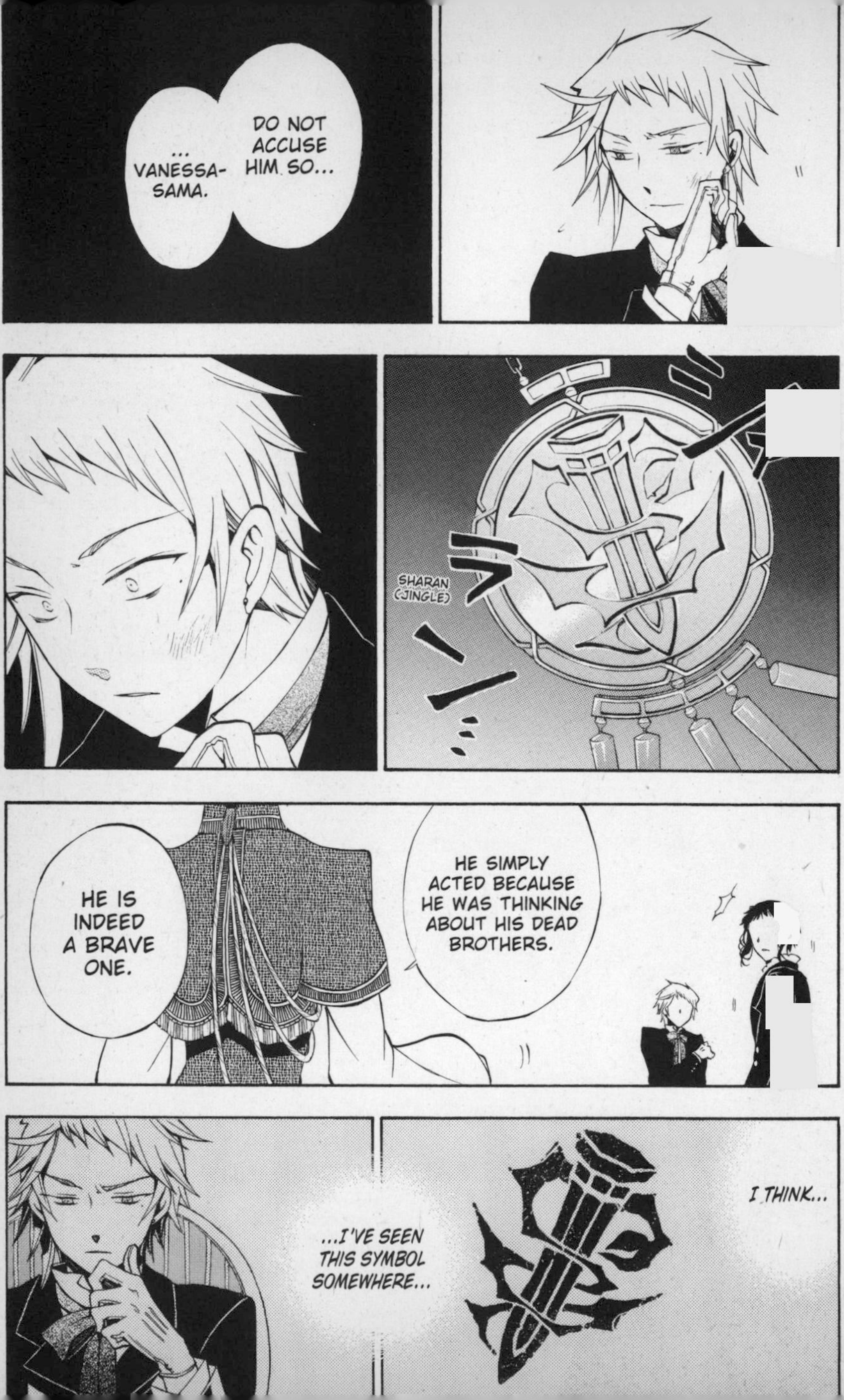
DO NOT ACCUSE HIM SO...
...VANESSA-SAMA.
SHARAN (JINGLE)
HE SIMPLY ACTED BECAUSE HE WAS THINKING ABOUT HIS DEAD BROTHERS.
HE IS INDEED A BRAVE ONE.
I THINK...
...I'VE SEEN THIS SYMBOL SOMEWHERE...

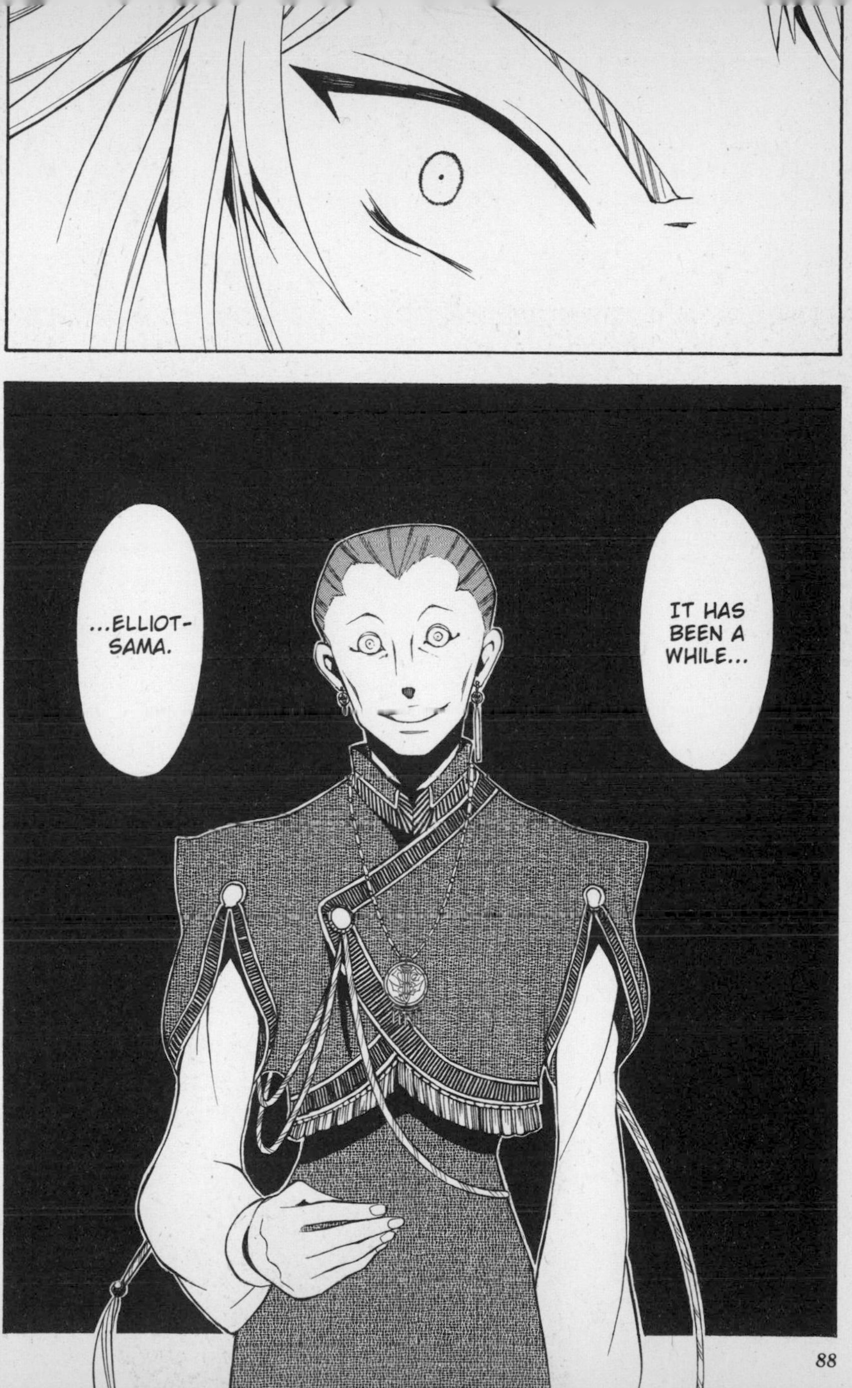
IT HAS BEEN A WHILE...
...ELLIOT-SAMA.

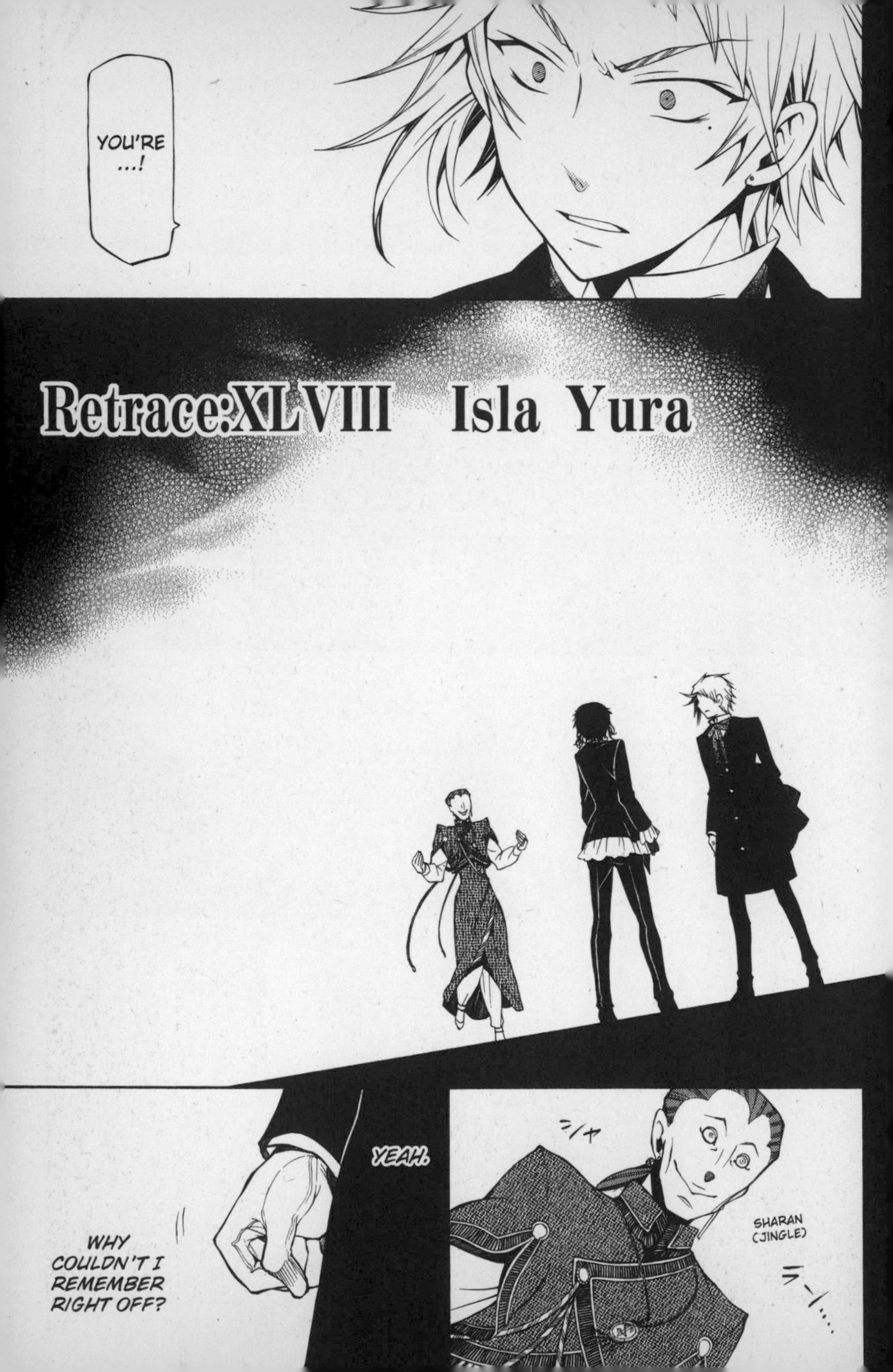
YOU'RE ...!
Retrace:XLVIII Isla Yura
SHARAN (JINGLE)
YEAH.
WHY COULDN'T I REMEMBER RIGHT OFF?

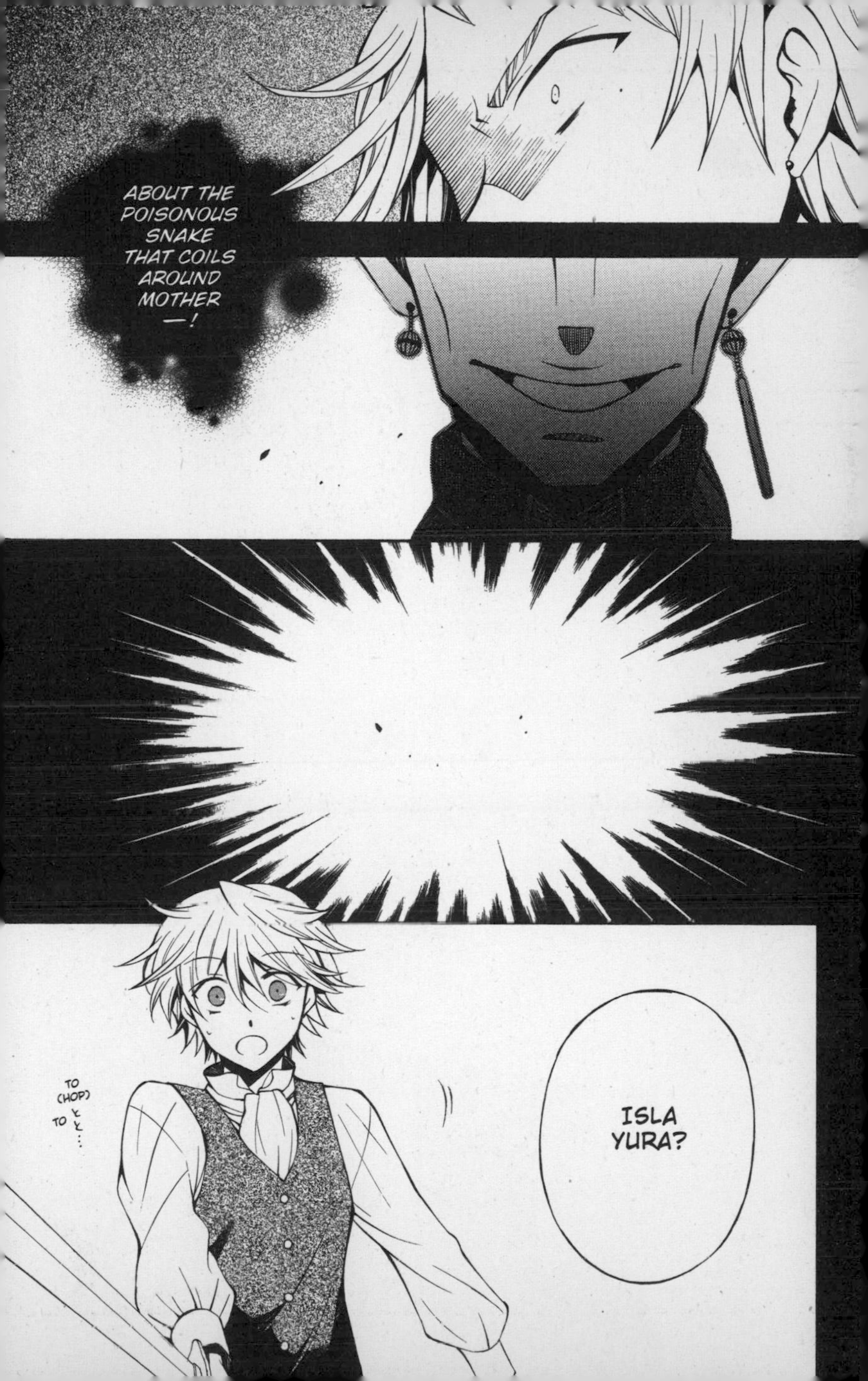
ABOUT THE POISONOUS SNAKE THAT COILS AROUND MOTHER —!
ISLA YURA?
TO (HOP) TO

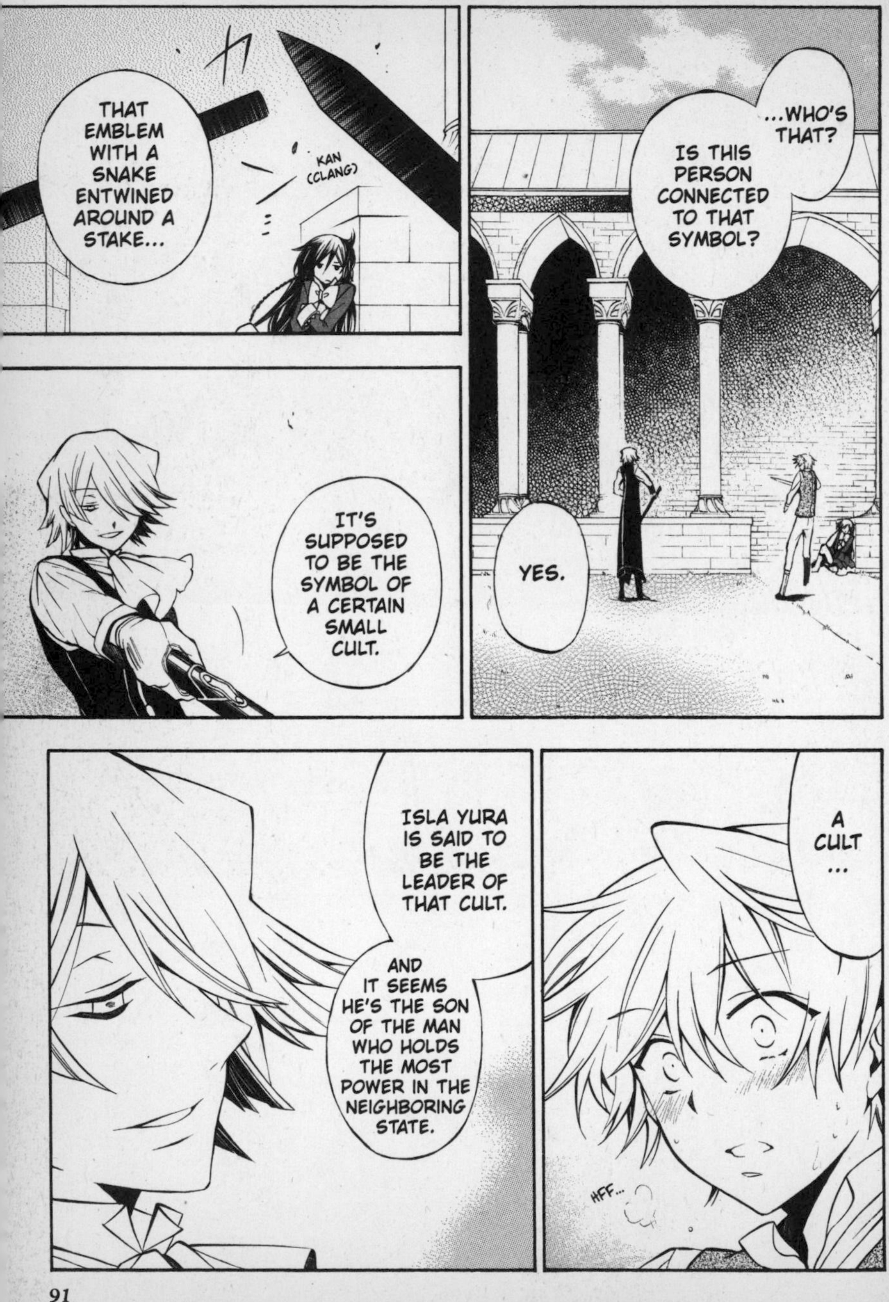
...WHO'S THAT?
IS THIS PERSON CONNECTED TO THAT SYMBOL?
YES.
THAT EMBLEM WITH A SNAKE ENTWINED AROUND A STAKE...
KAN (CLANG)
IT'S SUPPOSED TO BE THE SYMBOL OF A CERTAIN SMALL CULT.
A CULT ...
HFF...
ISLA YURA IS SAID TO BE THE LEADER OF THAT CULT.
AND IT SEEMS HE'S THE SON OF THE MAN WHO HOLDS THE MOST POWER IN THE NEIGHBORING STATE.

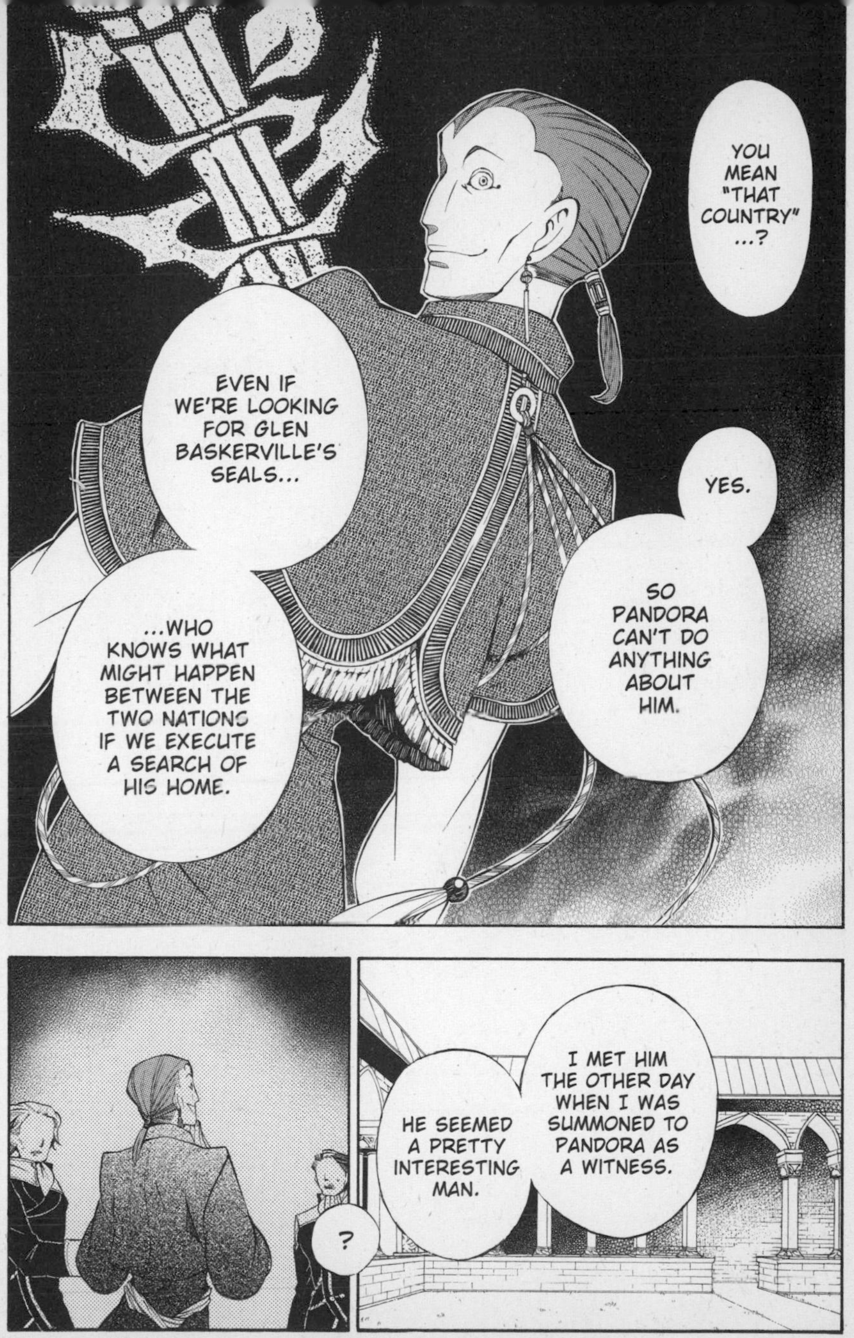
YOU MEAN "THAT COUNTRY" ...?
YES.
SO PANDORA CAN'T DO ANYTHING ABOUT HIM.
EVEN IF WE'RE LOOKING FOR GLEN BASKERVILLE'S SEALS...
...WHO KNOWS WHAT MIGHT HAPPEN BETWEEN THE TWO NATIONS IF WE EXECUTE A SEARCH OF HIS HOME.
I MET HIM THE OTHER DAY WHEN I WAS SUMMONED TO PANDORA AS A WITNESS.
HE SEEMED A PRETTY INTERESTING MAN.
?

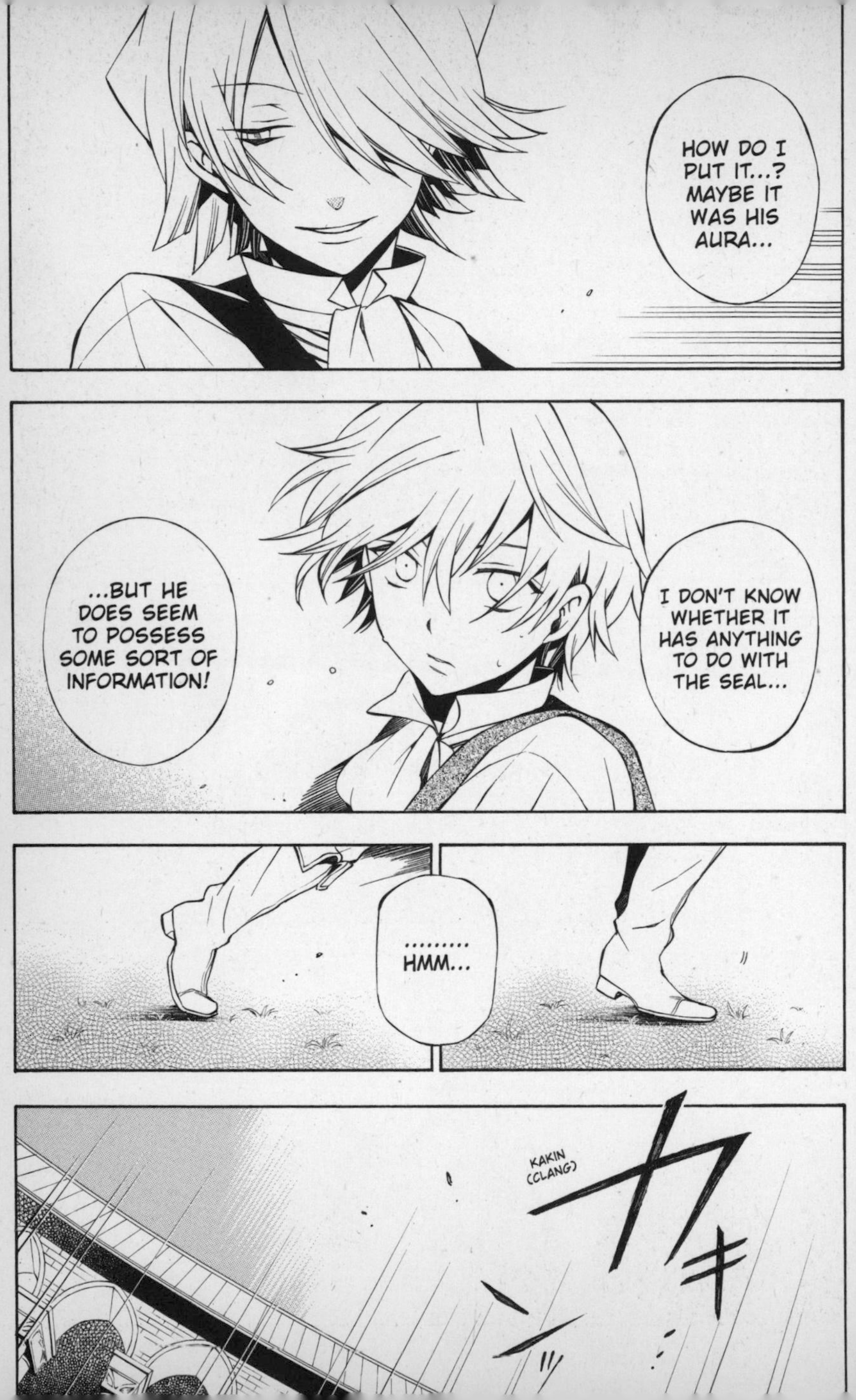
HOW DO I PUT IT...? MAYBE IT WAS HIS AURA...
I DON'T KNOW WHETHER IT HAS ANYTHING TO DO WITH THE SEAL...
...BUT HE DOES SEEM TO POSSESS SOME SORT OF INFORMATION!
....
HMM...
KAKIN (CLANG)

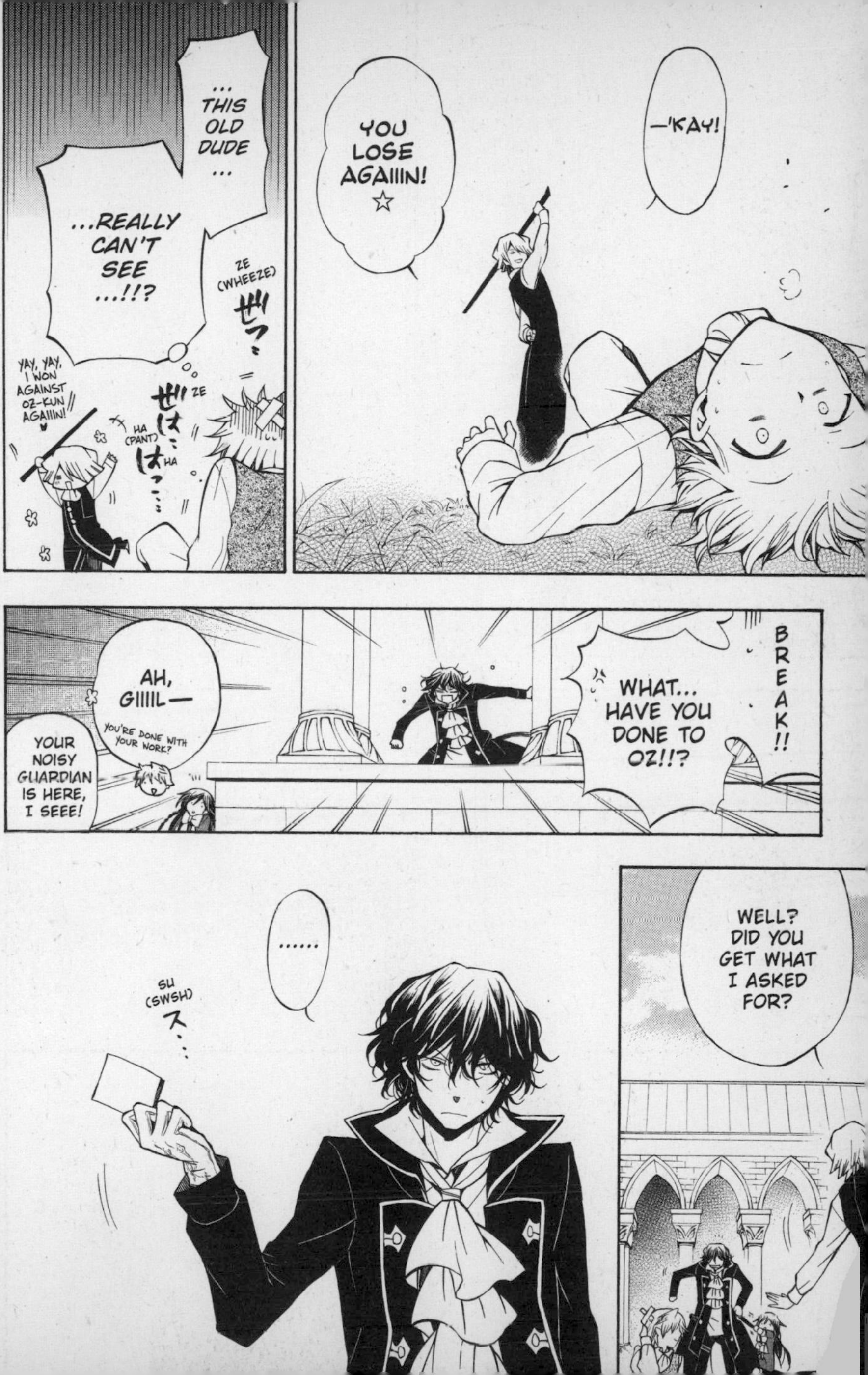
—'KAY!
YOU LOSE AGAIIIN! ☆
...THIS OLD DUDE...
...REALLY CAN'T SEE ...!!?
ZE (WHEEZE)
ぜっ
ZE
ぜはっ
HA (PANT) HA
はっ
YAY, YAY, I WON AGAINST OZ-KUN AGAIIIN!
BREAK!!
WHAT... HAVE YOU DONE TO OZ!!?
AH, GIIIL—
YOU'RE DONE WITH YOUR WORK?
YOUR NOISY GUARDIAN IS HERE, I SEEE!
WELL? DID YOU GET WHAT I ASKED FOR?
......
SU (SWSH)
ス…

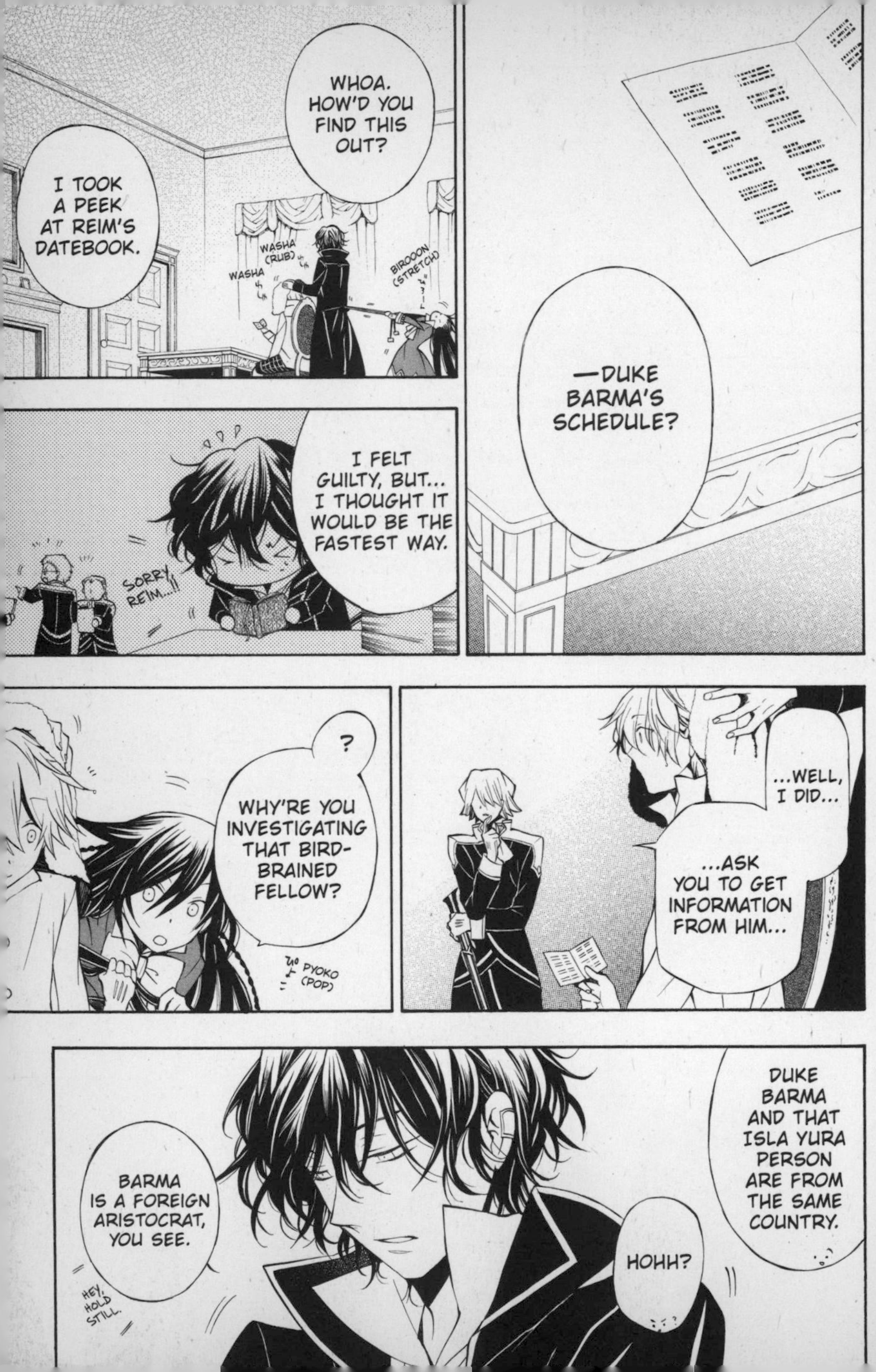
—DUKE BARMA'S SCHEDULE?
WHOA. HOW'D YOU FIND THIS OUT?
I TOOK A PEEK AT REIM'S DATEBOOK.
BIROOON (STRETCH)
WASHA (RUB)
WASHA
I FELT GUILTY, BUT... I THOUGHT IT WOULD BE THE FASTEST WAY.
SORRY REIM...!!
...WELL, I DID...
...ASK YOU TO GET INFORMATION FROM HIM...
?
WHY'RE YOU INVESTIGATING THAT BIRD-BRAINED FELLOW?
PYOKO (POP)
DUKE BARMA AND THAT ISLA YURA PERSON ARE FROM THE SAME COUNTRY.
HOHH?
BARMA IS A FOREIGN ARISTOCRAT, YOU SEE.
HEY, HOLD STILL.

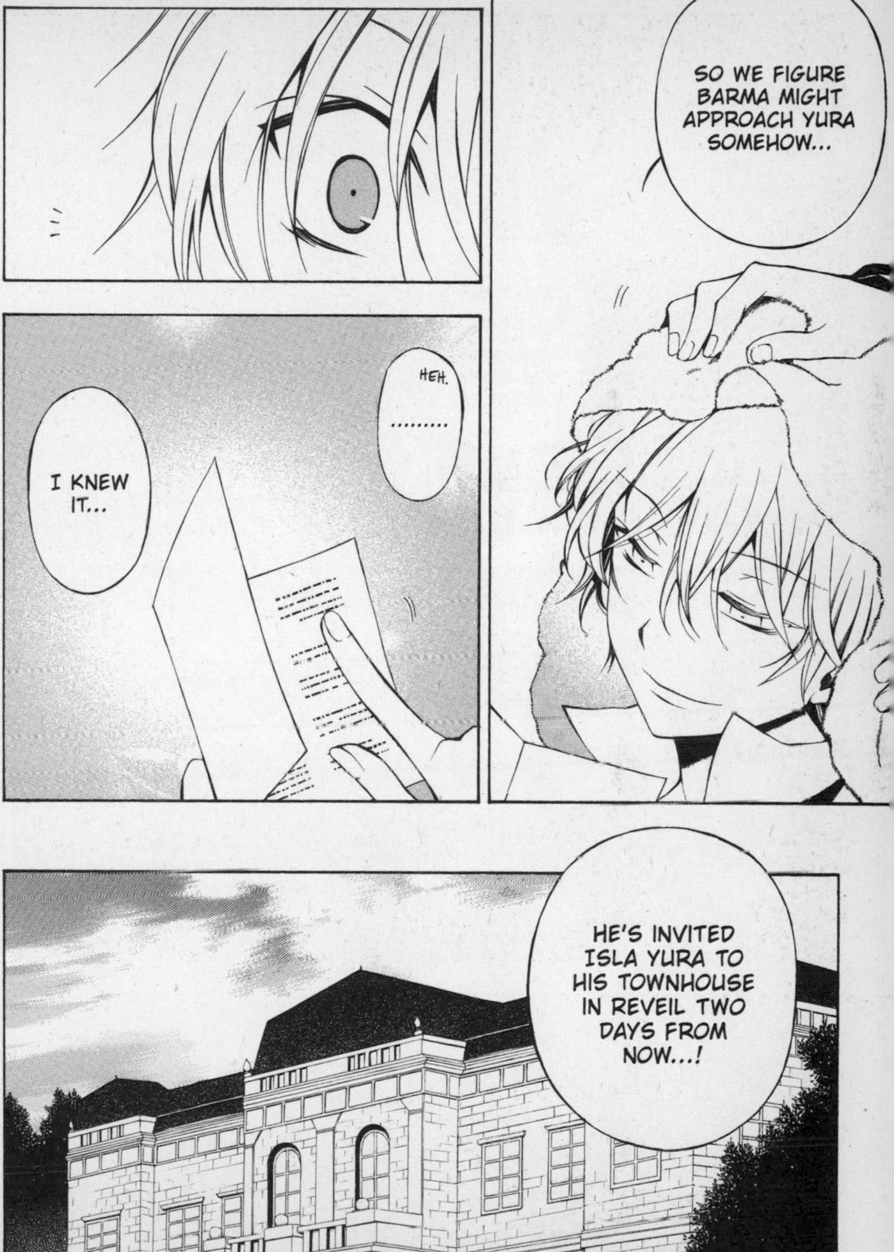
SO WE FIGURE BARMA MIGHT APPROACH YURA SOMEHOW...
HEH. ....
I KNEW IT...
HE'S INVITED ISLA YURA TO HIS TOWNHOUSE IN REVEIL TWO DAYS FROM NOW...!

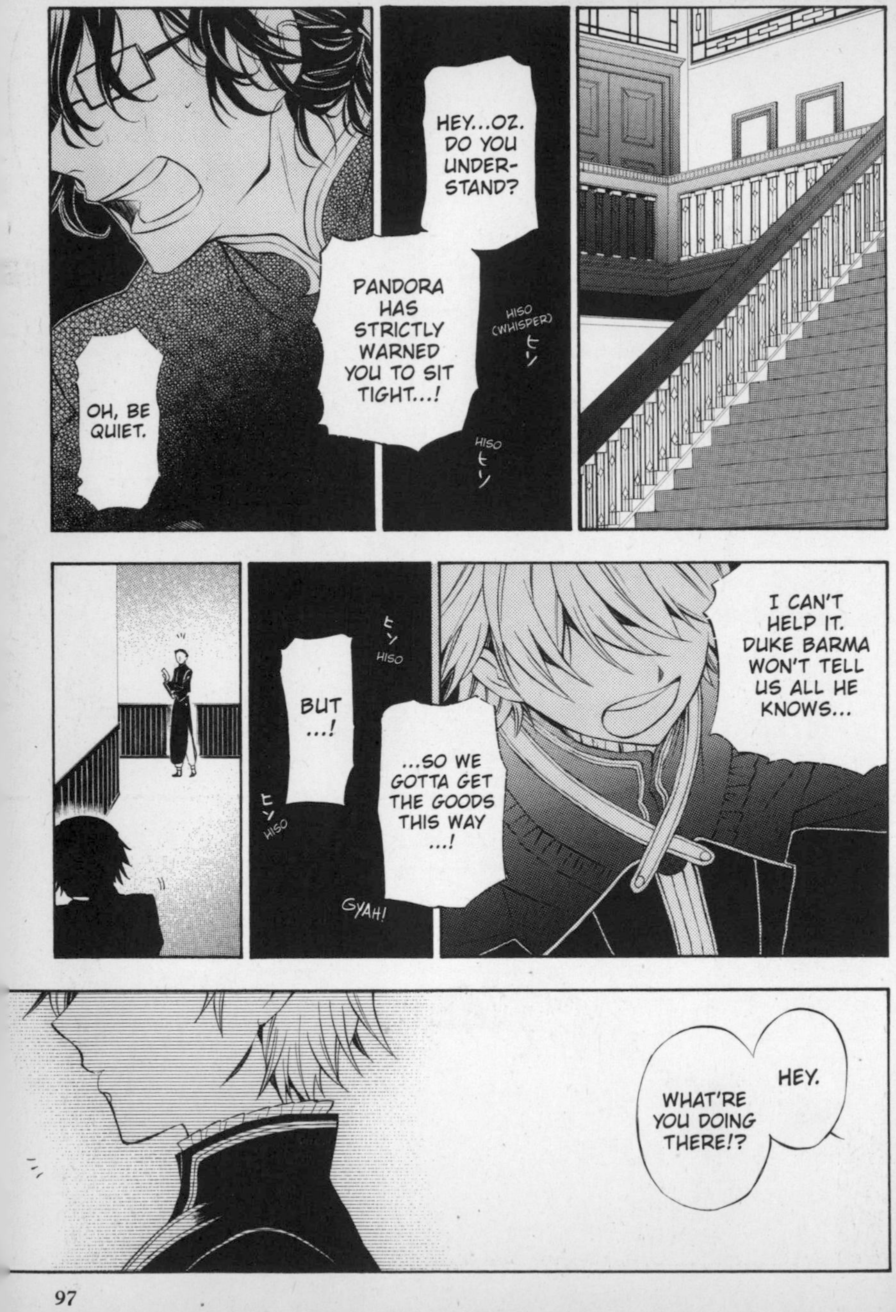
HEY...OZ. DO YOU UNDER-STAND?
PANDORA HAS STRICTLY WARNED YOU TO SIT TIGHT...!
HISO (WHISPER) ヒソ
HISO ヒソ
OH, BE QUIET.
I CAN'T HELP IT. DUKE BARMA WON'T TELL US ALL HE KNOWS...
...SO WE GOTTA GET THE GOODS THIS WAY ...!
ヒソ HISO
BUT ...!
ヒソ HISO
GYAH!
HEY.
WHAT'RE YOU DOING THERE!?

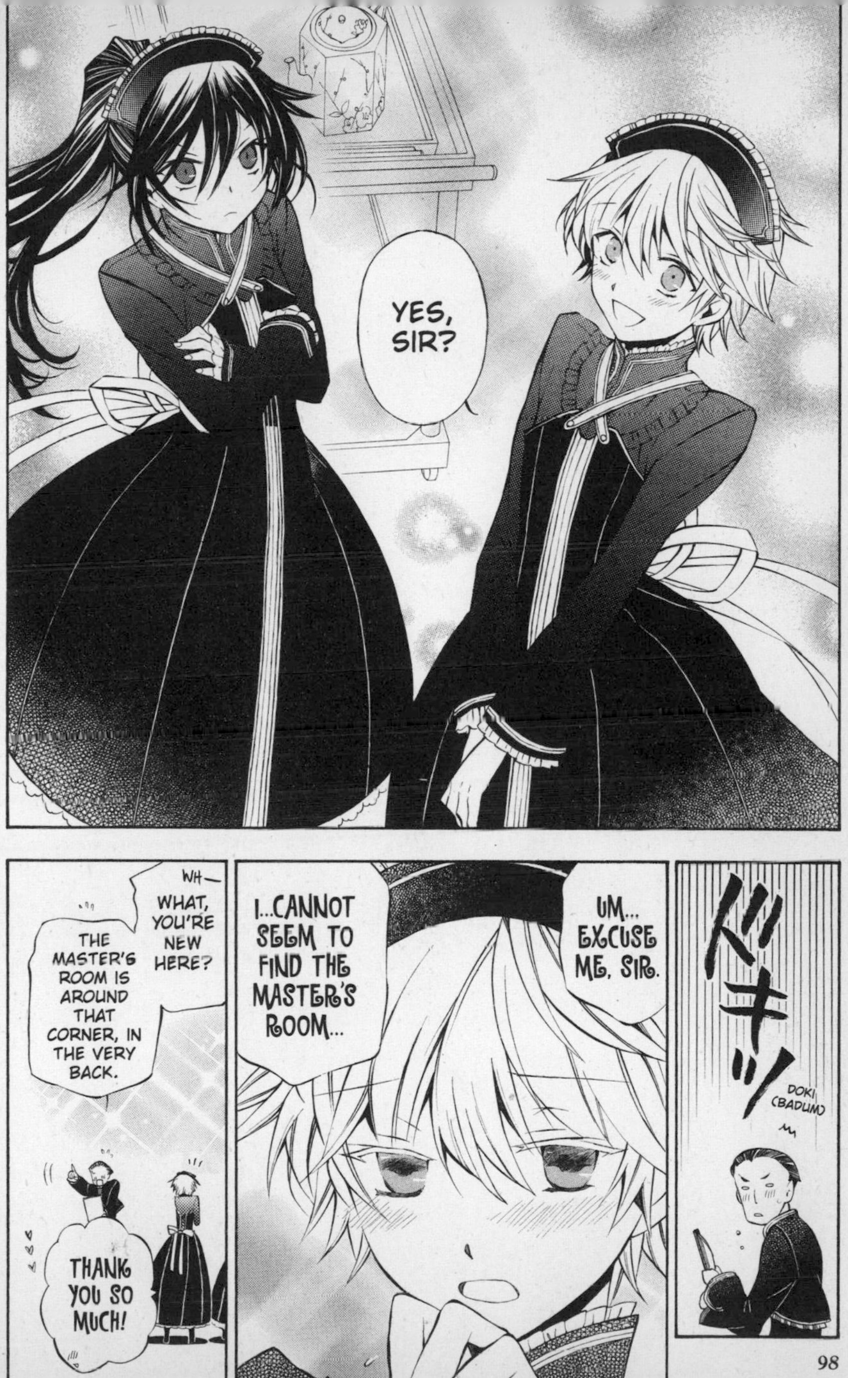
YES, SIR?
ドキッ
DOKI (BADUM)
UM... EXCUSE ME, SIR.
I...CANNOT SEEM TO FIND THE MASTER'S ROOM...
WH— WHAT, YOU'RE NEW HERE?
THE MASTER'S ROOM IS AROUND THAT CORNER, IN THE VERY BACK.
THANK YOU SO MUCH!

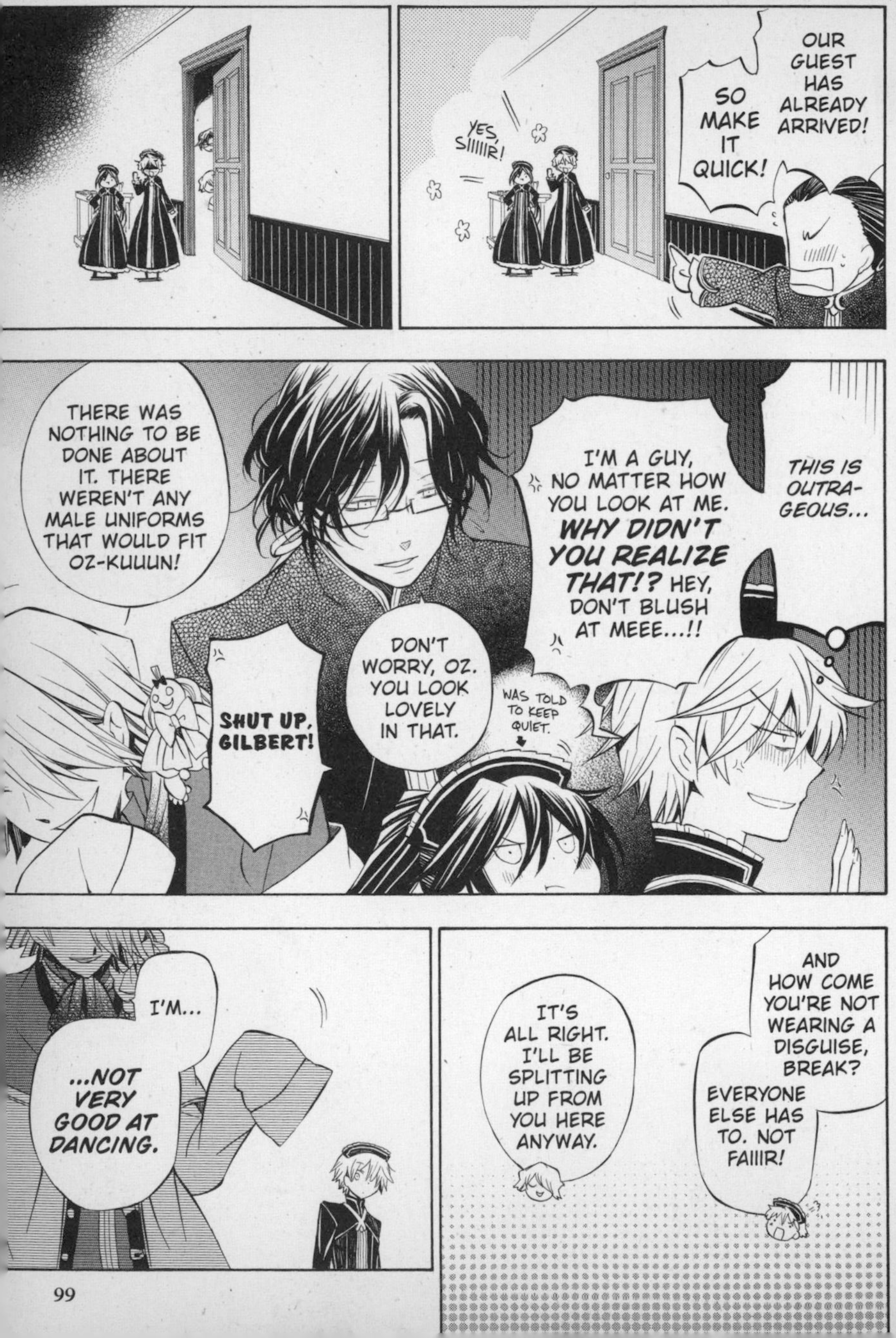
OUR GUEST HAS ALREADY ARRIVED!
SO MAKE IT QUICK!
YES, SIIIIR!
THIS IS OUTRAGEOUS...
I'M A GUY, NO MATTER HOW YOU LOOK AT ME. WHY DIDN'T YOU REALIZE THAT!? HEY, DON'T BLUSH AT MEEE...!!
DON'T WORRY, OZ. YOU LOOK LOVELY IN THAT.
WAS TOLD TO KEEP QUIET.
THERE WAS NOTHING TO BE DONE ABOUT IT. THERE WEREN'T ANY MALE UNIFORMS THAT WOULD FIT OZ-KUUUN!
SHUT UP, GILBERT!
AND HOW COME YOU'RE NOT WEARING A DISGUISE, BREAK?
EVERYONE ELSE HAS TO. NOT FAIIIR!
IT'S ALL RIGHT. I'LL BE SPLITTING UP FROM YOU HERE ANYWAY.
I'M...
...NOT VERY GOOD AT DANCING.

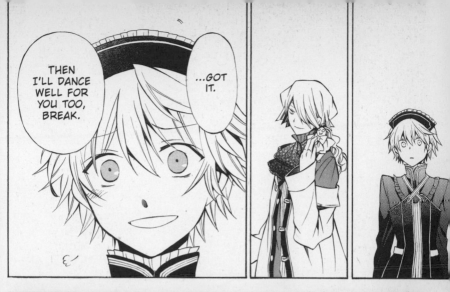

THEN I'LL DANCE WELL FOR YOU TOO, BREAK.

...GOT IT.

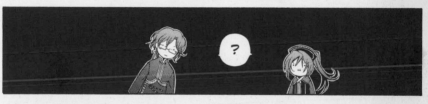

?

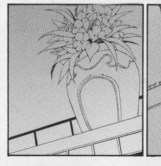

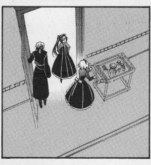

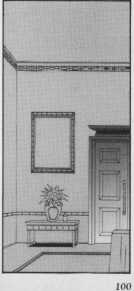

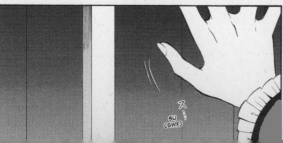

SU (SWF)

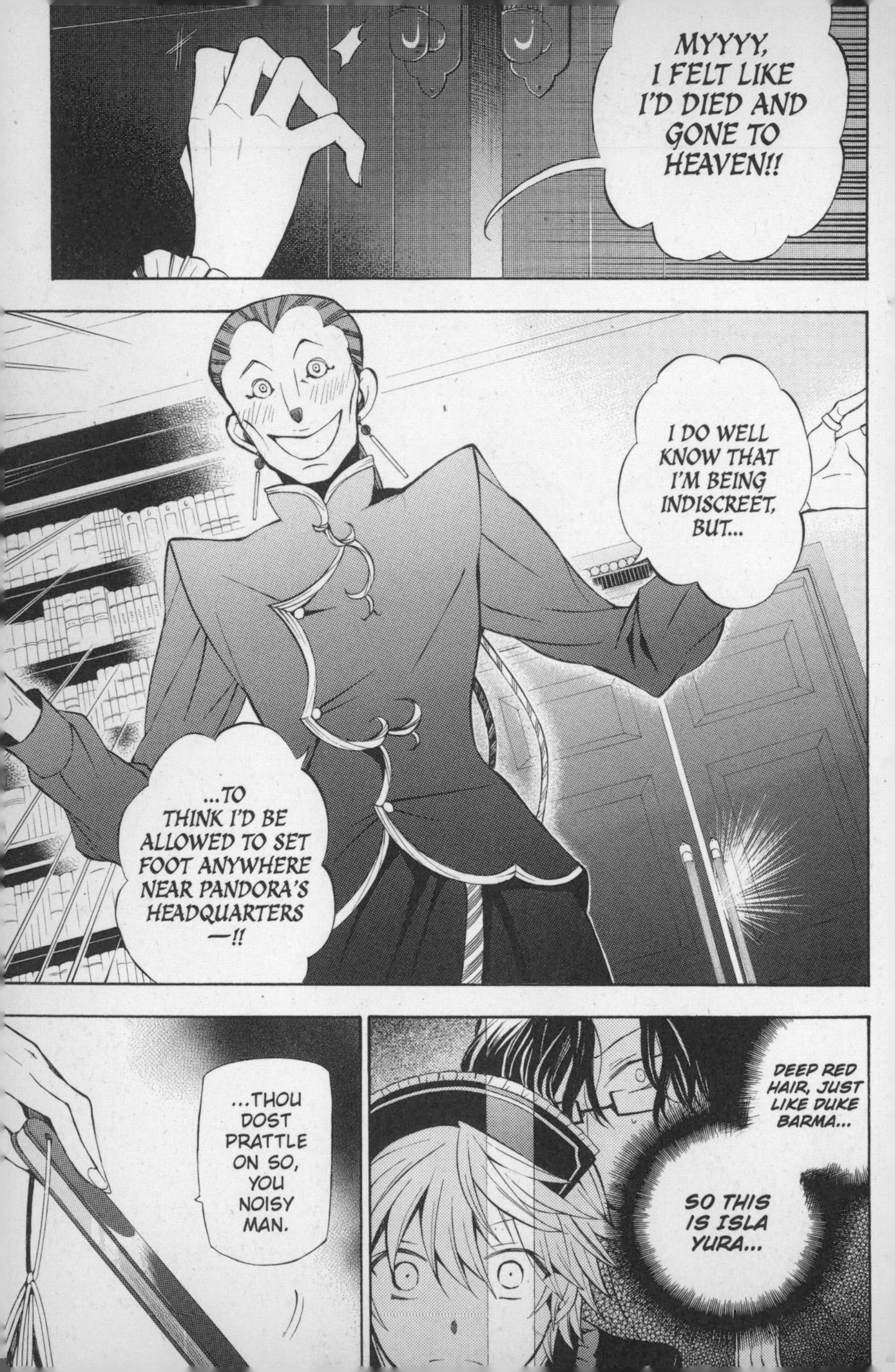
MYYYY, I FELT LIKE I'D DIED AND GONE TO HEAVEN!!
I DO WELL KNOW THAT I'M BEING INDISCREET, BUT...
...TO THINK I'D BE ALLOWED TO SET FOOT ANYWHERE NEAR PANDORA'S HEADQUARTERS—!!
DEEP RED HAIR, JUST LIKE DUKE BARMA...
SO THIS IS ISLA YURA...
...THOU DOST PRATTLE ON SO, YOU NOISY MAN.

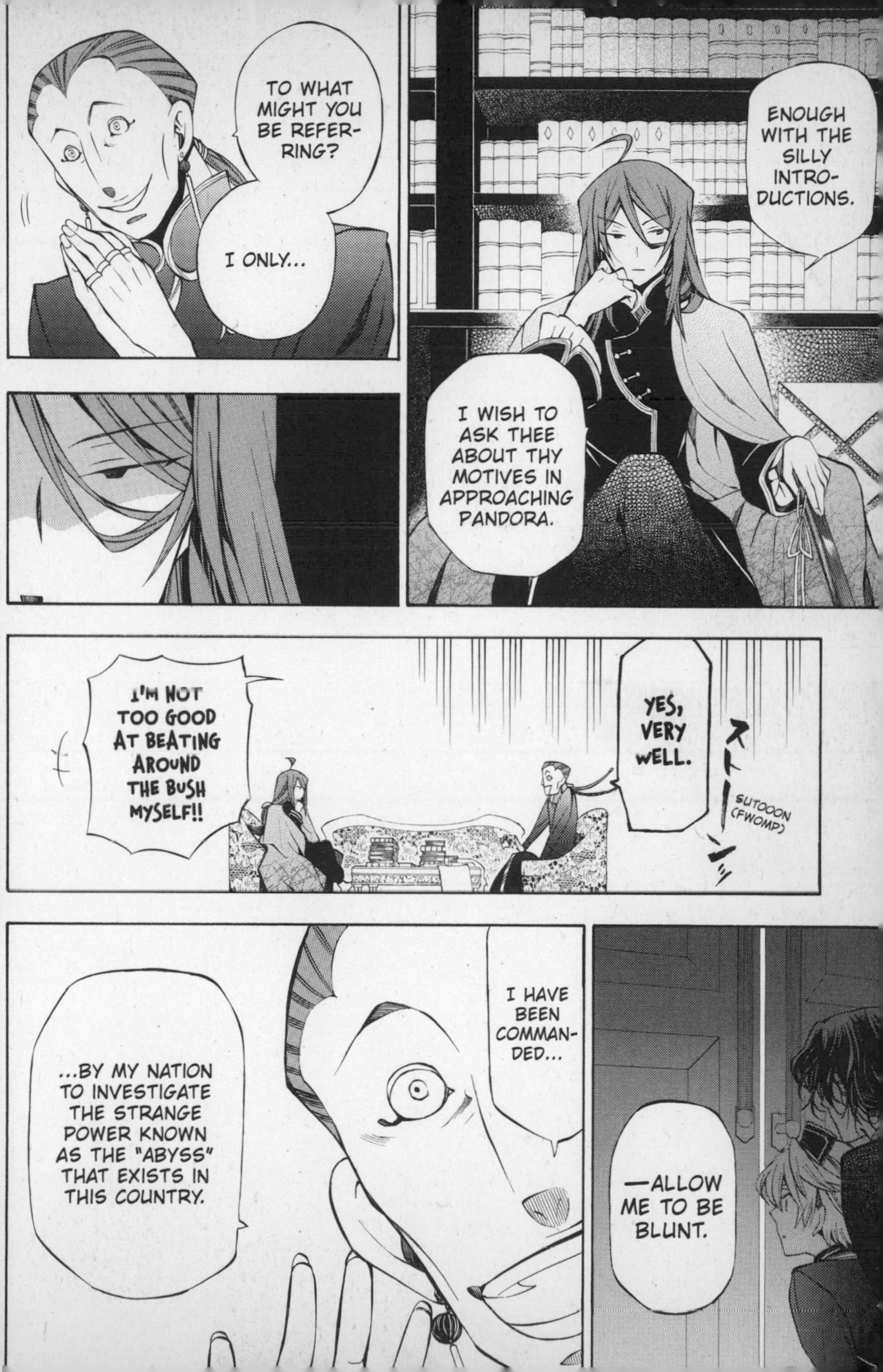
ENOUGH WITH THE SILLY INTRODUCTIONS.
I WISH TO ASK THEE ABOUT THY MOTIVES IN APPROACHING PANDORA.
TO WHAT MIGHT YOU BE REFERRING?
I ONLY...
YES, VERY WELL.
SUTOOON (FWOMP)
I'M NOT TOO GOOD AT BEATING AROUND THE BUSH MYSELF!!
—ALLOW ME TO BE BLUNT.
I HAVE BEEN COMMANDED...
...BY MY NATION TO INVESTIGATE THE STRANGE POWER KNOWN AS THE "ABYSS" THAT EXISTS IN THIS COUNTRY.

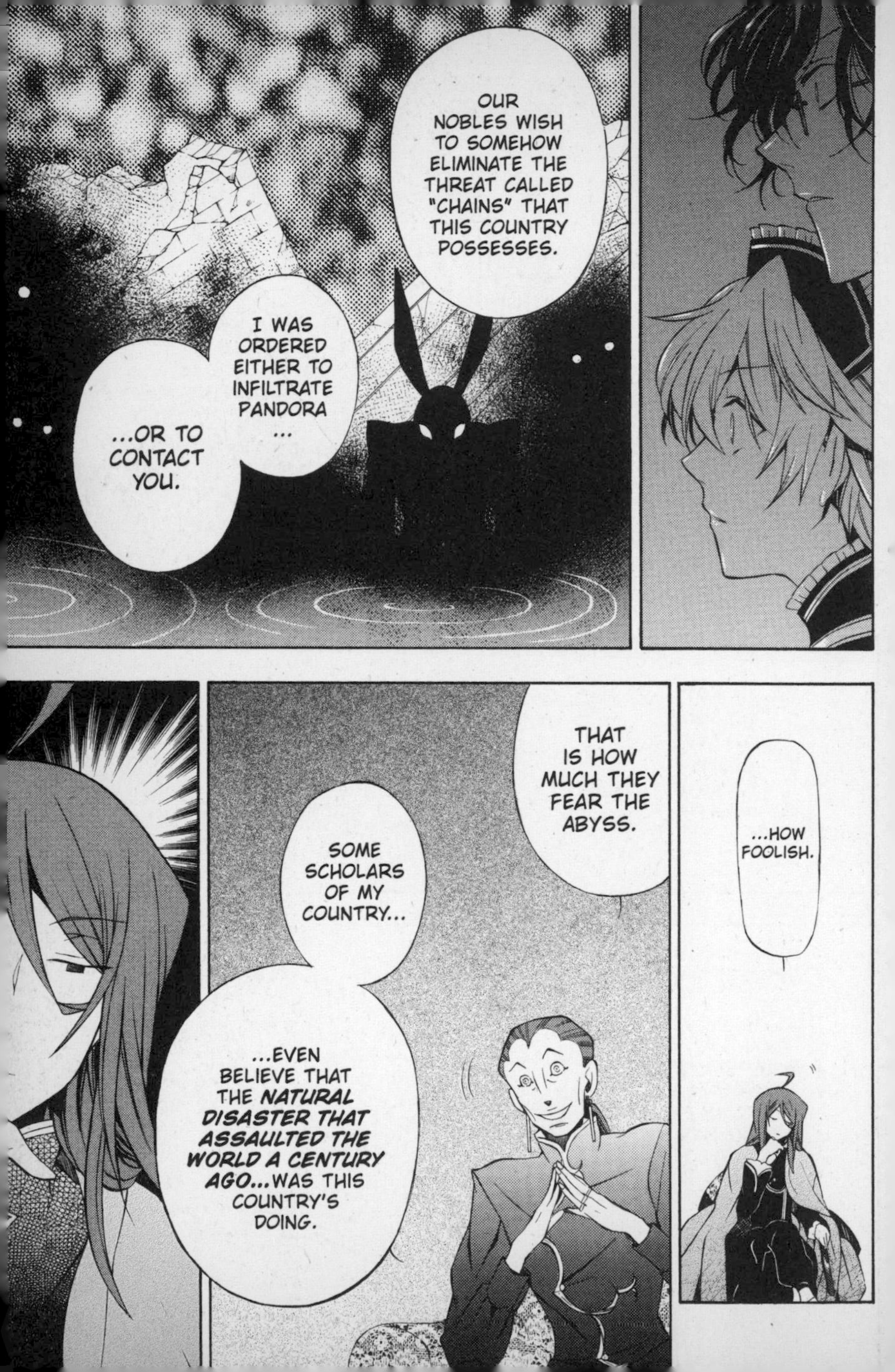
OUR NOBLES WISH TO SOMEHOW ELIMINATE THE THREAT CALLED "CHAINS" THAT THIS COUNTRY POSSESSES.
I WAS ORDERED EITHER TO INFILTRATE PANDORA ...
...OR TO CONTACT YOU.
...HOW FOOLISH.
THAT IS HOW MUCH THEY FEAR THE ABYSS.
SOME SCHOLARS OF MY COUNTRY...
...EVEN BELIEVE THAT THE NATURAL DISASTER THAT ASSAULTED THE WORLD A CENTURY AGO...WAS THIS COUNTRY'S DOING.

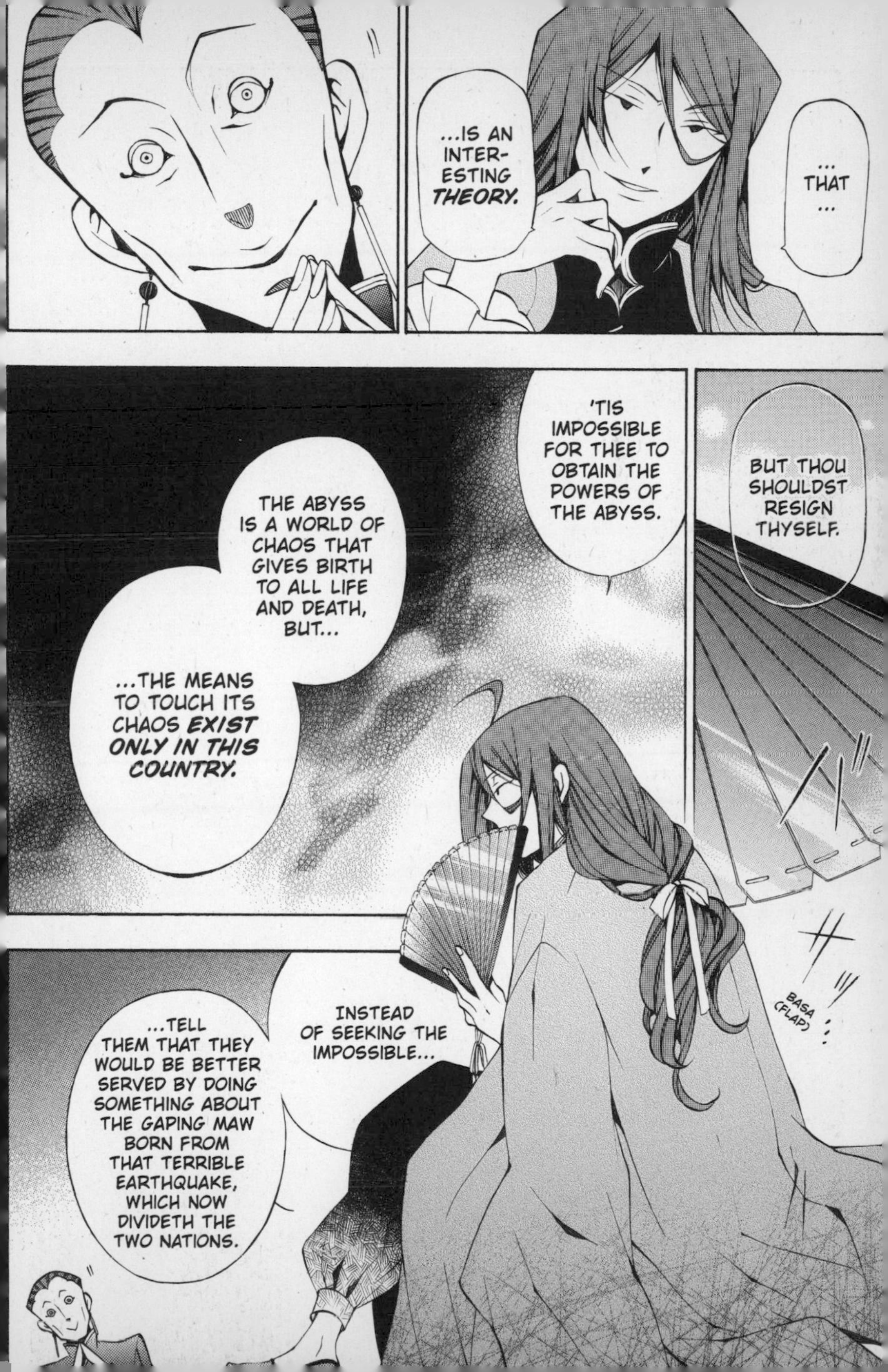
...THAT...
...IS AN INTER-ESTING *THEORY.*
BUT THOU SHOULDST RESIGN THYSELF.
'TIS IMPOSSIBLE FOR THEE TO OBTAIN THE POWERS OF THE ABYSS.
THE ABYSS IS A WORLD OF CHAOS THAT GIVES BIRTH TO ALL LIFE AND DEATH, BUT...
...THE MEANS TO TOUCH ITS CHAOS ***EXIST ONLY IN THIS COUNTRY.***
BASA (FLAP)
INSTEAD OF SEEKING THE IMPOSSIBLE...
...TELL THEM THAT THEY WOULD BE BETTER SERVED BY DOING SOMETHING ABOUT THE GAPING MAW BORN FROM THAT TERRIBLE EARTHQUAKE, WHICH NOW DIVIDETH THE TWO NATIONS.

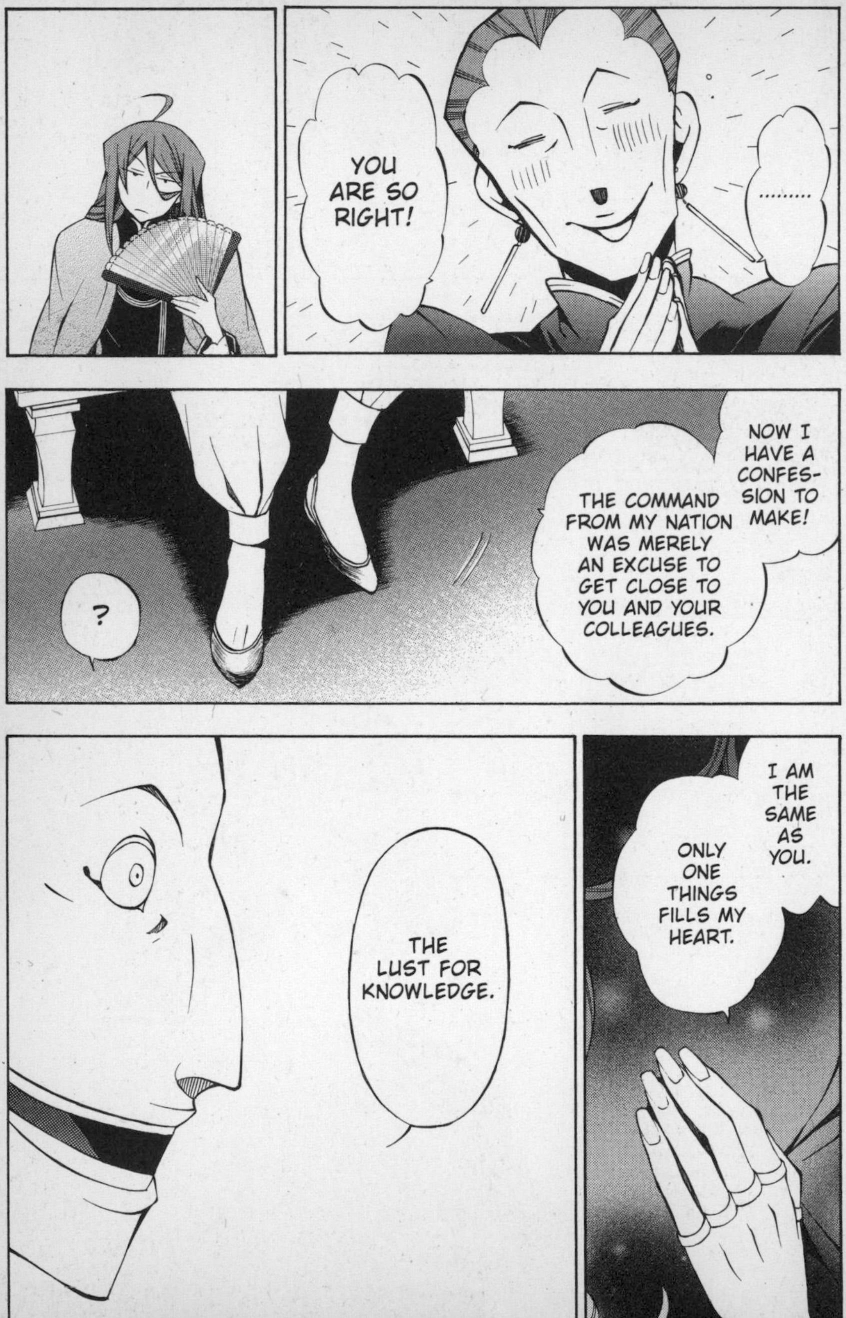
....
YOU ARE SO RIGHT!
NOW I HAVE A CONFES-SION TO MAKE!
THE COMMAND FROM MY NATION WAS MERELY AN EXCUSE TO GET CLOSE TO YOU AND YOUR COLLEAGUES.
?
I AM THE SAME AS YOU.
ONLY ONE THINGS FILLS MY HEART.
THE LUST FOR KNOWLEDGE.

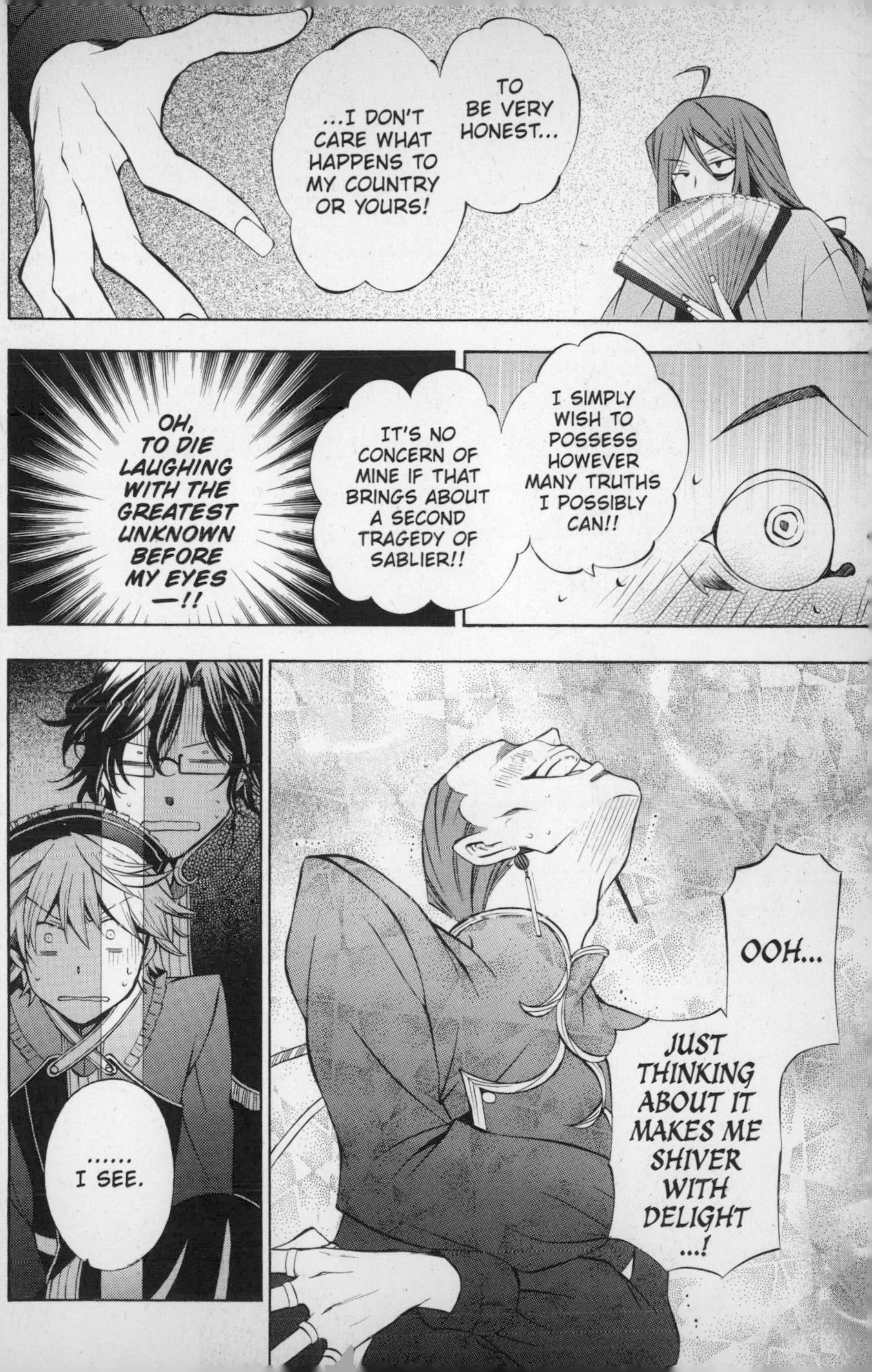

TO BE VERY HONEST...
...I DON'T CARE WHAT HAPPENS TO MY COUNTRY OR YOURS!
I SIMPLY WISH TO POSSESS HOWEVER MANY TRUTHS I POSSIBLY CAN!!
IT'S NO CONCERN OF MINE IF THAT BRINGS ABOUT A SECOND TRAGEDY OF SABLIER!!
OH, TO DIE LAUGHING WITH THE GREATEST UNKNOWN BEFORE MY EYES—!!
OOH...
JUST THINKING ABOUT IT MAKES ME SHIVER WITH DELIGHT...!
...... I SEE.

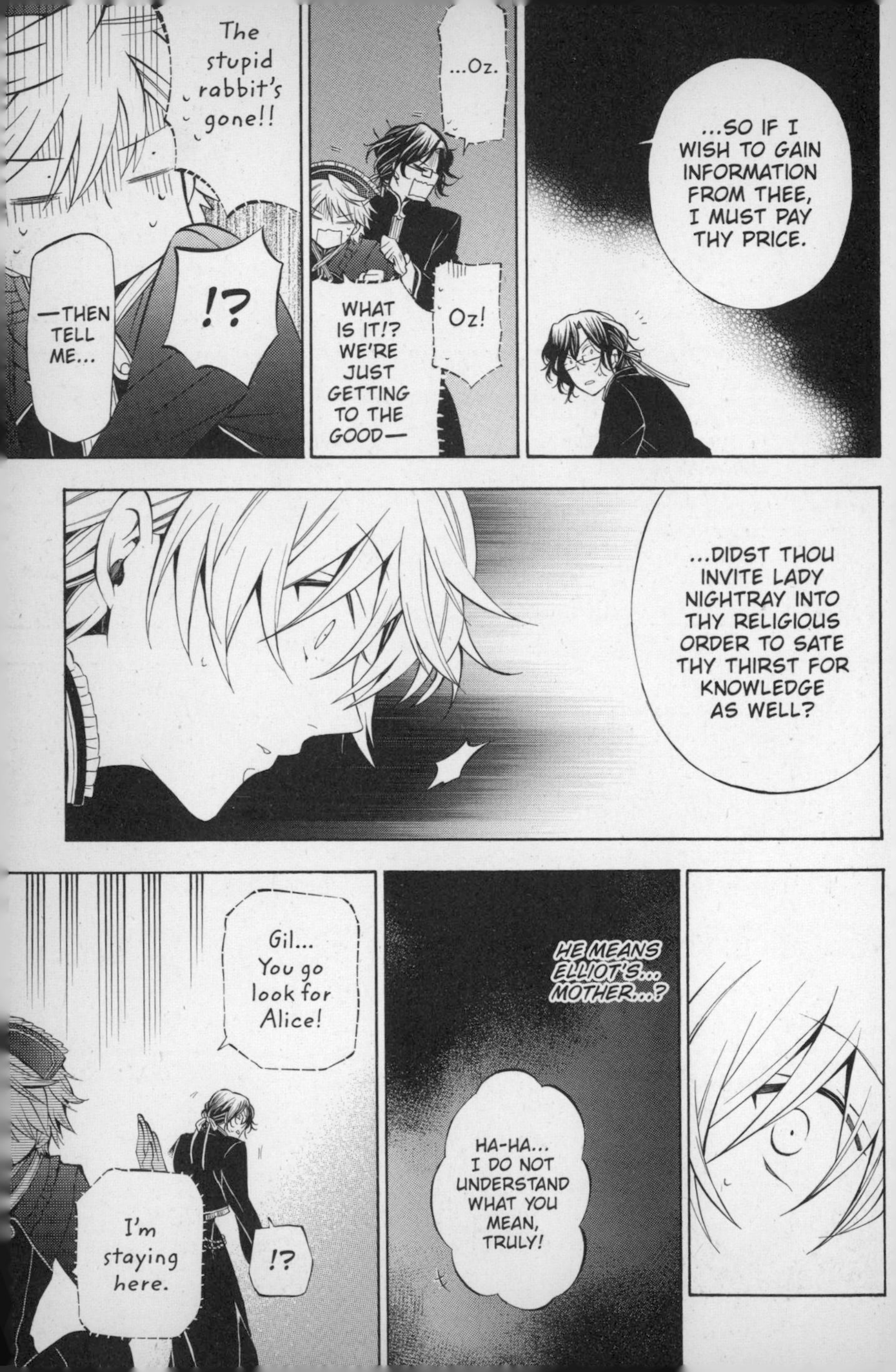
...SO IF I WISH TO GAIN INFORMATION FROM THEE, I MUST PAY THY PRICE.
...Oz.
Oz!
WHAT IS IT!? WE'RE JUST GETTING TO THE GOOD—
The stupid rabbit's gone!!
!?
—THEN TELL ME...
...DIDST THOU INVITE LADY NIGHTRAY INTO THY RELIGIOUS ORDER TO SATE THY THIRST FOR KNOWLEDGE AS WELL?
HE MEANS ELLIOT'S... MOTHER...?
HA-HA... I DO NOT UNDERSTAND WHAT YOU MEAN, TRULY!
Gil... You go look for Alice!
!?
I'm staying here.

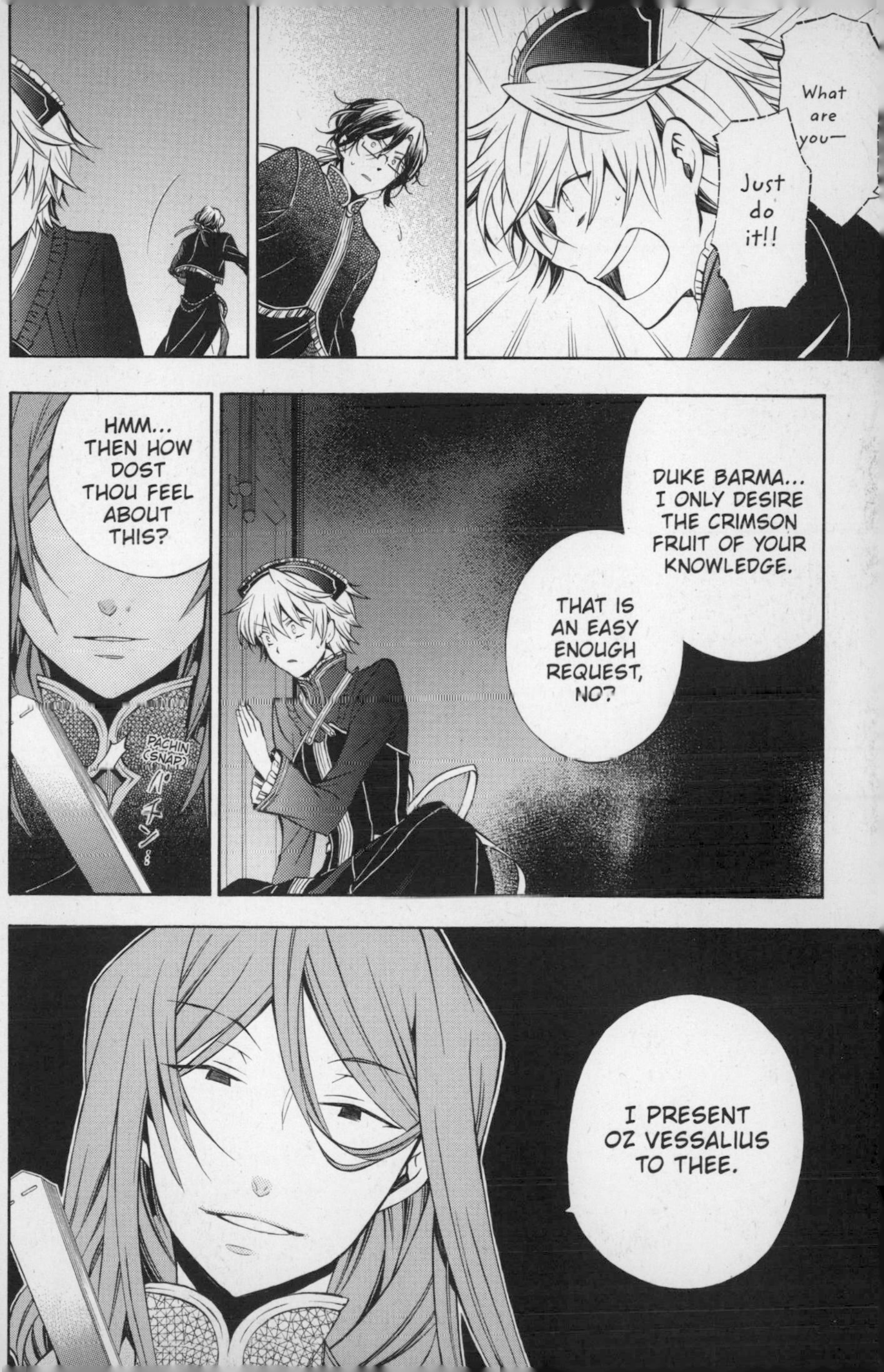
What are you—
Just do it!!
DUKE BARMA... I ONLY DESIRE THE CRIMSON FRUIT OF YOUR KNOWLEDGE.
THAT IS AN EASY ENOUGH REQUEST, NO?
HMM... THEN HOW DOST THOU FEEL ABOUT THIS?
PACHIN (SNAP)
パチン
I PRESENT OZ VESSALIUS TO THEE.

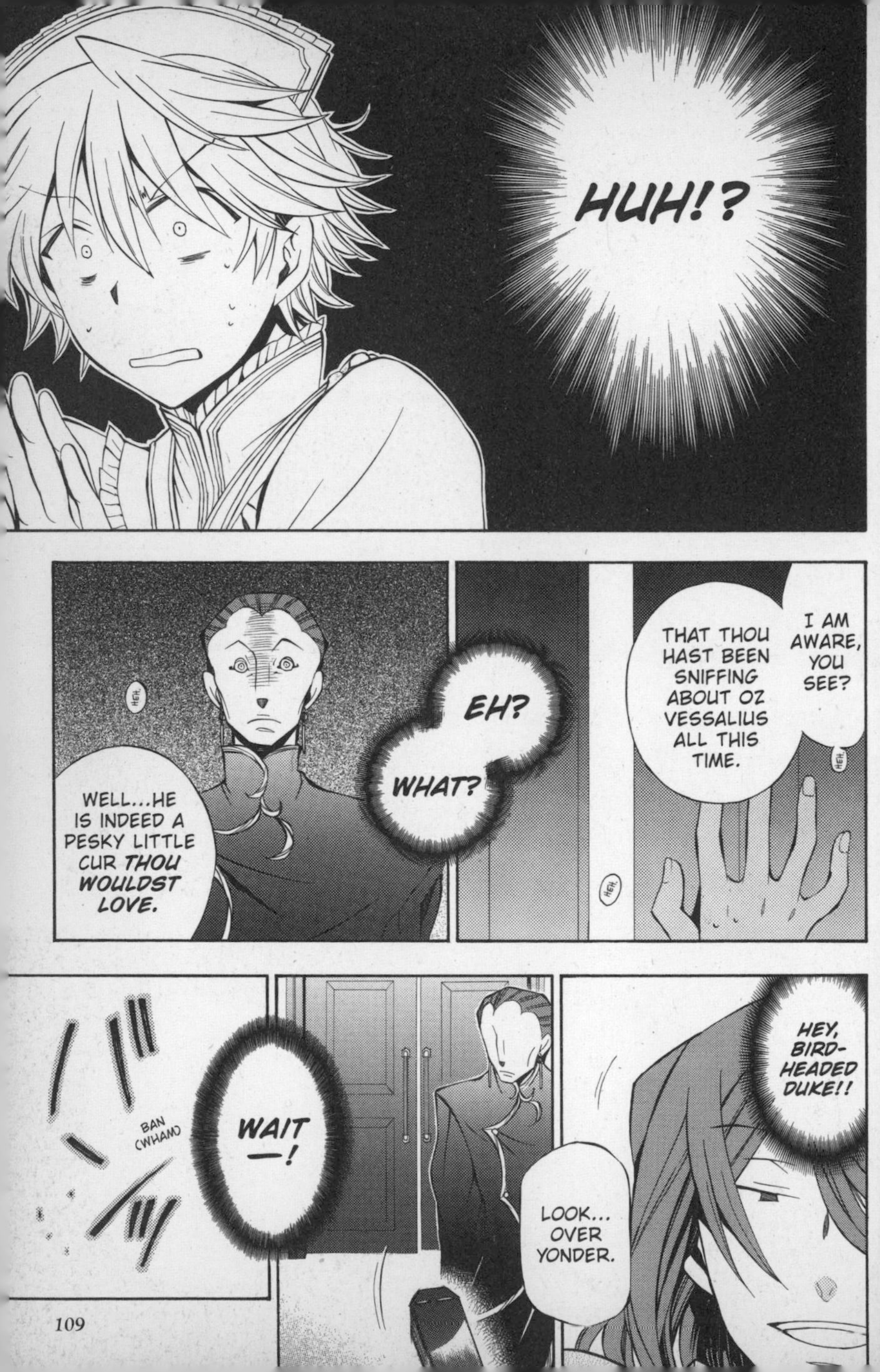
HUH!?
I AM AWARE, YOU SEE?
THAT THOU HAST BEEN SNIFFING ABOUT OZ VESSALIUS ALL THIS TIME.
HEH.
HEH.
EH?
WHAT?
HEH.
WELL...HE IS INDEED A PESKY LITTLE CUR *THOU WOULDST LOVE.*
HEY, BIRD-HEADED DUKE!!
LOOK... OVER YONDER.
WAIT—!
BAN (WHAM)

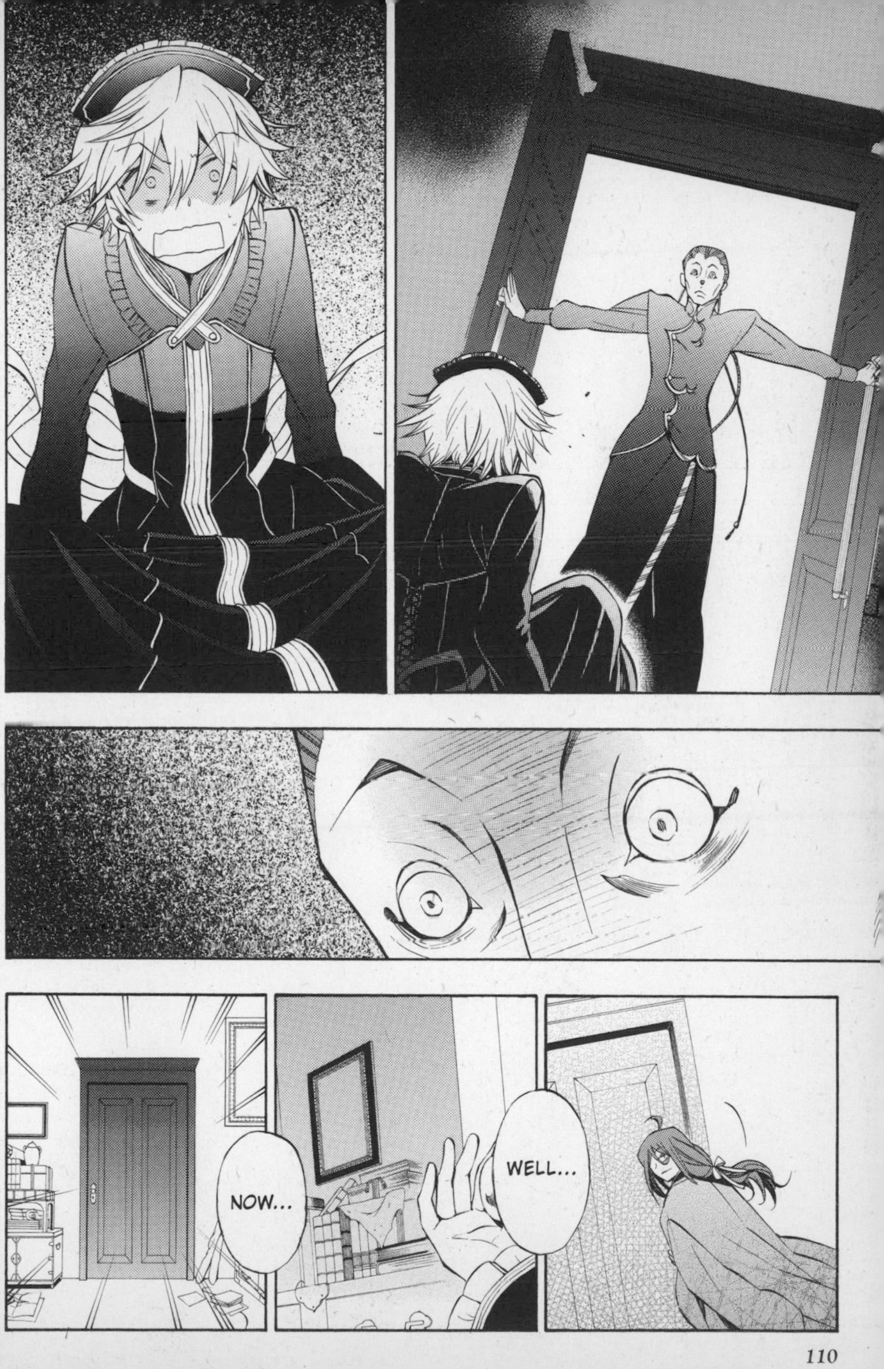
WELL...
NOW...

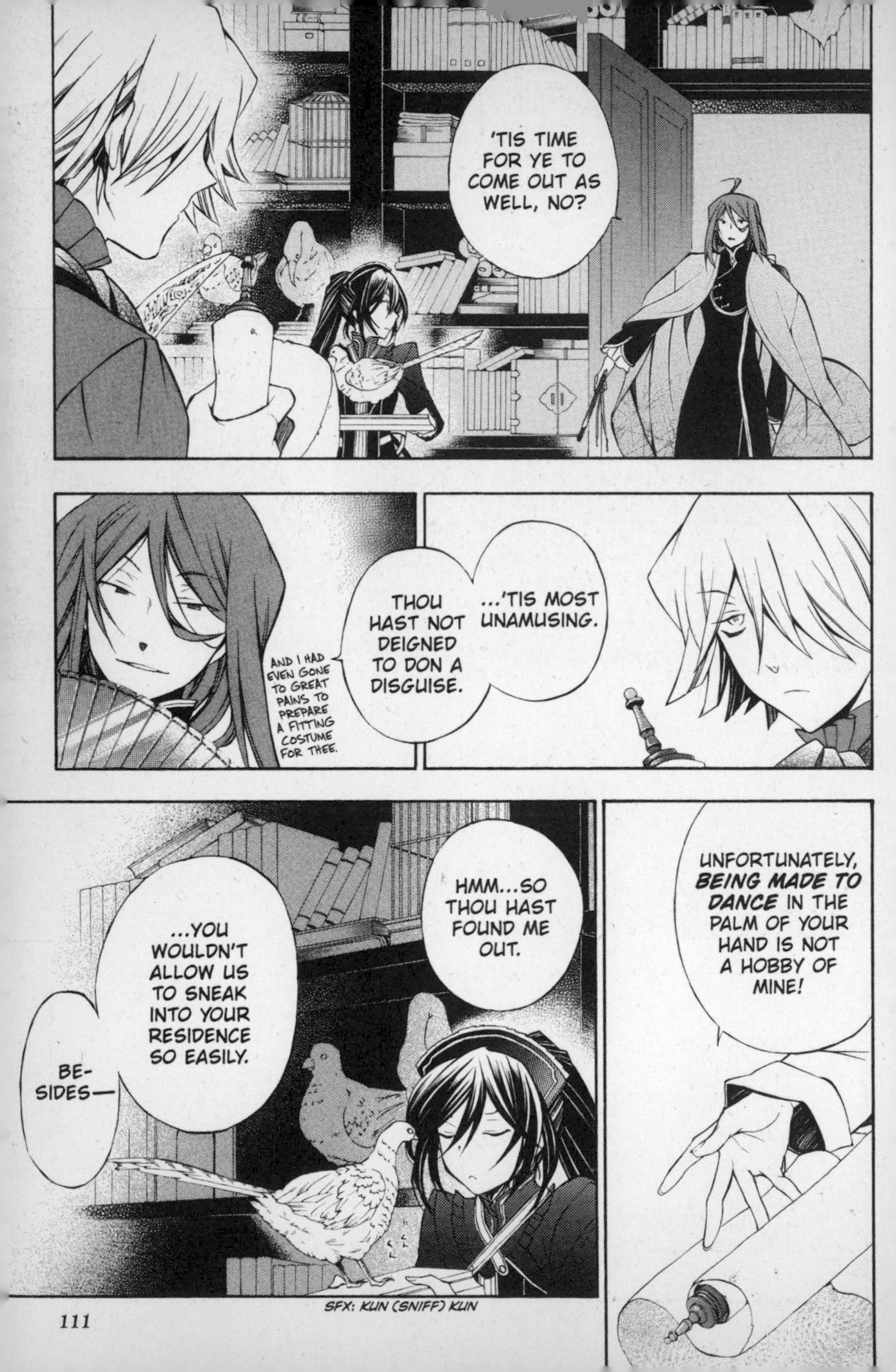
'TIS TIME FOR YE TO COME OUT AS WELL, NO?
THOU HAST NOT DEIGNED TO DON A DISGUISE.
...'TIS MOST UNAMUSING.
AND I HAD EVEN GONE TO GREAT PAINS TO PREPARE A FITTING COSTUME FOR THEE.
UNFORTUNATELY, ***BEING MADE TO DANCE*** IN THE PALM OF YOUR HAND IS NOT A HOBBY OF MINE!
HMM...SO THOU HAST FOUND ME OUT.
BE-SIDES—
...YOU WOULDN'T ALLOW US TO SNEAK INTO YOUR RESIDENCE SO EASILY.
SFX: KUN (SNIFF) KUN

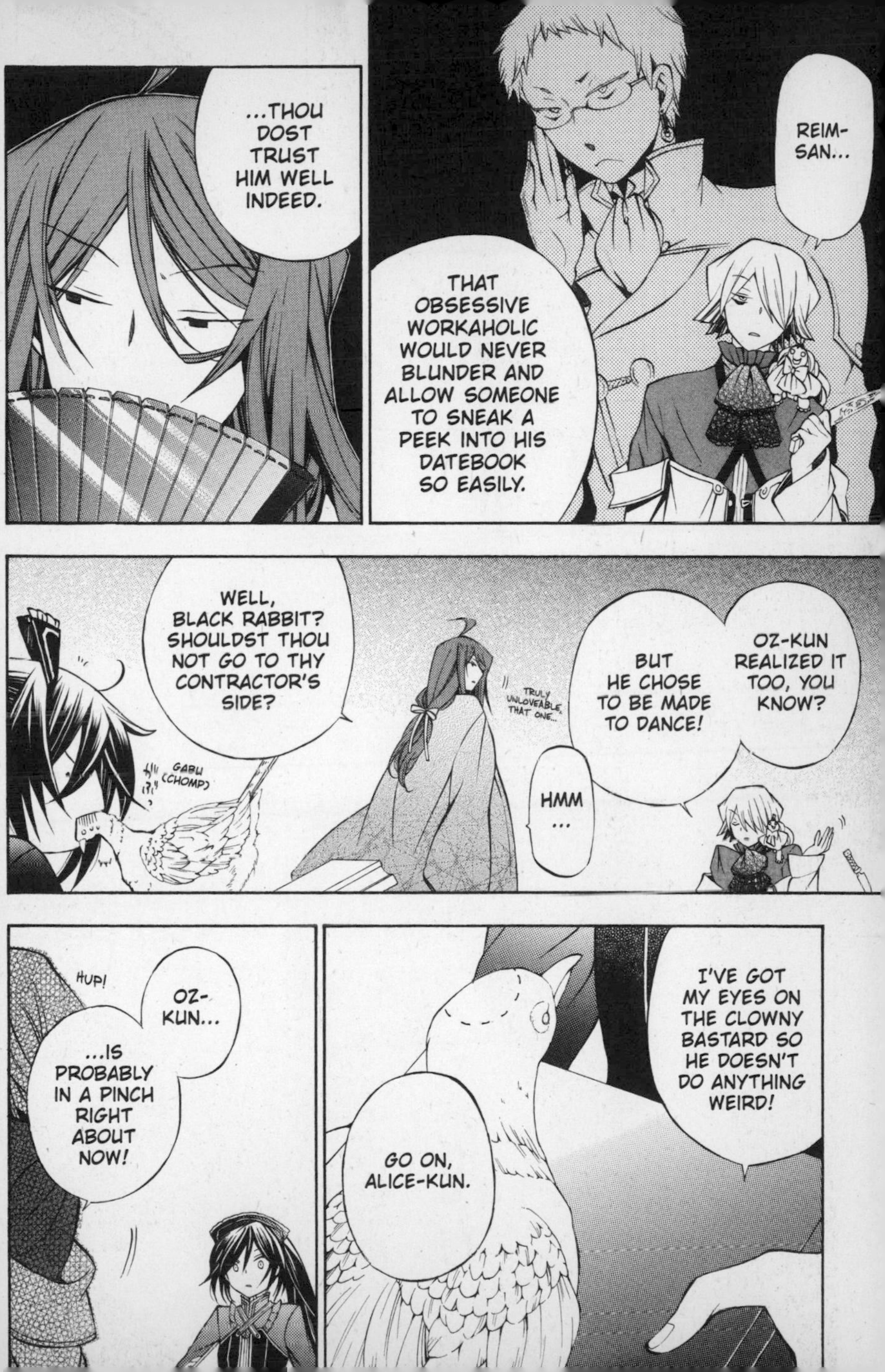
REIM-SAN...
THAT OBSESSIVE WORKAHOLIC WOULD NEVER BLUNDER AND ALLOW SOMEONE TO SNEAK A PEEK INTO HIS DATEBOOK SO EASILY.
...THOU DOST TRUST HIM WELL INDEED.
OZ-KUN REALIZED IT TOO, YOU KNOW?
BUT HE CHOSE TO BE MADE TO DANCE!
HMM...
TRULY UNLOVEABLE, THAT ONE...
WELL, BLACK RABBIT? SHOULDST THOU NOT GO TO THY CONTRACTOR'S SIDE?
GABU (CHOMP)
I'VE GOT MY EYES ON THE CLOWNY BASTARD SO HE DOESN'T DO ANYTHING WEIRD!
GO ON, ALICE-KUN.
HUP!
OZ-KUN...
...IS PROBABLY IN A PINCH RIGHT ABOUT NOW!

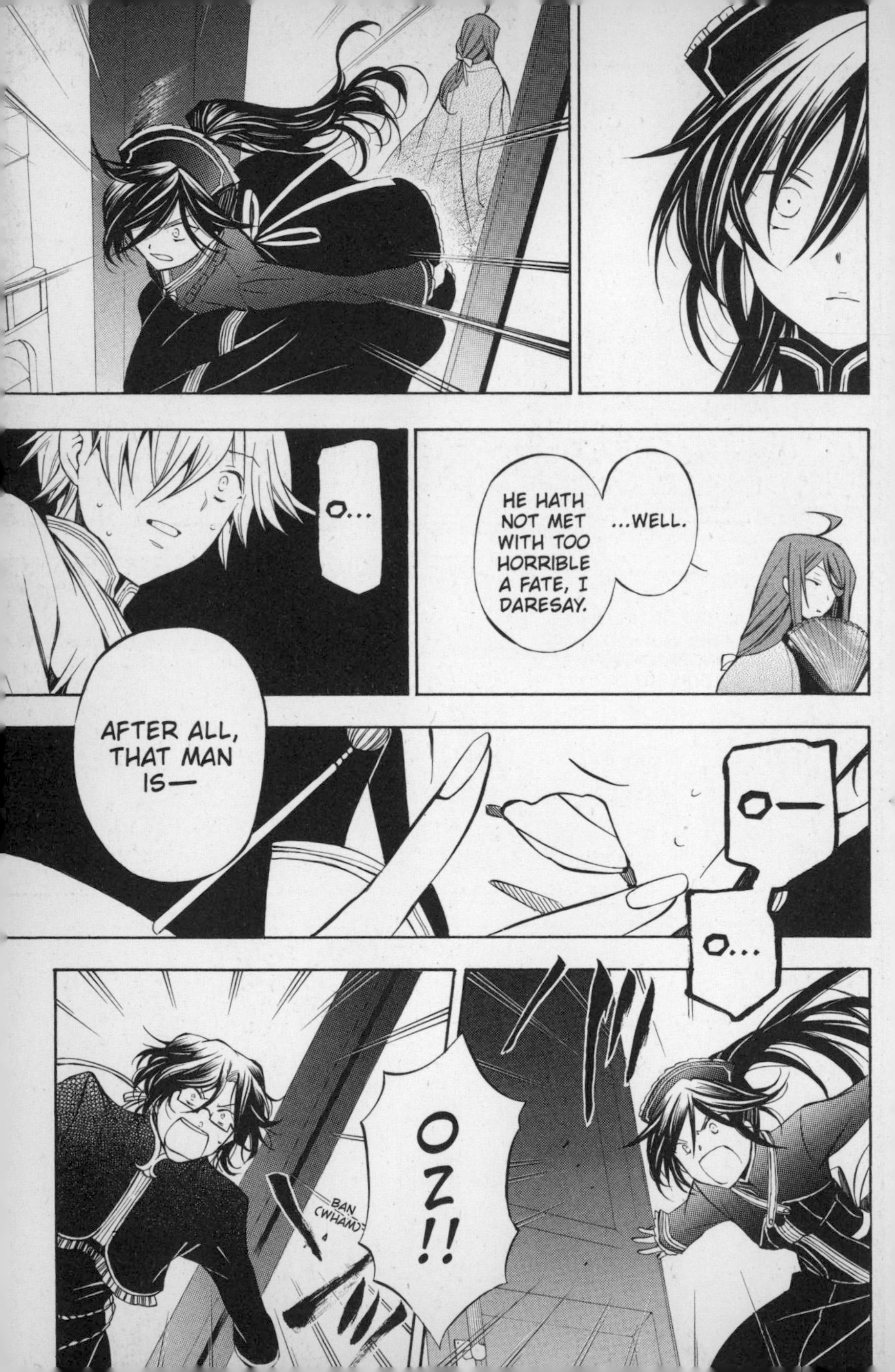
...WELL.
HE HATH NOT MET WITH TOO HORRIBLE A FATE, I DARESAY.
O...
AFTER ALL, THAT MAN IS—
O—
O...
OZ!!
BAN (WHAM)

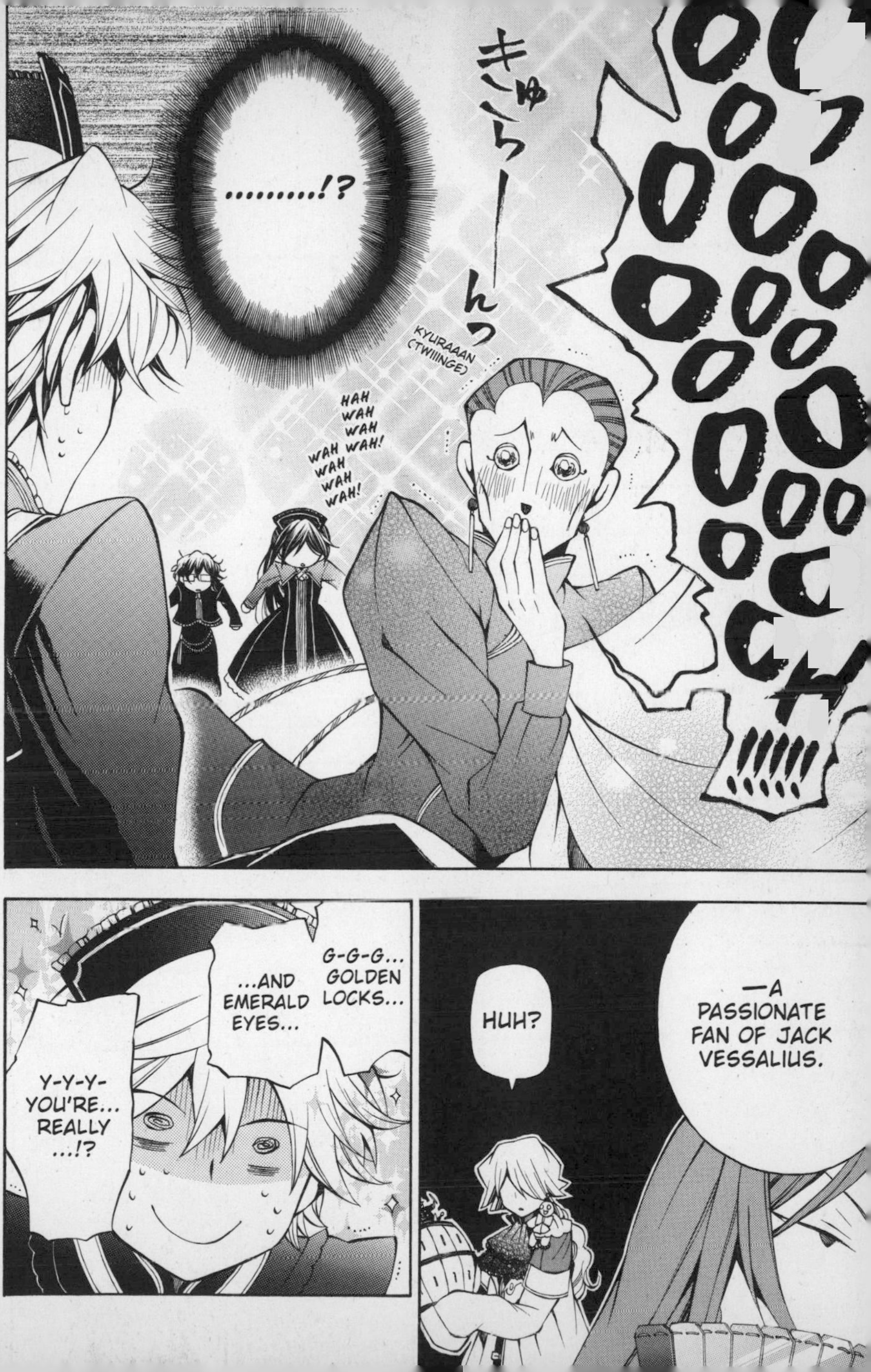
OOOOOOOOOOOOOOOOOOOOOOOOH!!!!!!
きゅらーーんっ
KYURAAAN (TWIIINGE)
HAH WAH WAH WAH WAH! WAH WAH WAH WAH!
.........!?
—A PASSIONATE FAN OF JACK VESSALIUS.
HUH?
G-G-G... GOLDEN LOCKS...
...AND EMERALD EYES...
Y-Y-Y-YOU'RE... REALLY ...!?

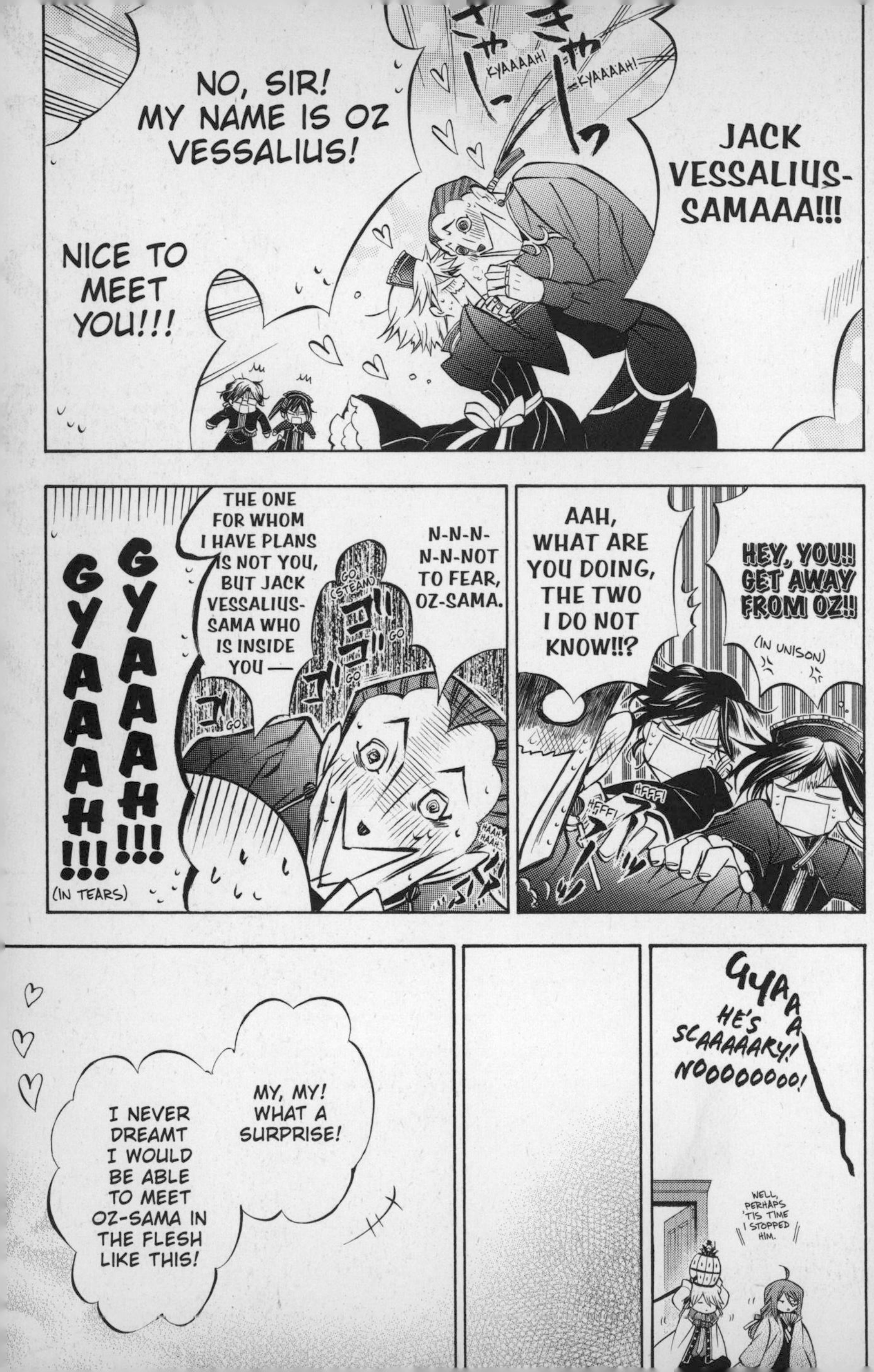
KYAAAAH!
KYAAAAH!
JACK VESSALIUS-SAMAAA!!!
NO, SIR! MY NAME IS OZ VESSALIUS!
NICE TO MEET YOU!!!
HEY, YOU!! GET AWAY FROM OZ!!
(IN UNISON)
AAH, WHAT ARE YOU DOING, THE TWO I DO NOT KNOW!!?
HFFF!
HFFF!
N-N-N-N-N-NOT TO FEAR, OZ-SAMA.
THE ONE FOR WHOM I HAVE PLANS IS NOT YOU, BUT JACK VESSALIUS-SAMA WHO IS INSIDE YOU—
GO (STEAM)
GO
GO
GO
HAAH HAAH
GYAAAAH!!!
GYAAAAH!!!
(IN TEARS)
GYAAAA
HE'S SCAAAAARY! NOOOOOOOO!
WELL, PERHAPS 'TIS TIME I STOPPED HIM.
MY, MY! WHAT A SURPRISE!
I NEVER DREAMT I WOULD BE ABLE TO MEET OZ-SAMA IN THE FLESH LIKE THIS!

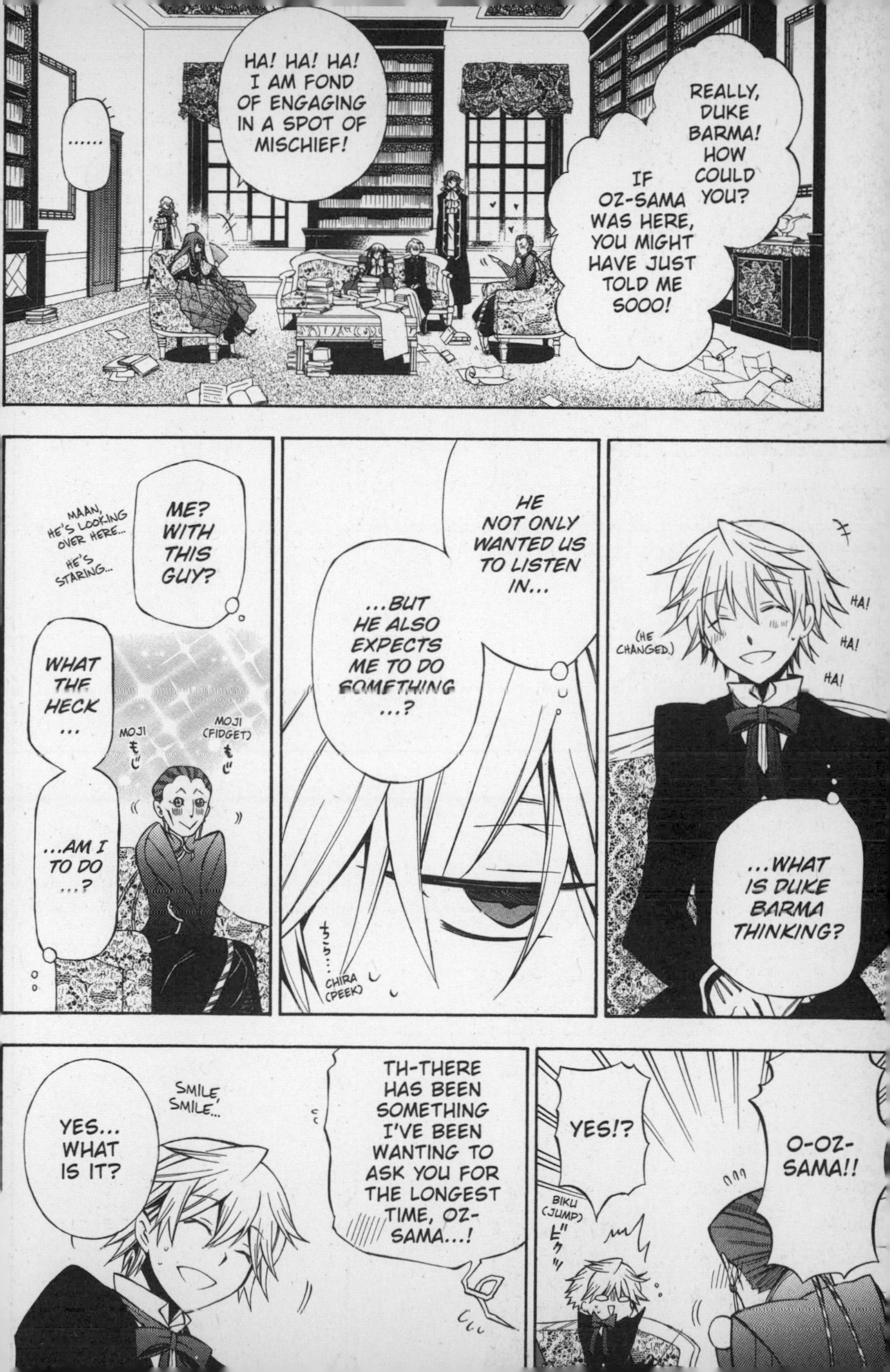
REALLY, DUKE BARMA! HOW COULD YOU?
IF OZ-SAMA WAS HERE, YOU MIGHT HAVE JUST TOLD ME SOOO!
HA! HA! HA! I AM FOND OF ENGAGING IN A SPOT OF MISCHIEF!
......
HA! HA! HA!
(HE CHANGED.)
...WHAT IS DUKE BARMA THINKING?
HE NOT ONLY WANTED US TO LISTEN IN...
...BUT HE ALSO EXPECTS ME TO DO SOMETHING...?
CHIRA (PEEK)
MAAN, HE'S LOOKING OVER HERE... HE'S STARING...
ME? WITH THIS GUY?
MOJI MOJI (FIDGET)
WHAT THE HECK...
...AM I TO DO...?
O-OZ-SAMA!!
YES!?
BIKU (JUMP)
TH-THERE HAS BEEN SOMETHING I'VE BEEN WANTING TO ASK YOU FOR THE LONGEST TIME, OZ-SAMA...!
SMILE, SMILE...
YES... WHAT IS IT?

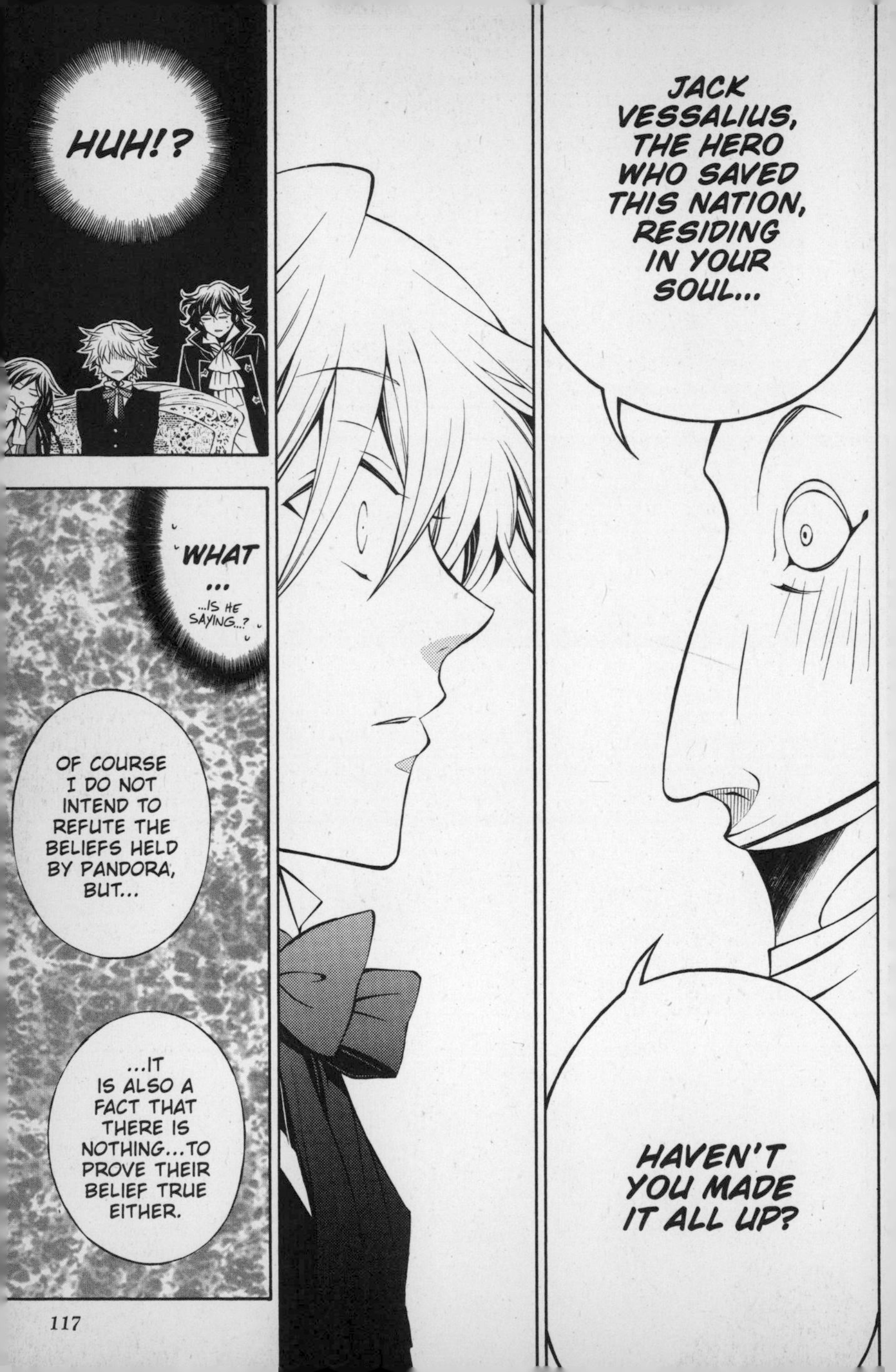
JACK VESSALIUS, THE HERO WHO SAVED THIS NATION, RESIDING IN YOUR SOUL...
HAVEN'T YOU MADE IT ALL UP?
HUH!?
WHAT ...
...IS HE SAYING...?
OF COURSE I DO NOT INTEND TO REFUTE THE BELIEFS HELD BY PANDORA, BUT...
...IT IS ALSO A FACT THAT THERE IS NOTHING...TO PROVE THEIR BELIEF TRUE EITHER.

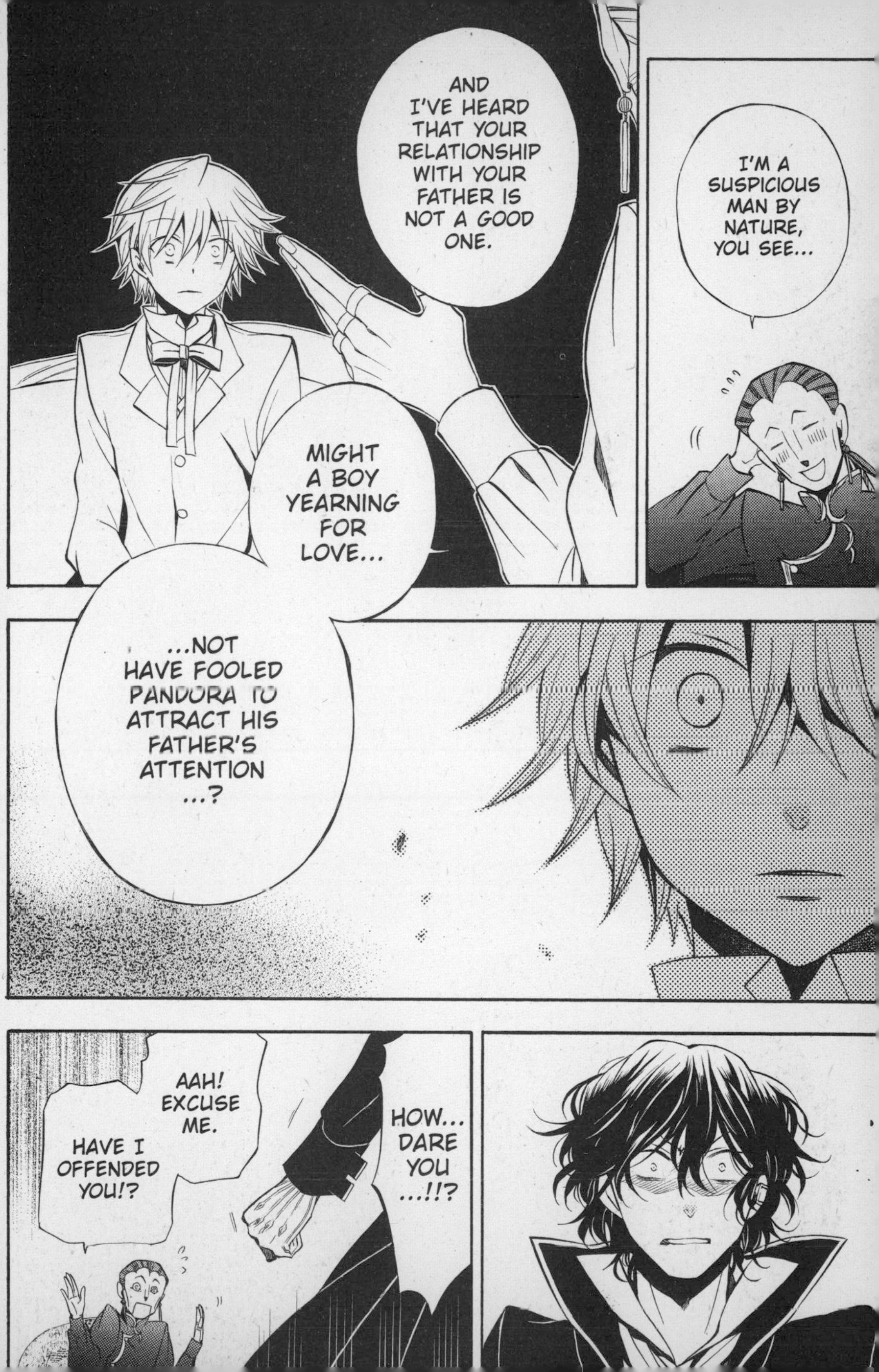
I'M A SUSPICIOUS MAN BY NATURE, YOU SEE...
AND I'VE HEARD THAT YOUR RELATIONSHIP WITH YOUR FATHER IS NOT A GOOD ONE.
MIGHT A BOY YEARNING FOR LOVE...
...NOT HAVE FOOLED PANDORA TO ATTRACT HIS FATHER'S ATTENTION ...?
HOW... DARE YOU ...!!?
AAH! EXCUSE ME.
HAVE I OFFENDED YOU!?

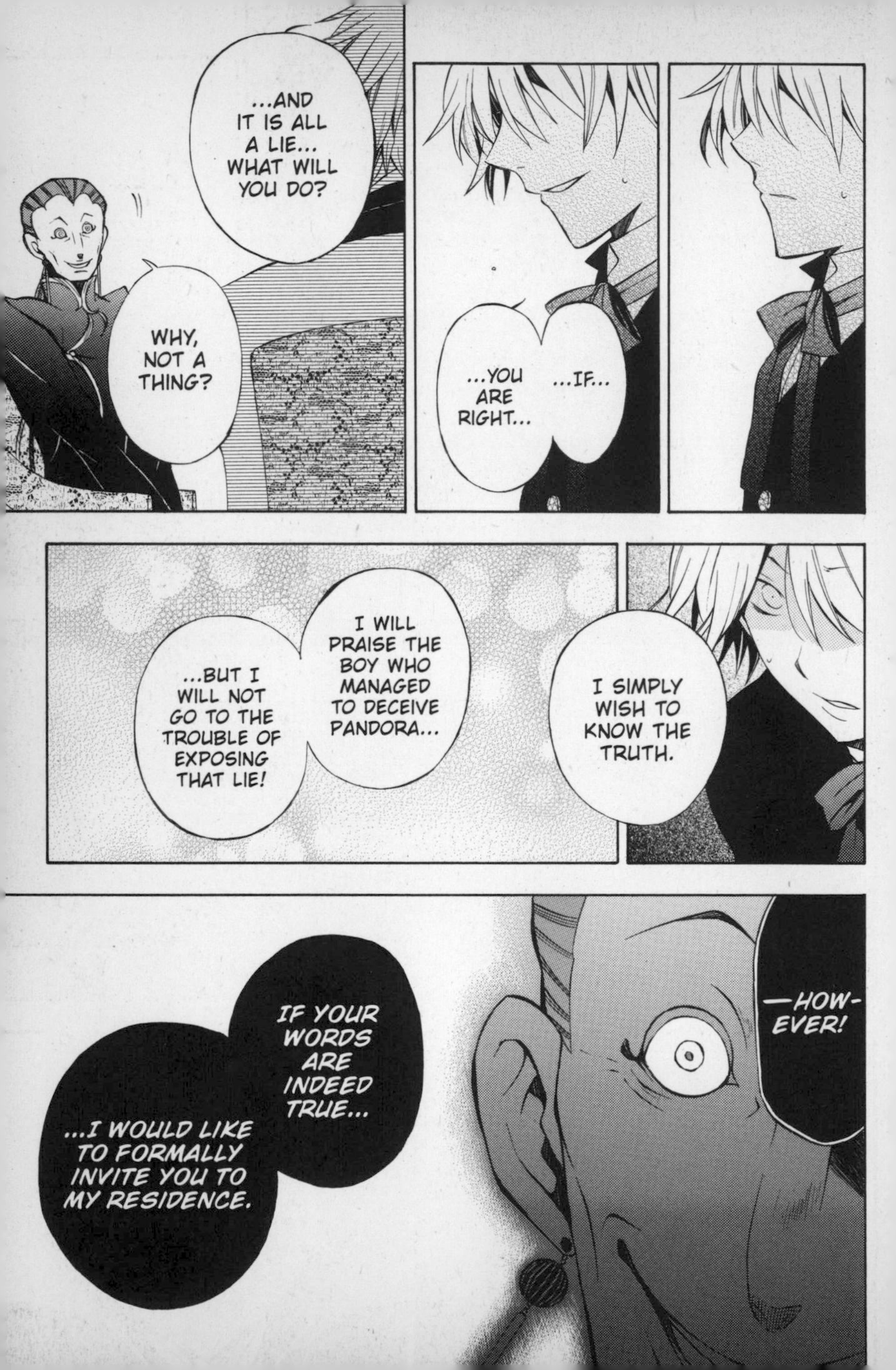
...IF...
...YOU ARE RIGHT...
...AND IT IS ALL A LIE... WHAT WILL YOU DO?
WHY, NOT A THING?
I SIMPLY WISH TO KNOW THE TRUTH.
I WILL PRAISE THE BOY WHO MANAGED TO DECEIVE PANDORA...
...BUT I WILL NOT GO TO THE TROUBLE OF EXPOSING THAT LIE!
—HOW-EVER!
IF YOUR WORDS ARE INDEED TRUE...
...I WOULD LIKE TO FORMALLY INVITE YOU TO MY RESIDENCE.

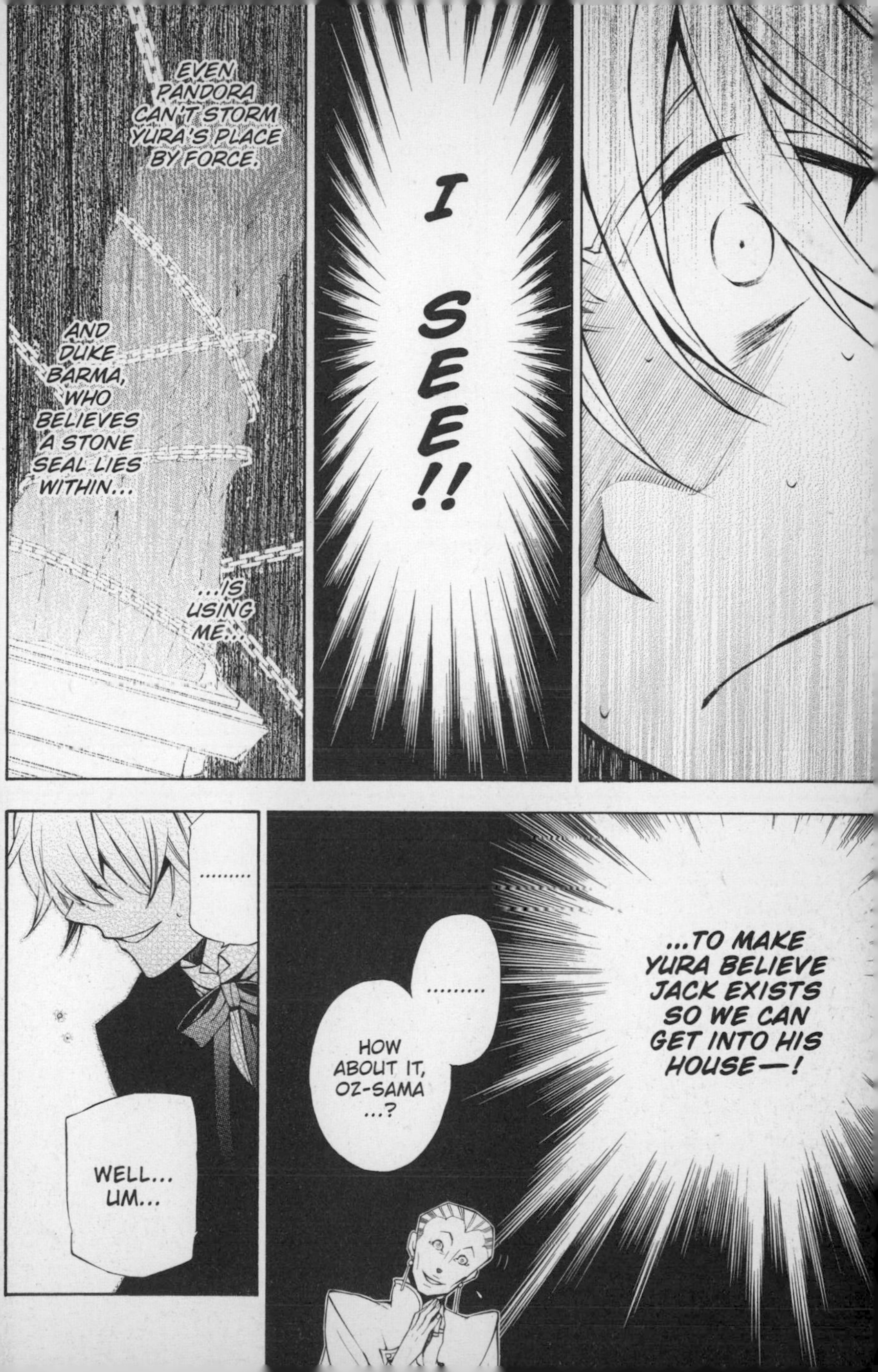
I SEE!!
EVEN PANDORA CAN'T STORM YURA'S PLACE BY FORCE.
AND DUKE BARMA, WHO BELIEVES A STONE SEAL LIES WITHIN...
...IS USING ME...
...TO MAKE YURA BELIEVE JACK EXISTS SO WE CAN GET INTO HIS HOUSE—!
....
HOW ABOUT IT, OZ-SAMA...?
....
WELL... UM...

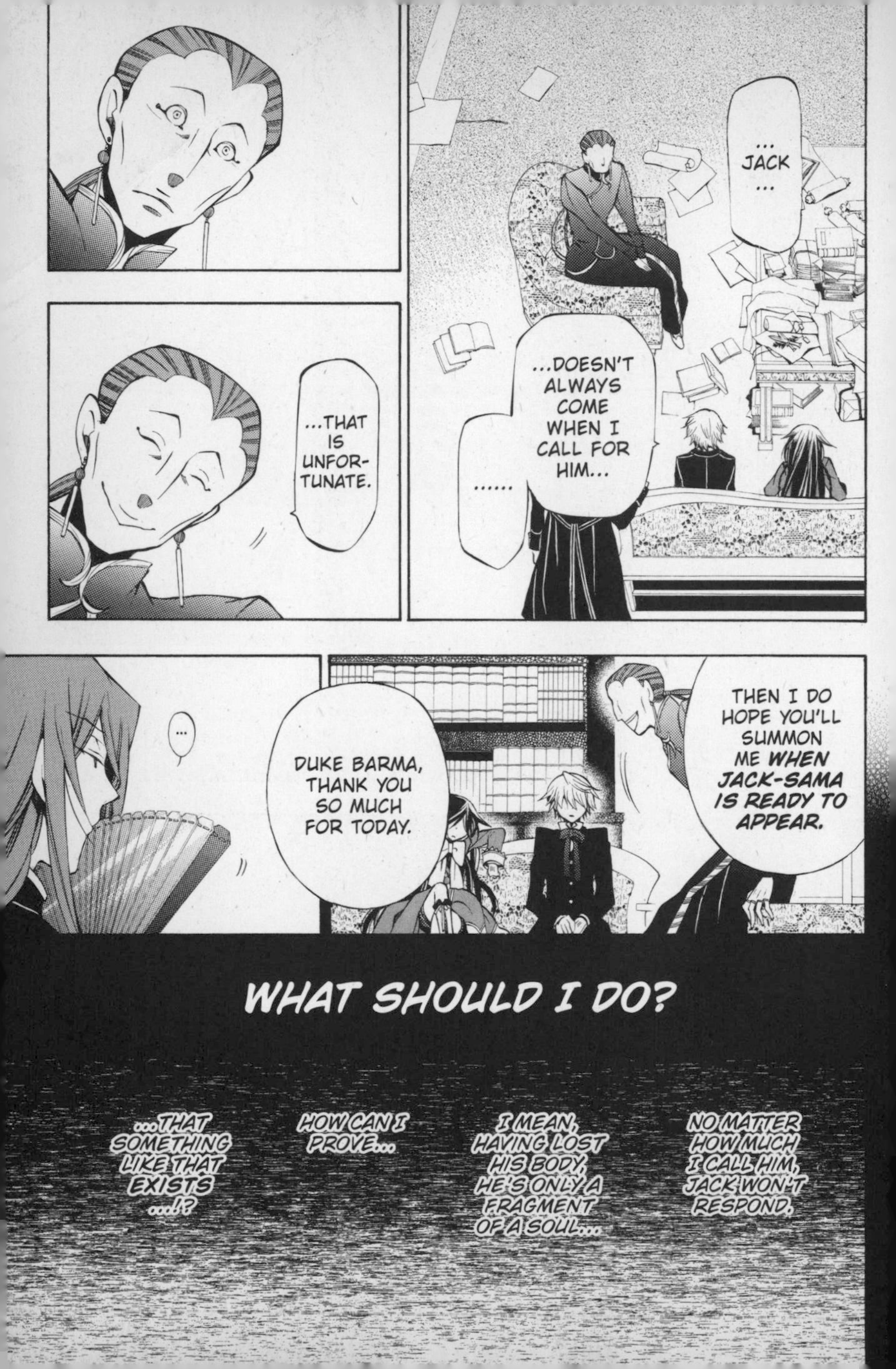
... JACK ...
...DOESN'T ALWAYS COME WHEN I CALL FOR HIM...
......
...THAT IS UNFOR-TUNATE.
THEN I DO HOPE YOU'LL SUMMON ME WHEN JACK-SAMA IS READY TO APPEAR.
DUKE BARMA, THANK YOU SO MUCH FOR TODAY.
...
WHAT SHOULD I DO?
NO MATTER HOW MUCH I CALL HIM, JACK WON'T RESPOND.
I MEAN, HAVING LOST HIS BODY, HE'S ONLY A FRAGMENT OF A SOUL...
HOW CAN I PROVE...
...THAT SOMETHING LIKE THAT EXISTS ...!?

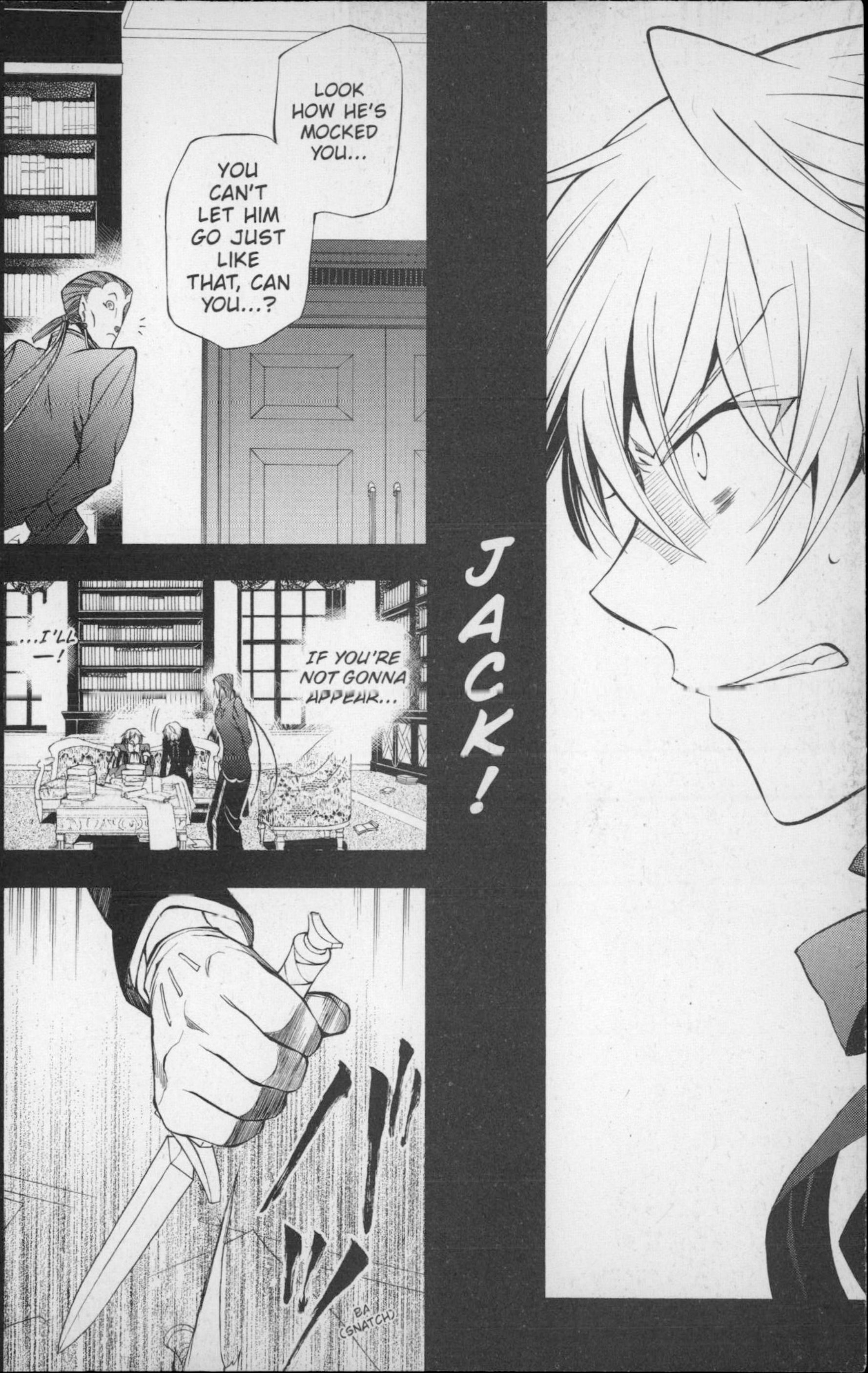
LOOK HOW HE'S MOCKED YOU...
YOU CAN'T LET HIM GO JUST LIKE THAT, CAN YOU...?
IF YOU'RE NOT GONNA APPEAR...
...I'LL —!
BA (SNATCH)
JACK!

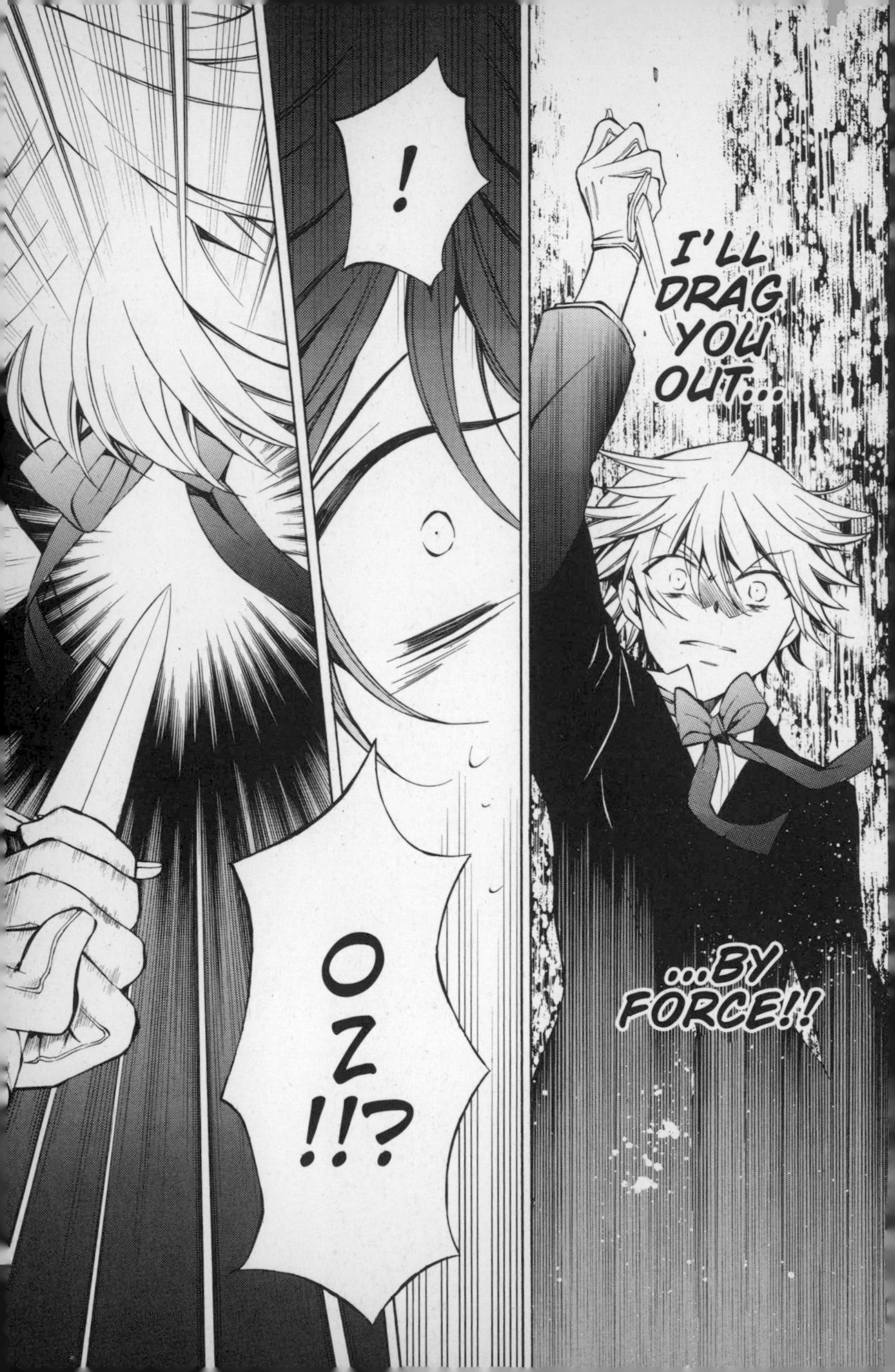
I'LL DRAG YOU OUT...
...BY FORCE!!
!
OZ!!?

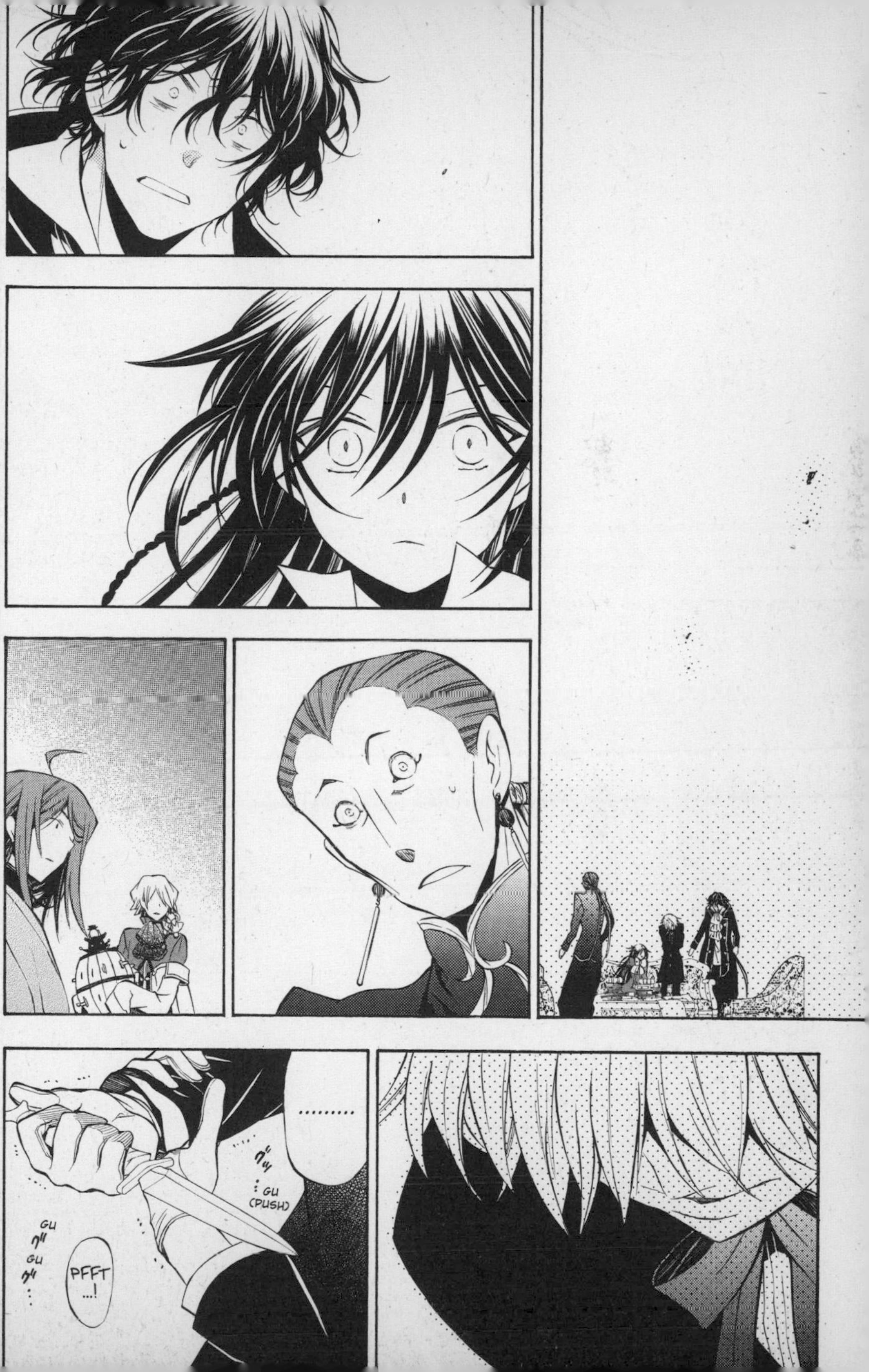

....
GU (PUSH)
GU
GU
PFFT ...!

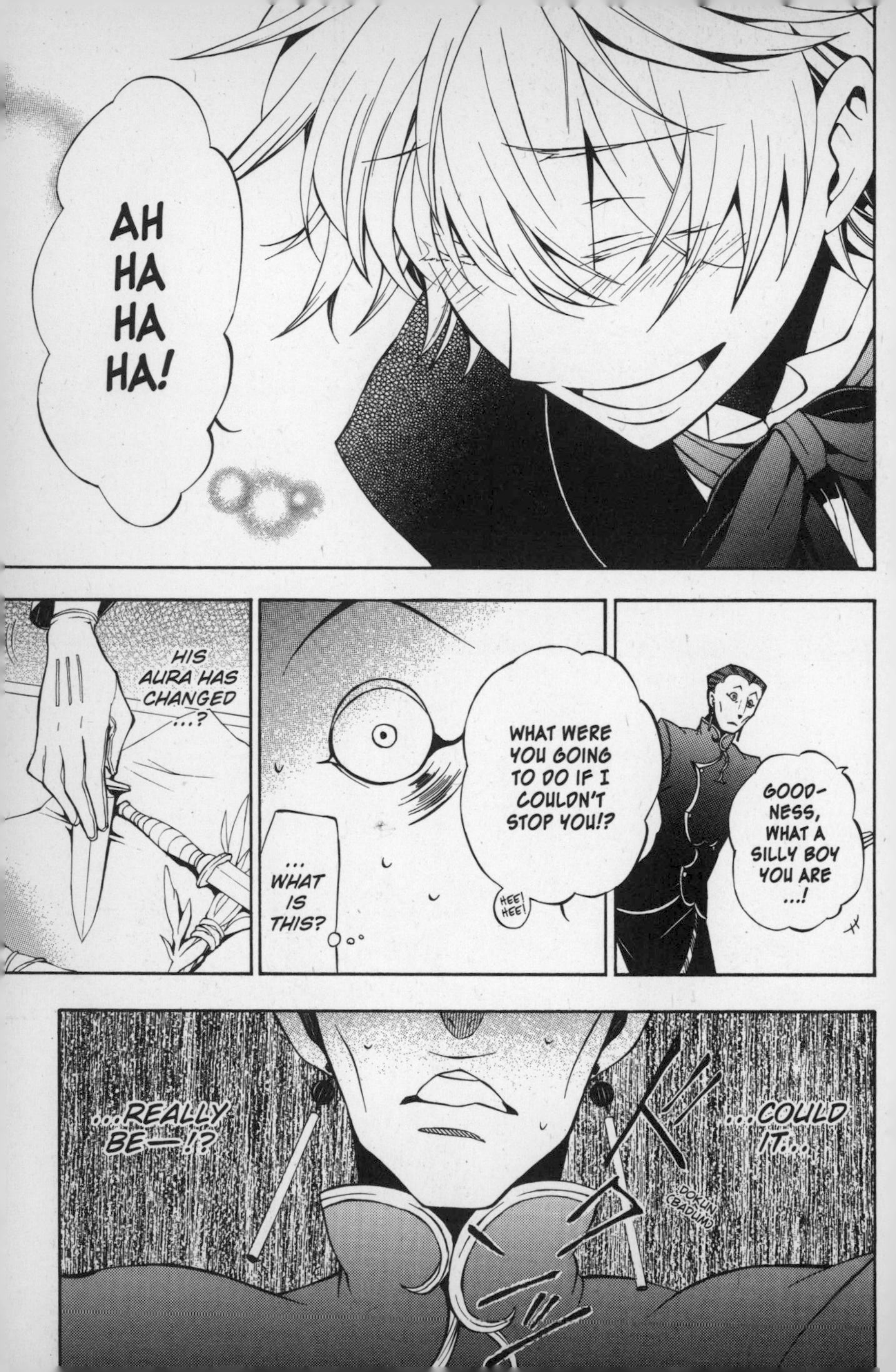
AH HA HA HA!
GOODNESS, WHAT A SILLY BOY YOU ARE...!
WHAT WERE YOU GOING TO DO IF I COULDN'T STOP YOU!?
HEE! HEE!
...WHAT IS THIS?
HIS AURA HAS CHANGED...?
...COULD IT...
DOKUN (BADUM)
...REALLY BE—!?

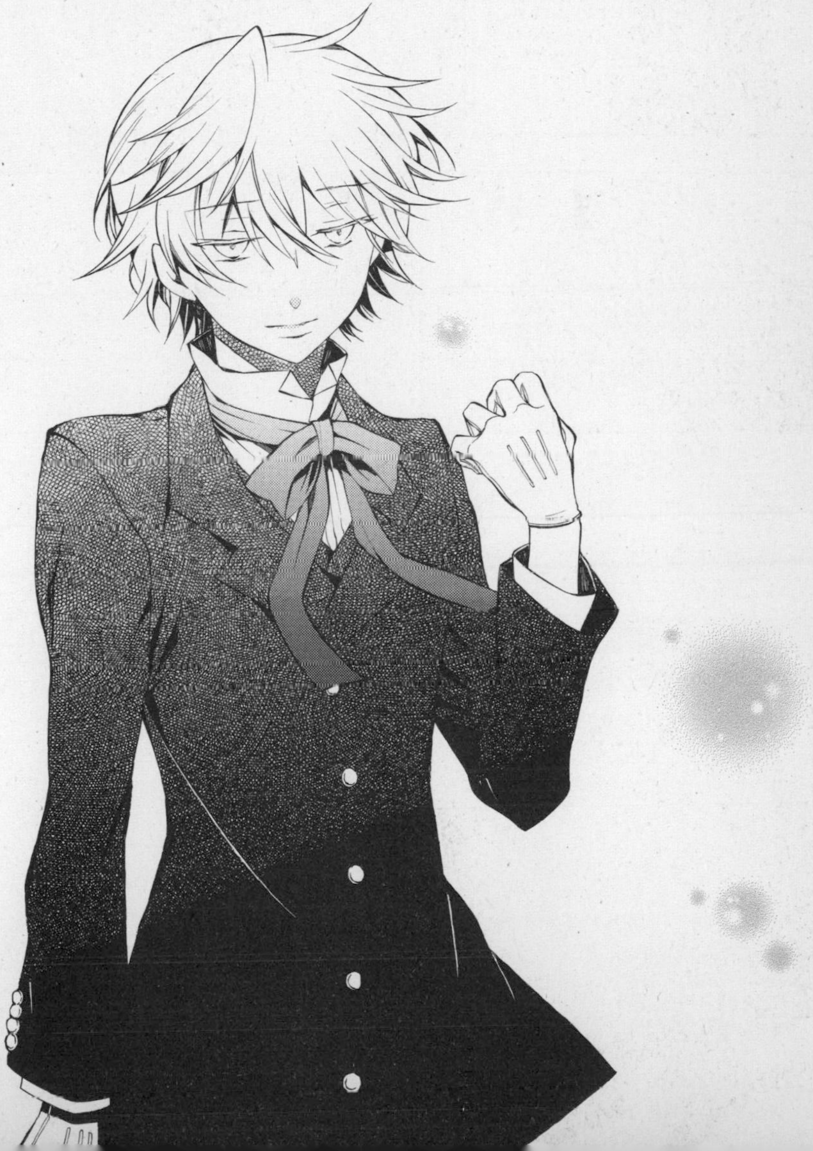

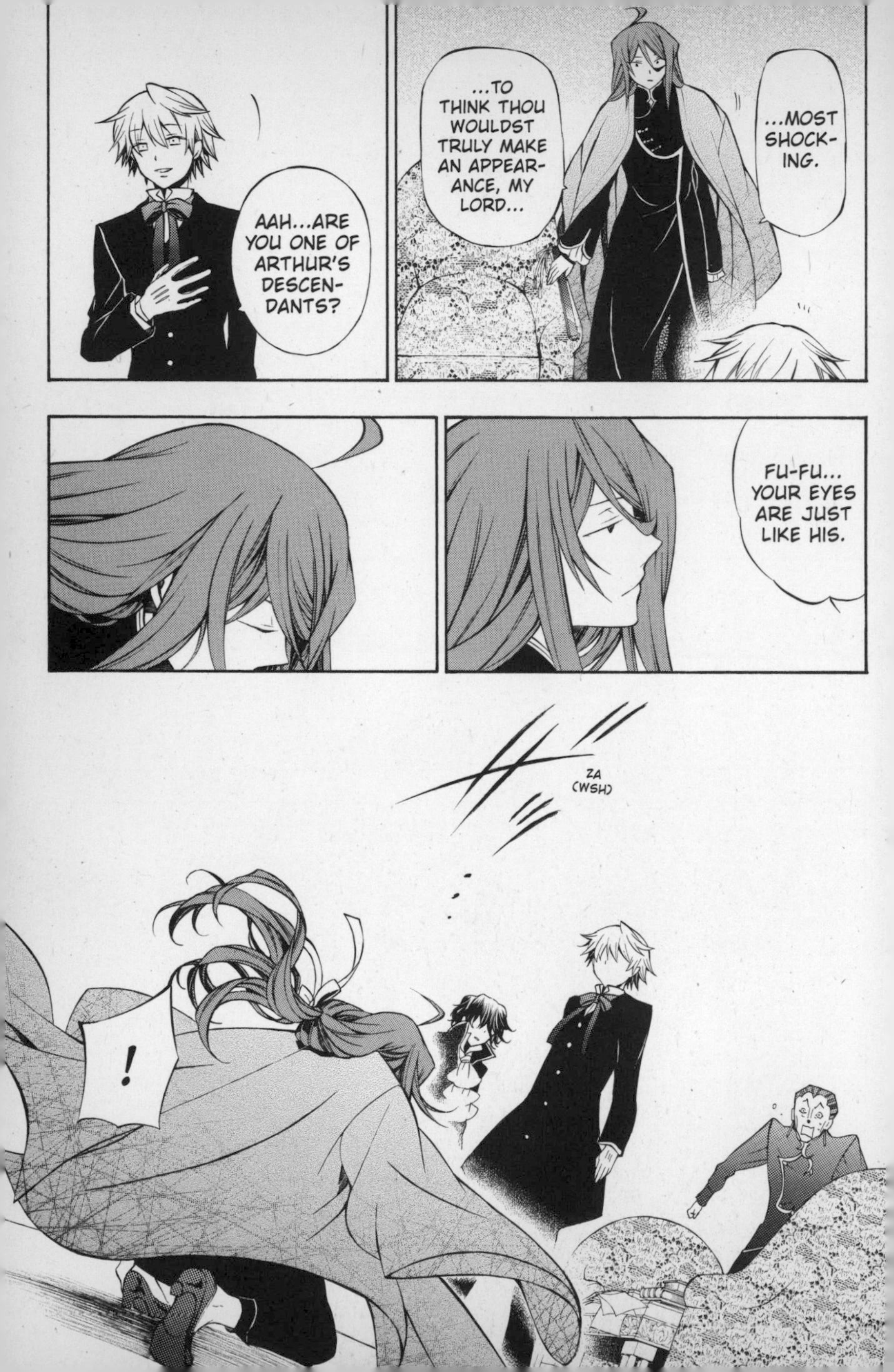
...MOST SHOCKING.
...TO THINK THOU WOULDST TRULY MAKE AN APPEARANCE, MY LORD...
AAH...ARE YOU ONE OF ARTHUR'S DESCENDANTS?
FU-FU... YOUR EYES ARE JUST LIKE HIS.
ZA (WSH)
!

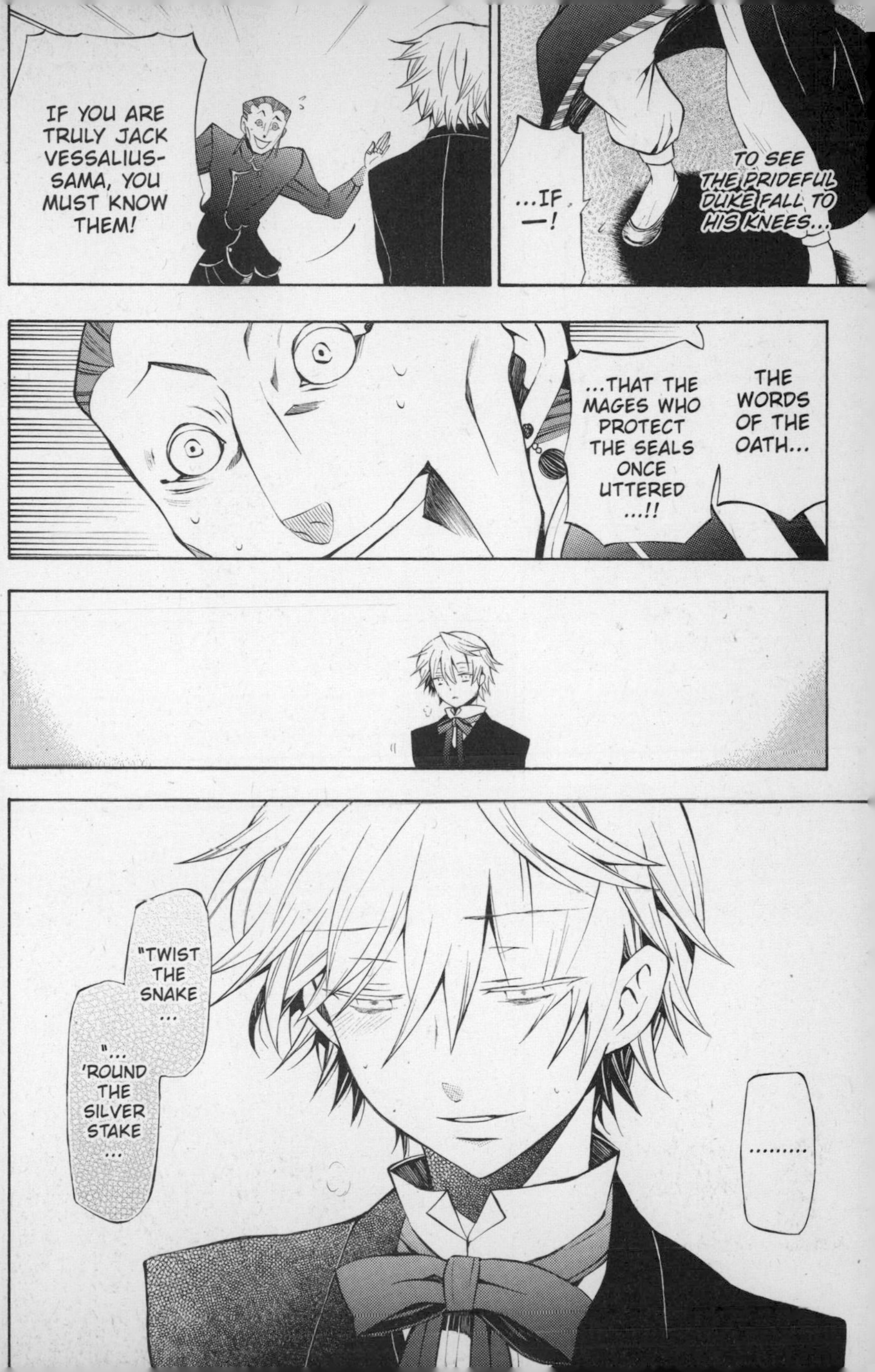
TO SEE THE PRIDEFUL DUKE FALL TO HIS KNEES...
...IF —!
IF YOU ARE TRULY JACK VESSALIUS-SAMA, YOU MUST KNOW THEM!
THE WORDS OF THE OATH...
...THAT THE MAGES WHO PROTECT THE SEALS ONCE UTTERED ...!!
....
"TWIST THE SNAKE ...
"... 'ROUND THE SILVER STAKE ...

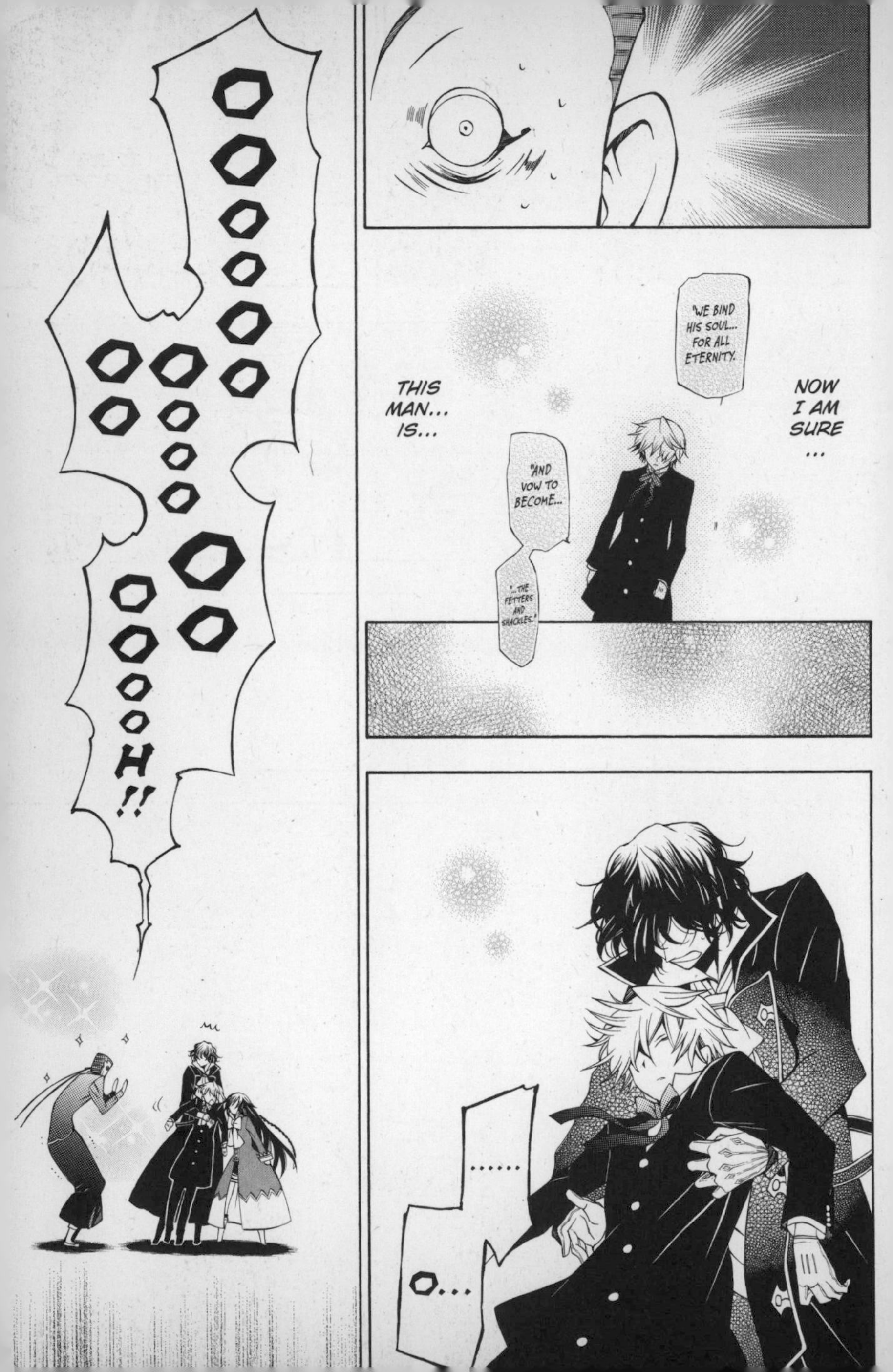
NOW I AM SURE ...
"WE BIND HIS SOUL... FOR ALL ETERNITY.
"AND VOW TO BECOME...
"...THE FETTERS AND SHACKLES."
THIS MAN... IS...
......
O...
OOOOOOOOOOOOOOOOOOH!!

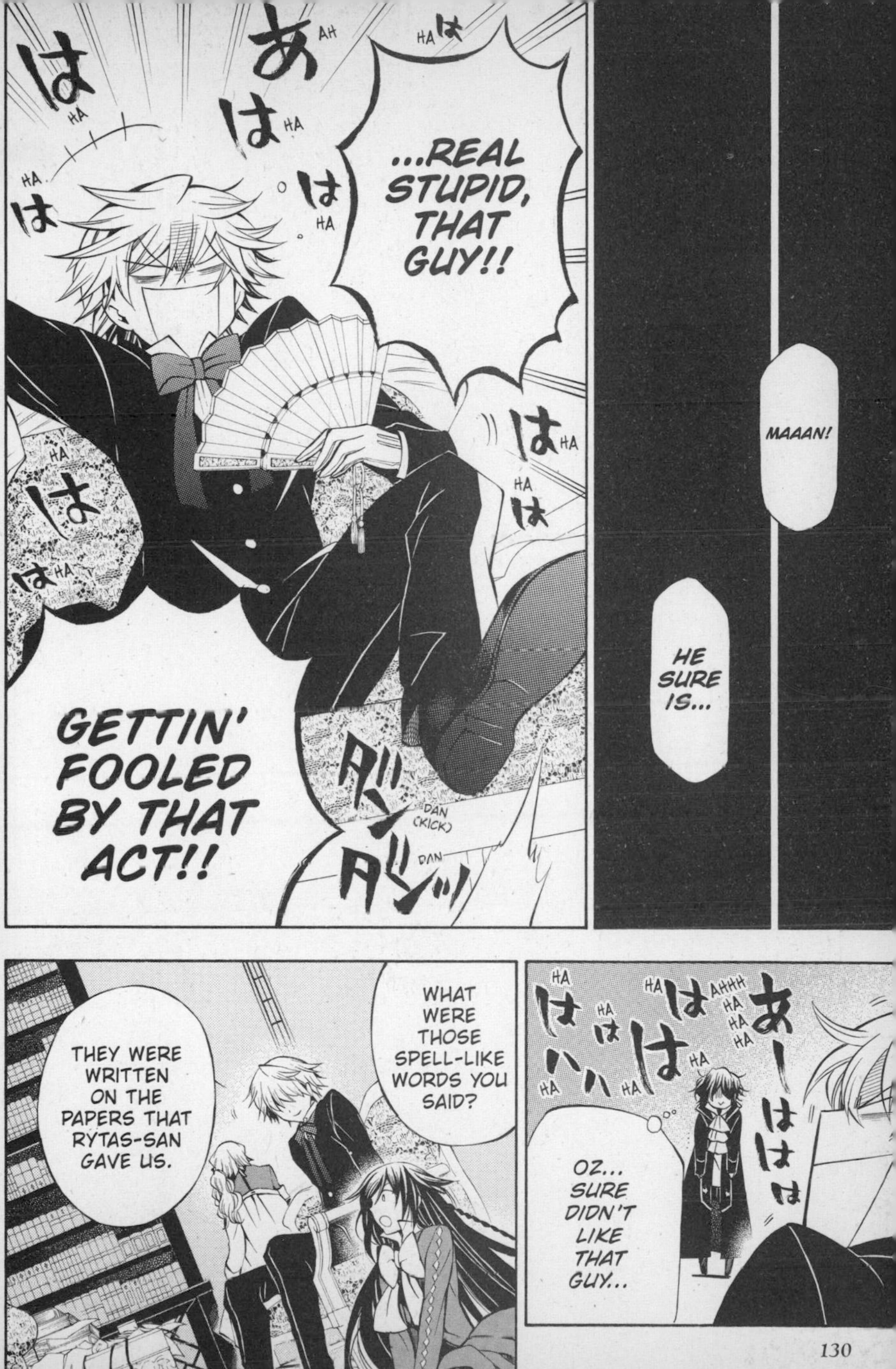
MAAAN!
HE SURE IS...
あはは AH HA
はははは HA HA HA HA
...REAL STUPID, THAT GUY!!
はは HA HA
ははは HA HA HA
GETTIN' FOOLED BY THAT ACT!!
ダン DAN (KICK)
ダンッ DAN
あーははは AHHH HA HA HA
ははは HA HA HA
はハハ HA HA HA
OZ... SURE DIDN'T LIKE THAT GUY...
WHAT WERE THOSE SPELL-LIKE WORDS YOU SAID?
THEY WERE WRITTEN ON THE PAPERS THAT RYTAS-SAN GAVE US.

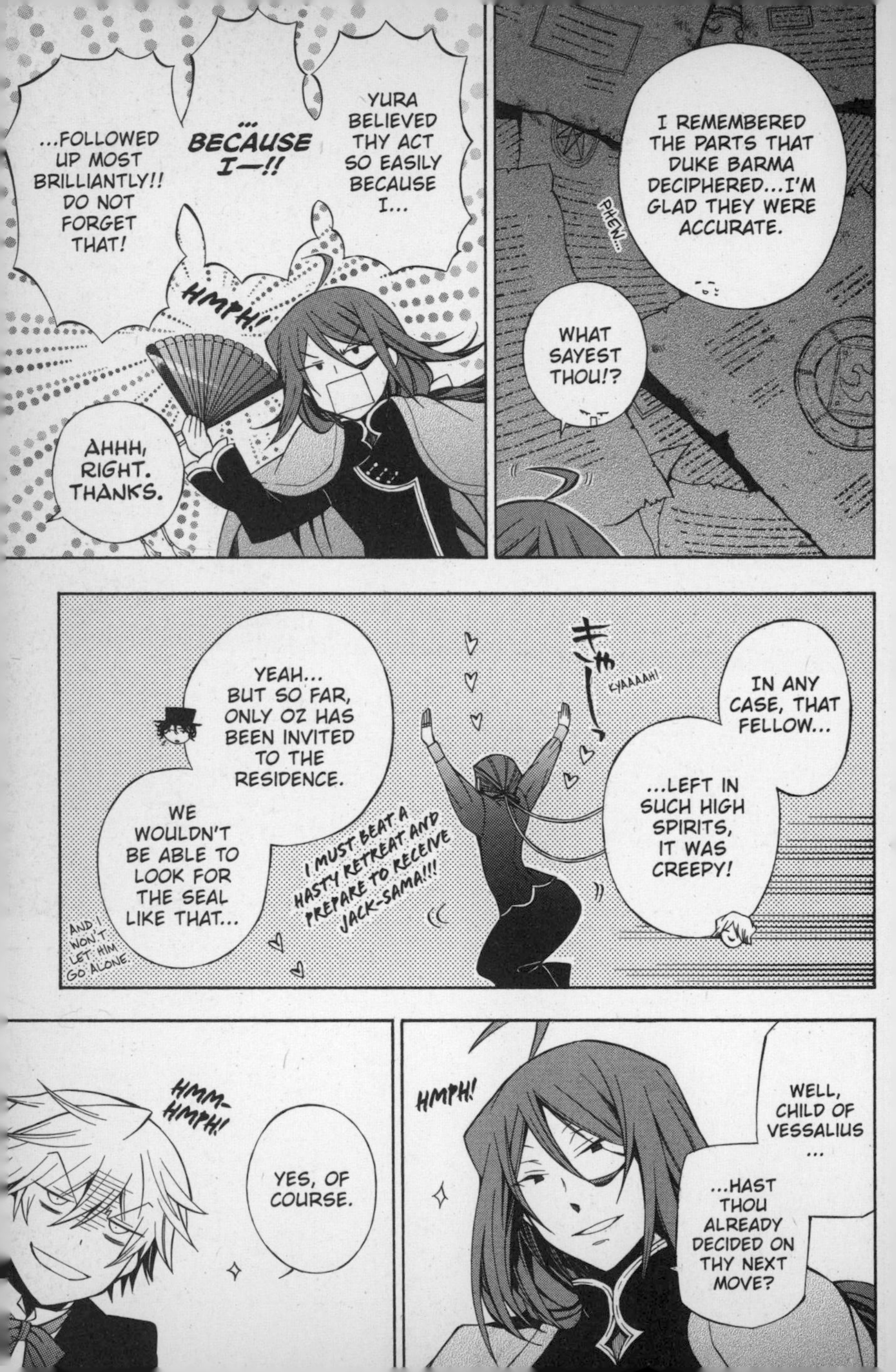
I REMEMBERED THE PARTS THAT DUKE BARMA DECIPHERED...I'M GLAD THEY WERE ACCURATE.
PHEW...
WHAT SAYEST THOU!?
YURA BELIEVED THY ACT SO EASILY BECAUSE I...
...BECAUSE I—!!
...FOLLOWED UP MOST BRILLIANTLY!! DO NOT FORGET THAT!
HMPH!
AHHH, RIGHT. THANKS.
IN ANY CASE, THAT FELLOW...
...LEFT IN SUCH HIGH SPIRITS, IT WAS CREEPY!
きゃー
KYAAAAH!
I MUST BEAT A HASTY RETREAT AND PREPARE TO RECEIVE JACK-SAMA!!!
YEAH... BUT SO FAR, ONLY OZ HAS BEEN INVITED TO THE RESIDENCE.
WE WOULDN'T BE ABLE TO LOOK FOR THE SEAL LIKE THAT...
AND I WON'T LET HIM GO ALONE.
WELL, CHILD OF VESSALIUS...
...HAST THOU ALREADY DECIDED ON THY NEXT MOVE?
HMPH!
HMM-HMPH!
YES, OF COURSE.

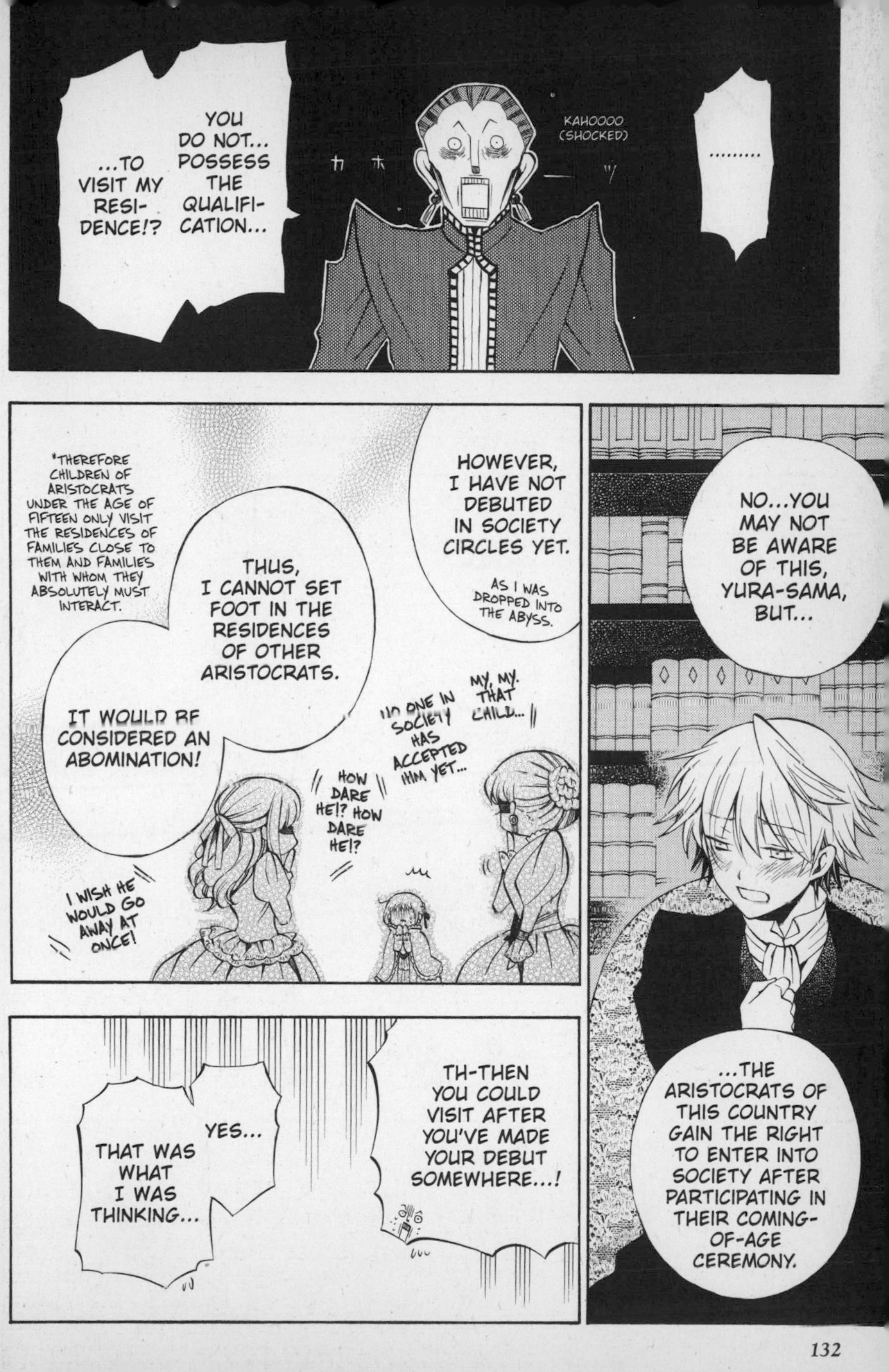
....
KAHOOOO (SHOCKED)
YOU DO NOT... POSSESS THE QUALIFICATION...
...TO VISIT MY RESIDENCE!?
NO...YOU MAY NOT BE AWARE OF THIS, YURA-SAMA, BUT...
...THE ARISTOCRATS OF THIS COUNTRY GAIN THE RIGHT TO ENTER INTO SOCIETY AFTER PARTICIPATING IN THEIR COMING-OF-AGE CEREMONY.
HOWEVER, I HAVE NOT DEBUTED IN SOCIETY CIRCLES YET.
AS I WAS DROPPED INTO THE ABYSS.
THUS, I CANNOT SET FOOT IN THE RESIDENCES OF OTHER ARISTOCRATS.
*THEREFORE CHILDREN OF ARISTOCRATS UNDER THE AGE OF FIFTEEN ONLY VISIT THE RESIDENCES OF FAMILIES CLOSE TO THEM AND FAMILIES WITH WHOM THEY ABSOLUTELY MUST INTERACT.
IT WOULD BE CONSIDERED AN ABOMINATION!
MY, MY. THAT CHILD...
NO ONE IN SOCIETY HAS ACCEPTED HIM YET...
HOW DARE HE!? HOW DARE HE!?
I WISH HE WOULD GO AWAY AT ONCE!
TH-THEN YOU COULD VISIT AFTER YOU'VE MADE YOUR DEBUT SOMEWHERE...!
YES... THAT WAS WHAT I WAS THINKING...

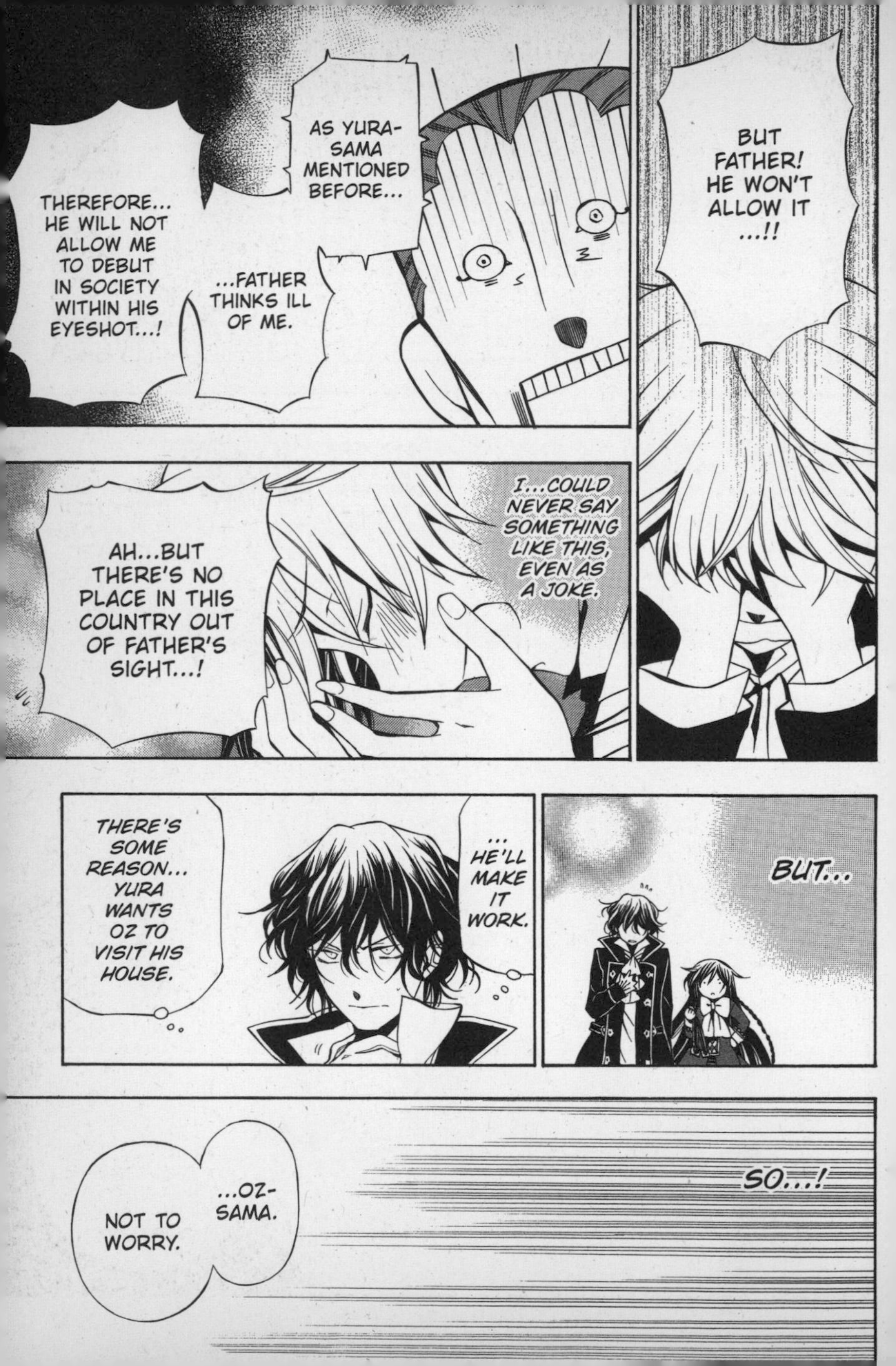
BUT FATHER! HE WON'T ALLOW IT ...!!
AS YURA-SAMA MENTIONED BEFORE...
...FATHER THINKS ILL OF ME.
THEREFORE... HE WILL NOT ALLOW ME TO DEBUT IN SOCIETY WITHIN HIS EYESHOT...!
I...COULD NEVER SAY SOMETHING LIKE THIS, EVEN AS A JOKE.
AH...BUT THERE'S NO PLACE IN THIS COUNTRY OUT OF FATHER'S SIGHT...!
BUT...
...HE'LL MAKE IT WORK.
THERE'S SOME REASON... YURA WANTS OZ TO VISIT HIS HOUSE.
SO...!
...OZ-SAMA.
NOT TO WORRY.

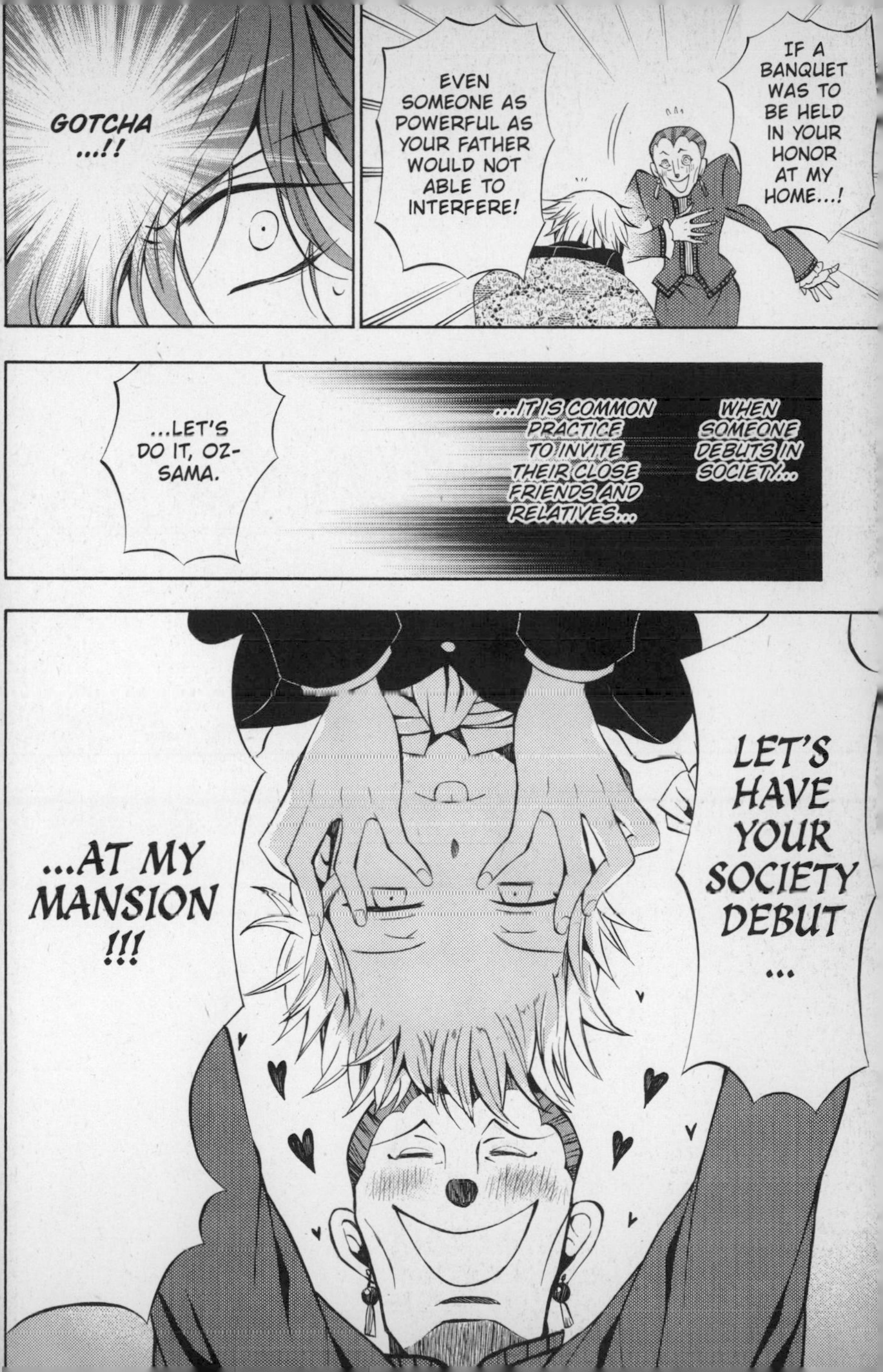
IF A BANQUET WAS TO BE HELD IN YOUR HONOR AT MY HOME...!
EVEN SOMEONE AS POWERFUL AS YOUR FATHER WOULD NOT ABLE TO INTERFERE!
GOTCHA ...!!
WHEN SOMEONE DEBUTS IN SOCIETY...
...IT IS COMMON PRACTICE TO INVITE THEIR CLOSE FRIENDS AND RELATIVES...
...LET'S DO IT, OZ-SAMA.
LET'S HAVE YOUR SOCIETY DEBUT...
...AT MY MANSION!!!

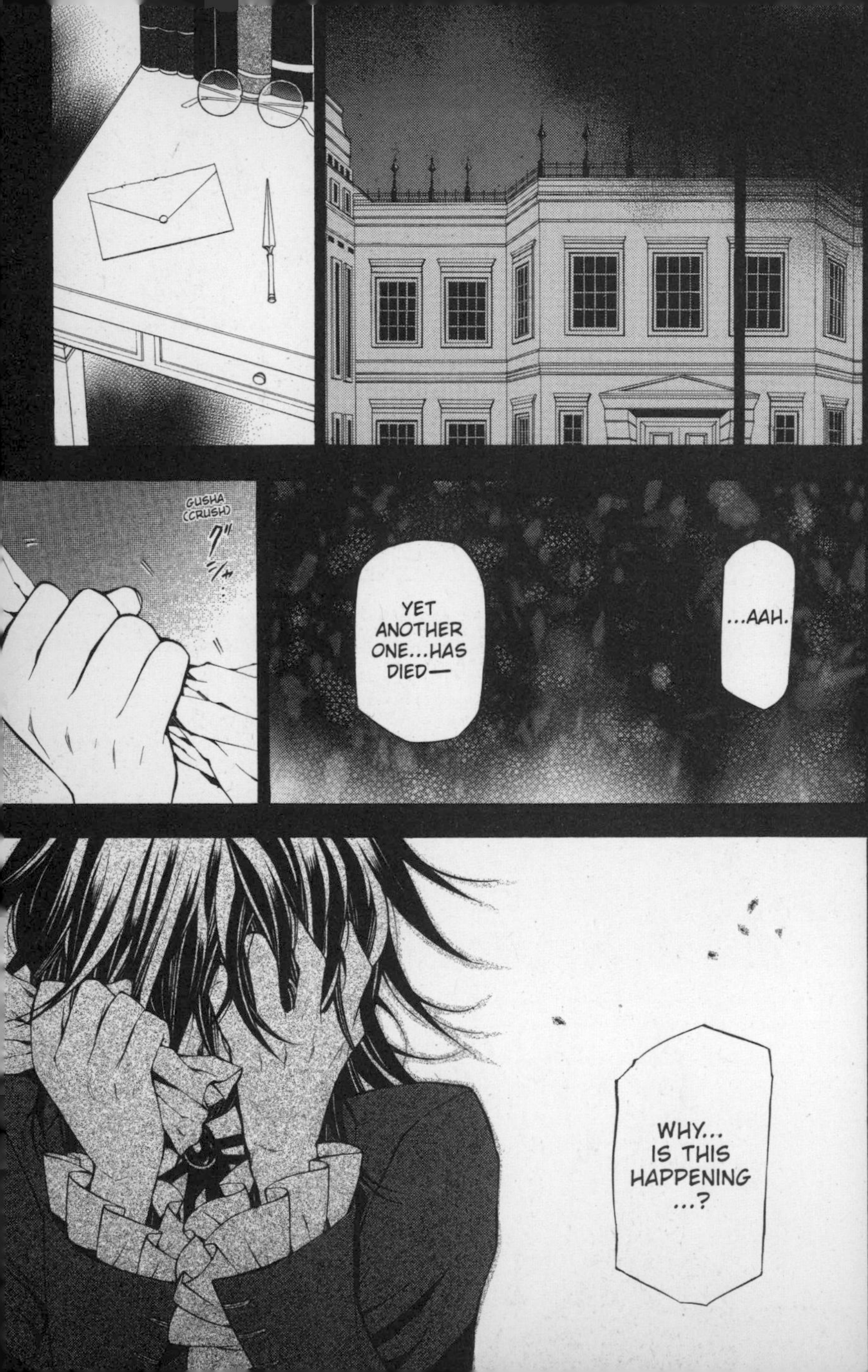
...AAH.
YET ANOTHER ONE...HAS DIED—
GUSHA (CRUSH)
WHY... IS THIS HAPPENING ...?

Retrace:XLIX Night in gale

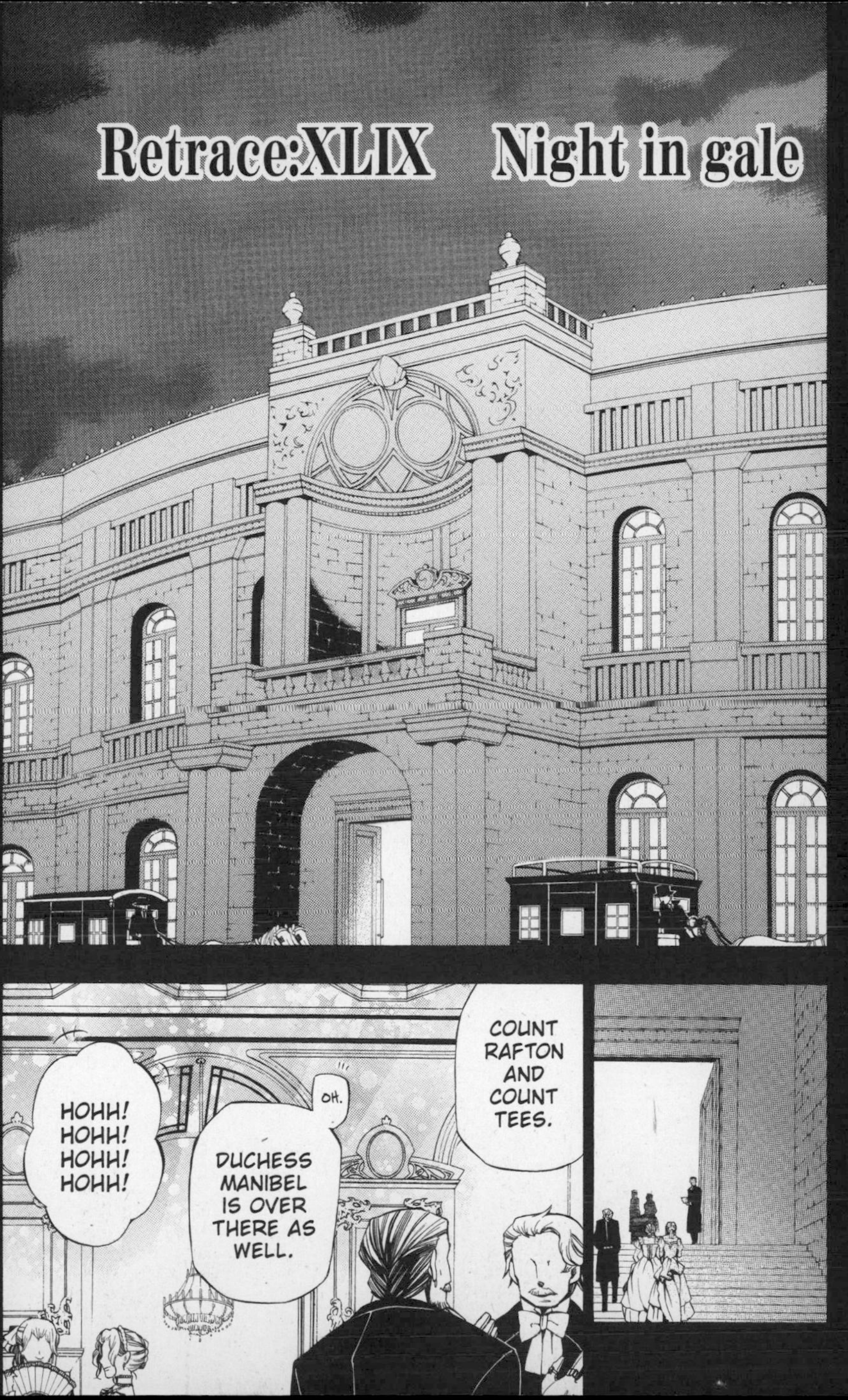
COUNT RAFTON AND COUNT TEES.
OH.
DUCHESS MANIBEL IS OVER THERE AS WELL.
HOHH! HOHH! HOHH! HOHH!

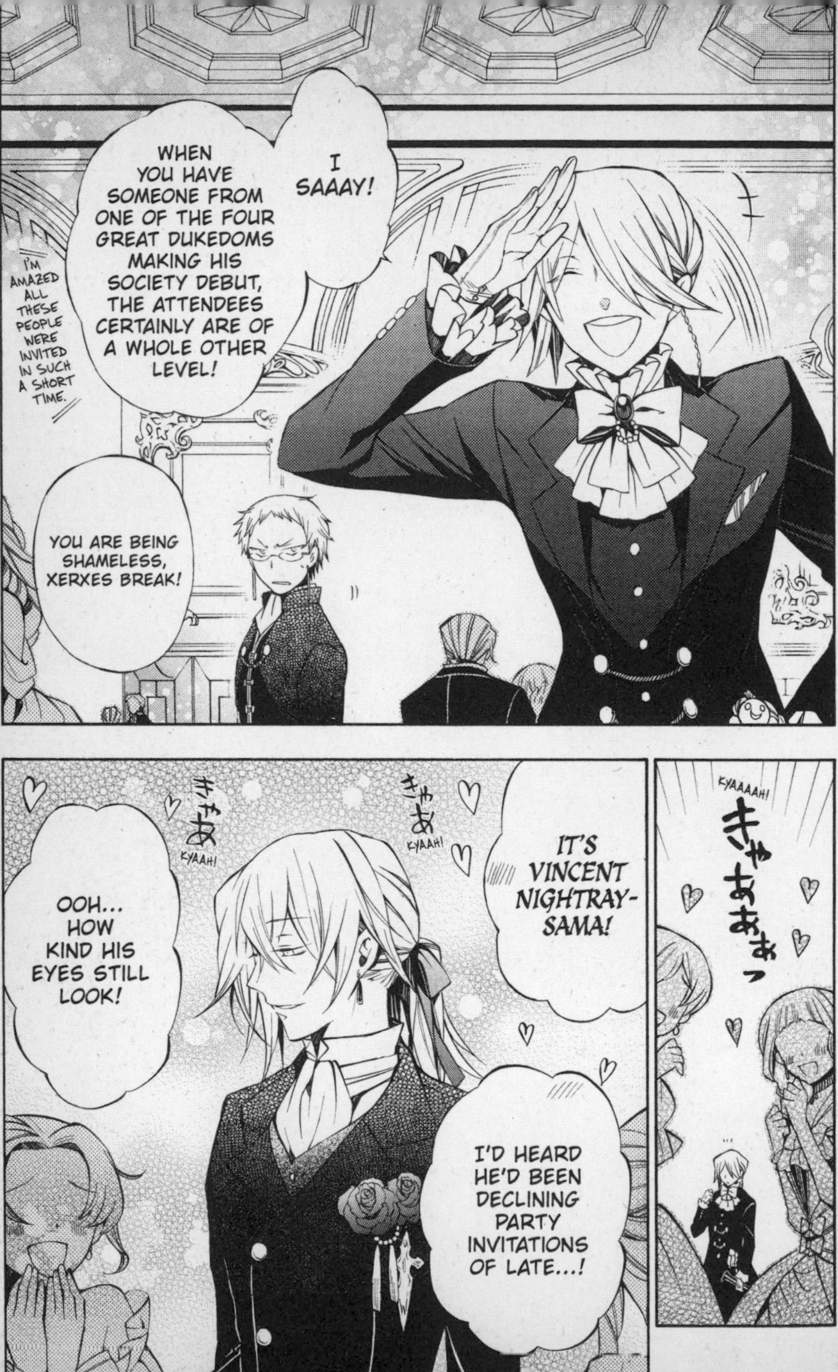
I SAAAY!
WHEN YOU HAVE SOMEONE FROM ONE OF THE FOUR GREAT DUKEDOMS MAKING HIS SOCIETY DEBUT, THE ATTENDEES CERTAINLY ARE OF A WHOLE OTHER LEVEL!
I'M AMAZED ALL THESE PEOPLE WERE INVITED IN SUCH A SHORT TIME.
YOU ARE BEING SHAMELESS, XERXES BREAK!
KYAAAAH!
きゃああああっ
IT'S VINCENT NIGHTRAY-SAMA!
きゃあ
KYAAH!
きゃあ
KYAAH!
OOH... HOW KIND HIS EYES STILL LOOK!
I'D HEARD HE'D BEEN DECLINING PARTY INVITATIONS OF LATE...!

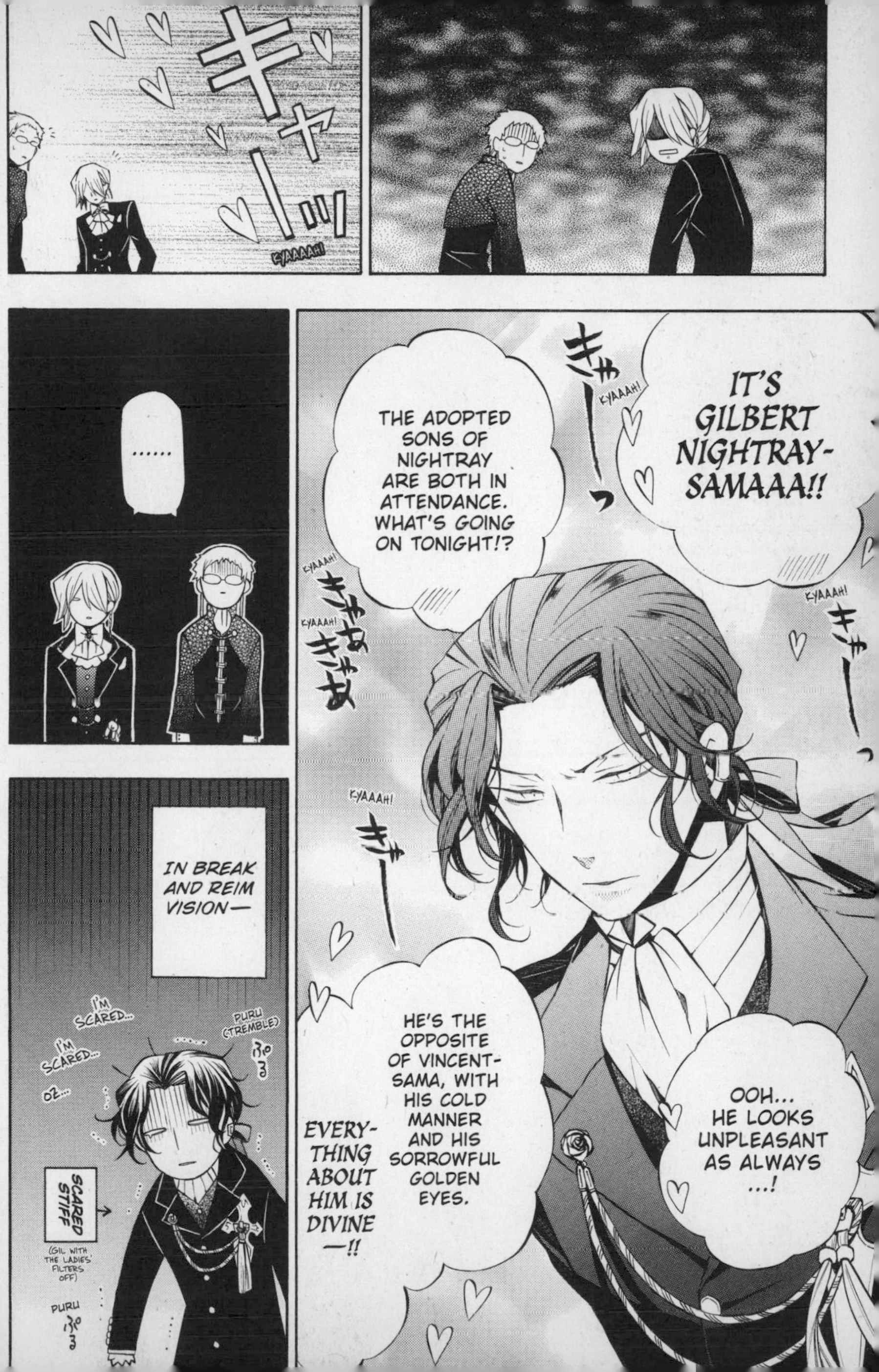

KYAAAAH!
IT'S GILBERT NIGHTRAY-SAMAAA!!
KYAAAH!
THE ADOPTED SONS OF NIGHTRAY ARE BOTH IN ATTENDANCE. WHAT'S GOING ON TONIGHT!?
KYAAAH!
KYAAAH!
KYAAAH!
KYAAAH!
OOH... HE LOOKS UNPLEASANT AS ALWAYS ...!
HE'S THE OPPOSITE OF VINCENT-SAMA, WITH HIS COLD MANNER AND HIS SORROWFUL GOLDEN EYES.
EVERY-THING ABOUT HIM IS DIVINE —!!
......
IN BREAK AND REIM VISION—
PURU (TREMBLE)
I'M SCARED...
I'M SCARED...
OZ...
SCARED STIFF
(GIL WITH THE LADIES' FILTERS OFF)
PURU

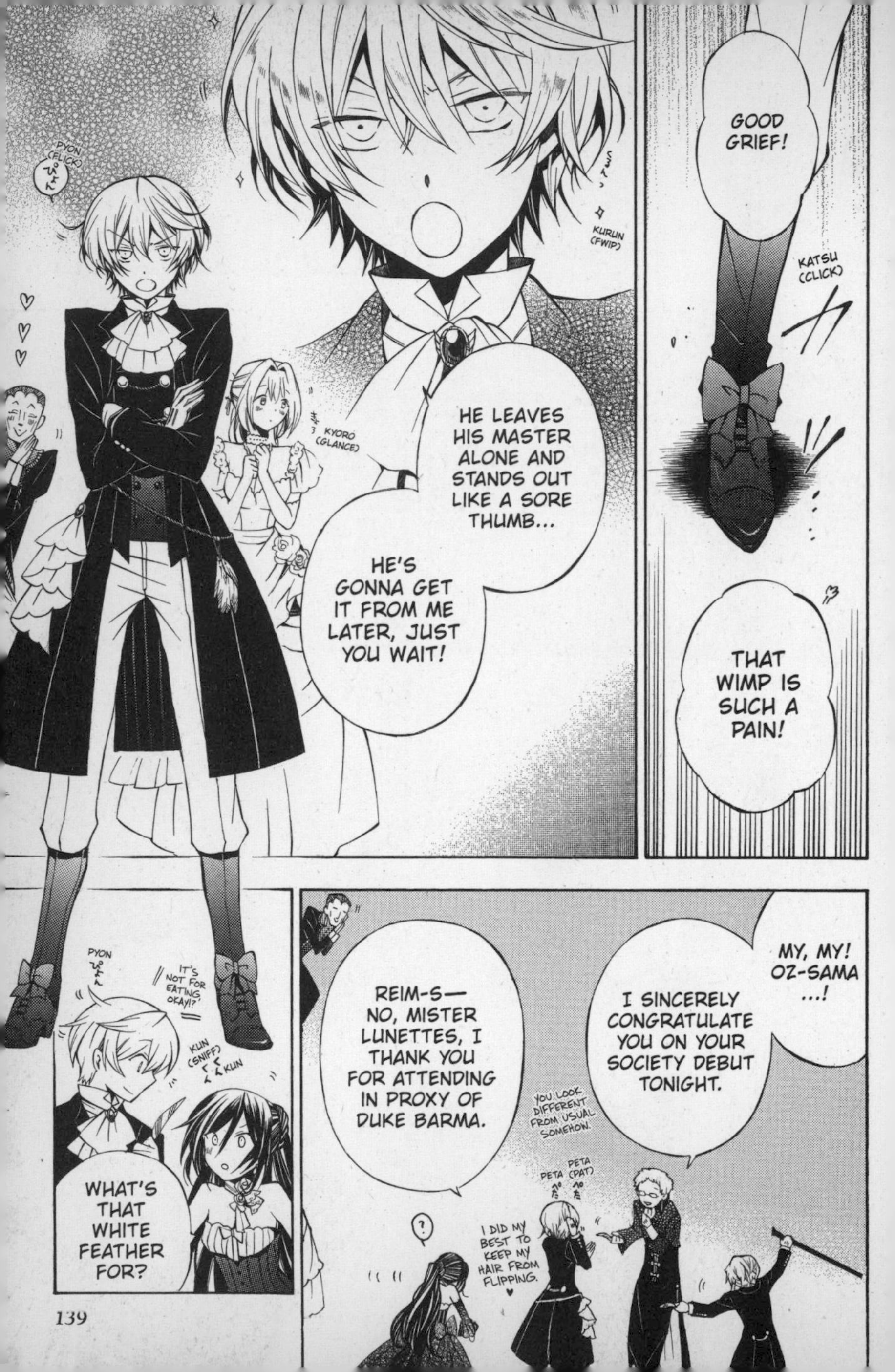
GOOD GRIEF!
KATSU (CLICK)
THAT WIMP IS SUCH A PAIN!
KURUN (FWIP)
HE LEAVES HIS MASTER ALONE AND STANDS OUT LIKE A SORE THUMB...
HE'S GONNA GET IT FROM ME LATER, JUST YOU WAIT!
KYORO (GLANCE)
PYON (FLICK)
MY, MY! OZ-SAMA ...!
I SINCERELY CONGRATULATE YOU ON YOUR SOCIETY DEBUT TONIGHT.
REIM-S— NO, MISTER LUNETTES, I THANK YOU FOR ATTENDING IN PROXY OF DUKE BARMA.
YOU LOOK DIFFERENT FROM USUAL SOMEHOW.
PETA PETA (PAT)
I DID MY BEST TO KEEP MY HAIR FROM FLIPPING.
?
PYON
IT'S NOT FOR EATING, OKAY!?
KUN (SNIFF) KUN
WHAT'S THAT WHITE FEATHER FOR?

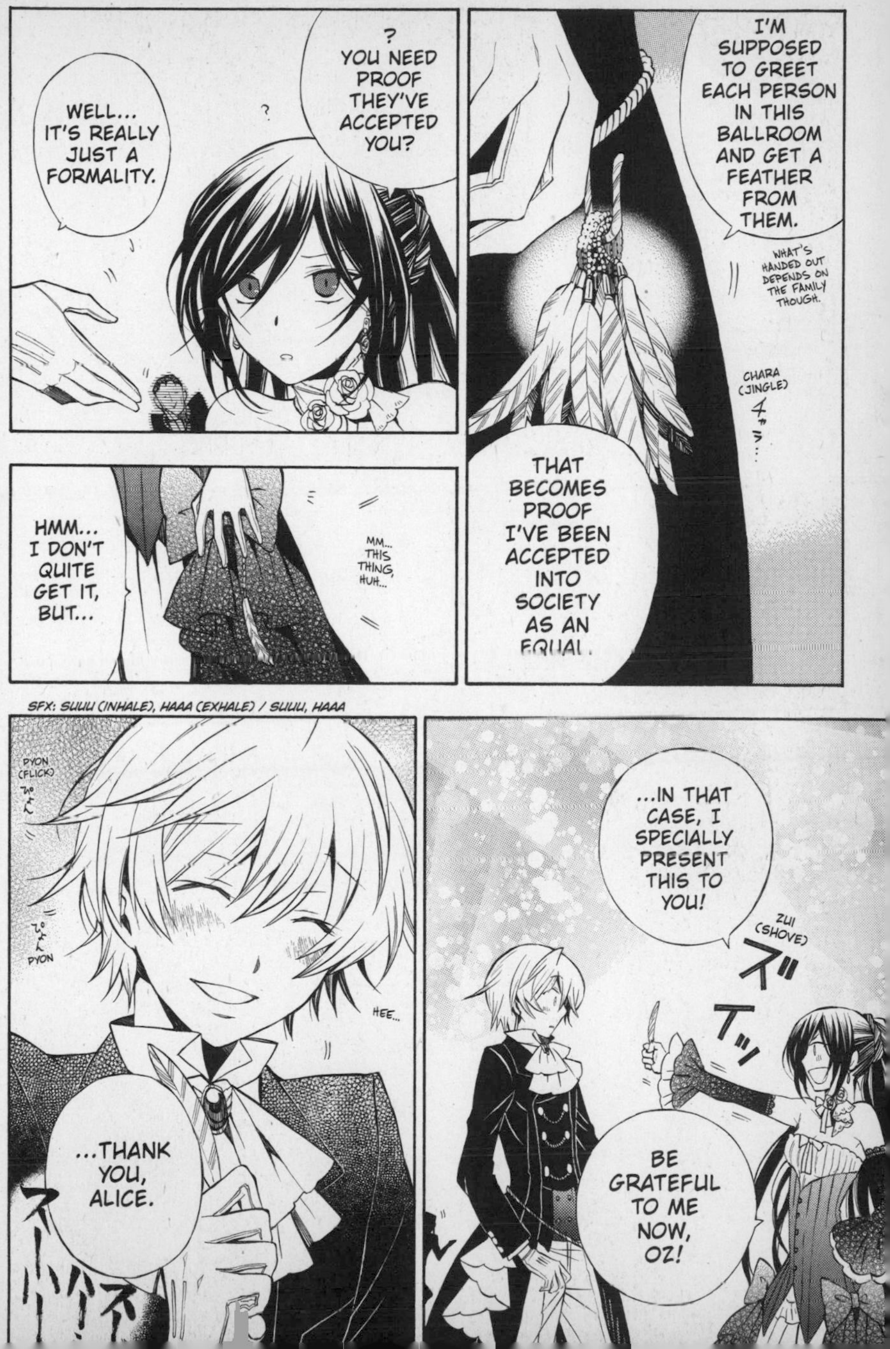
I'M SUPPOSED TO GREET EACH PERSON IN THIS BALLROOM AND GET A FEATHER FROM THEM.
WHAT'S HANDED OUT DEPENDS ON THE FAMILY THOUGH.
CHARA (JINGLE)
THAT BECOMES PROOF I'VE BEEN ACCEPTED INTO SOCIETY AS AN EQUAL.
? YOU NEED PROOF THEY'VE ACCEPTED YOU?
?
WELL... IT'S REALLY JUST A FORMALITY.
MM... THIS THING, HUH...
HMM... I DON'T QUITE GET IT, BUT...
SFX: SUUU (INHALE), HAAA (EXHALE) / SUUU, HAAA
...IN THAT CASE, I SPECIALLY PRESENT THIS TO YOU!
ZUI (SHOVE)
BE GRATEFUL TO ME NOW, OZ!
PYON (FLICK)
PYON
HEE...
...THANK YOU, ALICE.

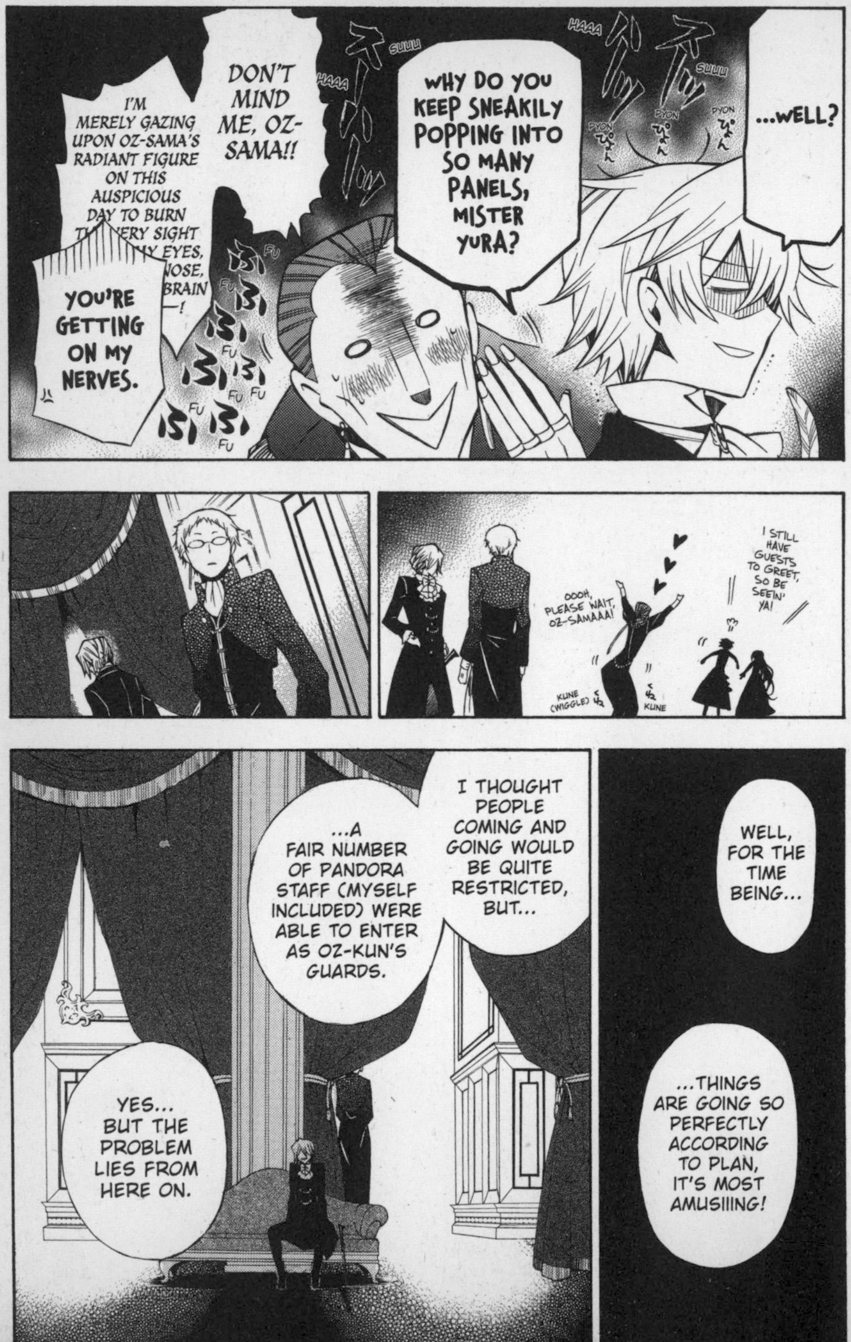
...WELL?
PYON
PYON
PYON
SUUU
HAAA
WHY DO YOU KEEP SNEAKILY POPPING INTO SO MANY PANELS, MISTER YURA?
SUUU
HAAA
DON'T MIND ME, OZ-SAMA!!
I'M MERELY GAZING UPON OZ-SAMA'S RADIANT FIGURE ON THIS AUSPICIOUS DAY TO BURN TH VERY SIGHT MY EYES, NOSE, BRAIN —!
FU FU FU FU FU FU
YOU'RE GETTING ON MY NERVES.
I STILL HAVE GUESTS TO GREET, SO BE SEEIN' YA!
OOOH, PLEASE WAIT, OZ-SAMAAA!
KUNE (WIGGLE)
KUNE
WELL, FOR THE TIME BEING...
...THINGS ARE GOING SO PERFECTLY ACCORDING TO PLAN, IT'S MOST AMUSIIING!
I THOUGHT PEOPLE COMING AND GOING WOULD BE QUITE RESTRICTED, BUT...
...A FAIR NUMBER OF PANDORA STAFF (MYSELF INCLUDED) WERE ABLE TO ENTER AS OZ-KUN'S GUARDS.
YES... BUT THE PROBLEM LIES FROM HERE ON.

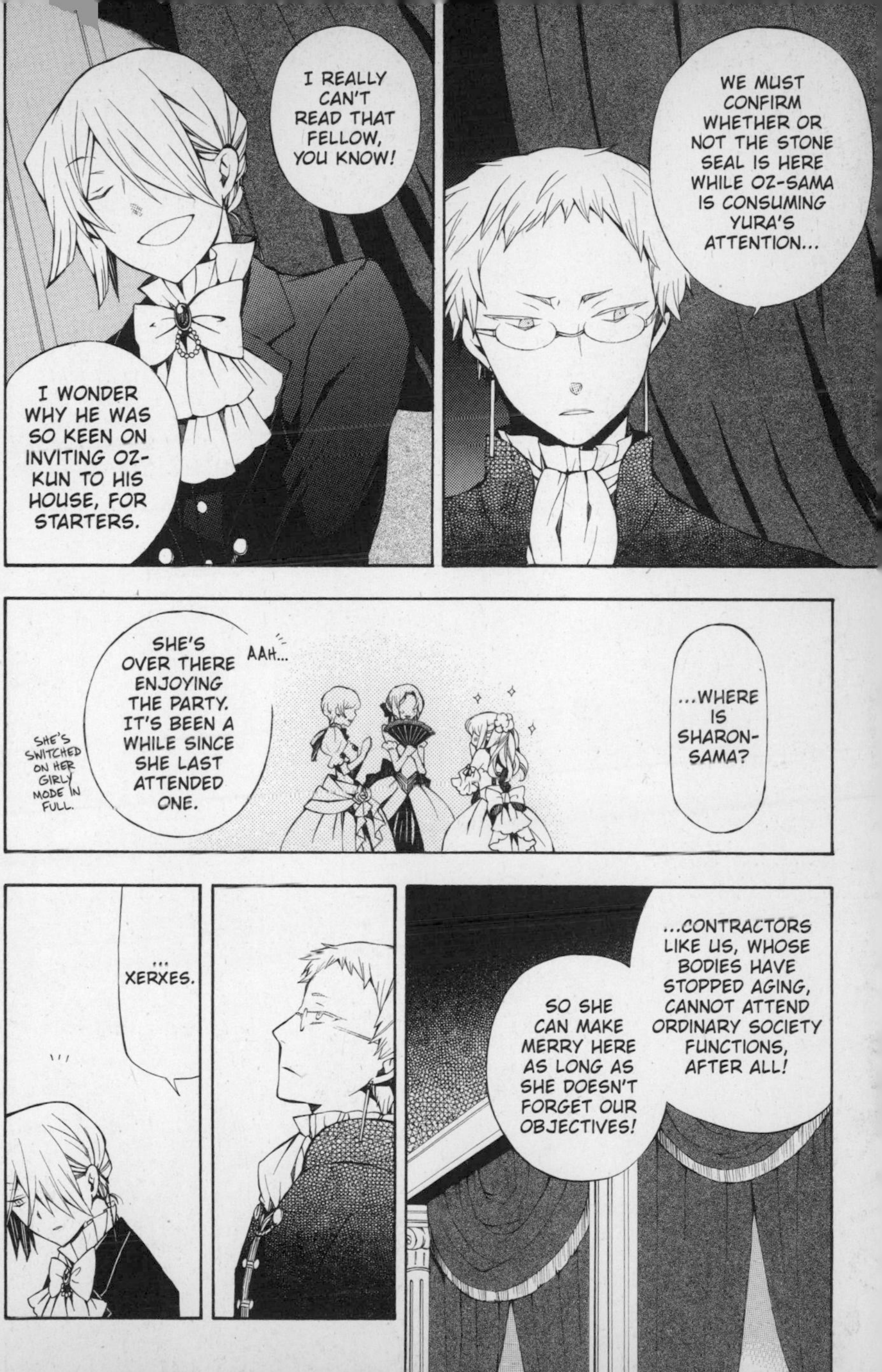
WE MUST CONFIRM WHETHER OR NOT THE STONE SEAL IS HERE WHILE OZ-SAMA IS CONSUMING YURA'S ATTENTION...
I REALLY CAN'T READ THAT FELLOW, YOU KNOW!
I WONDER WHY HE WAS SO KEEN ON INVITING OZ-KUN TO HIS HOUSE, FOR STARTERS.
...WHERE IS SHARON-SAMA?
AAH...
SHE'S OVER THERE ENJOYING THE PARTY. IT'S BEEN A WHILE SINCE SHE LAST ATTENDED ONE.
SHE'S SWITCHED ON HER GIRLY MODE IN FULL.
...CONTRACTORS LIKE US, WHOSE BODIES HAVE STOPPED AGING, CANNOT ATTEND ORDINARY SOCIETY FUNCTIONS, AFTER ALL!
SO SHE CAN MAKE MERRY HERE AS LONG AS SHE DOESN'T FORGET OUR OBJECTIVES!
... XERXES.

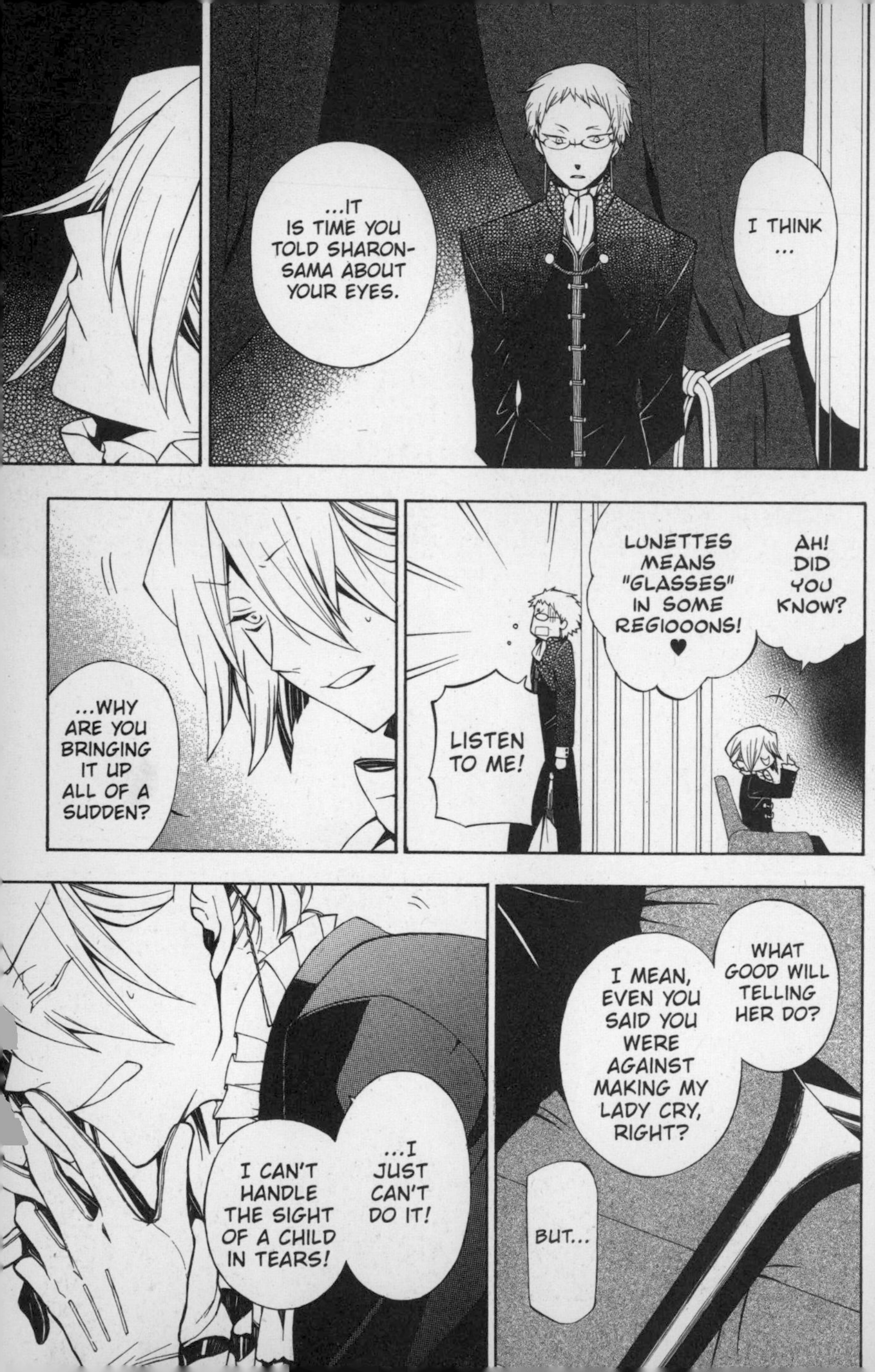
I THINK ...
...IT IS TIME YOU TOLD SHARON-SAMA ABOUT YOUR EYES.
AH! DID YOU KNOW?
LUNETTES MEANS "GLASSES" IN SOME REGIOOONS! ♥
LISTEN TO ME!
...WHY ARE YOU BRINGING IT UP ALL OF A SUDDEN?
WHAT GOOD WILL TELLING HER DO?
I MEAN, EVEN YOU SAID YOU WERE AGAINST MAKING MY LADY CRY, RIGHT?
BUT...
...I JUST CAN'T DO IT!
I CAN'T HANDLE THE SIGHT OF A CHILD IN TEARS!

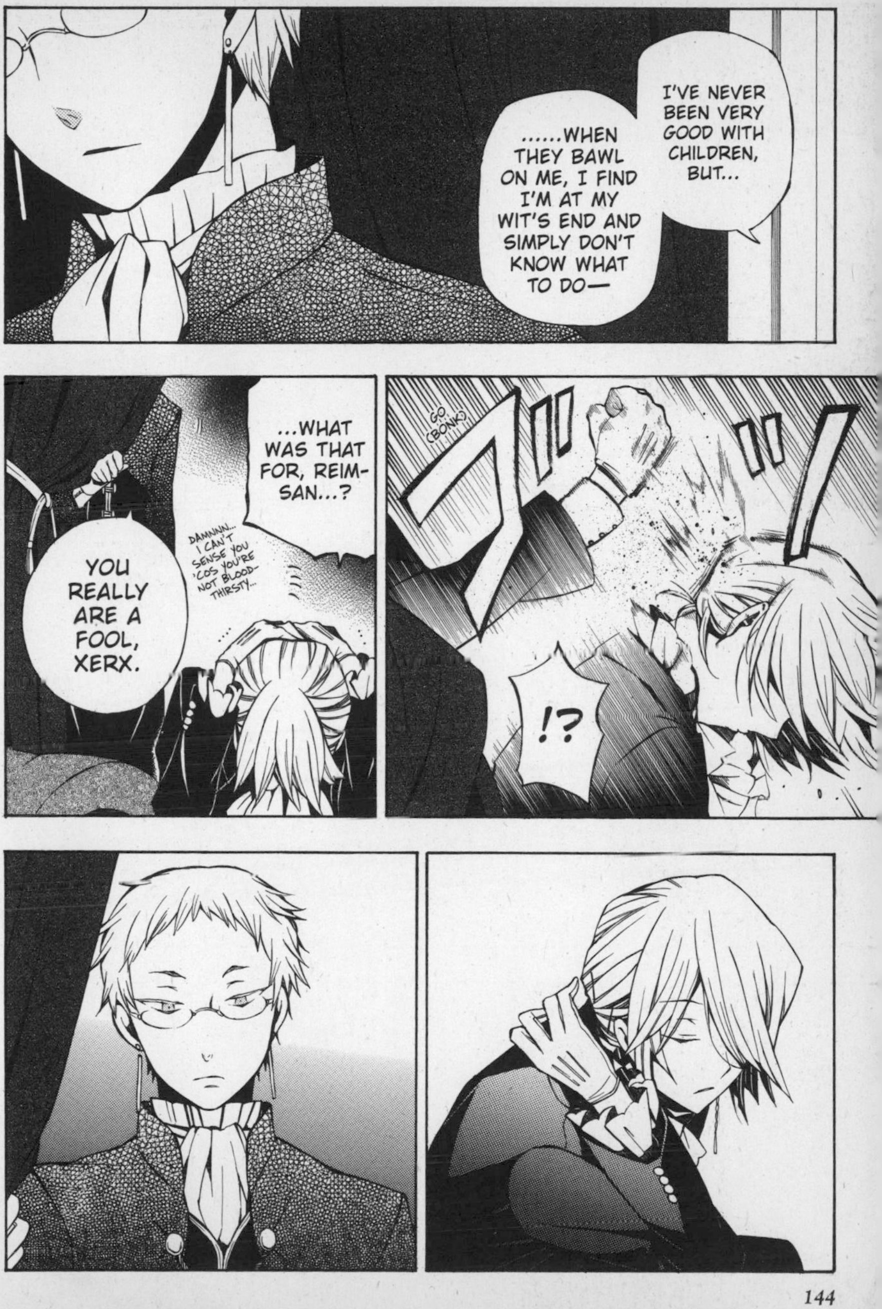
I'VE NEVER BEEN VERY GOOD WITH CHILDREN, BUT...
......WHEN THEY BAWL ON ME, I FIND I'M AT MY WIT'S END AND SIMPLY DON'T KNOW WHAT TO DO—
GO (BONK)
!?
...WHAT WAS THAT FOR, REIM-SAN...?
DAMNNN... I CAN'T SENSE YOU 'COS YOU'RE NOT BLOOD-THIRSTY...
YOU REALLY ARE A FOOL, XERX.

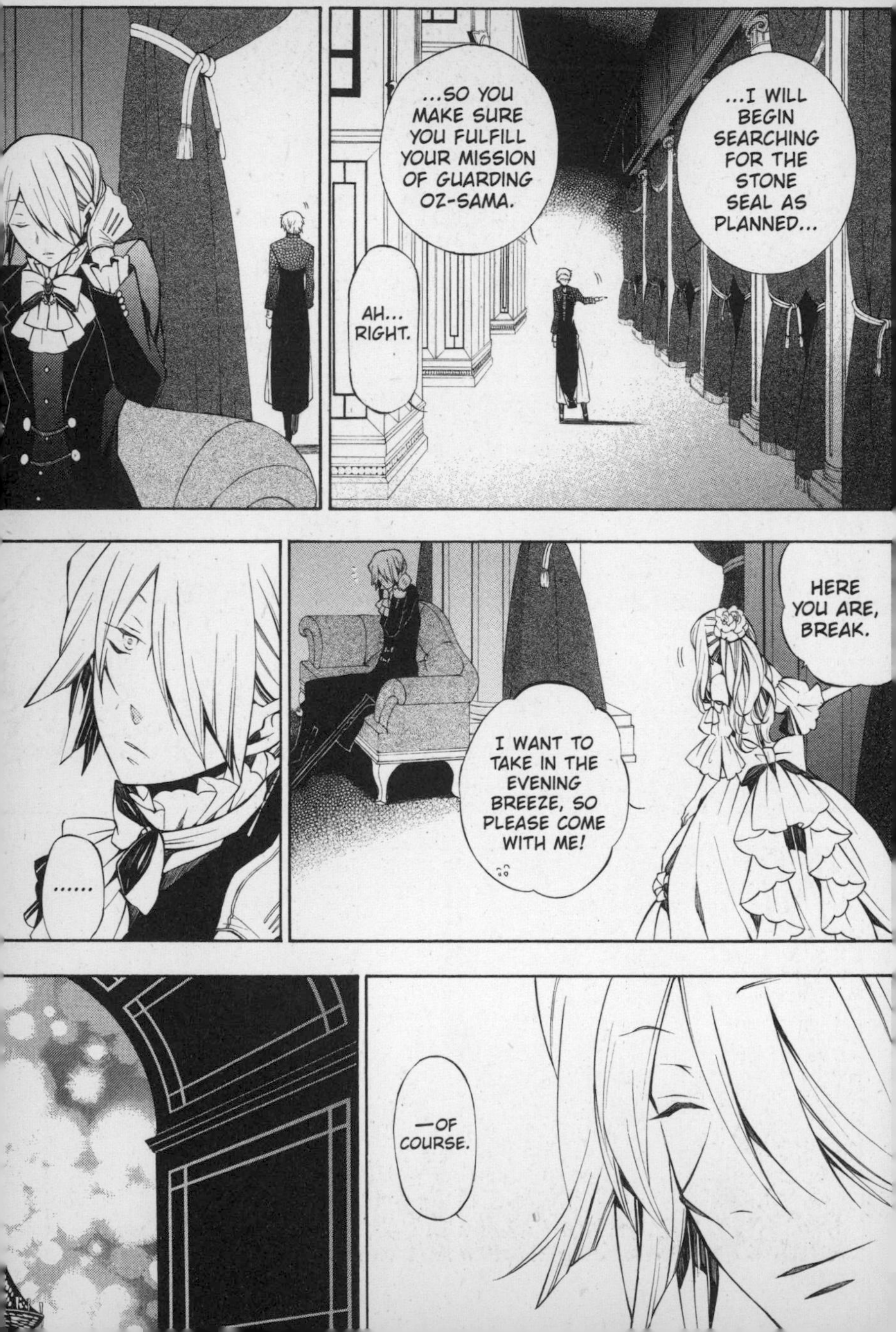
...I WILL BEGIN SEARCHING FOR THE STONE SEAL AS PLANNED...
...SO YOU MAKE SURE YOU FULFILL YOUR MISSION OF GUARDING OZ-SAMA.
AH... RIGHT.
HERE YOU ARE, BREAK.
I WANT TO TAKE IN THE EVENING BREEZE, SO PLEASE COME WITH ME!
......
—OF COURSE.

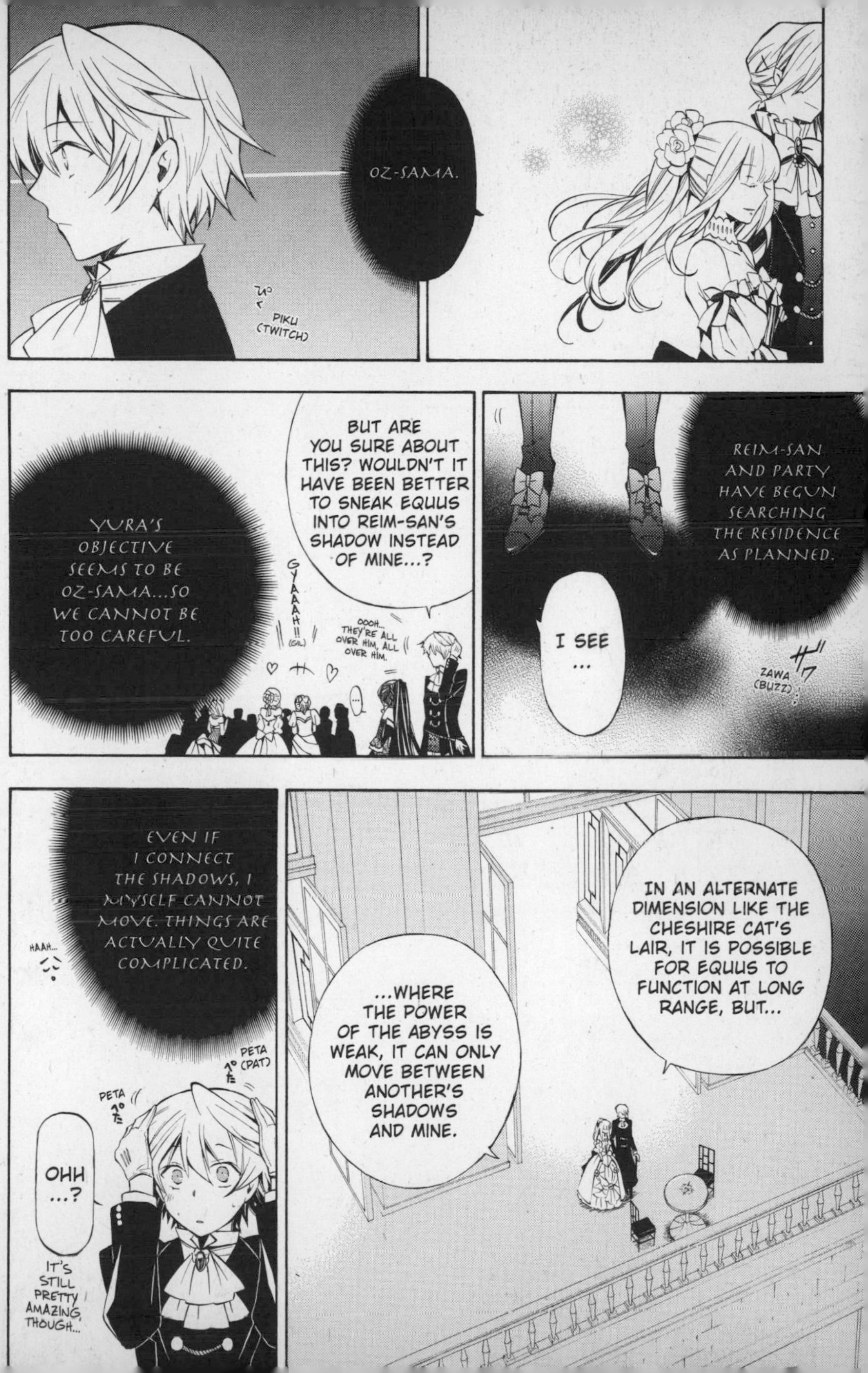
OZ-SAMA.
PIKU (TWITCH)
REIM-SAN AND PARTY HAVE BEGUN SEARCHING THE RESIDENCE AS PLANNED.
I SEE...
ZAWA (BUZZ)
BUT ARE YOU SURE ABOUT THIS? WOULDN'T IT HAVE BEEN BETTER TO SNEAK EQUUS INTO REIM-SAN'S SHADOW INSTEAD OF MINE...?
YURA'S OBJECTIVE SEEMS TO BE OZ-SAMA...SO WE CANNOT BE TOO CAREFUL.
GYAAAAH!! (GIL)
OOOH... THEY'RE ALL OVER HIM, ALL OVER HIM.
...
IN AN ALTERNATE DIMENSION LIKE THE CHESHIRE CAT'S LAIR, IT IS POSSIBLE FOR EQUUS TO FUNCTION AT LONG RANGE, BUT...
...WHERE THE POWER OF THE ABYSS IS WEAK, IT CAN ONLY MOVE BETWEEN ANOTHER'S SHADOWS AND MINE.
EVEN IF I CONNECT THE SHADOWS, I MYSELF CANNOT MOVE. THINGS ARE ACTUALLY QUITE COMPLICATED.
HAAH...
PETA (PAT)
PETA
OHH ...?
IT'S STILL PRETTY AMAZING THOUGH...

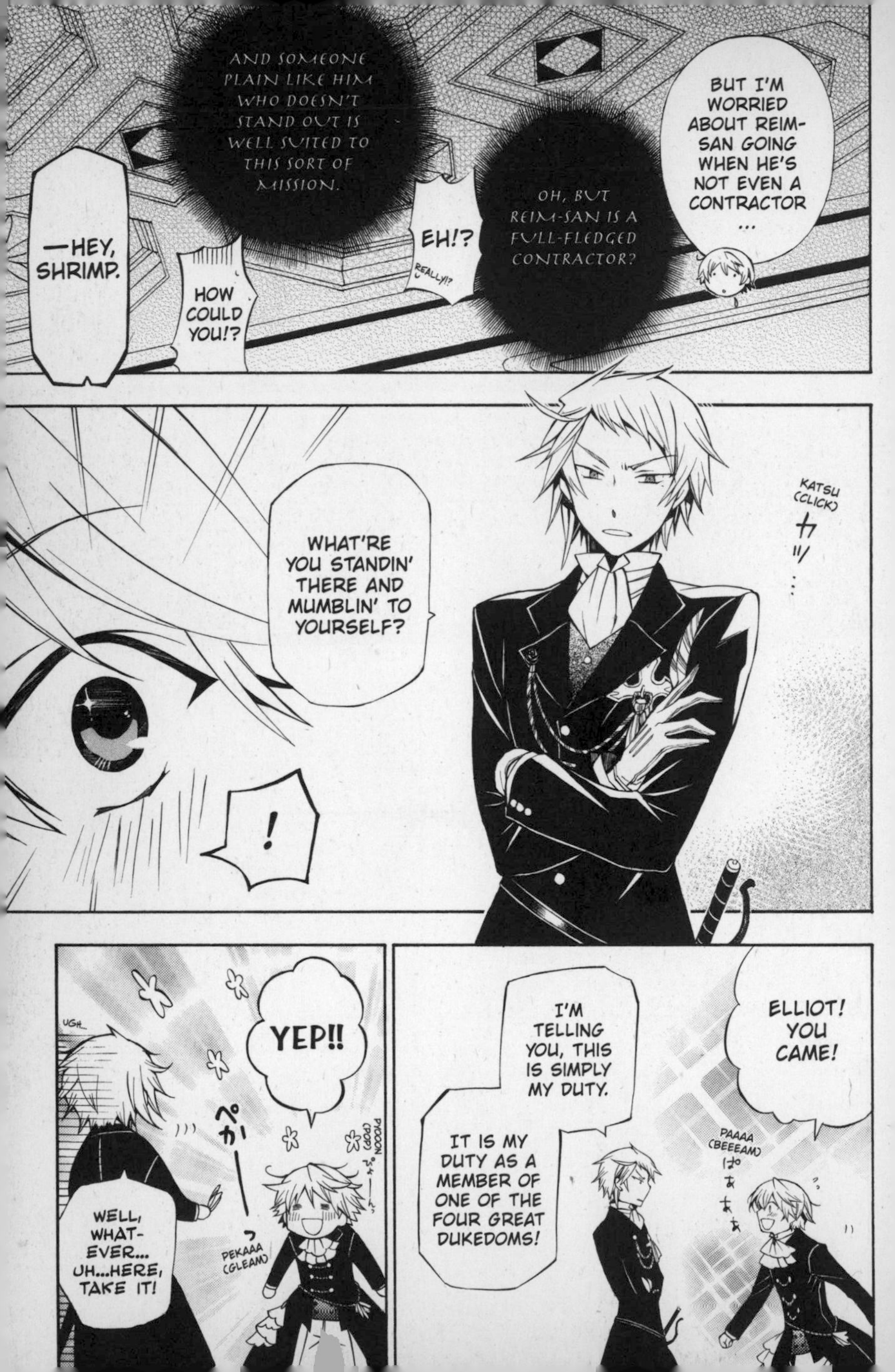
BUT I'M WORRIED ABOUT REIM-SAN GOING WHEN HE'S NOT EVEN A CONTRACTOR ...
OH, BUT REIM-SAN IS A FULL-FLEDGED CONTRACTOR?
EH!?
REALLY!?
AND SOMEONE PLAIN LIKE HIM WHO DOESN'T STAND OUT IS WELL SUITED TO THIS SORT OF MISSION.
HOW COULD YOU!?
—HEY, SHRIMP.
KATSU (CLICK)
カッ
WHAT'RE YOU STANDIN' THERE AND MUMBLIN' TO YOURSELF?
!
ELLIOT! YOU CAME!
PAAAA (BEEEAM)
ぱあぁ
I'M TELLING YOU, THIS IS SIMPLY MY DUTY.
IT IS MY DUTY AS A MEMBER OF ONE OF THE FOUR GREAT DUKEDOMS!
YEP!!
PYOOON (POP)
ぺか—
PEKAAA (GLEAM)
UGH...
WELL, WHAT-EVER... UH...HERE, TAKE IT!

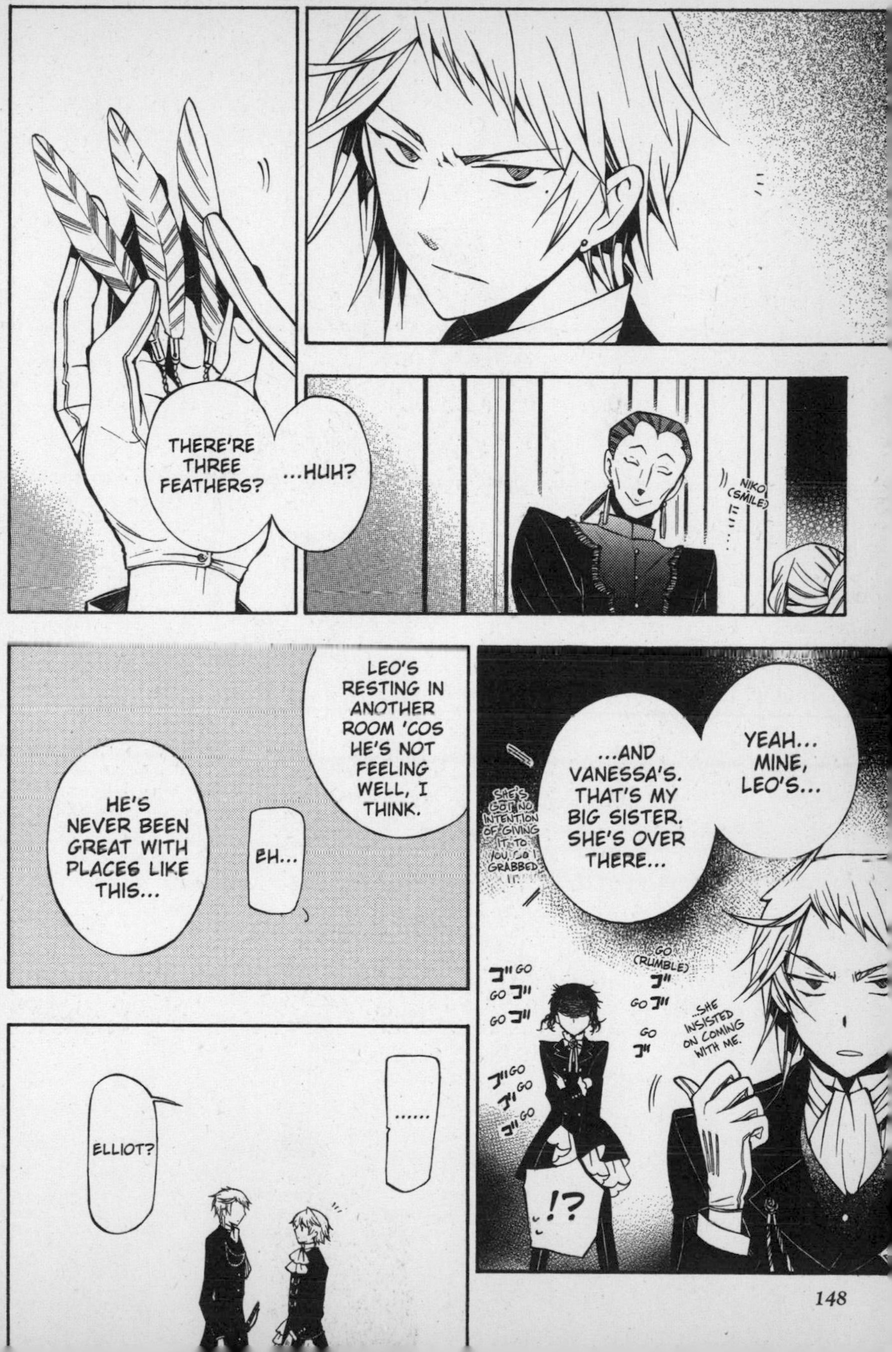
NIKO (SMILE)
...HUH?
THERE'RE THREE FEATHERS?
YEAH... MINE, LEO'S...
...AND VANESSA'S. THAT'S MY BIG SISTER. SHE'S OVER THERE...
SHE'S GOT NO INTENTION OF GIVING IT TO YOU, SO I GRABBED IT.
GO (RUMBLE)
...SHE INSISTED ON COMING WITH ME.
!?
LEO'S RESTING IN ANOTHER ROOM 'COS HE'S NOT FEELING WELL, I THINK.
EH...
HE'S NEVER BEEN GREAT WITH PLACES LIKE THIS...
......
ELLIOT?

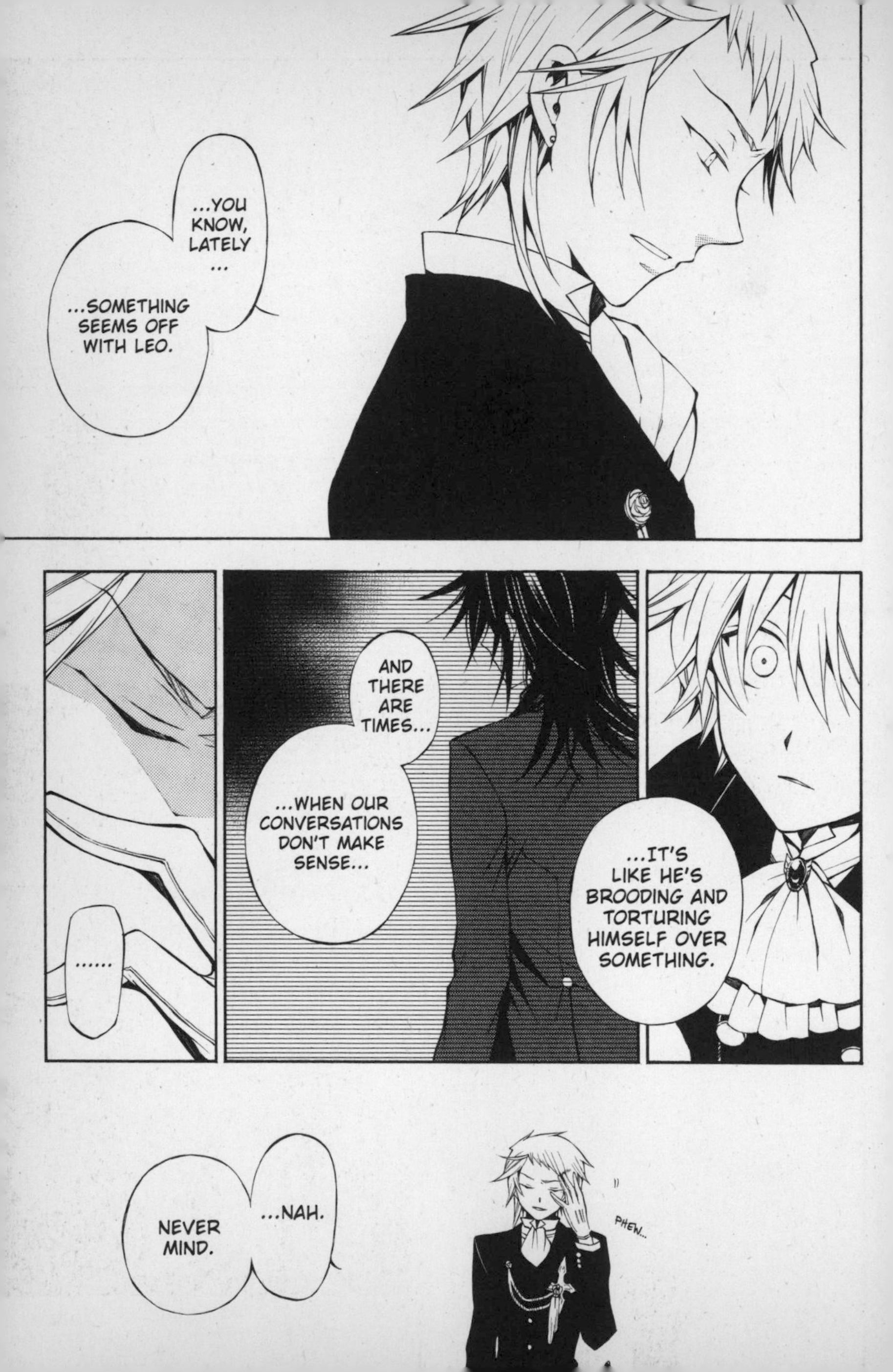

...YOU KNOW, LATELY ...
...SOMETHING SEEMS OFF WITH LEO.
AND THERE ARE TIMES...
...WHEN OUR CONVERSATIONS DON'T MAKE SENSE...
...IT'S LIKE HE'S BROODING AND TORTURING HIMSELF OVER SOMETHING.
......
...NAH.
NEVER MIND.
PHEW...

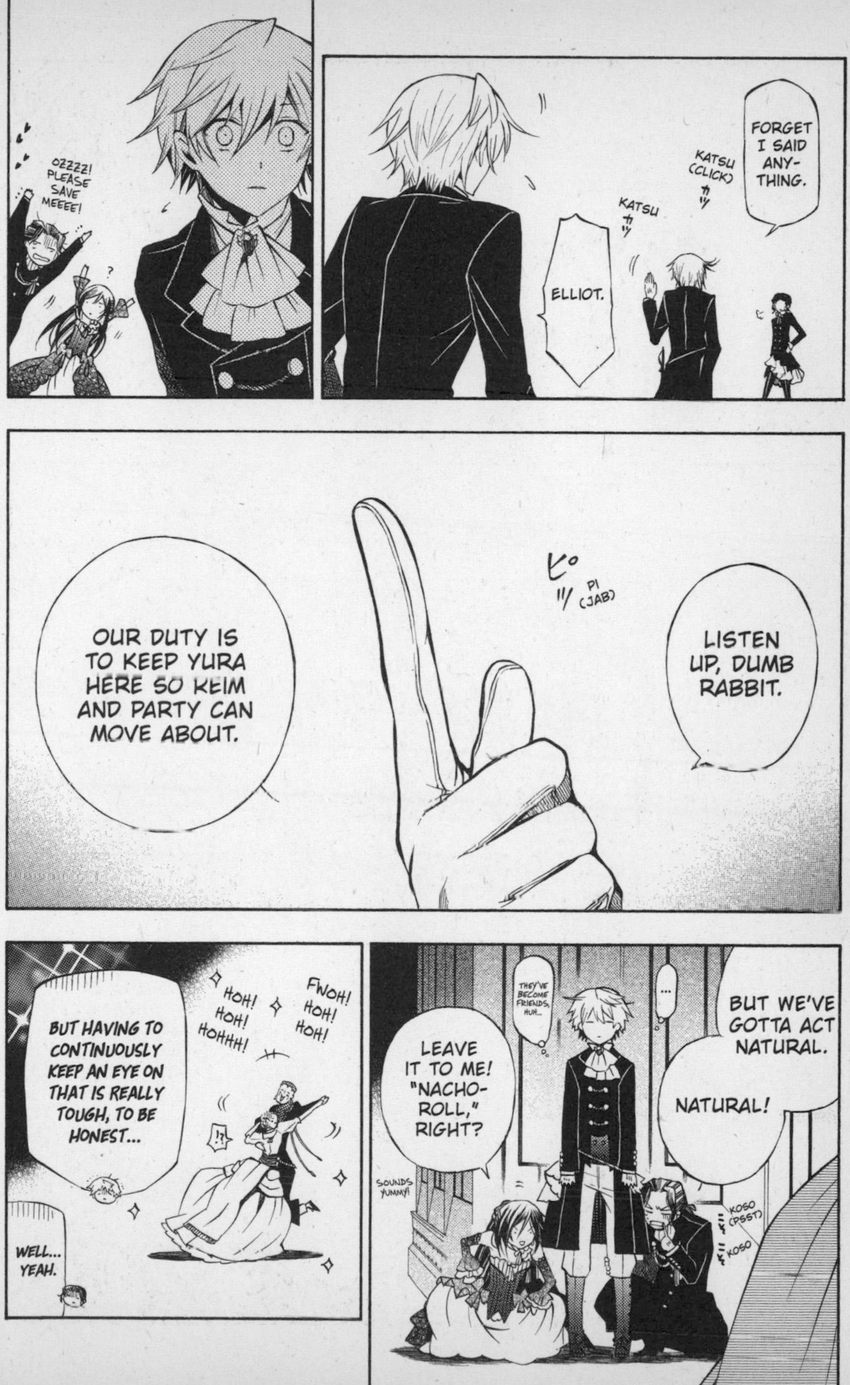
FORGET I SAID ANYTHING.
KATSU (CLICK)
KATSU
ELLIOT.
OZZZZ! PLEASE SAVE MEEEE!
LISTEN UP, DUMB RABBIT.
PI (JAB)
OUR DUTY IS TO KEEP YURA HERE SO KEIM AND PARTY CAN MOVE ABOUT.
BUT WE'VE GOTTA ACT NATURAL.
NATURAL!
...
THEY'VE BECOME FRIENDS, HUH...
LEAVE IT TO ME! "NACHO-ROLL," RIGHT?
KOSO (PSST)
KOSO
SOUNDS YUMMY!
FWOH! HOH! HOH!
HOH! HOH! HOHHHH!
!?
BUT HAVING TO CONTINUOUSLY KEEP AN EYE ON THAT IS REALLY TOUGH, TO BE HONEST...
WELL... YEAH.

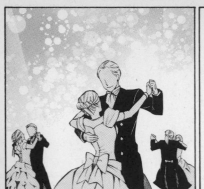

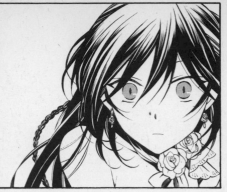

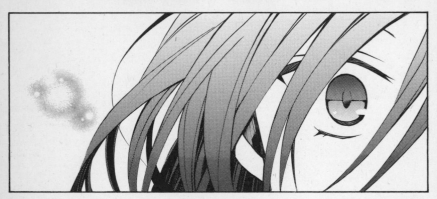

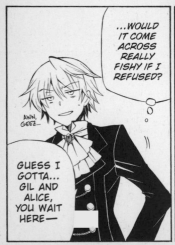

...WOULD IT COME ACROSS REALLY FISHY IF I REFUSED?

AWW, GEEZ...

GUESS I GOTTA... GIL AND ALICE, YOU WAIT HERE—

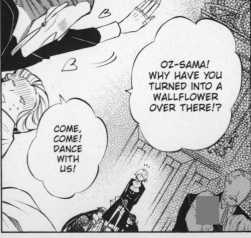

OZ-SAMA! WHY HAVE YOU TURNED INTO A WALLFLOWER OVER THERE!?

COME, COME! DANCE WITH US!

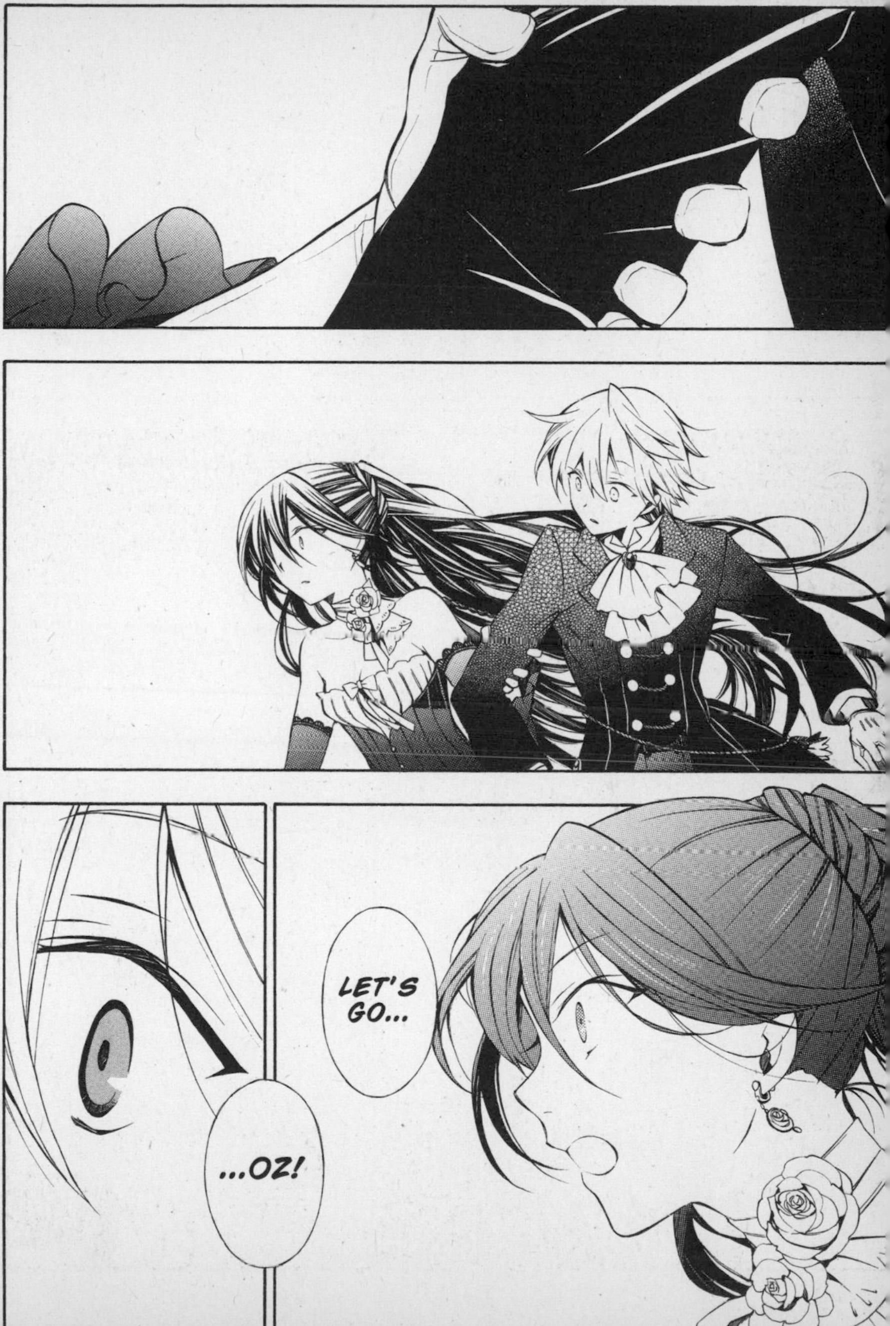
LET'S GO...
...OZ!

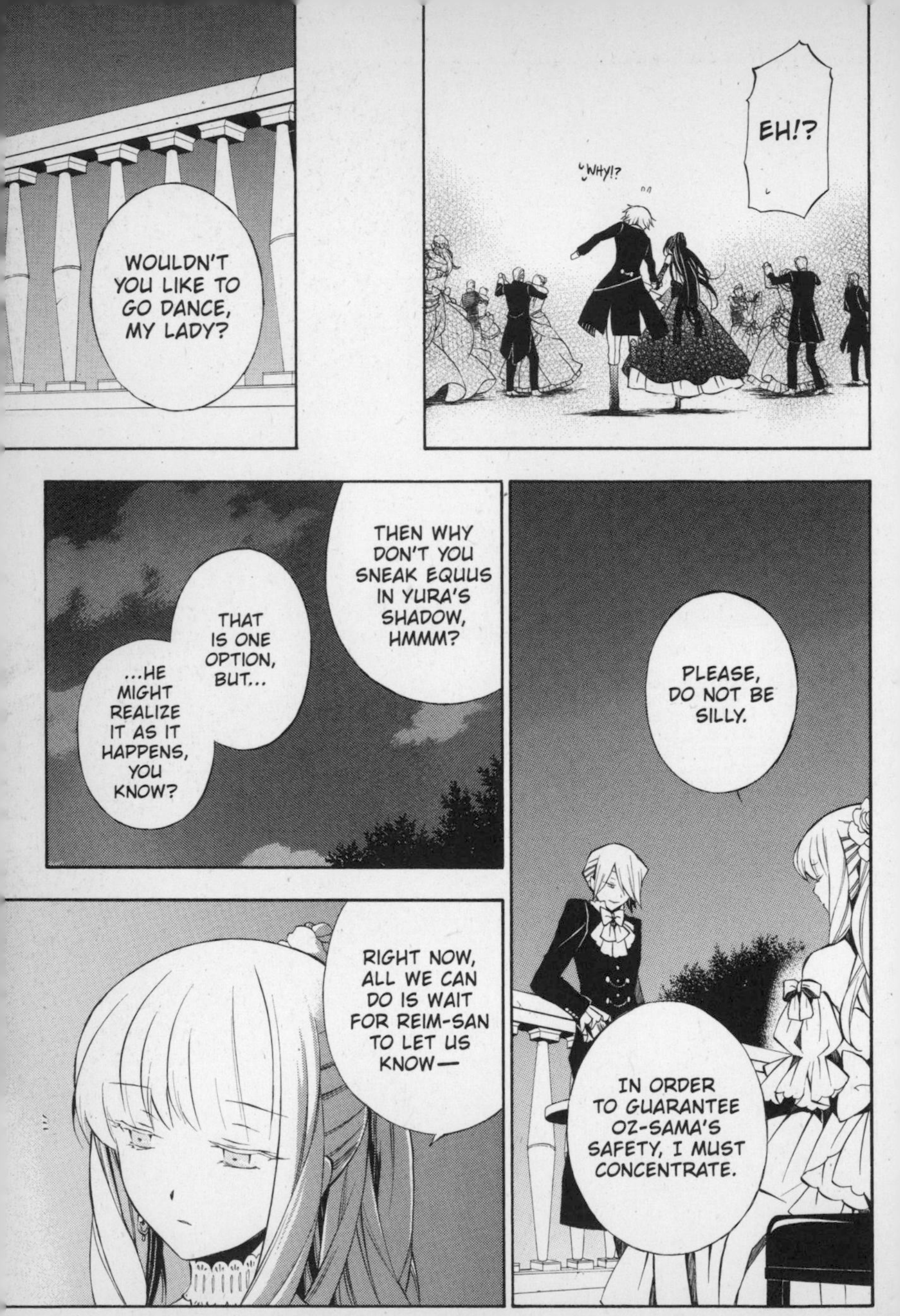
EH!?
WHY!?
WOULDN'T YOU LIKE TO GO DANCE, MY LADY?
PLEASE, DO NOT BE SILLY.
IN ORDER TO GUARANTEE OZ-SAMA'S SAFETY, I MUST CONCENTRATE.
THEN WHY DON'T YOU SNEAK EQUUS IN YURA'S SHADOW, HMMM?
THAT IS ONE OPTION, BUT...
...HE MIGHT REALIZE IT AS IT HAPPENS, YOU KNOW?
RIGHT NOW, ALL WE CAN DO IS WAIT FOR REIM-SAN TO LET US KNOW—

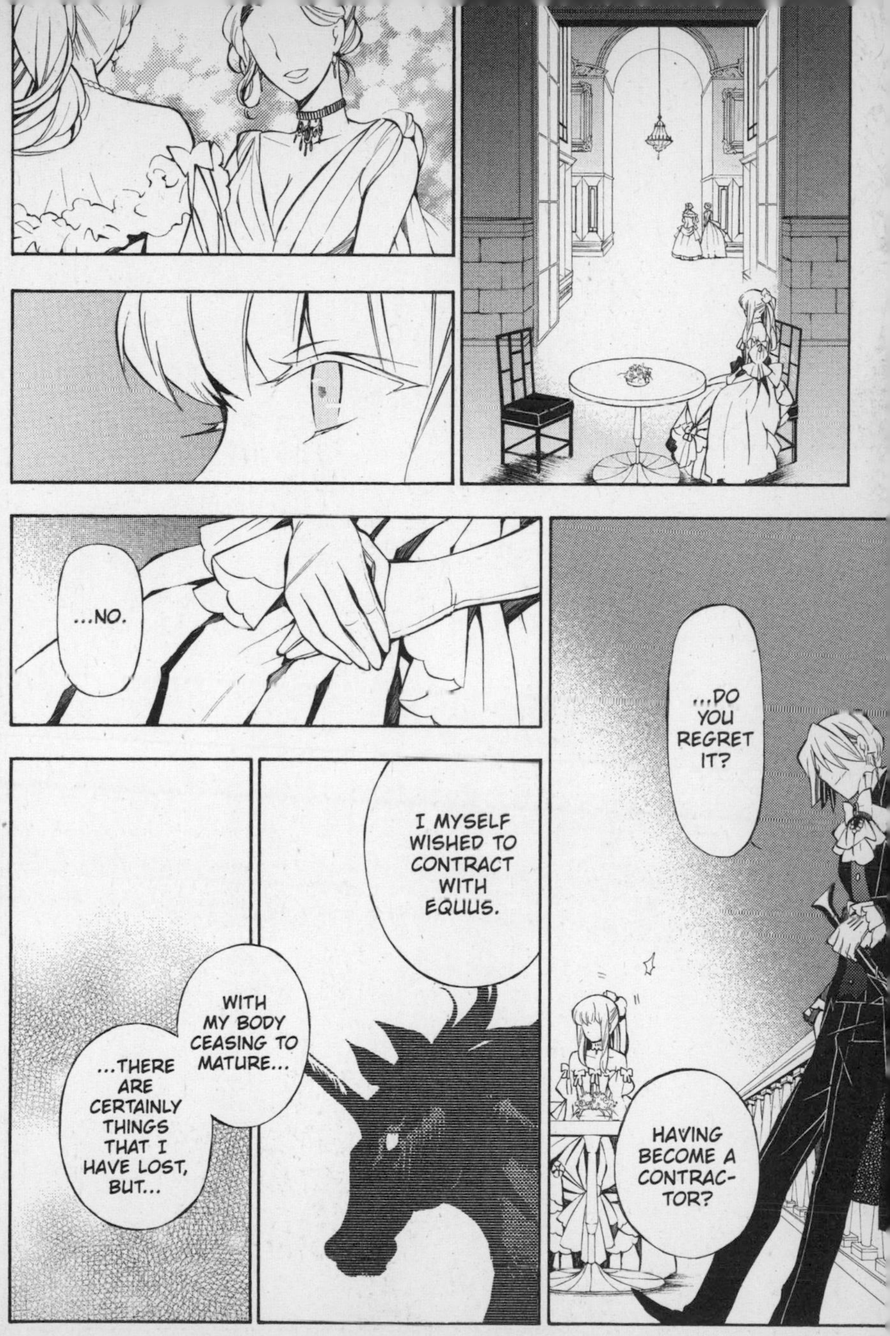
...DO YOU REGRET IT?
HAVING BECOME A CONTRAC-TOR?
...NO.
I MYSELF WISHED TO CONTRACT WITH EQUUS.
WITH MY BODY CEASING TO MATURE...
...THERE ARE CERTAINLY THINGS THAT I HAVE LOST, BUT...

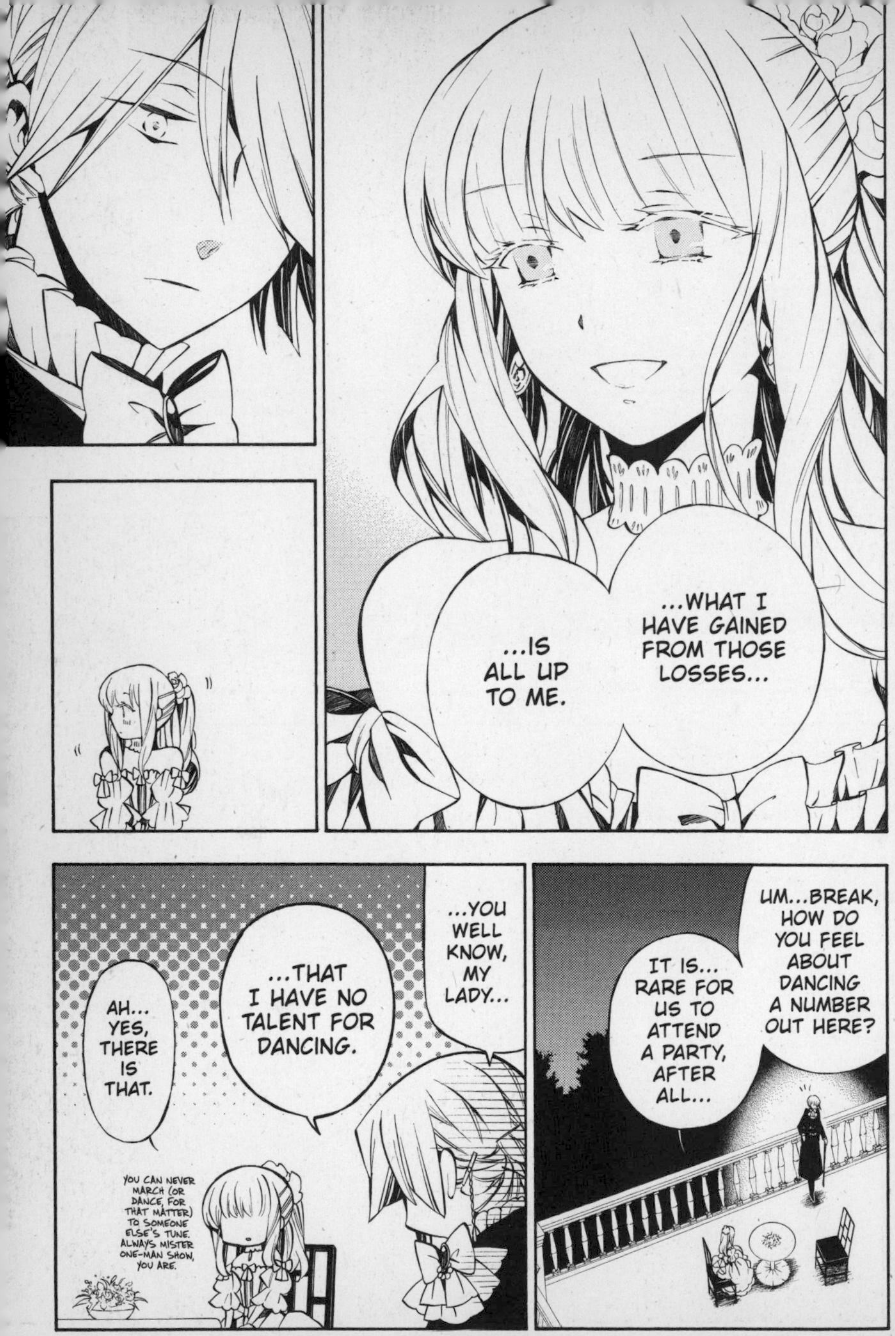
...WHAT I HAVE GAINED FROM THOSE LOSSES...
...IS ALL UP TO ME.
UM...BREAK, HOW DO YOU FEEL ABOUT DANCING A NUMBER OUT HERE?
IT IS... RARE FOR US TO ATTEND A PARTY, AFTER ALL...
...YOU WELL KNOW, MY LADY...
...THAT I HAVE NO TALENT FOR DANCING.
AH... YES, THERE IS THAT.
YOU CAN NEVER MARCH (OR DANCE, FOR THAT MATTER) TO SOMEONE ELSE'S TUNE. ALWAYS MISTER ONE-MAN SHOW, YOU ARE.

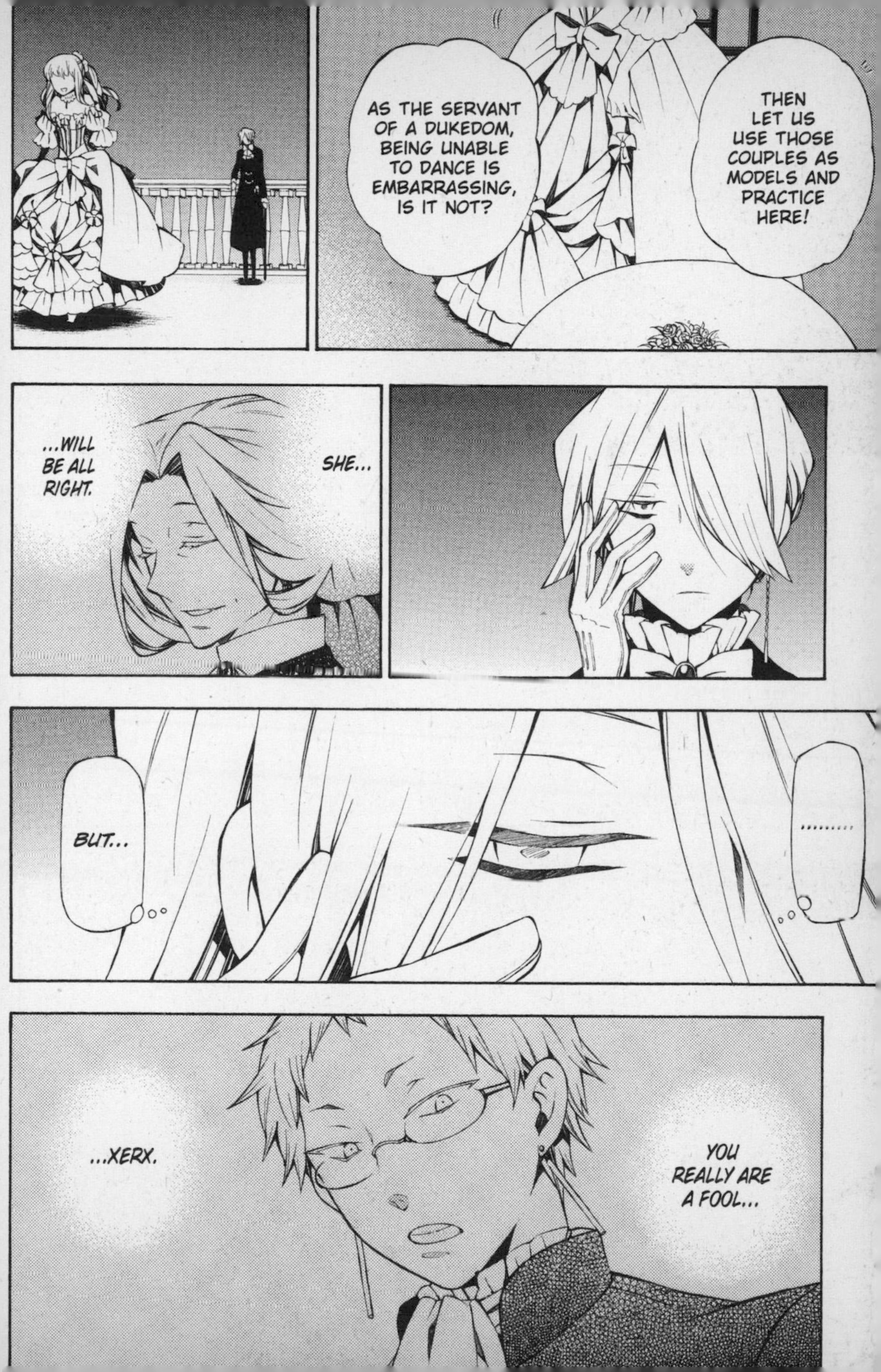
AS THE SERVANT OF A DUKEDOM, BEING UNABLE TO DANCE IS EMBARRASSING, IS IT NOT?
THEN LET US USE THOSE COUPLES AS MODELS AND PRACTICE HERE!
SHE...
...WILL BE ALL RIGHT.
....
BUT...
YOU REALLY ARE A FOOL...
...XERX.

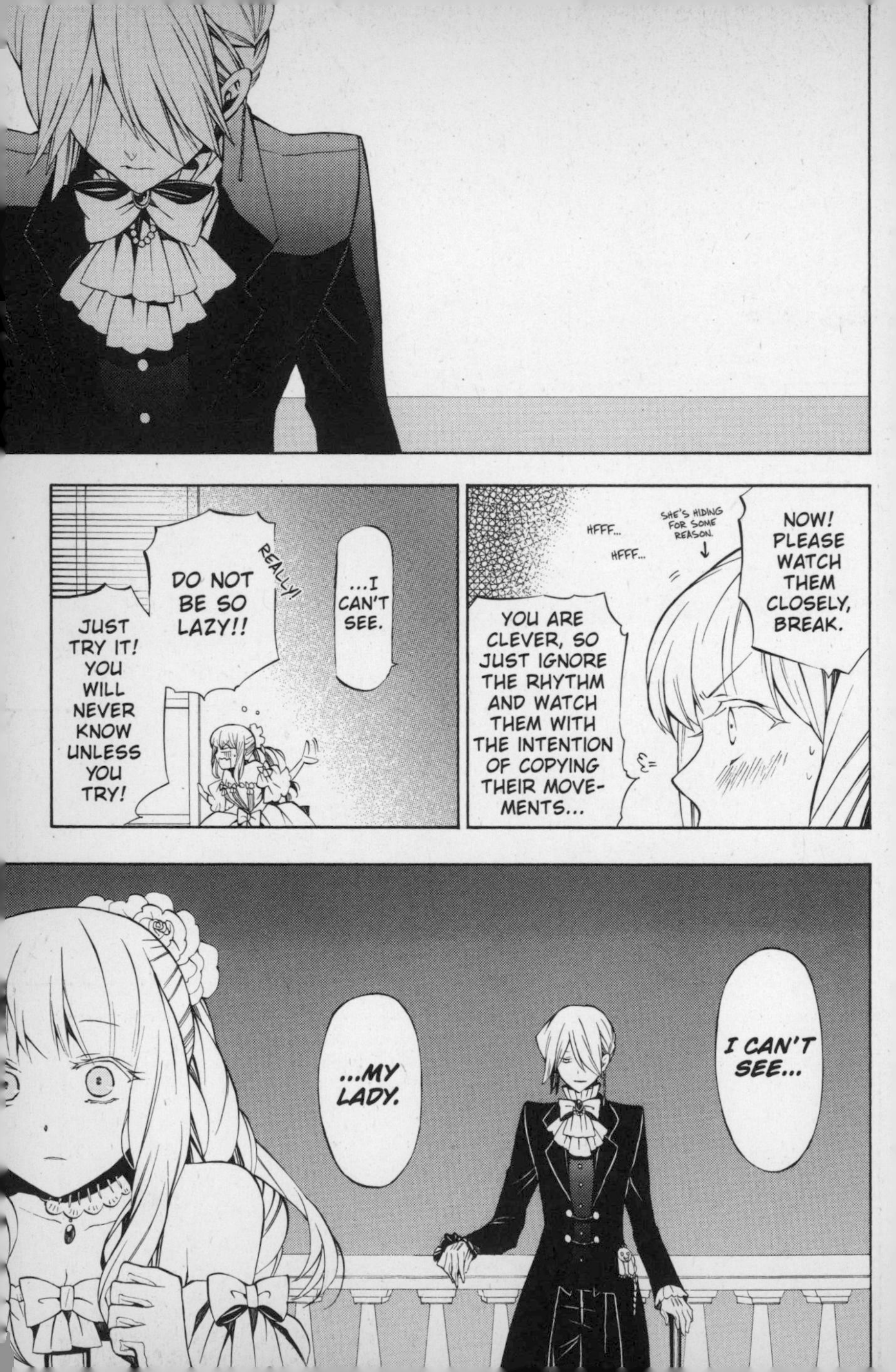
NOW! PLEASE WATCH THEM CLOSELY, BREAK.
SHE'S HIDING FOR SOME REASON.
HFFF...
HFFF...
YOU ARE CLEVER, SO JUST IGNORE THE RHYTHM AND WATCH THEM WITH THE INTENTION OF COPYING THEIR MOVE-MENTS...
...I CAN'T SEE.
DO NOT BE SO LAZY!!
REALLY!
JUST TRY IT! YOU WILL NEVER KNOW UNLESS YOU TRY!
I CAN'T SEE...
...MY LADY.

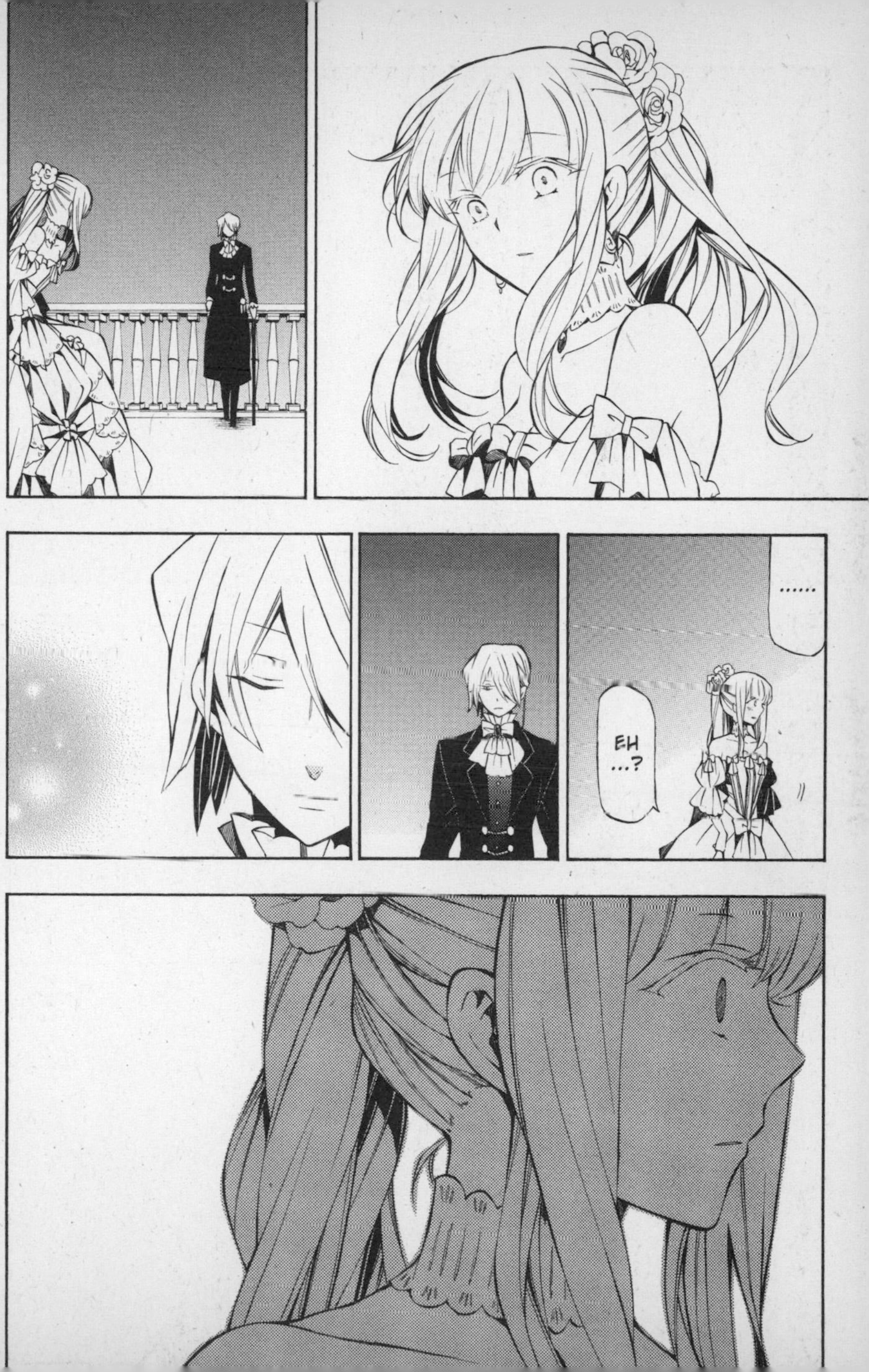
......
EH ...?

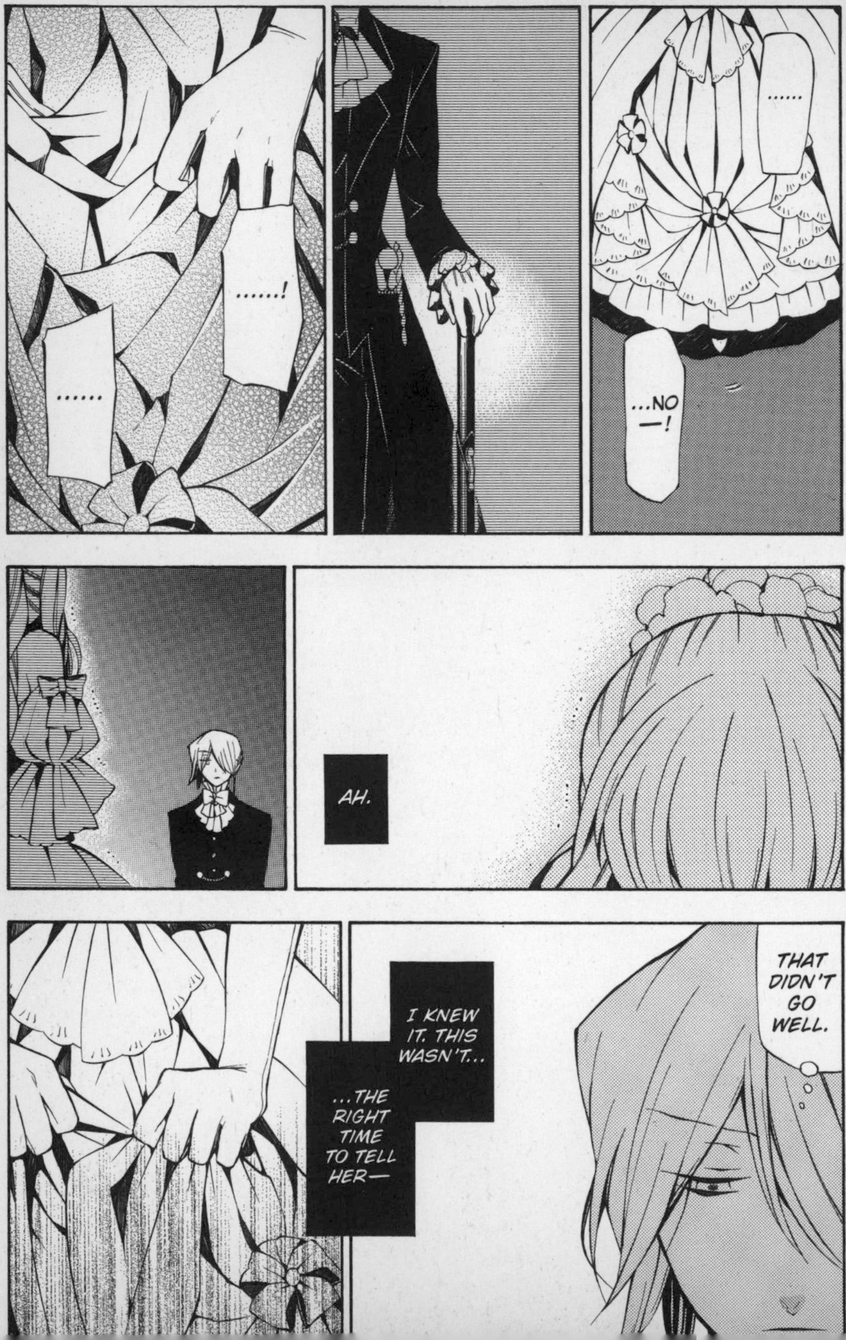
......
...NO —!
......!
......
AH.
THAT DIDN'T GO WELL.
I KNEW IT. THIS WASN'T...
...THE RIGHT TIME TO TELL HER—

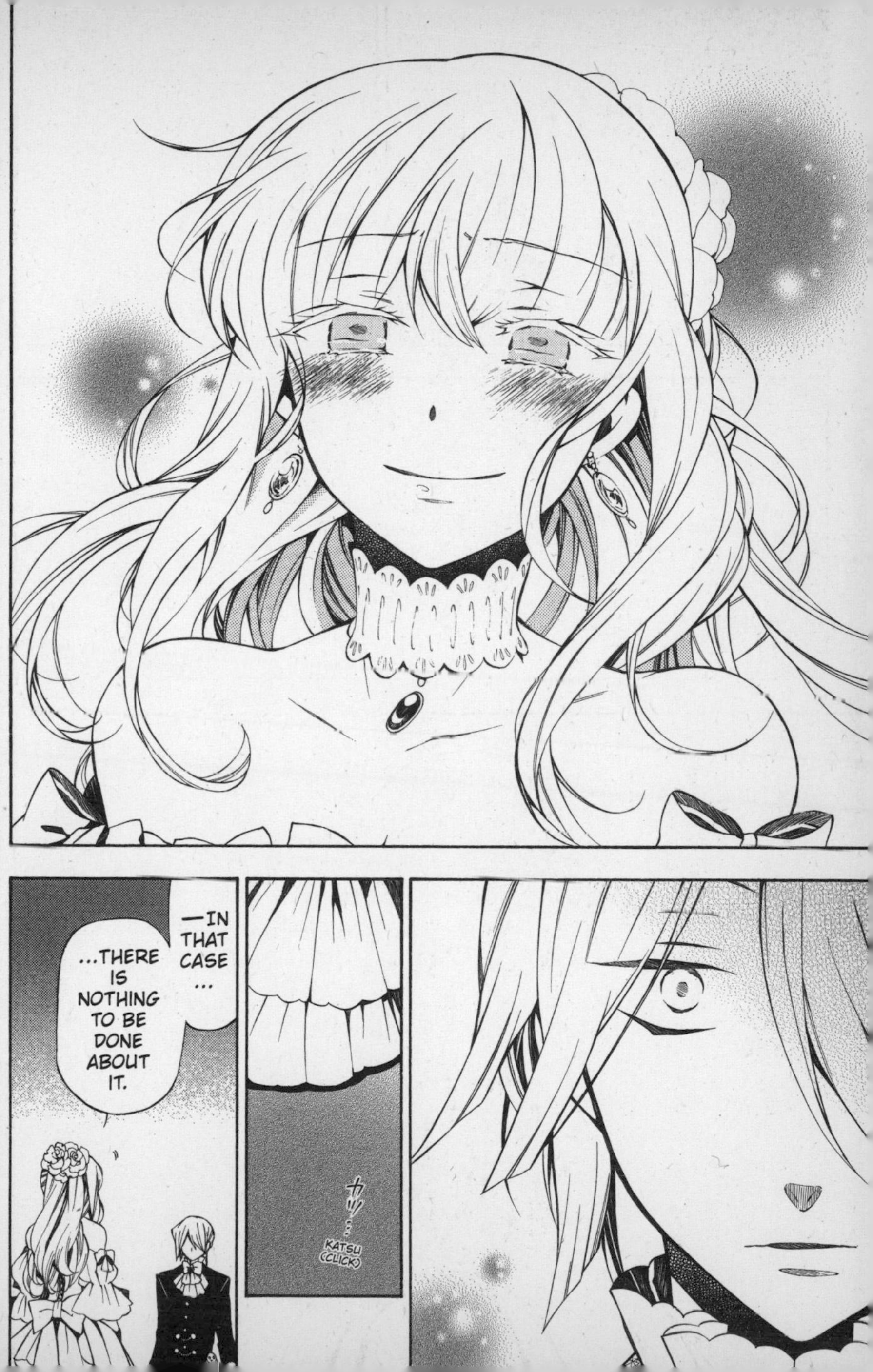
KATSU (CLICK)
—IN THAT CASE ...
...THERE IS NOTHING TO BE DONE ABOUT IT.

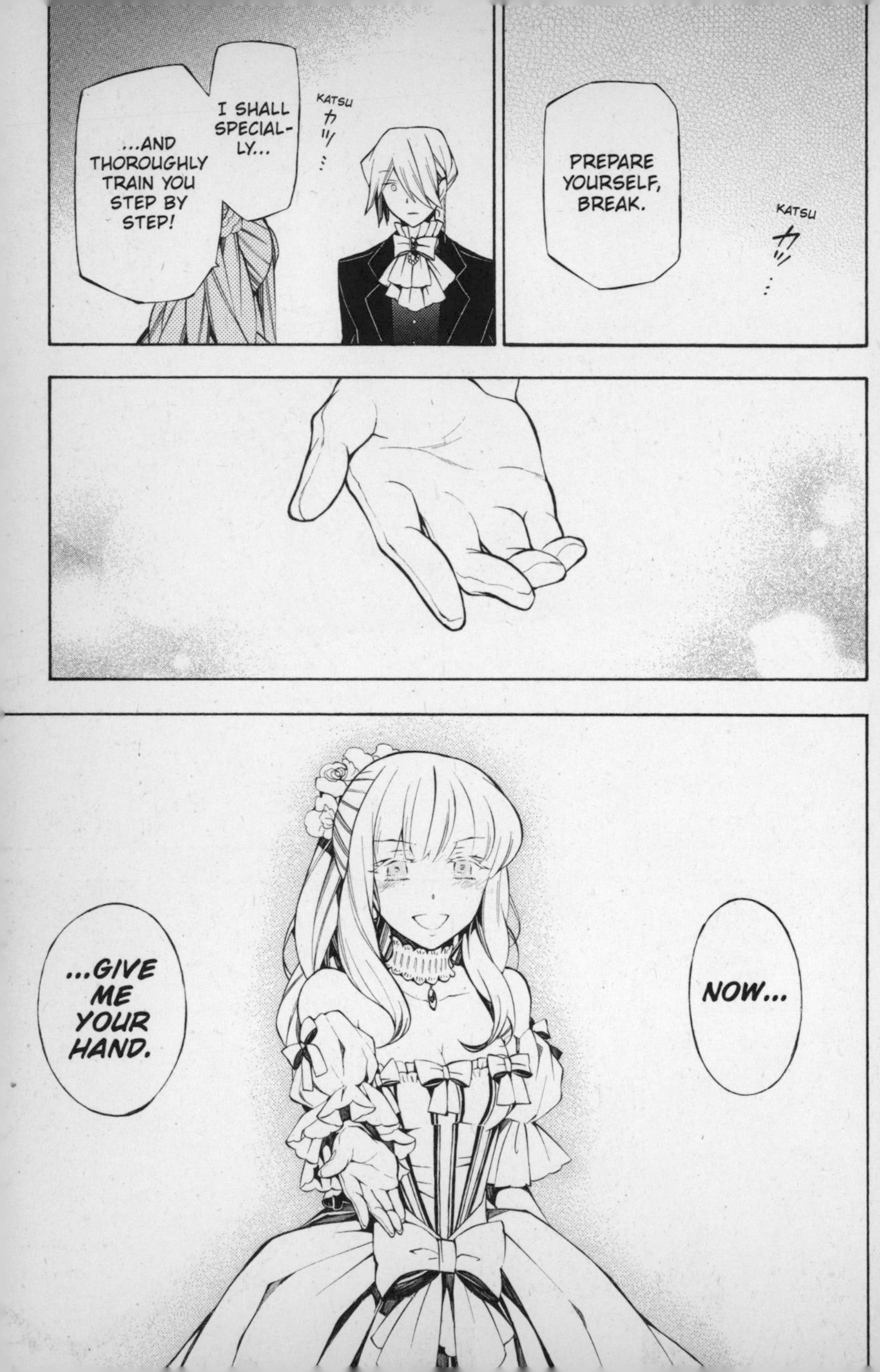
KATSU
PREPARE YOURSELF, BREAK.
I SHALL SPECIAL-LY...
...AND THOROUGHLY TRAIN YOU STEP BY STEP!
KATSU
NOW...
...GIVE ME YOUR HAND.

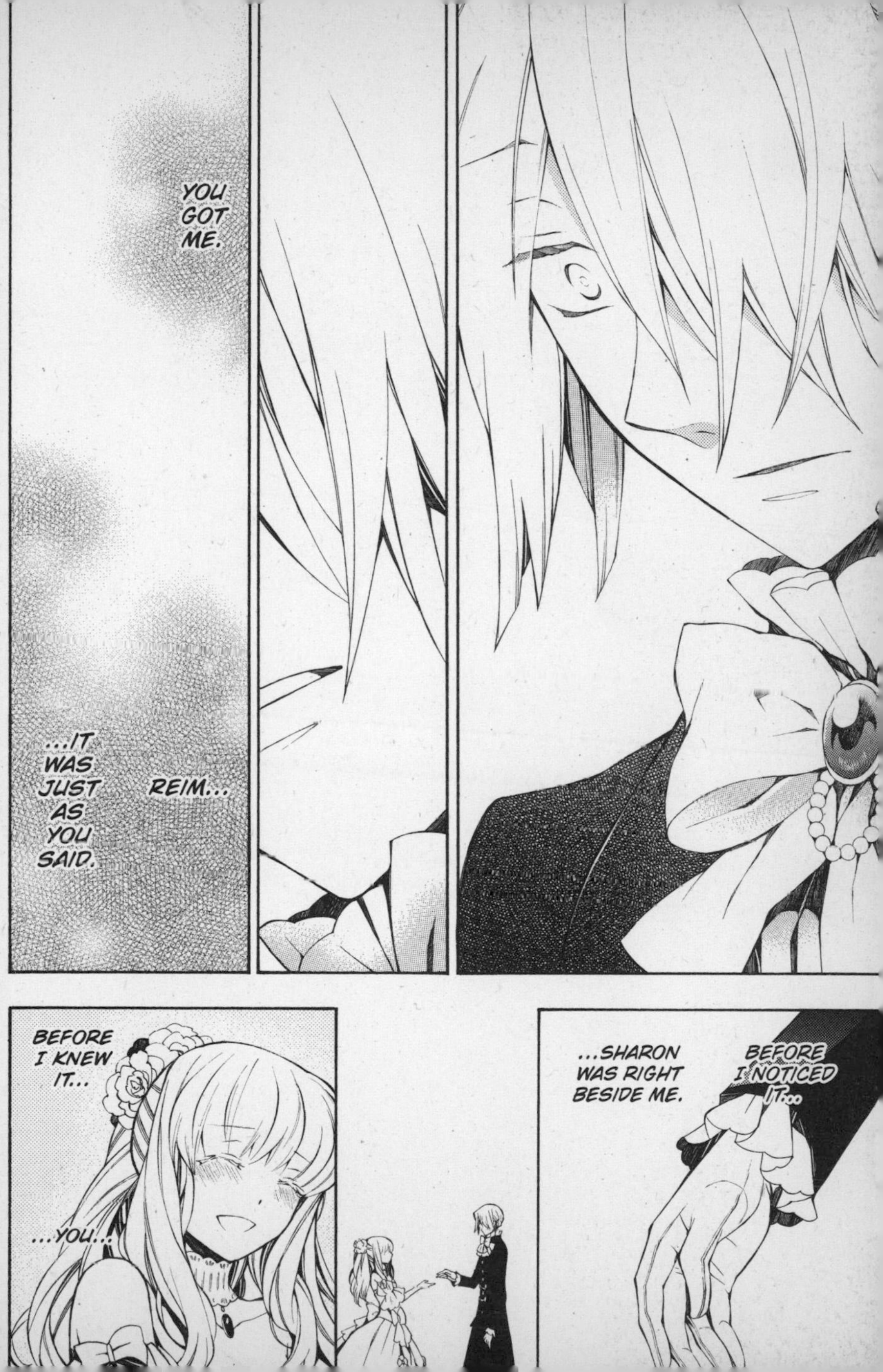
YOU GOT ME.
REIM...
...IT WAS JUST AS YOU SAID.
BEFORE I NOTICED IT...
...SHARON WAS RIGHT BESIDE ME.
BEFORE I KNEW IT...
...YOU...

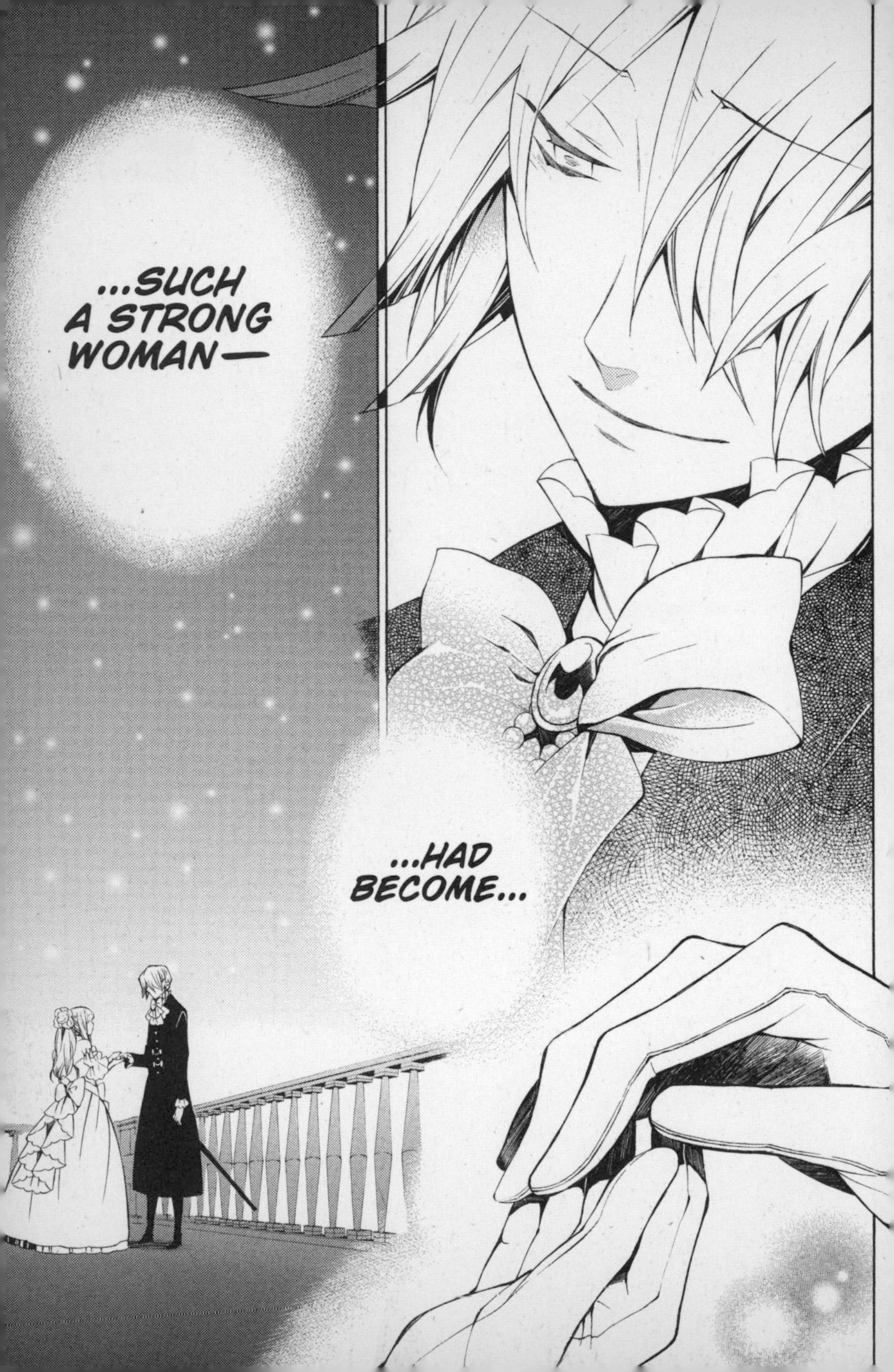
...HAD BECOME...
...SUCH A STRONG WOMAN—

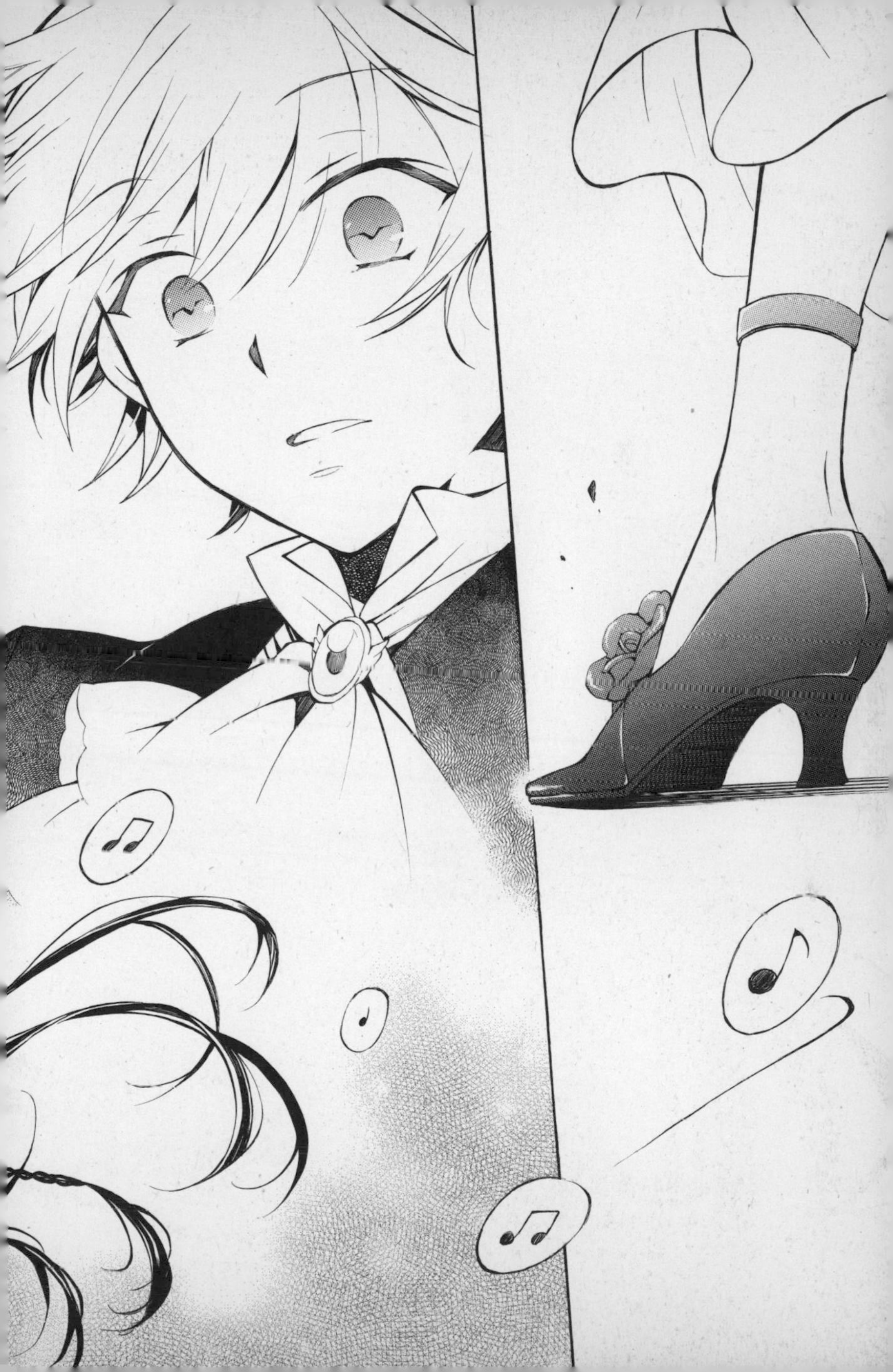

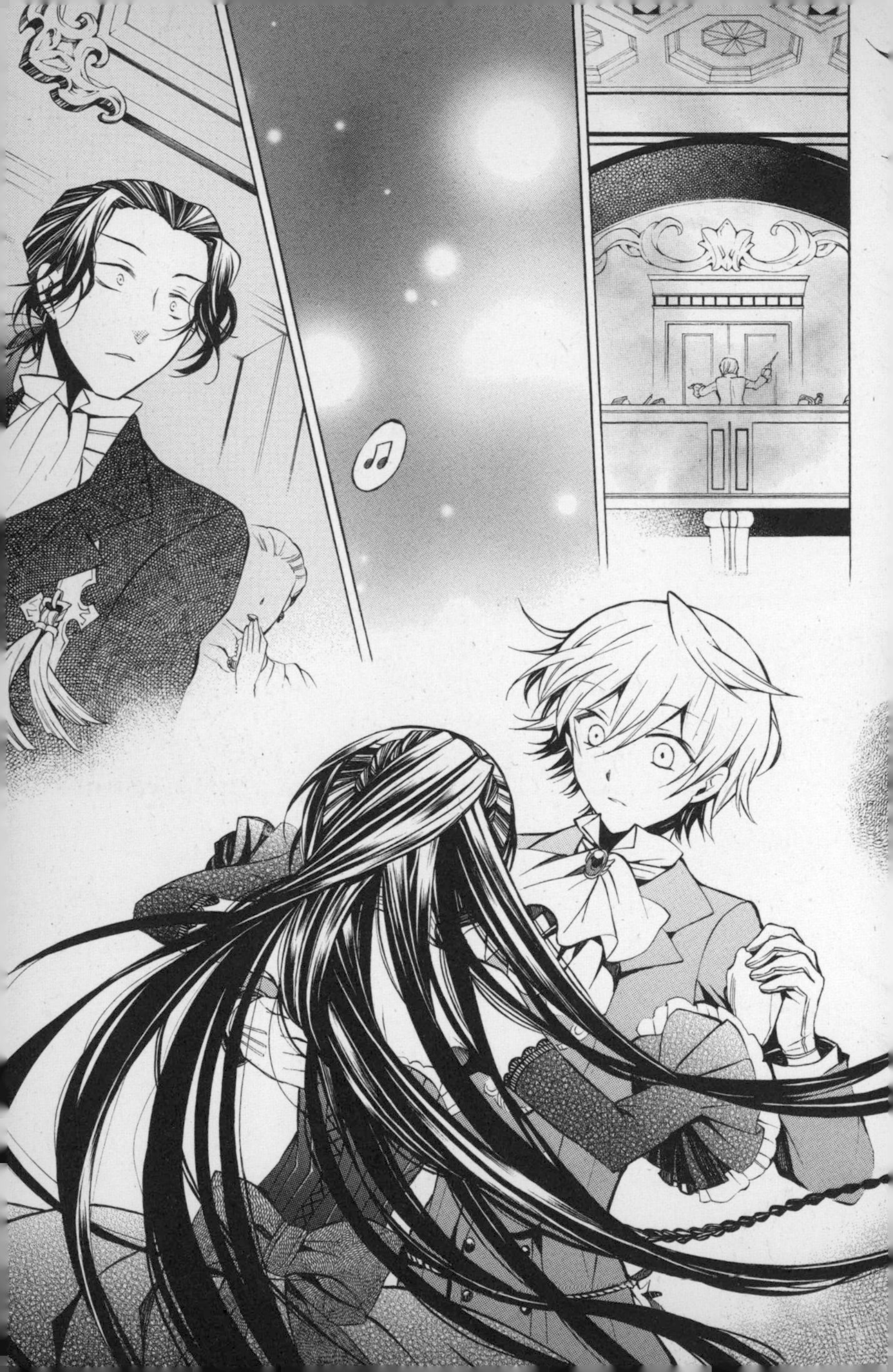

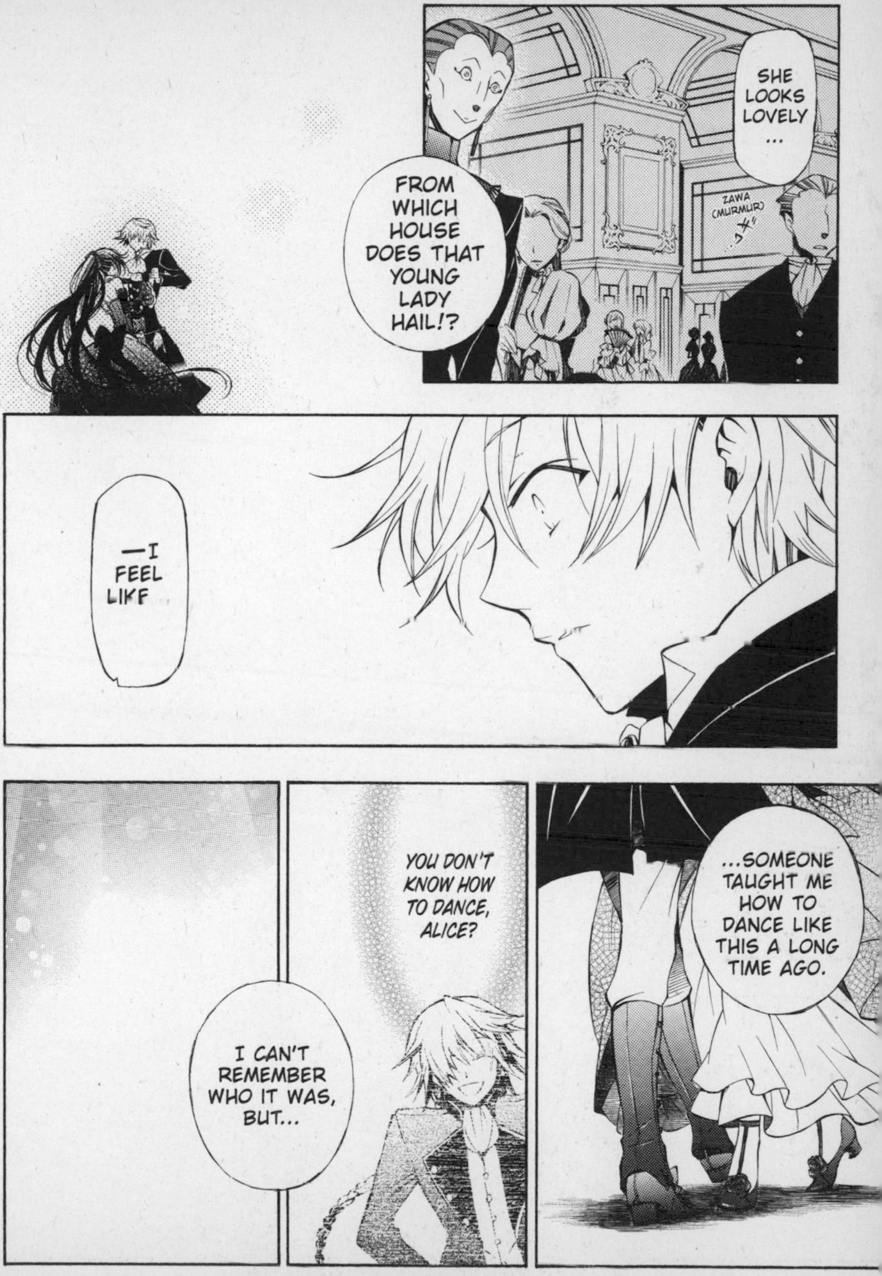
SHE LOOKS LOVELY ...
ZAWA (MURMUR)
FROM WHICH HOUSE DOES THAT YOUNG LADY HAIL!?
—I FEEL LIKE...
...SOMEONE TAUGHT ME HOW TO DANCE LIKE THIS A LONG TIME AGO.
YOU DON'T KNOW HOW TO DANCE, ALICE?
I CAN'T REMEMBER WHO IT WAS, BUT...

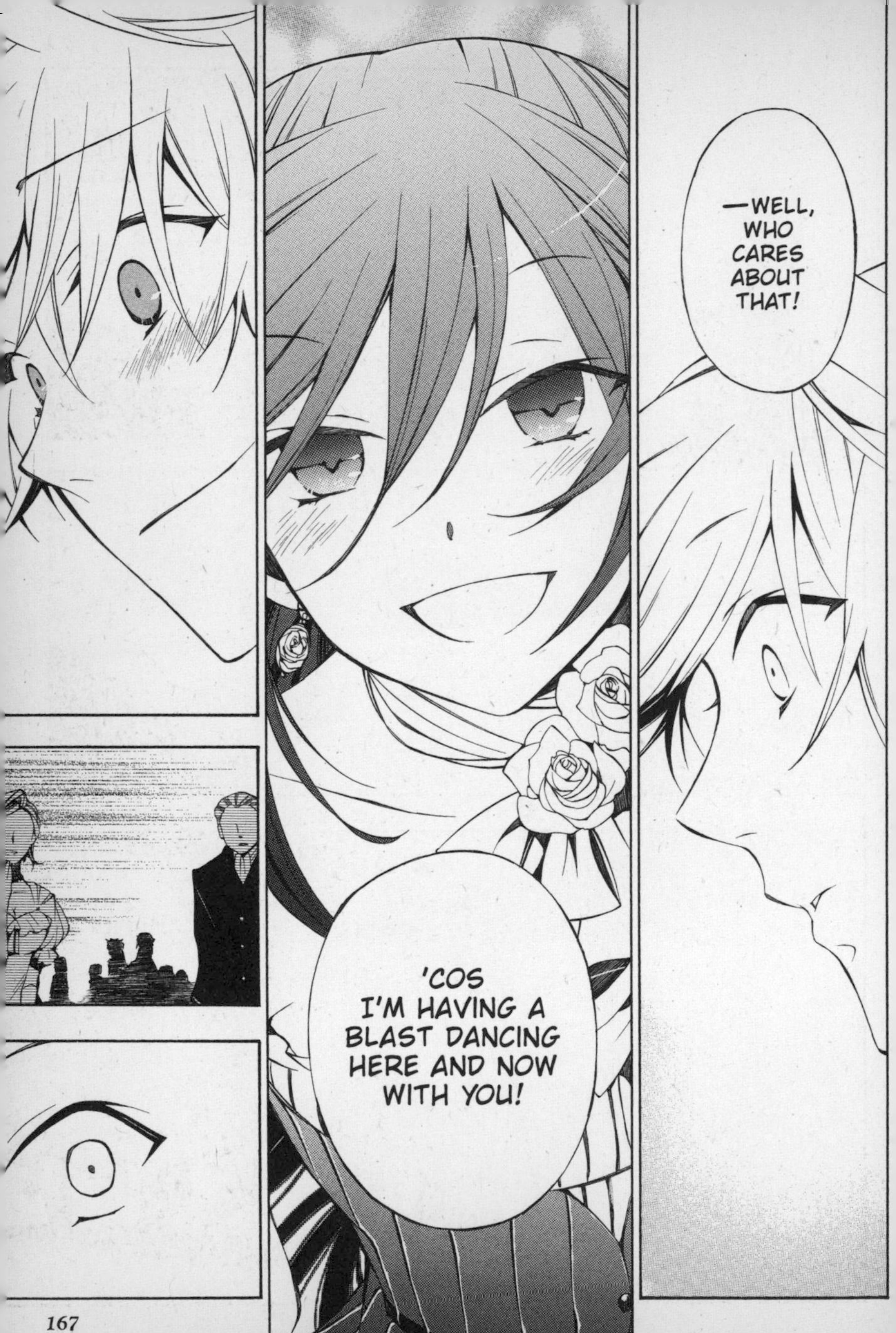
—WELL, WHO CARES ABOUT THAT!
'COS I'M HAVING A BLAST DANCING HERE AND NOW WITH YOU!

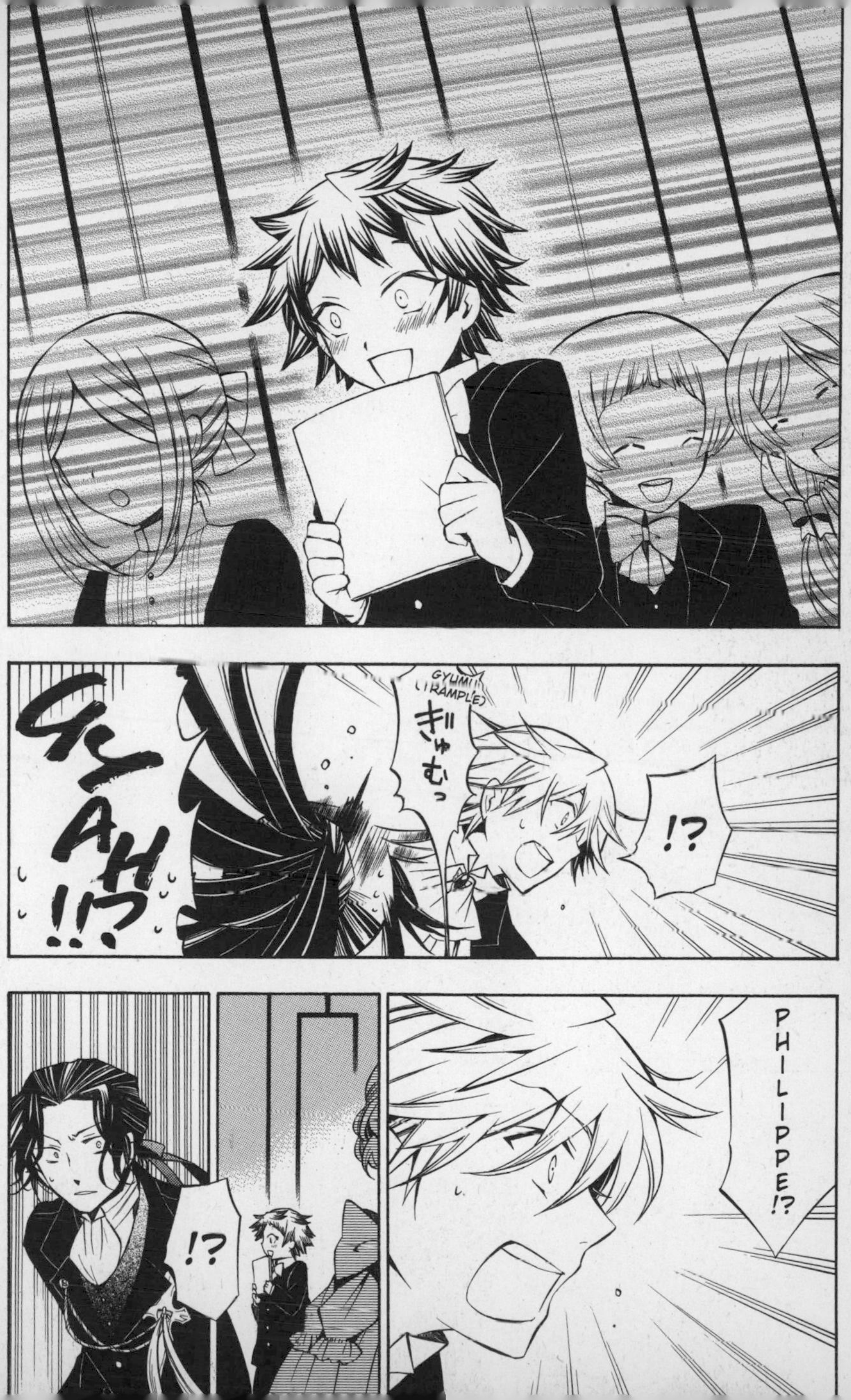
!?
GYUM!!
(RAMPLE)
ぎゅむっ
GYAH!!?
PHILIPPE!?
!?

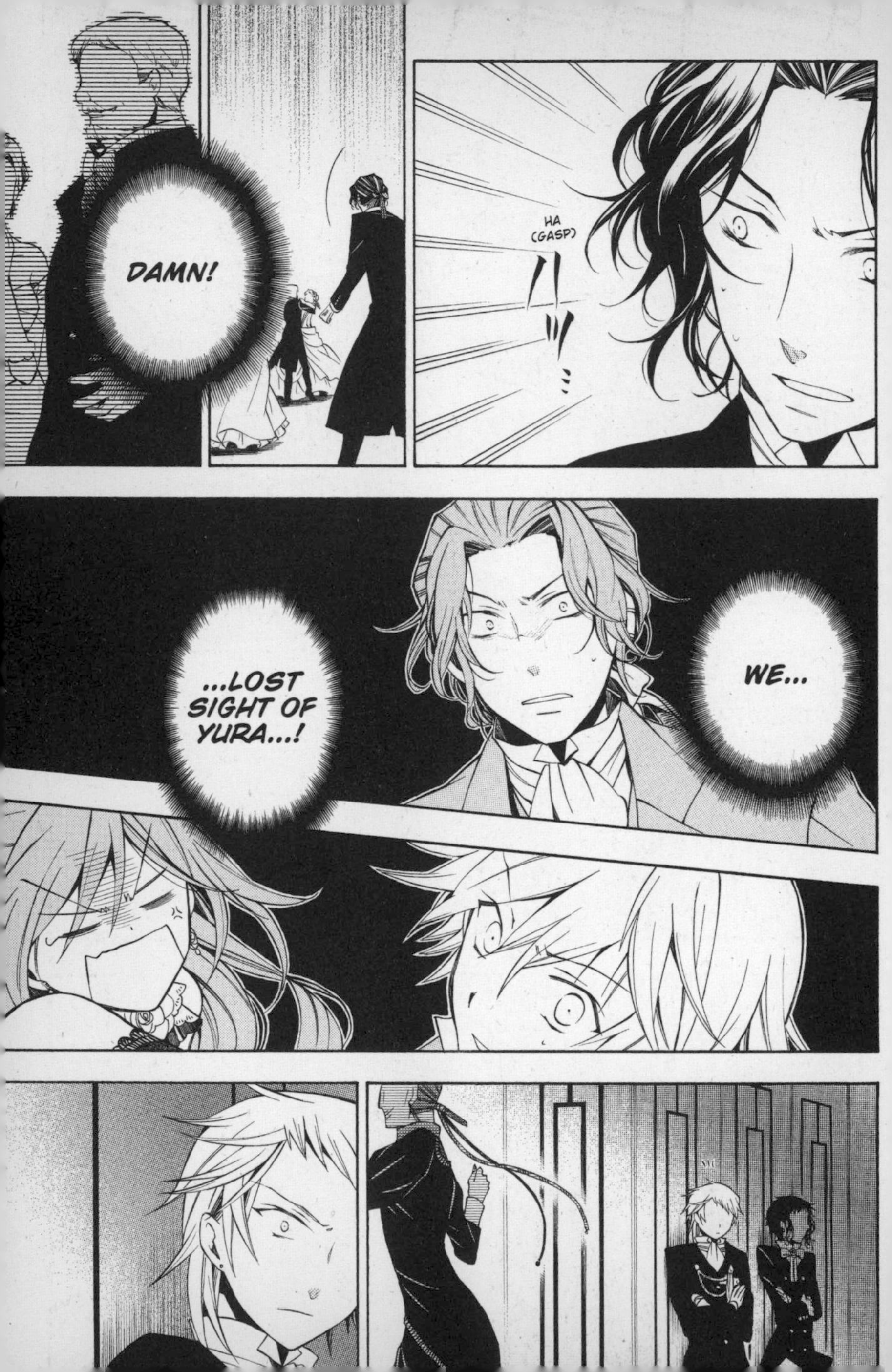
HA (GASP)
DAMN!
WE...
...LOST SIGHT OF YURA...!

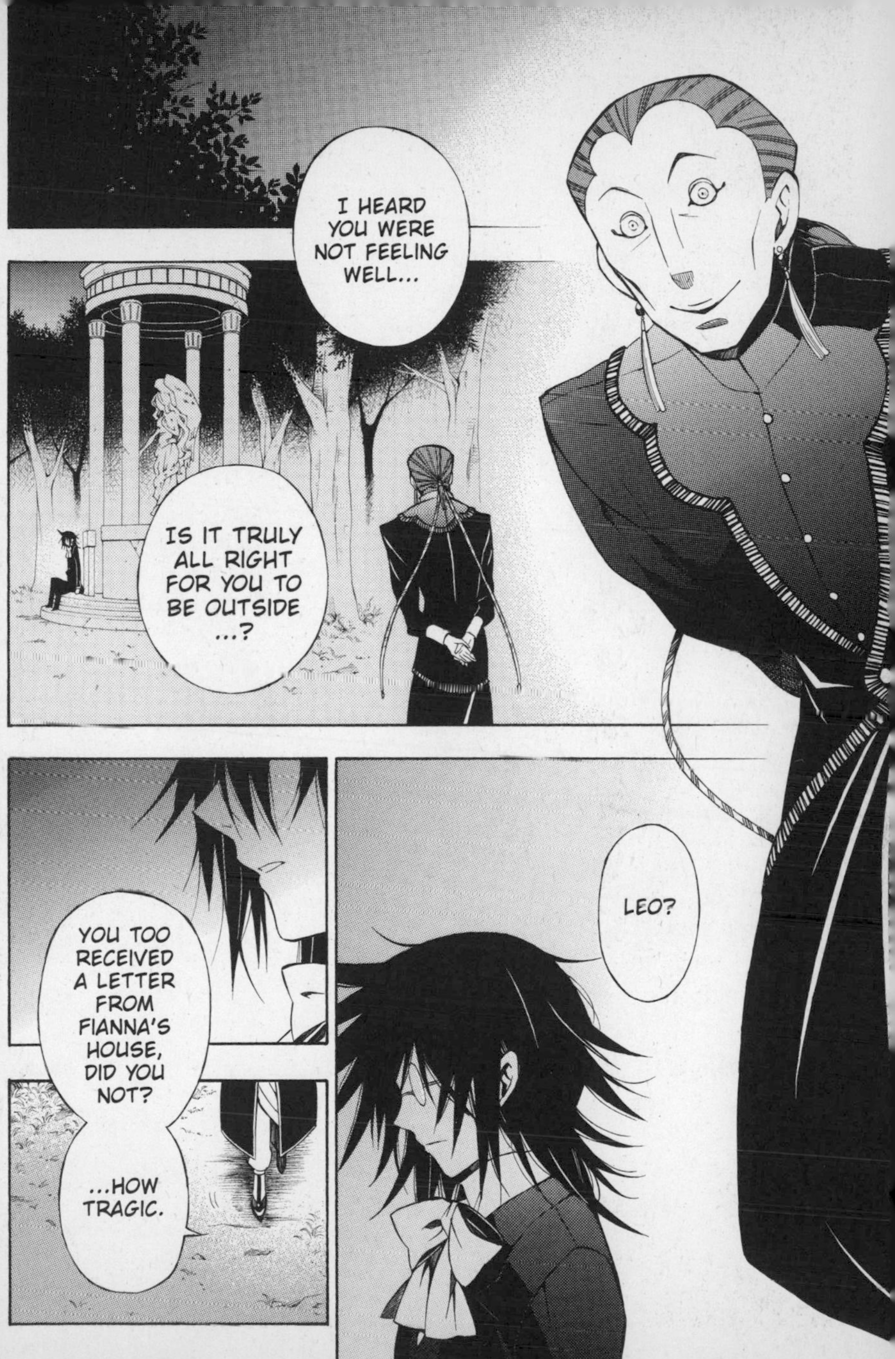
I HEARD YOU WERE NOT FEELING WELL...
IS IT TRULY ALL RIGHT FOR YOU TO BE OUTSIDE ...?
LEO?
YOU TOO RECEIVED A LETTER FROM FIANNA'S HOUSE, DID YOU NOT?
...HOW TRAGIC.

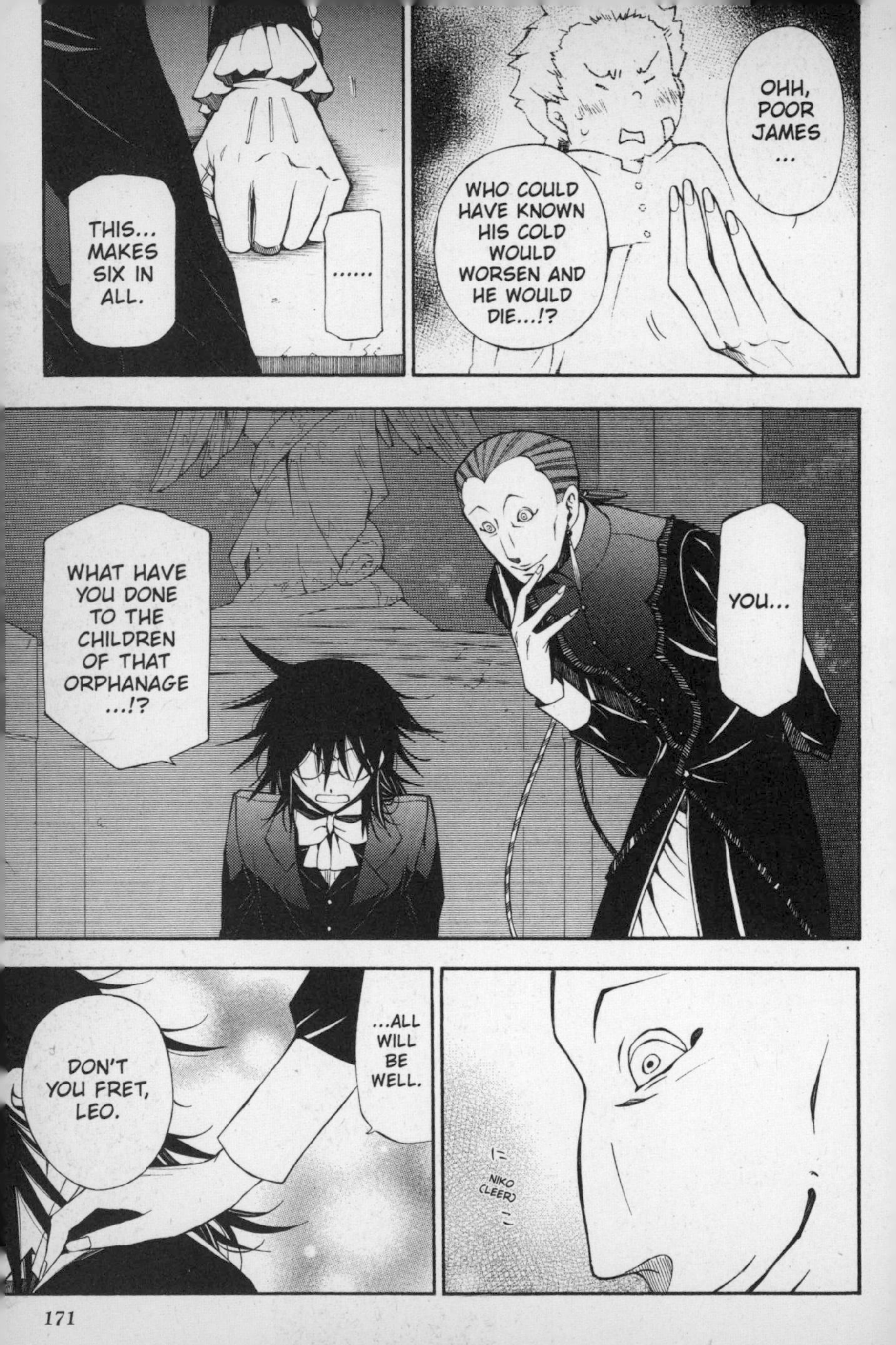
OHH, POOR JAMES ...
WHO COULD HAVE KNOWN HIS COLD WOULD WORSEN AND HE WOULD DIE...!?
......
THIS... MAKES SIX IN ALL.
YOU...
WHAT HAVE YOU DONE TO THE CHILDREN OF THAT ORPHANAGE ...!?
NIKO (LEER)
...ALL WILL BE WELL.
DON'T YOU FRET, LEO.

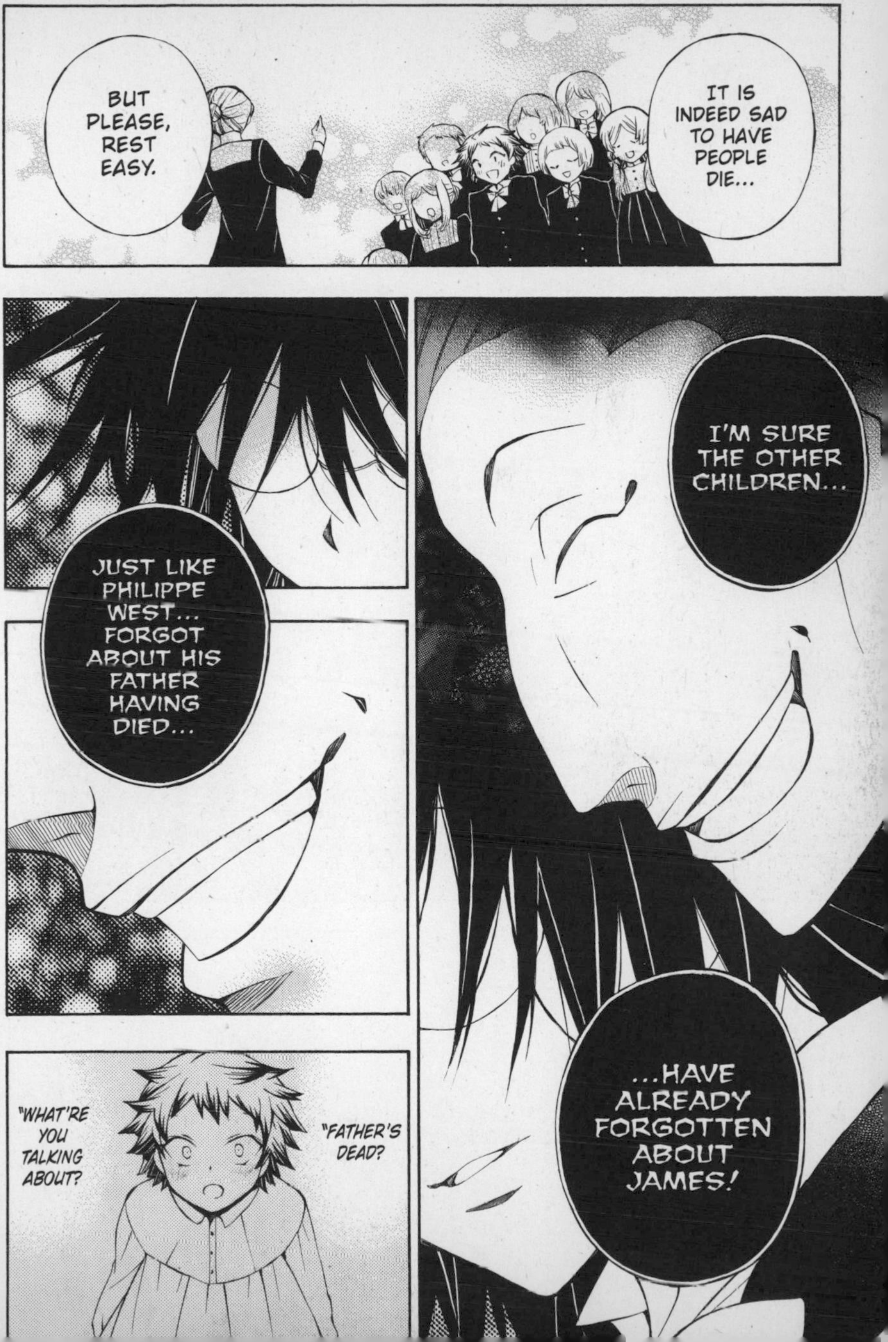
IT IS INDEED SAD TO HAVE PEOPLE DIE...
BUT PLEASE, REST EASY.
I'M SURE THE OTHER CHILDREN...
...HAVE ALREADY FORGOTTEN ABOUT JAMES!
JUST LIKE PHILIPPE WEST... FORGOT ABOUT HIS FATHER HAVING DIED...
"FATHER'S DEAD?
"WHAT'RE YOU TALKING ABOUT?

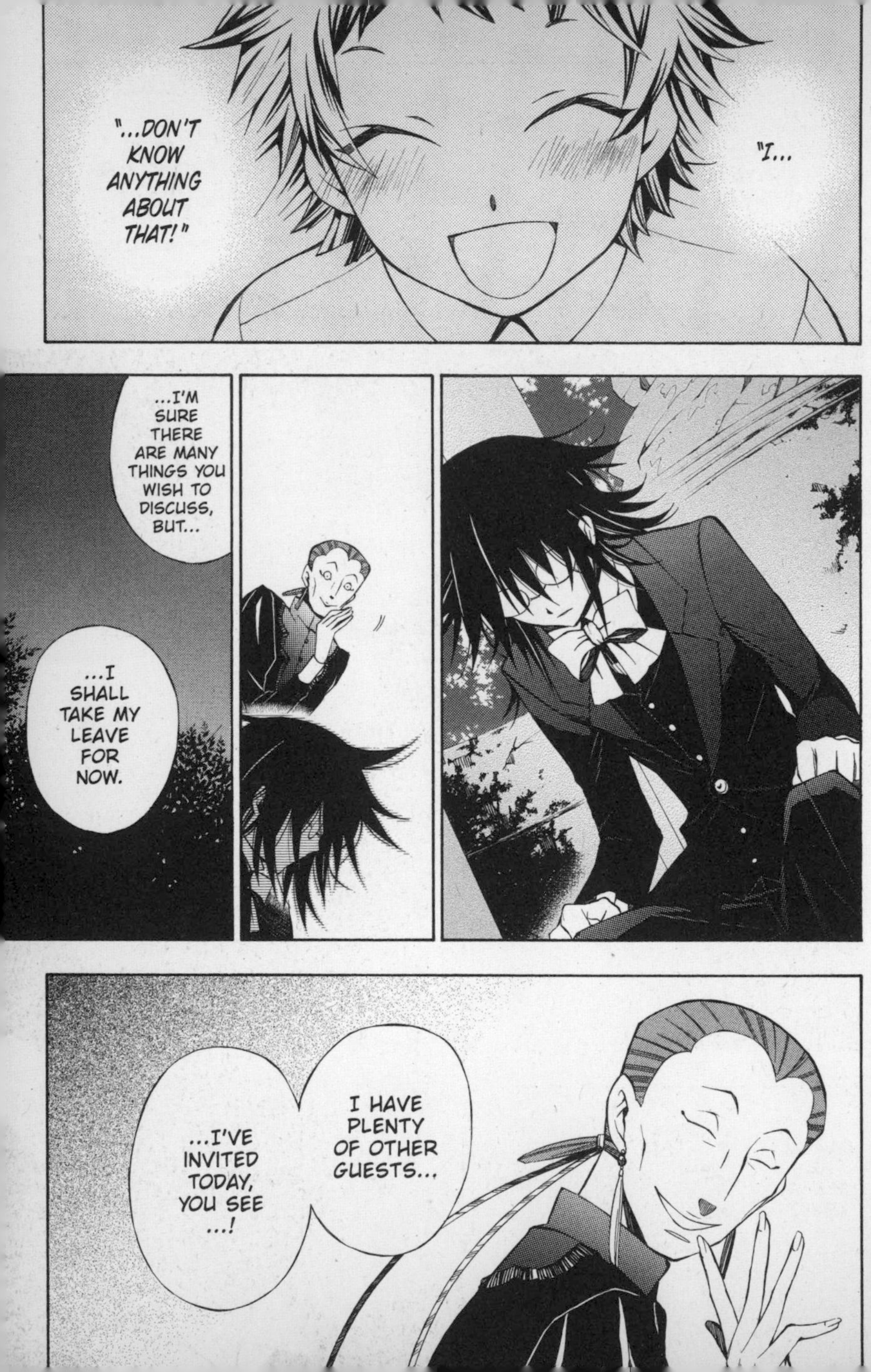
"I...
"...DON'T KNOW ANYTHING ABOUT THAT!"
...I'M SURE THERE ARE MANY THINGS YOU WISH TO DISCUSS, BUT...
...I SHALL TAKE MY LEAVE FOR NOW.
I HAVE PLENTY OF OTHER GUESTS...
...I'VE INVITED TODAY, YOU SEE ...!

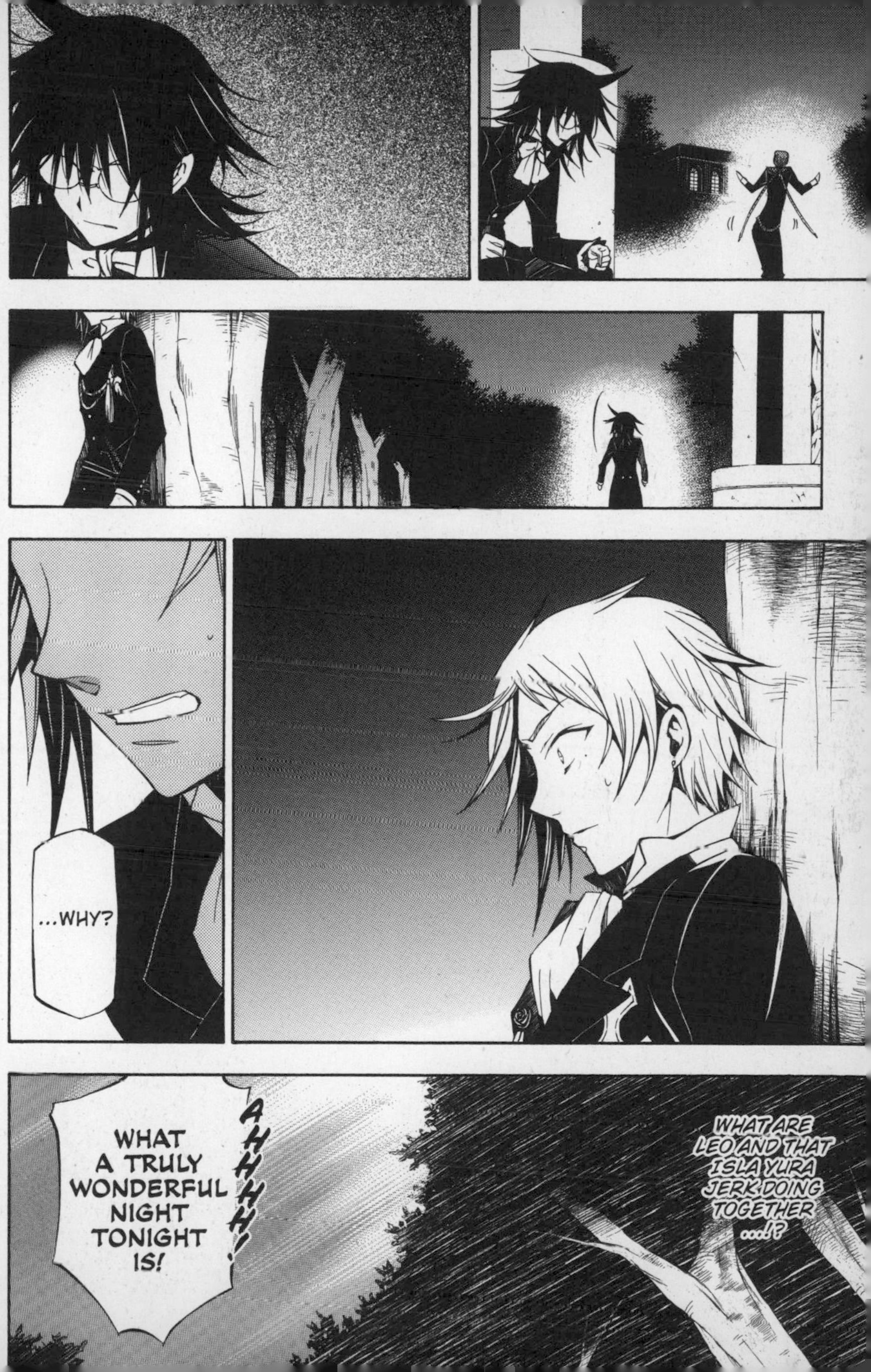
...WHY?
WHAT ARE LEO AND THAT ISLA YURA JERK DOING TOGETHER ...!?
AHHHHH!
WHAT A TRULY WONDERFUL NIGHT TONIGHT IS!

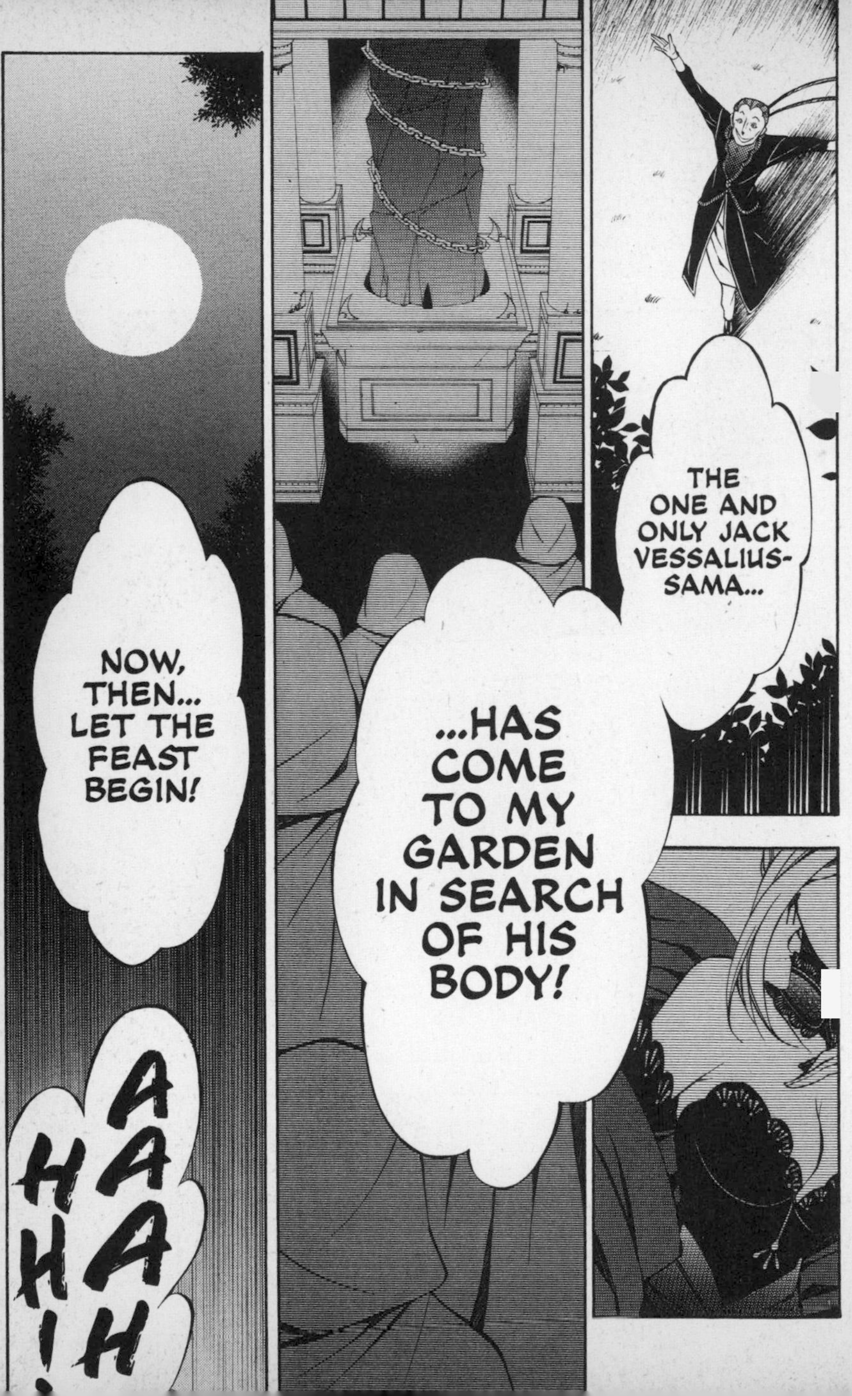
THE ONE AND ONLY JACK VESSALIUS-SAMA...
...HAS COME TO MY GARDEN IN SEARCH OF HIS BODY!
NOW, THEN... LET THE FEAST BEGIN!
AAAH
HH!

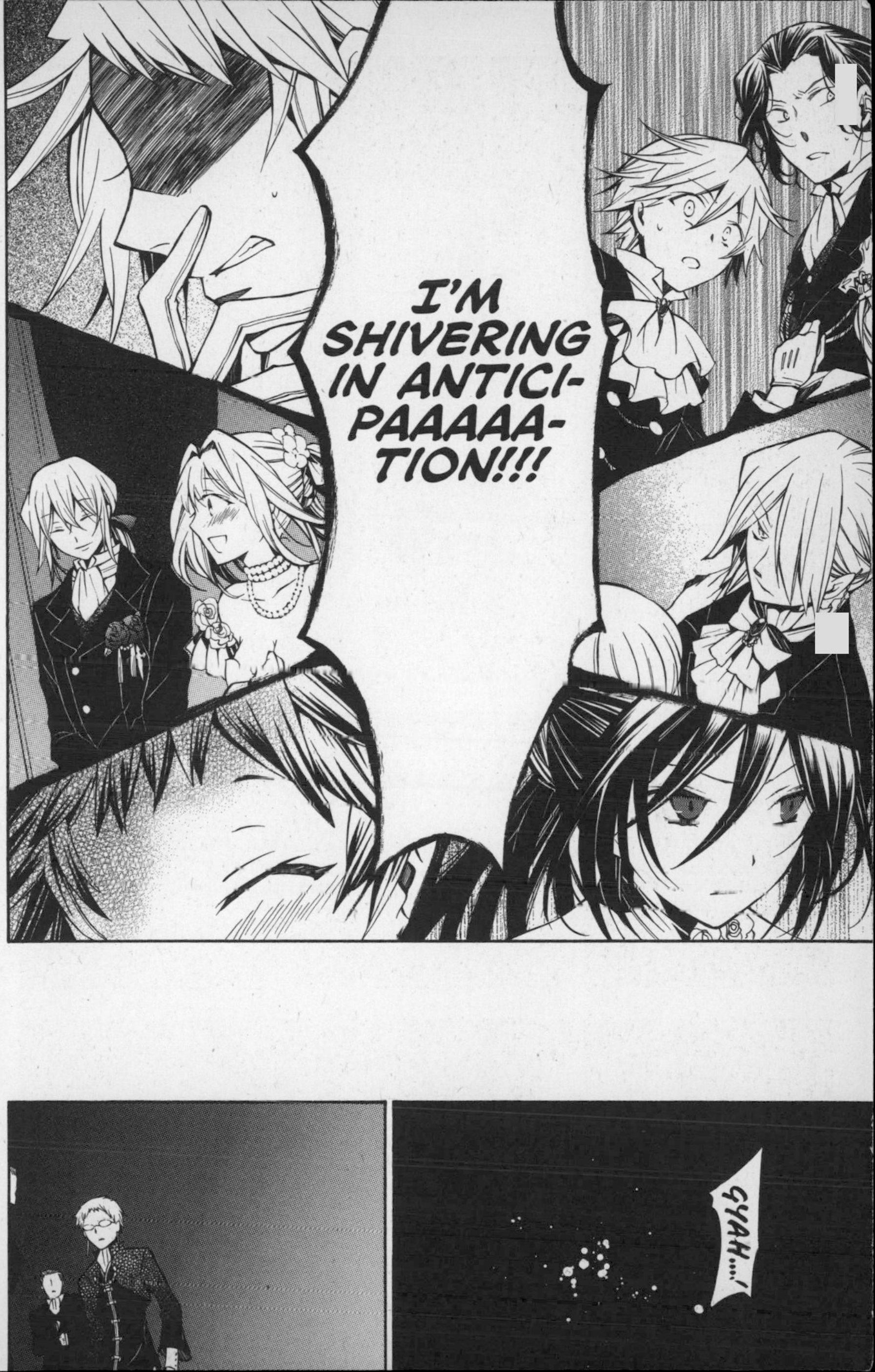
I'M SHIVERING IN ANTICI-PAAAAAA-TION!!!
GYAH...!

...WHAT IS IT?
IS SOMETHING-THING WRONG?
バキ
BAKI (SNAP)
グチュ…
GUCHU (GNAW)
AWW!
YOU MUSTN'T DO THAT, BANDER-SNATCH!
BARI (CRUNCH)
GUCHU

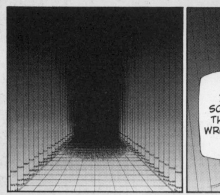

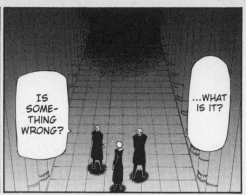

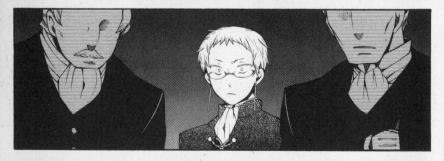

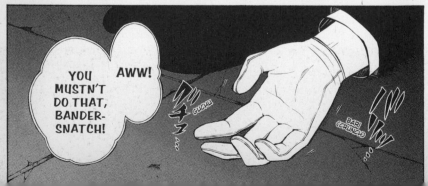

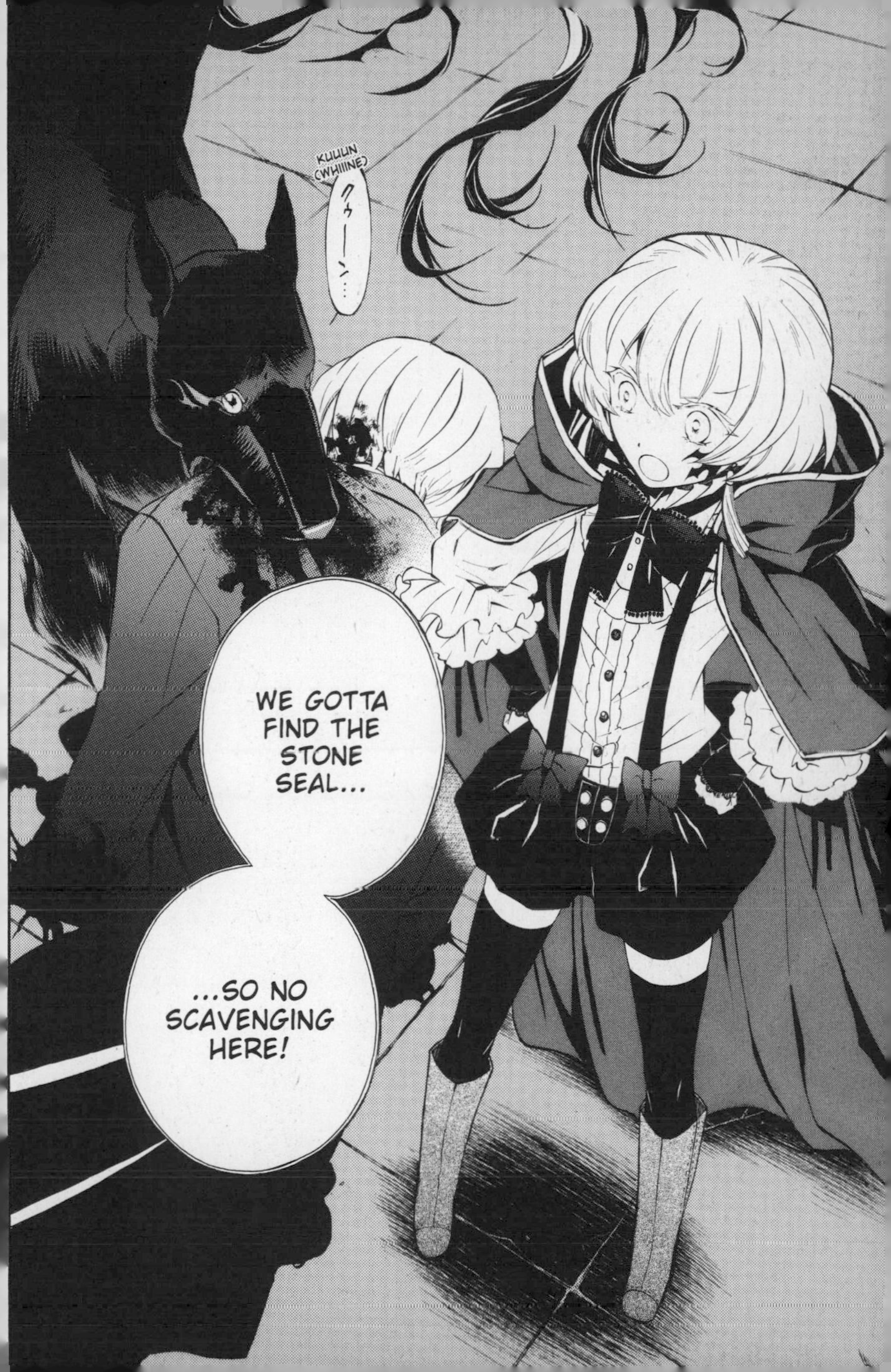
KUUUN (WHIIINE)
クゥーン…
WE GOTTA FIND THE STONE SEAL...
...SO NO SCAVENGING HERE!

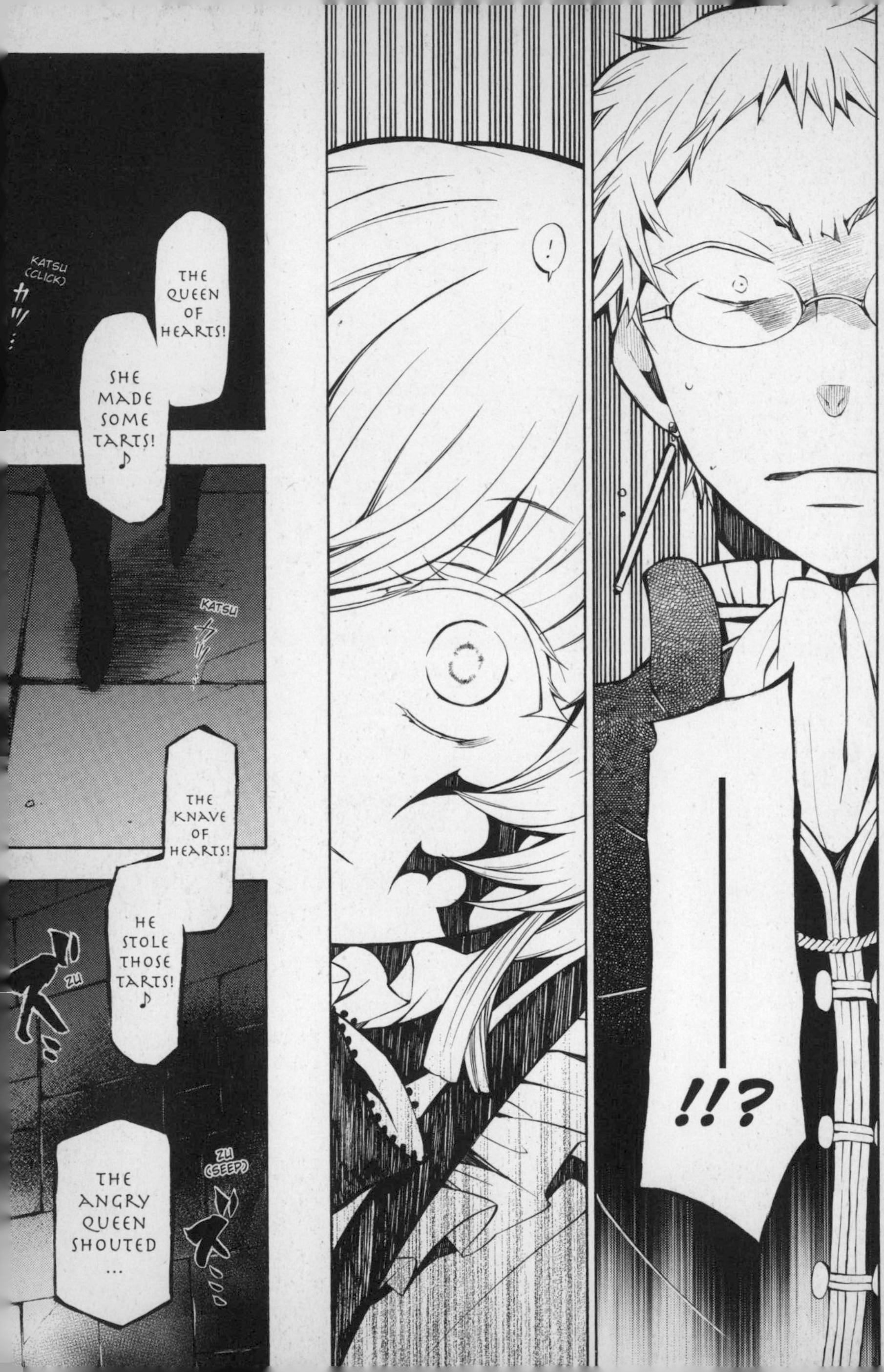
!!?
!
THE QUEEN OF HEARTS!
SHE MADE SOME TARTS! ♪
KATSU (CLICK)
KATSU
THE KNAVE OF HEARTS!
HE STOLE THOSE TARTS! ♪
ZU
ZU (SEEP)
THE ANGRY QUEEN SHOUTED ...

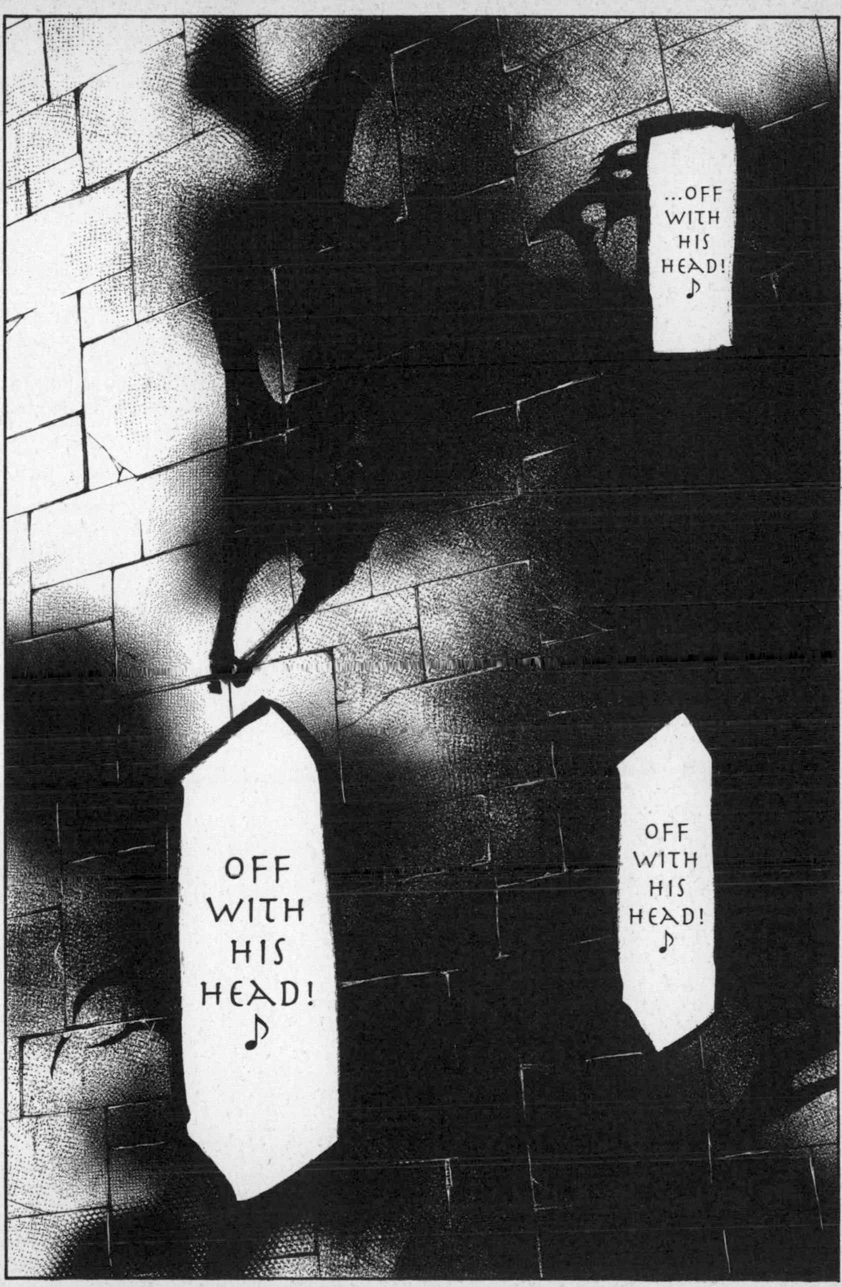
...OFF WITH HIS HEAD! ♪
OFF WITH HIS HEAD! ♪
OFF WITH HIS HEAD! ♪

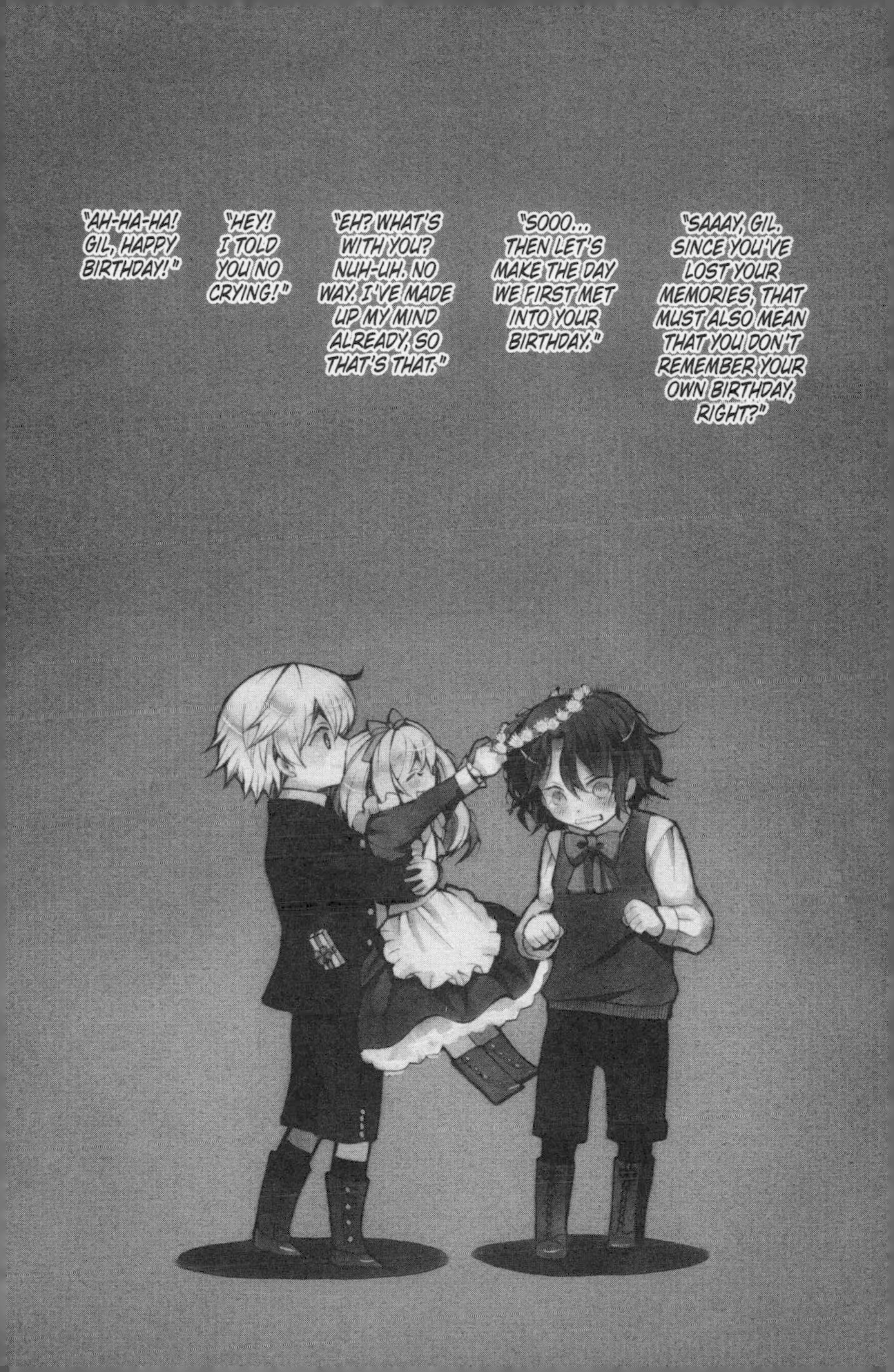
"SAAAY, GIL. SINCE YOU'VE LOST YOUR MEMORIES, THAT MUST ALSO MEAN THAT YOU DON'T REMEMBER YOUR OWN BIRTHDAY, RIGHT?"
"SOOO... THEN LET'S MAKE THE DAY WE FIRST MET INTO YOUR BIRTHDAY."
"EH? WHAT'S WITH YOU? NUH-UH. NO WAY. I'VE MADE UP MY MIND ALREADY, SO THAT'S THAT."
"HEY! I TOLD YOU NO CRYING!"
"AH-HA-HA! GIL, HAPPY BIRTHDAY!"

BONUS: "AN ORDINARY, PRECIOUS DAY"

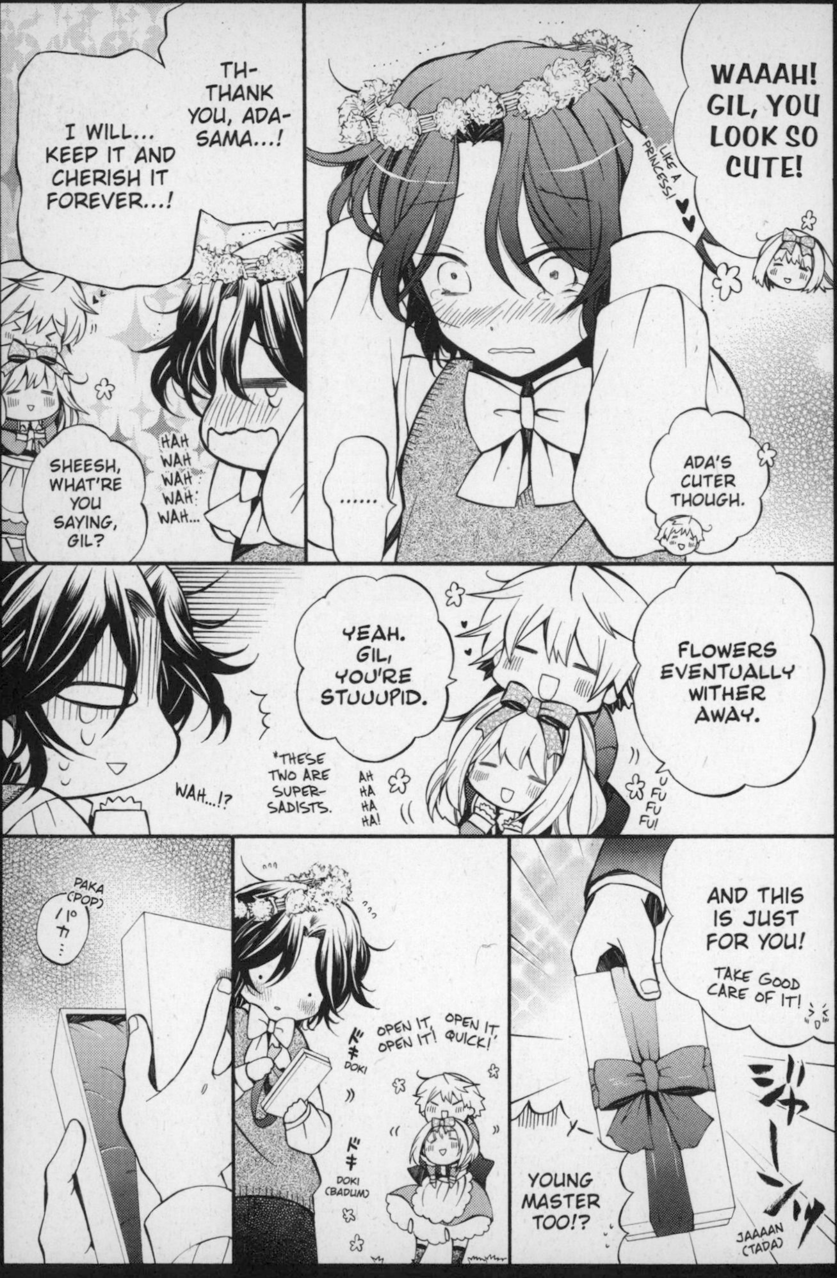

WAAAH! GIL, YOU LOOK SO CUTE!
LIKE A PRINCESS!
......
ADA'S CUTER THOUGH.
TH- THANK YOU, ADA-SAMA...!
I WILL... KEEP IT AND CHERISH IT FOREVER...!
HAH WAH WAH WAH WAH...
SHEESH, WHAT'RE YOU SAYING, GIL?
FLOWERS EVENTUALLY WITHER AWAY.
U FU FU FU!
YEAH. GIL, YOU'RE STUUUPID.
AH HA HA HA!
*THESE TWO ARE SUPER-SADISTS.
WAH...!?
AND THIS IS JUST FOR YOU!
TAKE GOOD CARE OF IT!
ジャーンッ
JAAAAN (TADA)
Y-
YOUNG MASTER TOO!?
OPEN IT, QUICK!
OPEN IT, OPEN IT!
ドキ
DOKI
ドキ
DOKI (BADUM)
パカ…
PAKA (POP)

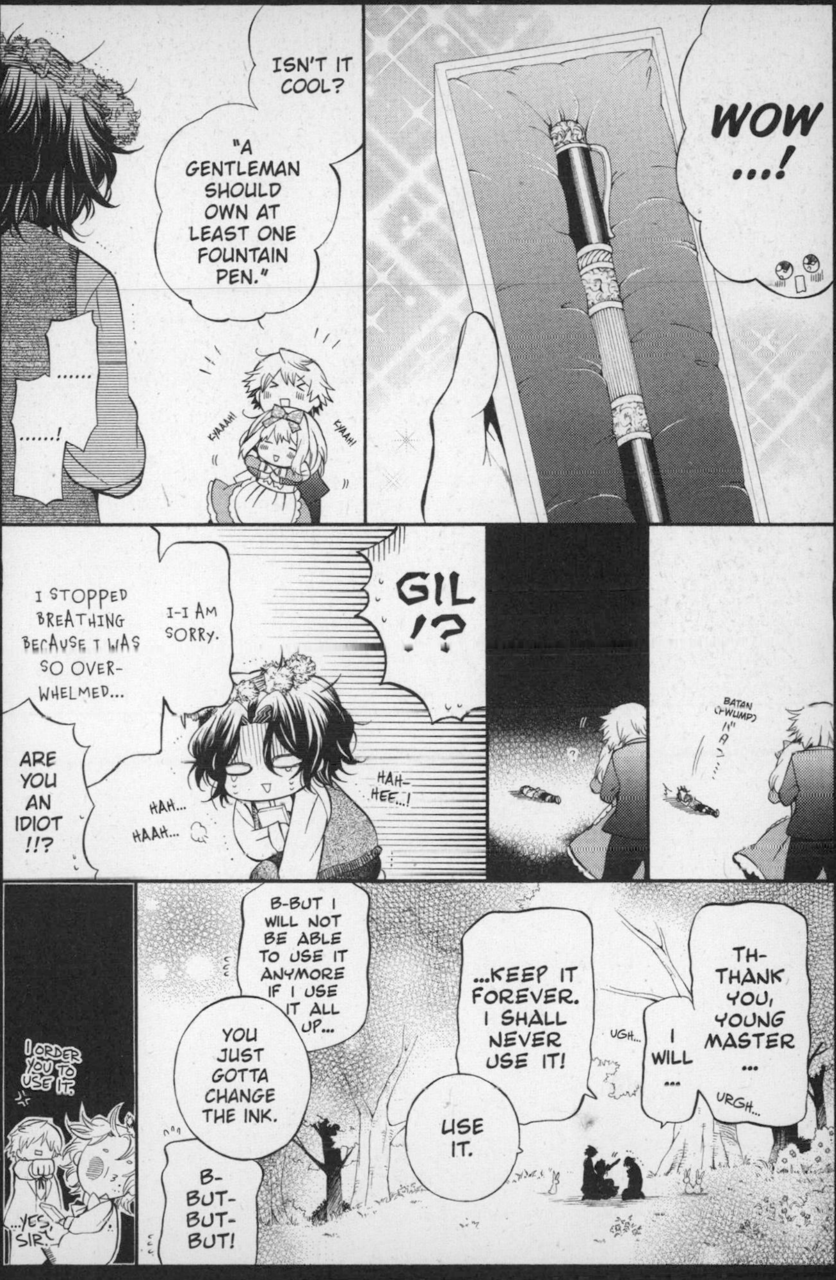
WOW ...!
ISN'T IT COOL?
"A GENTLEMAN SHOULD OWN AT LEAST ONE FOUNTAIN PEN."
KYAAAH!
KYAAH!
......
......!
BATAN (THWUMP)
GIL !?
HAH-HEE...!
I-I AM SORRY.
I STOPPED BREATHING BECAUSE I WAS SO OVERWHELMED...
HAH... HAAH...
ARE YOU AN IDIOT !!?
TH-THANK YOU, YOUNG MASTER ...
URGH...
I WILL ...
UGH...
...KEEP IT FOREVER. I SHALL NEVER USE IT!
USE IT.
B-BUT I WILL NOT BE ABLE TO USE IT ANYMORE IF I USE IT ALL UP...
YOU JUST GOTTA CHANGE THE INK.
B-BUT-BUT-BUT!
I ORDER YOU TO USE IT.
...YES, SIR.

END

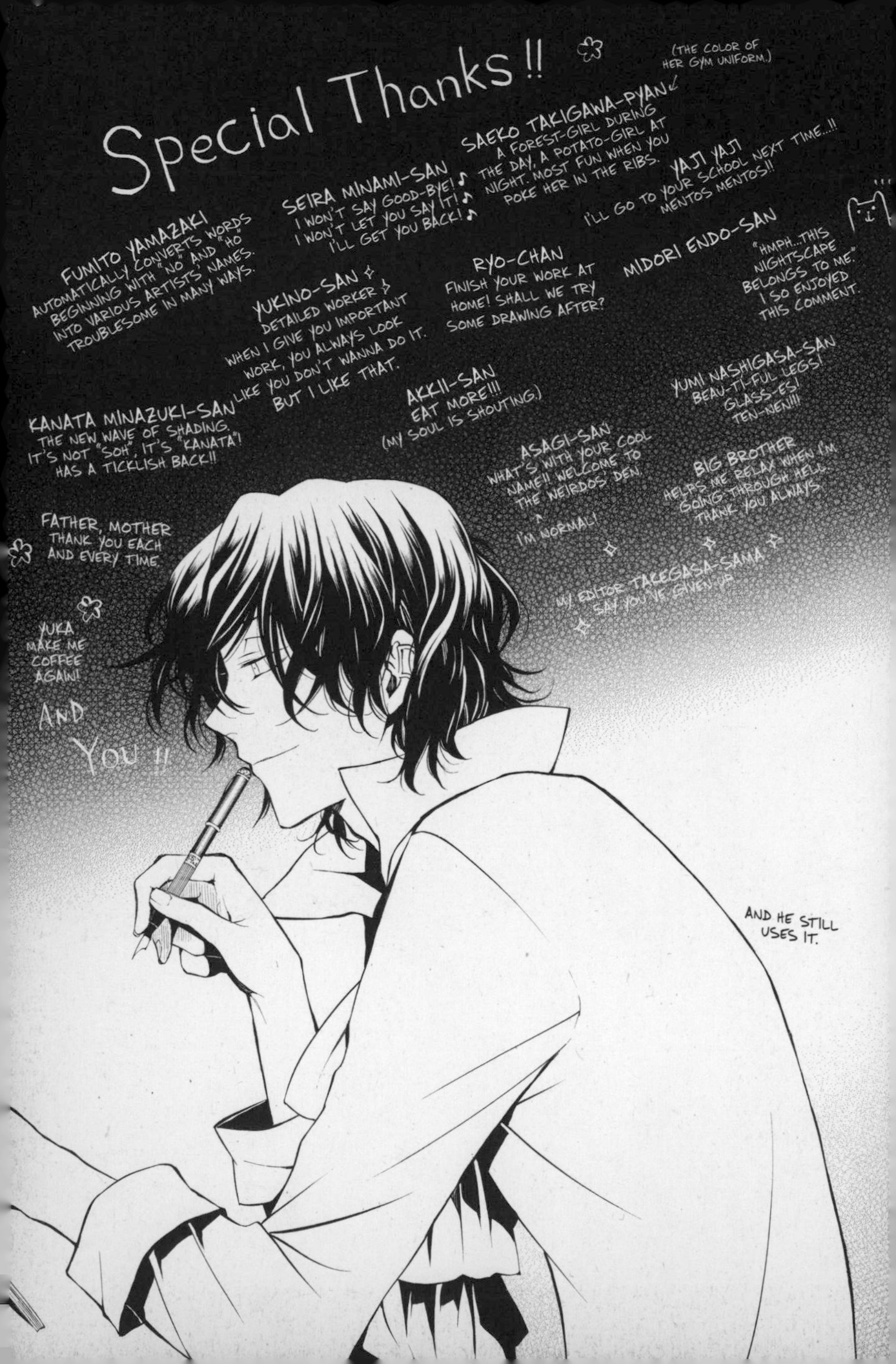

Special Thanks!!
(THE COLOR OF HER GYM UNIFORM.)
SAEKO TAKIGAWA-PYAN A FOREST-GIRL DURING THE DAY, A POTATO-GIRL AT NIGHT. MOST FUN WHEN YOU POKE HER IN THE RIBS.
YAJI YAJI I'LL GO TO YOUR SCHOOL NEXT TIME...!! MENTOS MENTOS!!
SEIRA MINAMI-SAN I WON'T SAY GOOD-BYE!♪ I WON'T LET YOU SAY IT!♪ I'LL GET YOU BACK!♪
FUMITO YAMAZAKI AUTOMATICALLY CONVERTS WORDS BEGINNING WITH "NO" AND "HO" INTO VARIOUS ARTISTS' NAMES. TROUBLESOME IN MANY WAYS.
MIDORI ENDO-SAN "HMPH...THIS NIGHTSCAPE BELONGS TO ME." I SO ENJOYED THIS COMMENT.
RYO-CHAN FINISH YOUR WORK AT HOME! SHALL WE TRY SOME DRAWING AFTER?
YUKINO-SAN DETAILED WORKER WHEN I GIVE YOU IMPORTANT WORK, YOU ALWAYS LOOK LIKE YOU DON'T WANNA DO IT. BUT I LIKE THAT.
YUMI NASHIGASA-SAN BEAU-TI-FUL LEGS! GLASS-ES! TEN-NEN!!!
AKKII-SAN EAT MORE!!! (MY SOUL IS SHOUTING.)
KANATA MINAZUKI-SAN THE NEW WAVE OF SHADING. IT'S NOT "SOH", IT'S "KANATA"! HAS A TICKLISH BACK!!
BIG BROTHER HELPS ME RELAX WHEN I'M GOING THROUGH HELL. THANK YOU ALWAYS.
ASAGI-SAN WHAT'S WITH YOUR COOL NAME!! WELCOME TO THE WEIRDOS' DEN.
I'M NORMAL!
MY EDITOR TAKEGASA-SAMA SAY YOU'VE GIVEN UP.
FATHER, MOTHER THANK YOU EACH AND EVERY TIME.
YUKA MAKE ME COFFEE AGAIN!
AND YOU!!
AND HE STILL USES IT.

DOKI-DOKI PANDORA ACADEMY

"I-IT'S NOT BECAUSE I'VE RUN OUT OF IDEAS" EDITION

CHARACTERS BREAKING DOWN ARE THE BEST!!

THIS TIME, OUR HERO HAS A SPLIT PERSONALITY!!!?

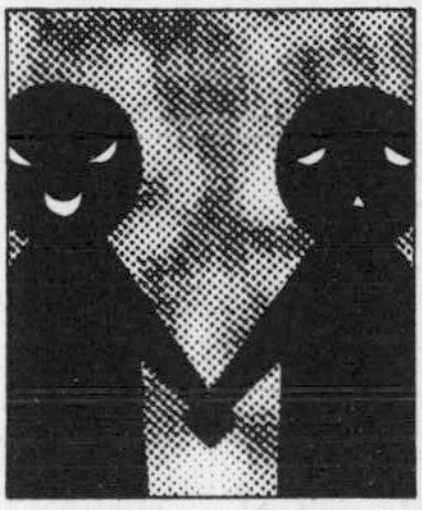

LIKE BEFORE, THE S&M METER SHOWS HOW SADISTIC OR MASOCHISTIC THE CHARACTER IS! IN ADDITION, YOU CAN NOW PRESS A BUTTON TO SWITCH BETWEEN "W (WHITE)" AND "B (BLACK)" MODE. DEPENDING ON WHO YOU'VE CHOSEN, WHAT HAPPENS WHEN YOU MAKE YOUR CHOICE DIFFERS SLIGHTLY. WHEN YOUR CHARACTER'S OBTAINED THE TITLE OF THE SUPER-SADIST, THE SUPER-MASOCHIST, WHEN BOTH PERSONALITIES HAVE BECOME SADISTS OR MASOCHISTS, ETC. ETC. DEPENDING ON YOUR CHARACTER'S ATTRIBUTES, THE RESPONSES OF THE OTHER CHARACTERS CHANGE ACCORDINGLY. THE POSSIBILITIES ARE INFINITE. **THAT'S THE PANDORA ACADEMY QUALITY!!**

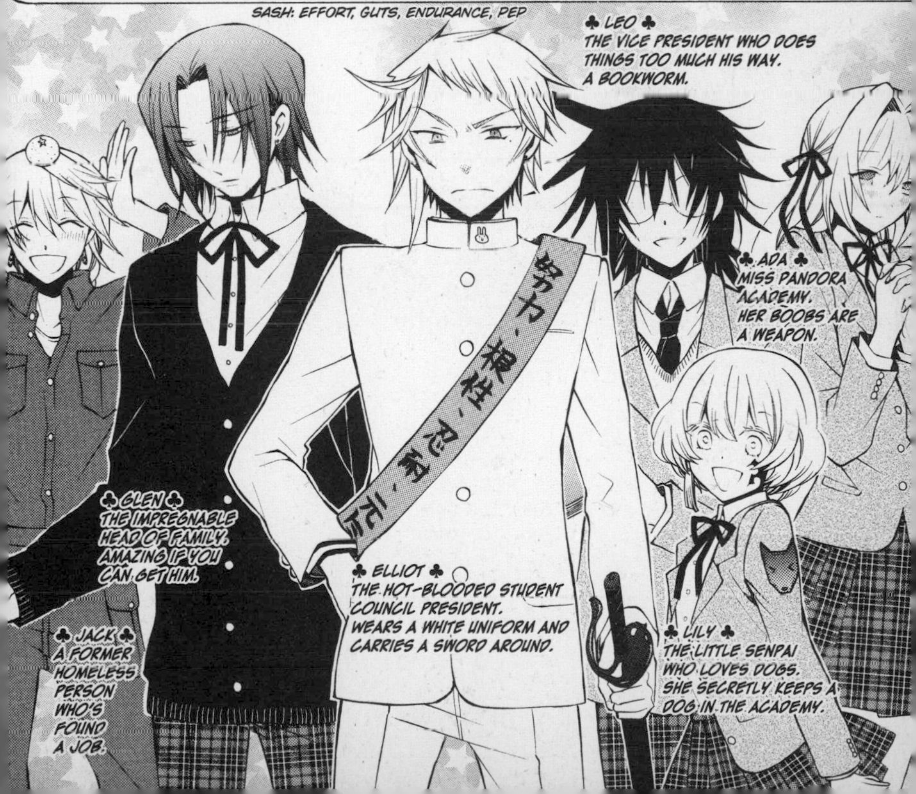
SASH: EFFORT, GUTS, ENDURANCE, PEP
♣ LEO ♣
THE VICE PRESIDENT WHO DOES THINGS TOO MUCH HIS WAY. A BOOKWORM.
♣ ADA ♣
MISS PANDORA ACADEMY. HER BOOBS ARE A WEAPON.
♣ GLEN ♣
THE IMPREGNABLE HEAD OF FAMILY. AMAZING IF YOU CAN GET HIM.
♣ ELLIOT ♣
THE HOT-BLOODED STUDENT COUNCIL PRESIDENT. WEARS A WHITE UNIFORM AND CARRIES A SWORD AROUND.
♣ JACK ♣
A FORMER HOMELESS PERSON WHO'S FOUND A JOB.
♣ LILY ♣
THE LITTLE SENPAI WHO LOVES DOGS. SHE SECRETLY KEEPS A DOG IN THE ACADEMY.

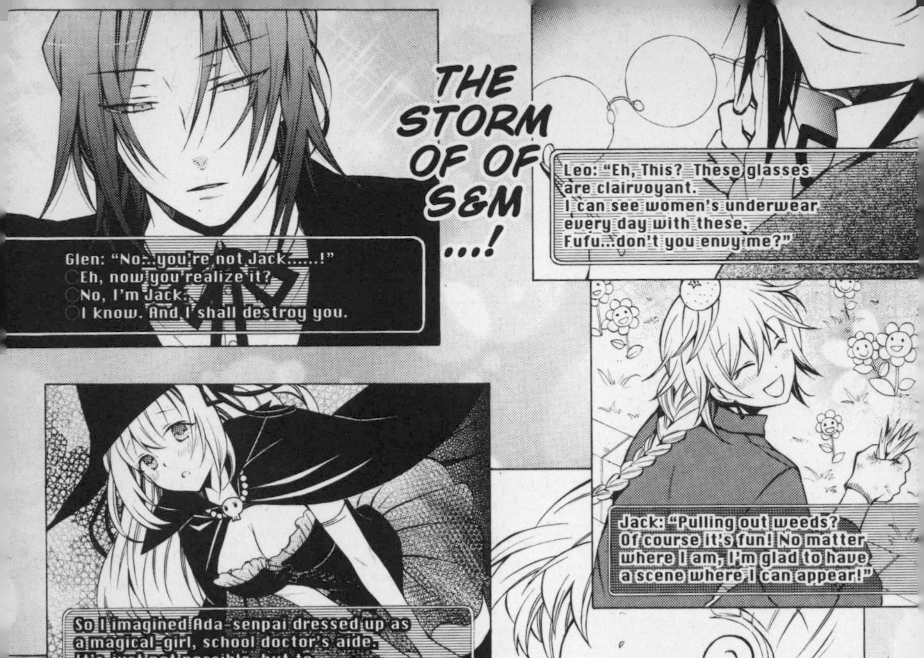
Leo: "Eh, This? These glasses
are clairvoyant.
I can see women's underwear
every day with these.
Fufu...don't you envy me?"
THE STORM OF OF S&M ...!
Glen: "No...you're not Jack......!"
○Eh, now you realize it?
○No, I'm Jack.
○I know. And I shall destroy you.
Jack: "Pulling out weeds?
Of course it's fun! No matter
where I am, I'm glad to have
a scene where I can appear!"
So I imagined Ada-senpai dressed up as
a magical-girl, school doctor's aide.
It's just not possible, but to
be honest......I like it.
...ONCE MORE!
Side W
Oz: "Yes, yes, yeees! ♥
I'm Oz.
I'm your handsome student teacheeeer!"
Sorry...I had an
unpleasant dream.
...........Um......won't you......
...........hold my hand?"

IF YOU RESERVE NOW, YOU GET THE
"PANDORA ACADEMY SCHOOL SONG" CD!!

CONTAINS: (EACH SONG HAS A DIFFERENT ARRANGEMENT!)

- PANDORA ACADEMY SCHOOL SONG: -OZ & GILBERT-
- PANDORA ACADEMY SCHOOL SONG -JACK & GLEN-
- PANDORA ACADEMY SCHOOL SONG -ADA & LILY-
- PANDORA ACADEMY SCHOOL SONG -ELLIOT & LEO-
- MINI-DRAMA "THE HEADHUNTER'S SCARY!"

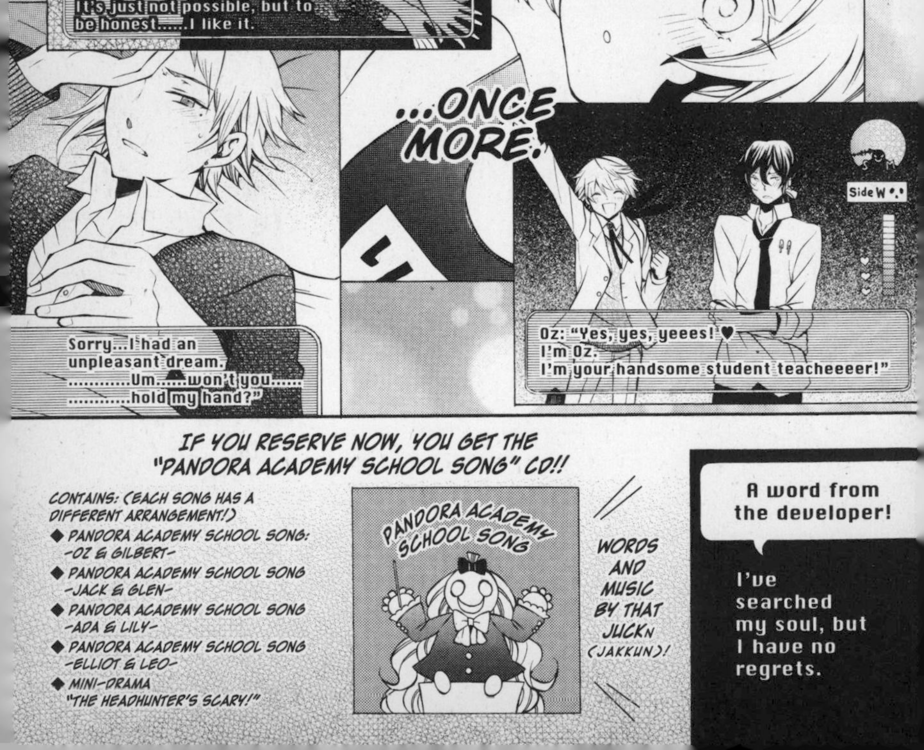
PANDORA ACADEMY SCHOOL SONG

WORDS AND MUSIC BY THAT JUCKn (JAKKUN)!

A word from the developer!

I've searched my soul, but I have no regrets.

COMMON HONORIFICS

no honorific: Indicates familiarity or closeness; if used without permission or reason, addressing someone in this manner would constitute an insult.

-san: The Japanese equivalent of Mr./Mrs./Miss. If a situation calls for politeness, this is the fail-safe honorific.

-sama: Conveys great respect; may also indicate that the social status of the speaker is lower than that of the addressee.

-kun: Used most often when referring to boys (though it can be applied to girls as well), this indicates affection or familiarity. Occasionally used by older men among their peers, but it may also be used by anyone referring to a person of lower standing.

-chan: An affectionate honorific indicating familiarity used mostly in reference to girls; also used in reference to cute persons or animals of either gender.

forest girl, potato girl   page 183

A forest girl, or *mori* girl, is a young woman who tends to wear natural colors and shapes and dresses with a very earthy, woodsy vibe. "Forest girl" is also the name of this specific type of Japanese street fashion. The word for potato (*imo*) can double as a colloquial word for "hick, bumpkin."

PandoraHearts

MOCHIZUKI'S MUSINGS

VOLUME 12

I feel like I drew with the greatest sense of calm I've ever had up till now, like I never got the urge to really break down in tears, like I've reached a juncture in the story—that's how Volume 12 is. Thanks for reading.

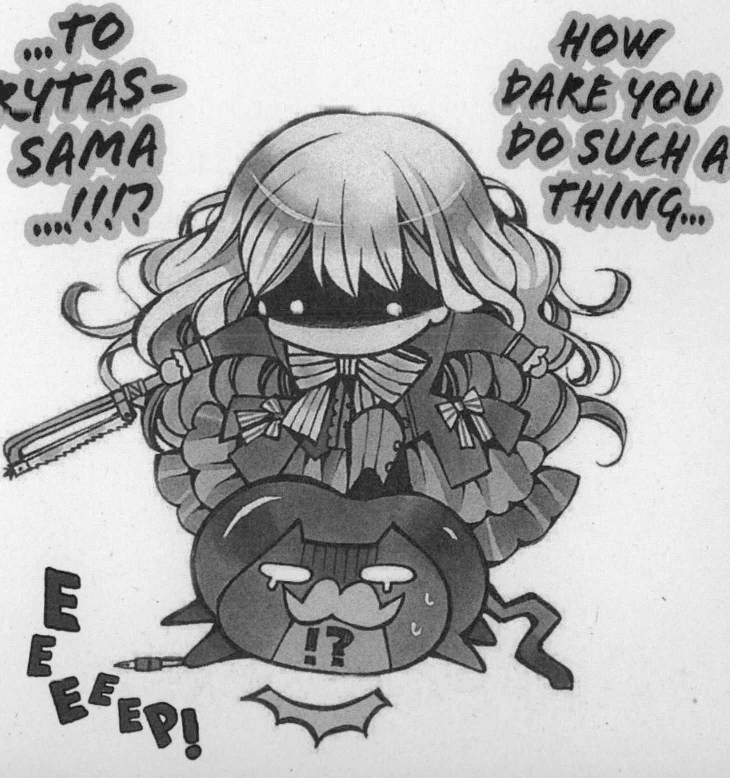
HOW DARE YOU DO SUCH A THING...
...TO RYTAS-SAMA ...!!!?
!?
EEEEEP!

PandoraHearts

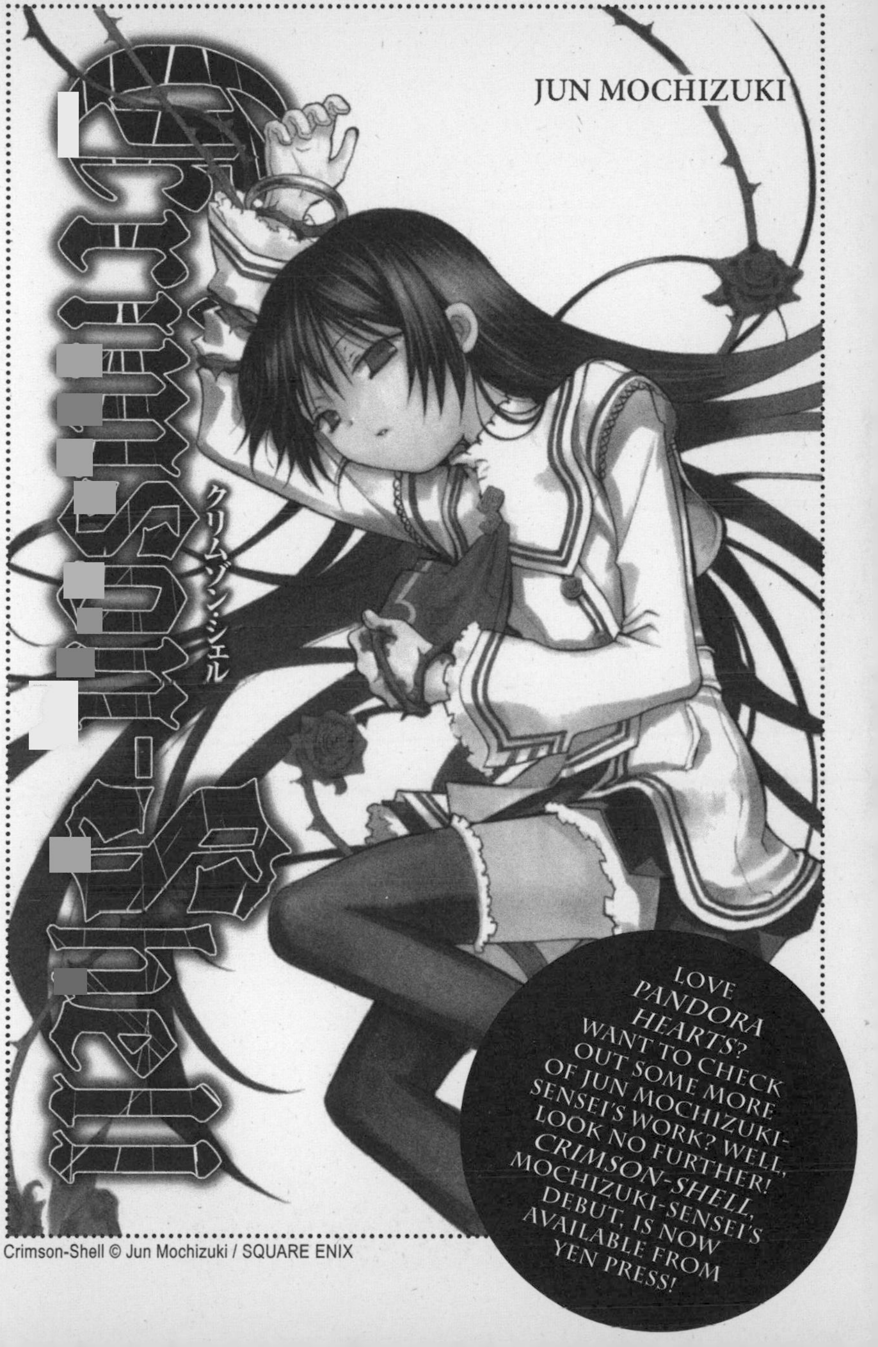
Crimson-Shell
クリムゾン・シェル
JUN MOCHIZUKI
LOVE *PANDORA HEARTS*? WANT TO CHECK OUT SOME MORE OF JUN MOCHIZUKI-SENSEI'S WORK? WELL, LOOK NO FURTHER! *CRIMSON-SHELL*, MOCHIZUKI-SENSEI'S DEBUT, IS NOW AVAILABLE FROM YEN PRESS!

PandoraHearts

PANDORA H

D0558988

Translation: Tomo Kimura • Lettering: Alexis Eckerman

PANDORA HEARTS Vol. 12 © 2010 Jun Mochizuki / SQUARE ENIX CO., LTD. All rights reserved. First published in Japan in 2010 by SQUARE ENIX CO., LTD. English translation rights arranged with SQUARE ENIX CO., LTD. and Hachette Book Group through Tuttle-Mori Agency, Inc.

Translation © 2012 by SQUARE ENIX CO., LTD.

Yen Press
Hachette Book Group
237 Park Avenue, New York, NY 10017

www.HachetteBookGroup.com
www.YenPress.com

Yen Press is an imprint of Hachette Book Group, Inc. The Yen Press name and logo are trademarks of Hachette Book Group, Inc.

First Yen Press Edition: October 2012

ISBN: 978-0-316-19731-1

10 9 8 7 6 5 4 3 2 1

BVG

Printed in the United States of America